THE CONCISE CATALOGUE
OF THE
SCOTTISH NATIONAL PORTRAIT GALLERY

John Miller Gray by Patrick William Adam, 1885
First Curator of the Scottish National Portrait Gallery

The Concise Catalogue
of the
Scottish National Portrait Gallery

COMPILED BY HELEN SMAILES

THE TRUSTEES OF THE NATIONAL GALLERIES OF SCOTLAND

EDINBURGH 1990

© The Trustees of the National Galleries of Scotland, 1990
Published by the Trustees of the National Galleries of Scotland
Designed by Cinamon and Kitzinger, London
Typeset by Rowland Phototypesetting Ltd, Bury St Edmunds, Suffolk
Printed in the Netherlands by Lecturis bv., Eindhoven

CONTENTS

FOREWORD

This newly revised and updated Concise Catalogue of the primary collections (excluding engravings and photographs) of the Scottish National Portrait Gallery has been compiled during 1989, the year which marks the one-hundredth anniversary of the opening of the Gallery. Since the last edition came out in 1977 the collection has grown considerably and now amounts to some 2800 items. In addition there are 340 long-term registered loans. During this period the Gallery's collecting policy has evolved to include, in addition to the basic collection of portraits of historically important Scots, topographical paintings (like the view of Falkland Palace painted by Alexander Keirincx about 1635) and depictions of great historical events (such as Tillemans's view of the Battle of Glenshiel in 1719). In addition, portraits that stand as landmarks in the history of Scottish portraiture, even when the sitter may not be especially eminent, are now collected. Another radical departure from previous policy has been, since 1983, the acquisition of portraits of distinguished contemporaries, many of them commissioned by the Gallery.

The Portrait Gallery which opened its doors to the public in the summer of 1889 was almost entirely the result of the munificence of John Ritchie Findlay, proprietor of the *Scotsman* newspaper and it is fitting that his name should be mentioned here. It was an extraordinary act of private patronage that has never been equalled in Scotland in the sphere of museums and galleries, involving the expenditure of some £70,000 on the elaborate red-sandstone, neo-Gothic building designed by Sir Robert Rowand Anderson.

The many ideas which, since the eighteenth century, were to lead to this new manifestation of national identity, came to fruition late in 1882 when the Board of Manufactures undertook responsibility for the foundation of a gallery devoted to national portraiture. The collection began to grow quite quickly and by 1885 some 156 portraits were on show in a temporary building on part of the site where the Portrait Gallery was being erected. However, of these only 95 items were the property of the Board, the remainder being loans from private collectors, although many of them would eventually be added to the permanent collection.

The first catalogue of the collection appeared in the same year and it and subsequent updated editions before his premature death in 1894 were the work of the Gallery's first curator, John Miller Gray, a former banker and dedicated antiquarian and art critic. His reputation as one of Scotland's finest art historians rests principally on his unsurpassed book on the portrait medallionists, James and William Tassie. Such was Gray's importance in the pioneering days of the Gallery that we have felt it appropriate to remember him by including his portrait as the frontispiece to the present catalogue.

Gray was the first of many staff in the Portrait Gallery who, over the years, have added to our knowledge and understanding of the ever-growing collections, often assisted by colleagues in the wider institution of which the Portrait Gallery is part, the National Galleries of Scotland. Our present compiler, Helen Smailes, has acknowledged the contribution of present colleagues and predecessors as she has worked during the past year making her own very considerable contribution. This new, and, for the first time, lavishly illustrated edition of the catalogue, is a measure of the historical breadth and aesthetic diversity of a great national collection.

TIMOTHY CLIFFORD   DUNCAN THOMSON
Director of the National   *Keeper of the Scottish*
Galleries of Scotland   *National Portrait Gallery*

EXPLANATORY NOTE

Inventory numbers: Each entry is preceded by an inventory number with the prefix 'PG' or 'PGL' in the case of long-term loans to the collection.

Names and titles: Noblemen are catalogued under their last title. Married women are catalogued under their last known married name with cross-references as appropriate. Italicised titles within the main body of the text correspond to exhibition titles of group portraits or finished pictures for which the Gallery possesses a sketch or study.

Groups: Portraits comprising four or more sitters have been included in the GROUPS section. Each entry is preceded by the exhibited title of the picture where known or by a generalised descriptive title. Cross-references to the principal identified sitters are given in the main body of the catalogue.

Support or medium: Oil paintings are described in terms of their support (eg canvas, panel, millboard); drawings and sculpture in terms of their medium (eg water-colour, marble, bronze).

Sizes: Measurements are given in centimetres followed by inches in brackets, height before width. Height measurements only are given for sculpture.

Dates: Where the date of a picture is separated from the name of the artist by a comma, this indicates that the work has been dated by the artist. If it is preceded by the word 'dated', the date has probably been applied by another hand or as part of a reproductive process (eg on medallions and coins.) Where an undated work can be dated reliably on external evidence, the date is preceded by the words 'painted', 'drawn', 'struck' or 'sculpted'.

Illustrations: An asterisk following the inventory number of a work indicates that it is illustrated. Portraits comprising two or three sitters are illustrated either under the principal sitter or under the sitter whose name appears first in alphabetical sequence.

CATALOGUE OF SUBJECTS

ABBOTSFORD
    PG 825*   (*Sir Walter Scott and his friends at Abbotsford.*) See GROUPS.
    PG 1193*   (*Gala Day at Abbotsford.*) See SCOTT, Sir Walter.
    PG 1303*   (*The Abbotsford family.*) See GROUPS.
    PG 1731   (Scott's death at Abbotsford.) See SCOTT, Sir Walter.
    PG 2660   (Plan of the hall pavement at Abbotsford.) See SCOTT, Sir Walter.

ABERCROMBY, Alexander Abercromby, Lord, 1745–95. *Judge*
    PG 1257   Paste medallion, h.7.3 (2⅞), by James Tassie. Dated 1791. Purchased 1935.

ABERCROMBY, Sir Ralph, 1734–1801. *General*
    PG 250*   Canvas, 242 x 151.4 (95¼ x 59⅝), by Colvin Smith. Transferred from the National Gallery of Scotland 1889.
    PG 765   (Death of Abercromby.) Copper medal, dia. 3.8 (1½), by unknown artist. Dated 1801. Purchased 1911.
    PG 989*   Canvas, 74.9 x 62.2 (29½ x 24½), by John Hoppner. Bequeathed by A. Abercromby Trotter 1925.
    PG 1232   (Centenary of the capture of Trinidad.) Bronze medal, dia. 4.7 (1⅞) by unknown artist. Dated 1897. Given by Major James W. Cursiter 1934.
    PG 1455   Enamel miniature, 13.5 x 10.7 (5¼ x 4¼), by Henry Bone after John Hoppner, signed. Dated 1808. Bequeathed by Sir St Clair Thomson 1944.
    PG 1549   (Tribute to the 42nd Regiment from the London Highland Society.) Silver medal, dia. 4.7 (1⅞) by G. F. Pidgeon after Benjamin West. Dated 1801. Given by Mrs Mary J. Robertson 1950.
    PG 2680*   (*The Battle of Alexandria, 21 March 1801*; death of Abercromby.) See GROUPS.
    PG 2681*   (*The Landing of British Troops at Aboukir, 8 March 1801.*) See GROUPS.

ABERDEEN, George Hamilton Gordon, 4th Earl of, 1784–1860. *Statesman*
    PG 1482*   Canvas, 76.2 x 63.5 (30 x 25), by Sir Martin Archer Shee. Painted *c.* 1838. Purchased 1946.

ABERDEEN AND TEMAIR, George Gordon, 2nd Marquess of, 1879–1965.
    PG 2392   Pencil drawing, 35.6 x 25.3 (14 x 10), by Sir William Oliphant Hutchison. Given by the executors of Margery, Lady Hutchison 1977.

ABERDEEN AND TEMAIR, John Campbell Gordon, 7th Earl and 1st Marquess of, 1847–1934. *Statesman*
    PG 1349   Bronze plaque, 36.2 x 26 (14¼ x 10¼), by Robert Tait MacKenzie. Dated 1921. Given by Dr R. Tait MacKenzie 1937.

ABOUKIR, LANDING OF BRITISH TROOPS AT; see GROUPS (PG 2681).

ABOYNE, Mary Douglas, Countess of, d. 1816. *Wife of 4th Earl of Aboyne*
PG 2233* (As a child.) See GROUPS.

ADAM, Alexander, 1741–1809. *Schoolmaster*
PG 2038* Canvas, 127 x 101.6 (50 x 40), by Sir Henry Raeburn. Painted *c.* 1805. Given by the sitter's surviving pupils to the National Gallery of Scotland in 1860 and transferred 1964.

ADAM, Jean Ramsay, Mrs John, fl. 1750–91. *Wife of the architect John Adam*
PG 1964* Paste medallion, h. 7.6 (3), by James Tassie. Dated 1791. Transferred from the National Gallery of Scotland 1960.

ADAM of Maryburgh, John, 1721–92. *Architect*
PG 1963* Paste medallion, h. 7.4 (2⅞), by James Tassie. Dated 1791. Transferred from the National Gallery of Scotland 1960.

ADAM, Patrick William, 1854–1929. *Artist*
PG 1587 Bronzed metal medallion, dia. 10.7 (4¼), by Charles Matthew, signed. Dated 1889. Given by the executors of Sir James and Lady Caw 1952.
PG 2583 Bronzed metal medallion, dia. 10.7 (4¼) by Charles Matthew, signed. Dated 1889. Bequeathed by J. M. Gray 1894.

ADAM, Robert, 1728–92. *Architect*
PG 201* Paste medallion, h. 7.3 (2⅞), by James Tassie. Transferred from the National Gallery of Scotland 1889.
PG 262* Paste medallion, h. 7.8 (3⅛), by James Tassie. Dated 1792. Purchased 1887.
PG 2590* Paste medallion, h. 7.9 (3⅛), by James Tassie. Dated 1792. Purchased 1983.

ADAM, William, 1688–1748. *Architect; father of Robert and John Adam*
PG 1033* Marble bust, h. 68.6 (27) by unknown artist. Purchased 1926.

ADAMSON, Patrick, 1537–92. *Prelate and statesman*
PG 757* Panel, 40.6 x 31.4 (16 x 12⅜), by unknown artist. Dated 1569. Purchased 1911.

ADAMSON, William, 1863–1936. *Labour Parliamentarian*
PG 1798* Black chalk drawing, 46.3 x 29.8 (18¼ x 11¾), by David Foggie, 1934, signed. Given by Mrs M. Foggie 1955.

ADELAIDE, Queen; Princess Adelaide Louisa Theresa Caroline Amelia of Saxe-Meiningen, 1792–1849. *Queen of William IV*
PG 956* Canvas, 76.2 x 63.5 (30 x 25), by Sir David Wilkie. Purchased 1923.

AGNEW of Lochnaw, Sir Andrew, 1687–1771. *Soldier*
PGL 173* Canvas, 77.4 x 62.9 (30½ x 24¾), by unknown artist. On loan from Lady Agnew.

AIKMAN, Colonel Thomas Stokes Robertson, 1860–1948. *Of Hamilton Curling Club*
  PG 1856* (*Curling at Carsebreck.*) See GROUPS.

AIKMAN, William, 1682–1731. *Artist*
  PG 309* Canvas, 75.9 x 63 (30 x 24⅞), self-portrait. Bequeathed by W. F. Watson
      1886.

AINSLIE, John, fl. 1816–35. *Artist*
  PG 1676* Pencil and chalk drawing, 38.1 x 27.3 (15 x 10¾), by unknown artist.
      Bequeathed by W. F. Watson 1886.

AINSLIE, W., fl. 1899. *Of Pitfour Curling Club*
  PG 1856* (*Curling at Carsebreck.*) See GROUPS.

AIRLIE, Anne Stewart, Countess of, d. 1798. *Wife of David Ogilvy, titular Earl of Airlie*
  PG 2584 (Silhouette album no. 50. See GROUPS.) Printed (?) silhouette, h. 7.3
      (2⅞), by unknown artist. Acquired *c.* 1951.

AIRTH, William Graham, 1st Earl of, 1589–1661. *President of the Privy Council*
  PG 1834* Canvas (conjoined with PG 1833, 1st Lord Napier), 106.7 x 128.3 (42 x
      50½), by George Jamesone, 1637, signed. Purchased 1956.

ALBANY, Charlotte Stewart, Duchess of, 1753–89. *Daughter of Prince Charles Edward
      Stewart*
  PG 623* Canvas, 25.7 x 22 (10⅛ x 8⅛), by Hugh Douglas Hamilton. Painted
      c. 1785–88. Purchased 1903.

ALBEMARLE, General George Monck, 1st Duke of, 1608–70. *Soldier and statesman*
  PG 900 Canvas, 223 x 130.2 (87¾ x 51¼), by Sir Peter Lely and studio. Purchased
      1919.

ALBERT, Prince; Prince Francis Albert Augustus Charles Emmanuel of Saxe Coburg and
      Gotha, 1819–61. *Consort of Queen Victoria*
  PG 1169 (With Queen Victoria, the Prince of Wales and the Princess Royal.) See
      GROUPS.
  PG 2417* (*The visit of Queen Victoria and Prince Albert to Hawthornden.*) See
      GROUPS.

ALDBOROUGH, Edward Augustus Stratford, 2nd Earl of, d. 1801. *Politician*
  PG 483 Medallion (plaster replica), h. 7.3 (3), after James Tassie. Cast from a
      medallion in possession of Jeffery Whitehead 1894.

ALEXANDER I, 1777–1825. *Emperor of Russia*
  PG 1928 (With the Grand Duke Constantine.) Medallion (plaster replica), h. 5.4
      (2⅛), after James Tassie. Modelled by the Empress Maria Feodorovna 1791.
      Provenance untraced.

Abercromby, Sir Ralph
PG 250

Abercromby, Sir Ralph
PG 989

Aberdeen, 4th Earl of
PG 1482

Adam, Alexander
PG 2038

Adam, Jean
PG 1964

Adam, John
PG 1963

Adam, Robert
PG 201

Adam, Robert
PG 262

Adam, Robert
PG 2590

Adam, William
PG 1033

Adamson, Patrick
PG 757

Adamson, William
PG 1798

Adelaide, Queen
PG 956

Agnew, Sir Andrew
PGL 173

Aikman, William
PG 309

ALEXANDER, Forrest, 1759–1833. *Edinburgh merchant and banker*
    PG 2145   Cut paper silhouette, h. 20.4 (8¹⁄₁₆), by Augustin Edouart, 1830, signed.
        Given by Mrs J. H. G. Ross 1969.

ALEXANDER, John, 1686/8–1757. *Artist*
    PG 1970*   Oil on copper, 7.2 x 5.7 (2⅞ x 2¼), self-portrait. Dated 1711. Purchased
        1960.

ALEXANDER, Robert, 1840–1923. *Artist*
    PG 1191   Canvas, 61 x 45.7 (24 x 18), by J. R. Abercromby, signed. Purchased 1932.
    PG 2627   Pencil drawing, 26.5 x 21.8 (10½ x 8⅝), by John Henry Lorimer, signed.
        Dated 1891. Provenance untraced.

ALEXANDER, Rev. William Lindsay, 1808–84. *Theologian*
    PG 93*   Canvas, 127 x 102.9 (50 x 41½), by Norman Macbeth. Given by the
        executors of Miss E. Fraser 1885.

ALEXANDRA, Queen; Princess Alexandra Caroline Marie Charlotte Louise Julie,
        1844–1925. *Daughter of Christian IX of Denmark; Queen of Edward VII*
    PG 1563   (Coronation 9 August 1902.) Bronze medal, dia. 5.4 (2⅛), by G. W. de
        Saulles. Dated 1902. Given by Mrs Stewart 1951.

ALEXANDRIA, BATTLE OF; see GROUPS (PG 2680)

ALISON, General Sir Archibald, 1826–1907. *Soldier*
    PG 944   Plaster bust, h. 76.2 (30), by Katherine Anne Fraser Tytler. Dated 1883.
        Given by Major J. F. Fraser Tytler 1923.

ALISON, Sir Archibald, 1792–1867. *Historian*
    PG 323*   Canvas, 56.5 x 41.9 (22¼ x 16½), by Robert Scott Lauder. Bequeathed by
        W. F. Watson 1886.
    PG 1291*   Marble bust, h. 83.8 (33), by Patric Park. Given by the Misses Brown 1935.

ALISON, Rev. Archibald, 1757–1839. *Essayist*
    PG 228   Bust (plaster replica), h. 79.4 (31¼), after Samuel Joseph. Dated 1841.
        Purchased 1888.
    PG 529   Porcelain medallion, h. 6.7 (2⅝), by John Henning. Dated 1802. Given by
        Miss Brown 1894.
    PG 1219*   Marble bust, h. 75.6 (29¾), by Samuel Joseph, 1841, signed. Transferred
        from the National Gallery of Scotland 1934.

ALISON, Henry Young, 1889–1972. *Artist*
    PG 2391*   Canvas, 92 x 71.7 (36¼ x 28¼), self-portrait, signed. Purchased 1977.

Ainslie, John
PG 1676

Airth, 1st Earl of (PG 1834),
and Napier, 1st Lord (PG 1833)

Albany, Duchess of
PG 623

Alexander, John
PG 1970

Alexander, Rev. William
Lindsay   PG 93

Alison, Sir Archibald
PG 323

Alison, Sir Archibald
PG 1291

Alison, Rev. Archibald
PG 1219

Alison, Henry Young
PG 2391

Allan, David
PG 731

Allan, David
PGL 227

Allan, Shirley
PG 2600

Allan, Sir William
PG 1022

Allan, Sir William
PG 1048

ALLAN, David, 1744–96. *Artist*

PG 261   Paste medallion, h. 6.3 (2½), by James Tassie. Dated 1781. Transferred from the National Gallery of Scotland 1889.

PG 325   Canvas, 35.6 x 26.4 (14 x 10⅜), by John Medina after David Allan. Bequeathed by W. F. Watson 1886.

PG 731*   Canvas, 74.3 x 61.3 (29¼ x 24⅛), by Domenico Corvi. Dated 1774. Given by the Royal Scottish Academy 1910.

PGL 227*   Canvas, 126.4 x 98.4 (49¾ x 38¾), self-portrait, 1770, signed. On loan from the Royal Scottish Academy.

ALLAN, Robert Weir, 1852–1942. *Artist*

PG 1292   Canvas, 61 x 50.8 (24 x 20), self-portrait, 1935, signed. Given by the artist 1935.

ALLAN, Shirley Welsh, Mrs David, d. 1821. *Religious writer and wife of the painter David Allan*

PG 2600*   Paste medallion, h. 6.8 (2¹¹⁄₁₆), by James Tassie. Dated 1791. Purchased 1983.

ALLAN, Sir William, 1782–1850. *Artist*

PG 825*   (*Sir Walter Scott and his friends at Abbotsford.*) See GROUPS.

PG 1022*   (In Circassian dress.) Canvas, 91.4 x 71.4 (36 x 28⅛), by William Nicholson. Painted 1818. Purchased 1925.

PG 1048*   Chalk drawing, 53.3 x 38.1 (21 x 15), by William Bewick. Dated 1824. Purchased 1927.

ALLOA

PGL 243*   (Alloa House, seat of 7th Earl of Mar.) See GROUPS.

ALLOWAY

PG 1060   (Burns's cottage at Alloway.) See BURNS, Robert.

AMHERST, Jeffrey Amherst, 1st Baron, 1717–97. *Field-Marshal*

PG 456   Medallion (plaster replica), h. 9.2 (3¾), after James Tassie. Given by J. M. Gray 1893.

ANCRAM, Robert Kerr, 1st Earl of, 1578–1654.

PGL 210*   Canvas, 62.2 x 51.4 (24½ x 20¼), by Jan Lievens. Painted 1654. On loan from the Marquess of Lothian.

ANDERSON, Alexander, 1582–c. 1619. *Mathematician*

PG 2115   Ink drawing, 11.7 x 9 (4⅝ x 3½), copy by unknown artist. Transferred from the National Gallery of Scotland 1950.

ANDERSON, Alexander, 1845–1909. *Poet*
PG 697*   Canvas, 40 x 27.6 (15¾ x 10⅞), by Charles Martin Hardie, 1883, signed.
            Purchased 1910.
PG 1720   Pencil drawing, 17.8 x 10.9 (7 x 4¼), by J. D. Gilruth, signed. Given by
            Dr Gilruth.
PG 2460*   (*Friendly Critics*) See GROUPS.

ANDERSON, Archibald, fl. 1830. *Director of the Commercial Bank*
PG 2146   Cut paper silhouette, h. 20.2 (8), by Augustin Edouart, 1830, signed. Given
            by Mrs J. H. G. Ross 1969.

ANDERSON of Finzeauch, David, 1577–1629. *Architect and merchant*
PGL 19*   Canvas, 61 x 47.6 (24 x 18¾), by unknown artist. Dated 1627. On loan from
            the National Museums of Scotland.

ANDERSON, George, b. 1722. *Burgess of Paisley*
PG 1944   Plaster medallion, h. 7.9 (3), by John Henning. Dated 1801. Provenance
            untraced.

ANDERSON, James, 1739–1808. *Author and agriculturist*
PG 370   Medallion (plaster replica), h. 7.7 (3⅛), after James Tassie. Dated 1793.
            Cast from a medallion in possession of W. G. Patterson 1889.

ANDERSON, James Robertson, 1811–95. *Actor*
PG 648*   Water-colour, 43.8 x 31.7 (17¼ x 12½), by Daniel Maclise. Purchased
            1905.

ANDERSON, Professor John, 1726–96. *Professor of Oriental Languages*
PG 327   Panel, 30.8 x 24.8 (12⅛ x 9¾), by unknown artist. Bequeathed by
            W. F. Watson 1886.
PG 371   Medallion (plaster replica), h. 7.5 (2⅞), after James Tassie. Cast from a
            medallion in possession of W. G. Patterson 1889.

ANDERSON, Joseph, 1832–1916. *Antiquary*
PG 865   Canvas, 109.2 x 92.7 (43 x 36½), by Henry Wright Kerr, signed.
            Bequeathed by Dr J. Anderson 1917.
PG 1695*   Pencil drawing, 37.4 x 33.6 (14¾ x 13¼), by W. Graham Boss. Given by
            the artist 1895.

ANDERSON, R. S., fl. 1899. *Of Peebles Curling Club*
PG 1856*   (*Curling at Carsebreck.*) See GROUPS.

ANDERSON, Robert, 1750–1830. *Writer; editor of the* Edinburgh Magazine
PG 436   Wax medallion, h. 10.4 (4⅛), by unknown artist. Purchased 1893.

ANDERSON, Sir Robert Rowand, 1834–1921. *Architect; designer of the Scottish National Portrait Gallery*

PG 985*   Bronze bust, h. 61 (24), by James Pittendrigh Macgillivray. Dated 1921. Purchased by commission 1925.

PG 1699*   Pencil drawing, 37.5 x 33.6 (14¾ x 13¼), by W. Graham Boss. Given by the artist 1895.

ANDERSON, William, d. 1785. *Antiquary*

PGL 67   Pencil drawing, 50.8 x 35.6 (20 x 14), by John Brown. On loan from the National Museums of Scotland.

ANDERSON, William, 1766–1846. *Horticulturist*

PG 2498   Paste medallion, h. 5.5 (2⅛), by John Henning. Dated 1810. Purchased 1981.

ANNAN, James Craig, 1864–1946. *Photographer*

PG 2205*   Chalk and water-colour drawing, 32.2 x 20.1 (12¹¹⁄₁₆ x 7¹⁵⁄₁₆), by William Strang, 1902, signed. Purchased 1972.

ANNE OF DENMARK, 1574–1619. *Queen of James VI and I*

PG 340   Panel, 49.5 x 30.5 (19½ x 12), by unknown artist. Bequeathed by W. F. Watson 1886.

PG 1110*   Panel, dia. 11.4 (4½), attributed to Adrian Vanson. Dated 1595. Bequeathed by A. W. Inglis 1929.

PG 1649   Water-colour, 8.9 x 5.9 (3½ x 2¼), copy by unknown artist. Bequeathed by W. F. Watson 1886.

PG 1653   Water-colour, 46.9 x 31 (18½ x 12¼), copy by unknown artist. Bequeathed by W. F. Watson 1886.

ANNE, Queen, 1665–1714. *Reigned 1702–1714*

PG 184   Canvas, 124.5 x 100.3 (49 x 39½), by unknown artist after Sir Godfrey Kneller. Given by R. P. Stuart 1887.

PG 443   Medallion (plaster replica), h. 5.2 (2⅛), after James Tassie after John O'Brisset. Given by the Trustees of the British Museum 1893.

PG 761   (Union of England and Scotland 1707.) Silver medal, dia. 3.5 (1⅜), by John Croker. Struck 1707. Purchased 1911.

PG 917   (Union of England and Scotland 1707.) Silver medal, dia. 4.7 (1⅞), by John Croker. Dated 1707. Purchased 1920.

PG 939*   Canvas 199.4 x 128.3 (78½ x 50½), by Willem Wissing and Jan van der Vaardt. Purchased 1922.

PG 2373   (Attempted invasion of Scotland 1708.) Copper medal, dia. 4 (1⁹⁄₁₆), by John Croker. Purchased 1976.

PG 2768   (Attempted invasion of Scotland 1708.) Silver medal, dia. 4 (1⁹⁄₁₆), by George Hautsch. Purchased 1989.

PG 2772   (Attempted invasion of Scotland 1708.) White metal medal, dia. 4.7 (1⅞), by Martin Smeltzing. Purchased 1989.

Ancram, 1st Earl of
PGL 210

Anderson, Alexander
PG 697

Anderson, David
PGL 19

Anderson, James
Robertson   PG 648

Anderson, Joseph
PG 1695

Anderson, Sir Robert Rowand
PG 985

Anderson, Sir Robert Rowand
PG 1699

Annan, James Craig
PG 2205

Anne of Denmark
PG 1110

Anne, Queen
PG 939

Anstruther, Sir John
PG 589

Arab Princess
PG 1604

Arbuthnot, John
PG 92

Argyll, Countess of
PG 1409

ANSON, George Anson, 1st Baron, 1697–1762. *Admiral*
    PG 503   Medallion (plaster replica), h. 6.7 (2⅝), after James Tassie. Cast from a medallion in possession of R. W. Cochran Patrick 1894.

ANSON, General George, 1797–1857. *Commander-in-Chief in India*
    PG 2291   Black chalk drawing, 26 x 19.1 (10¼ x 7½), by unknown artist. Given by Aberdeen University.

ANSTRUTHER, Sir John, 1753–1811. *Politician and Indian Judge*
    PG 589*   Pencil drawing, 26 x 19.7 (10¼ x 7¾), by George Dance, 1797, signed. Purchased 1900.

ARAB PRINCESS, fl. 1628. *'Wife' of Sir John Henderson of Fordell*
    PG 1604*   (With black maid.) Canvas, 66 x 123.2 (26 x 48½), by Walter Frier after unknown artist. Dated 1731. On loan from the Earl of Buckinghamshire.

ARBUTHNOT, John, 1667–1735. *Physician and wit*
    PG 92*   Canvas, 75.6 x 63.5 (29¾ x 25), by William Robinson, signed. Purchased 1885.

ARCHER, James, 1823–1904. *Artist*
    PG 725   Canvas on millboard, 19.3 x 14.9 (7¾ x 5⅞), self-portrait. Given by the Royal Scottish Academy 1910.

ARGYLL, Lady Agnes Douglas, Countess of, c. 1574–1607. *Wife of the 7th Earl of Argyll*
    PG 1409*   Canvas, 86.4 x 77.5 (34 x 30½), by unknown artist. Dated 1599. Bequeathed by the Marquess of Lothian 1941.

ARGYLL, Archibald Campbell, 1st Marquess of, 1598–1661. *Statesman*
    PG 583   Canvas, 48.9 x 35.5 (19¼ x 14), by unknown artist after David Scougall. Given by the trustees of Sir William Fraser 1899.
    PG 1408*   Canvas, 73.7 x 67.3 (29 x 26½), by David Scougall. Bequeathed by the Marquess of Lothian 1941.

ARGYLL, Archibald Campbell, 9th Earl of, 1629–85. *Confederate of the Duke of Monmouth*
    PG 1197   Oil miniature, 8.3 x 5.8 (3¼ x 2¼), attributed to David Loggan. Given by Sir Hew Hamilton-Dalrymple 1933.
    PG 1412   Canvas, 69.8 x 57.1 (27½ x 22½), by unknown artist. Bequeathed by the Marquess of Lothian 1941.
    PG 1611*   Canvas, 127 x 101.6 (50 x 40), attributed to L. Schuneman. Purchased 1954.
    PG 2765   (Execution of the Duke of Monmouth and the 9th Earl of Argyll.) Silver medal, dia. 6.2 (2⁷⁄₁₆), by Regnier Arondeaux. Purchased 1989.

ARGYLL, Archibald Campbell, 3rd Duke of, 1682–1761. *Statesman*
> PG 908   Canvas, 74.3 x 61.6 (29¼ x 24¼), attributed to Allan Ramsay. Purchased 1920.
> PG 1293* Canvas, 127 x 101.6 (50 x 40), by Allan Ramsay. Purchased 1936.

ARGYLL, George Campbell, 6th Duke of, 1768–1839. *Hereditary Master of the Household in Scotland*
> PG 1040* (*The Entrance of George IV at Holyroodhouse*.) See GROUPS.

ARGYLL, George Douglas Campbell, 8th Duke of, 1823–1900. *Statesman*
> PG 857   Canvas, 31.8 x 23.5 (12½ x 9¼), by John Pettie. Purchased 1916.

ARGYLL, John Campbell, 4th Duke of, c. 1693–1770. *Soldier*
> PG 1596* Canvas, 235 x 154.3 (92½ x 60¾), by Thomas Gainsborough. Purchased 1953.

ARGYLL, Lady Margaret Douglas, Marchioness of, 1610–78. *Wife of the 1st Marquess of Argyll*
> PG 1413* Canvas, 72.4 x 63.5 (28½ x 25), by George Jamesone. Dated 1634. Bequeathed by the Marquess of Lothian 1941.

ARGYLL AND GREENWICH, John Campbell, 2nd Duke of, 1678–1743. *Soldier and Statesman*
> PG 692*   Canvas, 74.9 x 62.2 (29½ x 24½), by William Aikman. Purchased 1909.
> PG 1456   Enamel miniature, 5.7 x 4.6 (2¼ x 1⅞), by Christian Friedrich Zincke, 1719, signed. Bequeathed by Sir St Clair Thomson 1944.
> PGL 186   Bronze medal, dia. 5.4 (2⅛), by Jacques Antoine Dassier. Struck 1743. On loan from the National Museums of Scotland.

ARMOUR, George Denholm, 1864–1949. *Artist*
> PG 1248   Panel, 36.5 x 27.6 (14⅜ x 10⅞), self-portrait, signed. Given by the artist 1935.

ARNISTON, Robert Dundas, Lord, 1713–87. *Lord President of the Court of Session*
> PG 1664   a. Wash drawing, 14.3 x 10.5 (5⅝ x 4⅛), by unknown artist after Sir Henry Raeburn. Bequeathed by W. F. Watson 1886.
> b. (View of the sitter's house in Adam Square, Edinburgh.) Water-colour drawing, 9.5 x 19.5 (3¾ x 7¹¹⁄₁₆), by unknown artist. Bequeathed by W. F. Watson 1886.

ARROL, Sir William, 1839–1913. *Engineer*
> PG 613   (Probably the artist's plaster.) Plaster bust, h. 78.7 (31) by David Watson Stevenson. Purchased 1903.

ASPINALL, Mr, fl. 1804.
> PG 2578   Silhouette in ink on plaster, h. 8.5 (3⅜), by or after John Miers. Drawn 1804. Transferred from the National Gallery of Scotland 1982.

ASQUITH; see OXFORD AND ASQUITH

ATHOLL, Lady Charlotte Murray, Duchess of, 1731–1805. *Wife of the 3rd Duke of Atholl; later Baroness Strange*
  PG 1872 Medallion (plaster replica), h. 3.4 (1⅜), after James Tassie. Provenance untraced.

ATHOLL, James Murray, 2nd Duke of, *c.* 1690–1764. *Lord Privy Seal*
  PG 925* Canvas, 73.7 x 61 (29 x 24), by Allan Ramsay, 1743, signed. Purchased 1921.

ATHOLL, John Murray, 3rd Duke of, 1729–74.
  PG 702 (Death of Atholl.) Silver medal, dia. 3.8 (1½), by John Kirk. Dated 1774. Purchased 1910.

ATKINSON, James, 1780–1852. *Persian scholar*
  PG 435 Water-colour on ivory, 9.9 x 7.9 (3⅞ x 3⅛), by Mrs Marmaduke Browne, signed. Given by Canon Atkinson 1893.

ATKINSON, Thomas, *c.* 1801–33. *Poet*
  PG 785 Cut paper silhouette, h. 20 (8), by Augustin Edouart. Purchased 1912.

AULD, Hugh, d. 1855. *Banker*
  PG 2147 Cut paper silhouette, h. 20.7 (8⅛), by Augustin Edouart, 1830, signed. Given by Mrs J. H. G. Ross 1969.

AYTOUN, Professor William Edmondstoune, 1813–65. *Lawyer and author*
  PG 125* Pencil and water-colour, 25.6 x 19.9 (10 x 7⅞), by James Archer, 1855, signed. Bequeathed by W. F. Watson 1886.
  PG 286* Marble bust, h. 83.8 (34), by John Rhind after Patric Park. Given by the Misses Aytoun 1890.

Argyll, 1st Marquess of
PG 1408

Argyll, 9th Earl of
PG 1611

Argyll, 3rd Duke of
PG 1293

Argyll, 4th Duke of
PG 1596

Argyll, Marchioness of
PG 1413

Argyll and Greenwich,
2nd Duke of   PG 692

Atholl, 2nd Duke of
PG 925

Aytoun, Professor William
Edmondstoune   PG 125

Aytoun, Professor William
Edmondstoune   PG 286

BAILEY, Philip James, 1816–1902. *Poet*
PG 242   Marble bust, h.74.3 (29¼), by John Alexander MacBride. Given by
W. G. Patterson 1889.

BAILLIE, Joanna, 1762–1851. *Dramatist and poet*
PG 2036*   Pencil and water-colour drawing, 27.9 x 20.1 (11 x 8), by Mary Ann Knight.
Purchased 1964.

BAILLIE, Very Rev. John Baillie, 1886–1960. *Principal of New College, Edinburgh and*
Professor of Divinity at Edinburgh University
PG 2393   Pencil drawing on tissue, 37.3 x 27 (14⅝ x 10⅝), by Sir William Oliphant
Hutchison. Given by the executors of Margery, Lady Hutchison 1977.

BAIN, Sir James, 1817–98. *Lord Provost of Glasgow*
PG 1687   Ink drawing, 17.5 x 11 (7 x 4¼), by Sir Daniel Macnee. Given by
G. R. Halkett 1886.

BAIRD, General Sir David, 1757–1829. *Soldier*
PG 644*   (Study for *Sir David Baird discovering the body of Tipu Sahib.*) Canvas,
75.6 x 62.8 (29¾ x 24¾), by Sir David Wilkie. Painted 1837–8. Given by
General Stirling 1906.
PG 2683   c. (Study related to *The Battle of Alexandria* and *The Landing of British*
Troops at Aboukir.) Water-colour, 10.7 x 8.9 (4³⁄₁₆ x 3½), attributed to
Philip James de Loutherbourg. Purchased 1986.
PGL 331*   Marble bust, h. 74.3 (29¼), by Lawrence Macdonald. Sculpted c.1828.
On loan from Andrew Gordon Duff.

BAIRD, John George Alexander, 1854–1917. *Politician*
PG 2708*   Pencil drawing, 28 x 21.7 (11 x 8⁹⁄₁₆), by Frederick Sargent. Purchased 1986.

BAIRD, John Logie, 1888–1946. *Television pioneer*
PG 1437*   Pencil drawing, 50.5 x 37.7 (17⅞ x 14⅞), by James Kerr-Lawson, signed.
Purchased 1943.

BALFOUR OF BURLEIGH, Alexander Hugh Bruce, 6th Lord, 1849–1921. *Statesman*
PG 872*   Canvas on millboard, 33.9 x 23.7 (13⅜ x 9⅜), by Charles Martin Hardie,
1899, signed. Purchased 1917.
PG 1856*   (*Curling at Carsebreck.*) See GROUPS.

BALFOUR, Arthur James Balfour, 1st Earl of, 1848–1930. *Statesman*
PG 691*   (Artist's plaster.) Plaster bust, h. 75.9 (29⅞), by Edward Onslow Ford.
Executed c. 1892. Given by Miss Alice Balfour 1909.
PG 924   (British intrigues in Sweden.) Bronze medal, dia. 5.6 (2¼), by Karl Goetz,
1916. Purchased 1920.
PG 1098*   Panel, 73.6 x 48.3 (29 x 19), by Charles Sims, signed. Painted c. 1923.
Purchased 1928.

PG 1132*   Canvas, 142.2 x 88.9 (56 x 35), by Sir James Guthrie; study for portrait in *Statesmen of the Great War* (National Portrait Gallery, London). Given by W. G. Gardiner and Sir Frederick Gardiner 1930.

PG 1466*   (*Some Statesmen of the Great War.*) See GROUPS.

PG 1856*   (*Curling at Carsebreck.*) See GROUPS.

BALFOUR, Sir James, 1600–57. *Historian and Lord Lyon King-of-Arms*

    PG 1551*   Canvas, 73.6 x 61 (29 x 24), by unknown artist. Purchased 1950.

BALFOUR, James, 1681–1737. *Manufacturer and first Laird of Pilrig*

    PG 1187   Water-colour on ivory, 7 x 5.1 (2¾ x 2), by unknown artist after James Jemely. Purchased 1932.

BALFOUR, John Hutton, 1808–84. *Botanist*

    PG 1442   Canvas, 92.1 x 71.1 (36¼ x 28), by John Horsburgh, 1878, signed. Purchased 1943.

BALLANTYNE, James, 1772–1833. *Printer of Scott's works*

    PG 825*   (*Sir Walter Scott and his friends at Abbotsford.*) See GROUPS.

BALLANTYNE, James, 1808–77. *Artist and author*

    PG 1370   Canvas, 75.9 x 63.2 (28⅞ x 24⅞), by unknown artist. Purchased 1938.

    PG 1589*   (With Sir William Fettes Douglas and Thomas Faed.) Wash drawing, 16.2 x 20.2 (6⅜ x 8), by John Faed, signed. Given by J. A. Faed 1952.

BALLANTYNE, John, 1774–1821. *Publisher*

    PG 1142*   Canvas, 76.2 x 63.5 (30 x 25), by unknown artist. Given by Miss Ballantyne 1930.

    PG 1673   Pencil, ink and water-colour drawing, 11.4 x 9.7 (4½ x 3¹³⁄₁₆), by unknown artist. Bequeathed by W. F. Watson 1886.

BARCLAY, Rev. George, 1731–95. *Minister of Haddington*

    PGL 68*   Pencil drawing, 51.2 x 34.8 (20⅛ x 13¾), by John Brown. On loan from the National Museums of Scotland.

BARCLAY, Rev. John, 1758–1826. *Anatomist*

    PG 1830*   Canvas, 90.2 x 68.6 (35½ x 27), by John Syme, 1816, signed. Transferred from the National Gallery of Scotland 1956.

BARCLAY, John Maclaren, 1811–86. *Artist*

    PG 2141*   Canvas, 91.5 x 71 (36 x 28), self-portrait. Given by A. F. B. Bridges 1968.

BARCLAY, Oswald, d. 1942. *Baillie of Holyroodhouse*

    PG 1818   Black chalk drawing, 47 x 29.2 (18½ x 11½), by David Foggie, 1933, signed. Given by Mrs M. Foggie 1955.

BARCLAY, William, c. 1546–1608. *Professor of Civil Law at Angers*
  PG 2091   Ink drawing, 19.2 x 16 (7½ x 6⅜), copy by unknown artist after engraving
             from Lorenzo Crasso's *Elogii d'huomini letterati*. Published 1666.
             Transferred from the National Gallery of Scotland 1950.

BARJARG AND ALVA, , James Erskine, Lord, 1722–96. *Scottish judge*
  PG 2216*   Canvas, 76.2 x 63.8 (30 x 25⅛), by Allan Ramsay, 1750, signed.
             Bequeathed by 13th Baron Elibank 1973.

BARNES, George Nicoll, 1859–1940. *Statesman*
  PG 1134*   Canvas, 111.7 x 86.4 (44 x 34), by Sir James Guthrie; study for portrait in
             Statesmen of the Great War (National Portrait Gallery, London). Given by
             W. G. Gardiner and Sir Frederick C. Gardiner 1930.

BARNES, Sir Harry Jefferson, 1915–82. *Artist; Director of Glasgow School of Art*
  PG 2516   Pencil drawing, 25.3 x 18.4 (10 x 7¼), by Edgar Holloway, signed.
             Purchased 1982.
  PG 2517   Pencil drawing, 38.2 x 27.9 (15 x 11), by Edgar Holloway, signed. Dated
             1940. Purchased 1982.
  PG 2518   Water-colour and pencil drawing, 37.8 x 28 (14⅞ x 11), by Edgar Holloway,
             signed. Purchased 1982.

BARNES, John Seton, Lord, d. 1594. *Master of the Horse and First Master of the Royal
             Household*
  PG 1020   (With his father, 5th Lord Seton, his brothers and sister.) See GROUPS.
  PGL 312*   (With his father, 5th Lord Seton, his brothers and sister.) See GROUPS.

BARNETT, Rev. Thomas Ratcliffe, 1868–1946. *Historian and topographer*
  PG 1791   Black chalk drawing, 43.5 x 27 (17⅛ x 10⅝), by David Foggie, 1935, signed.
             Given by Mrs M. Foggie 1955.

BARRIE, Sir James Matthew, 1860–1937. *Author*
  PG 1309*   Canvas, 76.2 x 63.5 (30 x 25), by Sir John Lavery, signed. Given by the
             artist 1936.
  PG 1438*   Canvas, 58.4 x 52.7 (23 x 20¾), by Sir William Nicholson, 1904, signed.
             Purchased with assistance from the National Art-Collections Fund 1943.

BARROWFIELD, Lady; see WALKINSHAW, Katherine (PGL 311)

BARTHOLOMEW, John George, 1860–1920. *Cartographer*
  PG 1994*   Canvas, 137.2 x 111.7 (54 x 44), by Edward Arthur Walton, signed. Painted
             c. 1911. Given by Mrs Bartholomew 1962.

BATTENBERG, Prince Henry Maurice of, d. 1896. *Husband of Princess Beatrice*
  PG 1306*   (*The Baptism of Prince Maurice of Battenberg*.) See GROUPS.

Baillie, Joanna
PG 2036

Baird, Sir David
PG 644

Baird, Sir David
PGL 331

Baird, John George Alexander
PG 2708

Baird, John Logie
PG 1437

Balfour of Burleigh,
6th Lord   PG 872

Balfour, 1st Earl of
PG 691

Balfour, 1st Earl of
PG 1098

Balfour, 1st Earl of
PG 1132

Balfour, Sir James
PG 1551

Ballantyne, James, with Thomas Faed
and Sir William Fettes Douglas   PG 1589

Ballantyne, John
PG 1142

Barclay, Rev. George
PGL 68

Barclay, Rev. John
PG 1830

Barclay, John MacLaren
PG 2141

BATTENBERG, Prince Maurice Victor Donald of, 1891–1914. *Son of Prince Henry of Battenberg and Princess Beatrice*
  PG 1306*   (*The Baptism of Prince Maurice of Battenberg.*) See GROUPS.

BAXTER, Alexander, fl. 1798. *Merchant in London*
  PG 1962   Paste medallion, h. 8.9 (3⅝), by James Tassie. Dated 1798. Transferred from the National Gallery of Scotland 1960.

BAXTER, John, d. 1796. *Architect*
  PGL 69*   Pencil drawing, 49.8 x 34 (19⅝ x 13⅜), by John Brown. On loan from the National Museums of Scotland.

BEATON, Mary. *Lady in waiting to Mary, Queen of Scots*
  PG 826   Canvas, 95.2 x 70.5 (37½ x 27¾), by unknown artist. Purchased 1913.

BEATRICE, Princess; Princess Beatrice Mary Victoria Feodore, 1857–1944. *Youngest daughter of Queen Victoria*
  PG 1306*   (*The Baptism of Prince Maurice of Battenberg.*) See GROUPS.

BEATTIE, James, 1735–1803. *Poet and moral philosopher*
  PG 132   Paste medallion, h. 7.7 (3¹⁄₁₆), by James Tassie. Dated 1789. Purchased 1886.

BEATTIE, Professor William, 1903–86. *Librarian of the National Library of Scotland*
  PG 2450   Ball-point drawing, 30.5 x 24.1 (12 x 9½) (irregular), by Jean Isabel Beattie (Mrs Tom Hunt), signed. Dated 1977. Given by the sitter 1979.

BEATTY, David Beatty, 1st Earl, 1871–1936. *Admiral*
  PG 1036*   Canvas, 76.2 x 63.5 (30 x 25), by Sir William Orpen, signed. Purchased 1926.

BECKFORD, William, 1759–1844. *Author of* Vathek
  PG 342   Canvas, 21.3 x 17.5 (8¼ x 6⅞), by unknown artist. Bequeathed by W. F. Watson 1886.

BEGG, Isabella Burns, Mrs John, 1771–1858. *Youngest sister of Robert Burns*
  PG 112   Chalk and water-colour drawing, 18.5 x 14.2 (7¼ x 5⅝), by or after William Bonnar. Bequeathed by W. F. Watson 1886.
  PG 1350*   Millboard, 25.9 x 20.7 (10³⁄₁₆ x 8³⁄₁₆), by William Bonnar, 1843, signed. Purchased 1937.

BEGG, Rev. James, 1808–83. *Free Church Minister*
  PG 437*   Canvas, 142.2 x 111.7 (56 x 44), by Sir Daniel Macnee, 1869, signed. Given by the family of the sitter 1893.

Barjarg and Alva, Lord
PG 2216

Barnes, George Nicoll
PG 1134

Barrie, Sir James
PG 1309

Barrie, Sir James
PG 1438

Bartholomew, John George
PG 1994

Baxter, John
PGL 69

Beatty, 1st Earl
PG 1036

Begg, Isabella Burns
PG 1350

Begg, Rev. James
PG 437

Belhaven, 1st Baron, with Lady Belhaven
PG 1054

Bell, Andrew
PG 307

Bell, Sir Charles
PG 1294

Bell, Henry
PG 911

Bell, Henry Glassford
PG 843

BELHAVEN, John Hamilton, 1st Baron, d. 1679. *Royalist*
   PG 1054*   (With his wife Margaret Hamilton.) Canvas, 124.5 x 146.7 (49 x 57¾),
           from the studio of Sir Anthony Van Dyck. Bequeathed by Mrs Nisbet
           Hamilton Ogilvy 1921.

BELHAVEN, John Hamilton, 2nd Baron, 1656–1708. *Statesman*
   PG 907   Canvas, 75.4 x 61.9 (29¾ x 24⅜), by unknown artist after Sir Godfrey
           Kneller. Purchased 1919.
   PG 1553   Canvas, 76.2 x 63.5 (30 x 25), by John Medina after Sir Godfrey Kneller.
           Purchased 1950.
   PG 1639   Chalk drawing, 34.6 x 24.2 (13⅝ x 9½), by the 11th Earl of Buchan after
           unknown artist. Bequeathed by W. F. Watson 1886.

BELL, Andrew, 1726–1809. *Engraver*
   PG 307*   Canvas, 88.9 x 68.6 (35 x 27), by George Watson. Bequeathed by
           W. F. Watson 1886.

BELL, Benjamin, 1749–1806. *Surgeon*
   PG 2780   Paste medallion, h. 7.9 (3⅛), by James Tassie, 1792. Purchased 1989.

BELL, Sir Charles, 1774–1842. *Surgeon and anatomist*
   PG 1294*   Canvas, 76.2 x 63.5 (30 x 25), by unknown artist. Purchased 1936.

BELL, Dr Charles, 1805–91. *Specialist in midwifery*
   PG 1543   Water-colour on ivory, 11.2 x 8.8 (4⅜ x 3½), by unknown artist.
           Bequeathed by Miss Ida M. Hayward 1950.

BELL, Professor George Joseph, 1770–1843. *Jurist*
   PG 562   Canvas, 91.4 x 71.1 (36 x 28), by James Tannock. Given by W. K. Dickson
           1897.
   PG 2306   (Crombie Sketchbook, fo. 7r. Study for *Modern Athenians*, pl. 12.) Pencil
           drawing, 15.6 x 20 (6⅛ x 7⅞), by Benjamin William Crombie. Purchased
           1938.

BELL, Henry, 1767–1830. *Marine engineer*
   PG 911*   Canvas, 76.2 x 63.5 (30 x 25), by James Tannock. Purchased 1920.

BELL, Henry Glassford, 1803–74. *Sheriff and man of letters*
   PG 843*   Marble bust, h. 85.7 (33¾), by John Mossman, 1874, signed. Bequeathed
           by Mrs Glassford Bell 1915.

BELL, John, 1745–1832. *Publisher*
   PG 2265   (Possibly John Bell.) Pencil and water-colour drawing, 37.8 x 32.7
           (14⅞ x 12⅞), by William Douglas. Provenance untraced.

BELLANY, John, b. 1942. *Artist*
　　PG 2632*　(With Alan Davie.) Canvas, 213.3 x 165 (84 x 65), self-portrait, signed.
　　　　　　　Dated 1983. Purchased 1984.

BELSCHES, Williamina, d. 1810. *Wife of Sir William Forbes of Pitsligo*
　　PGL 172　Paste medallion, h. 5.4 (2⅛), by unknown artist. On loan from Miss
　　　　　　　Adelaide Traill.

BENSON, Martin, 1689–1752. *Bishop of Gloucester*
　　PG 302　Medallion (plaster replica), h. 5.9 (2⅜), after W. Whitley; also known in
　　　　　　　Tassie paste. Cast from a medallion in the possession of W. G. Patterson
　　　　　　　1891.

BERGMAN, Torbern Olaf, 1735–84. *Chemist*
　　PG 1875　Medallion (plaster replica), h. 7.3 (2⅞), after unknown artist; also known in
　　　　　　　Tassie paste. Provenance untraced.

BERRY, William, 1730–83. *Seal engraver*
　　PG 114　Pencil drawing, 25.7 x 19.2 (10⅛ x 7⁹⁄₁₆), by Archibald Skirving, 1797,
　　　　　　　signed, after William Delacour. Bequeathed by W. F. Watson 1886.

BEUGO, John, 1759–1841. *Engraver*
　　PG 102*　Canvas, 74.9 x 62.2 (29½ x 24½), by George Willison. Given by John
　　　　　　　Ritchie Findlay 1885.
　　PG 117　Pencil drawing, 11.1 x 7.9 (4⅜ x 3¼), by R. C. Bell, 1822, signed.
　　　　　　　Bequeathed by W. F. Watson 1886.
　　PG 129　Pencil drawing, 18.2 x 14.5 (7⅛ x 5¾), by R. C. Bell. Given by R. P. Bell
　　　　　　　1886.

BIKANER, Sri Ganga Singh Bahadur, the Maharaja of, 1880–1943. *Statesman*
　　PG 1130*　Canvas, 111.2 x 86.8 (43⅞ x 34⅛), by Sir James Guthrie; study for portrait
　　　　　　　in *Statesmen of the Great War* (National Portrait Gallery, London). Given
　　　　　　　by W. G. Gardiner and Sir Frederick Gardiner 1930.

BINNING, Charles Hamilton, Lord, 1697–1732. *Knight Marischal of Scotland*
　　PG 2081　Water-colour, 18 x 15 (7 x 5⅞), copy by unknown artist. Transferred from
　　　　　　　the National Gallery of Scotland 1950.

BLACK, Adam, 1784–1874. *Politician and Lord Provost of Edinburgh*
　　PG 1691　Chalk drawing, 12.3 x 10 (4¾ x 3⅞), by unknown artist. Given by Sir
　　　　　　　William Fettes Douglas 1888.

BLACK, John, 1783–1855. *Journalist; editor of the* Morning Chronicle
　　PG 321　Canvas, 24.6 x 19.4 (9¾ x 7⅞), by W. H. Worthington. Bequeathed by
　　　　　　　W. F. Watson 1886.

BLACK, Professor Joseph, 1728–99. *Chemist*
  PG 153   Wedgwood medallion, h. 6.8 (2¹¹⁄₁₆), after James Tassie. Purchased 1886.
  PG 283   Chalk drawing, 44.4 x 57.1 (17½ x 22½), by unknown artist. Purchased
             1890.
  PG 2591*   Paste medallion, h. 7.4 (2⅞), by James Tassie. Dated 1788. Purchased 1983.
  PGL 259*   Canvas, 126.8 x 102 (50 x 40⅛), by David Martin, 1787, signed. On loan
             from the Royal Medical Society, Edinburgh.

BLACK, William, 1841–98. *Novelist*
  PG 932*   (Study for *A knight of the seventeenth century* in Glasgow Art Gallery.)
             Canvas, 51.2 x 44.6 (20⅛ x 17½). Painted *c.* 1877. Given by Henry
             J. Brown 1921.

BLACKADDER, Colonel John, 1664–1729. *Deputy Governor of Stirling Castle*
  PG 1534*   Canvas, 114.3 x 96.5 (45 x 38), by unknown artist. Given by Mrs Kemp
             1949.

BLACKIE, Professor John Stuart, 1809–95. *Scholar and poet*
  PG 676*   Canvas, 116.8 x 81.3 (46 x 32), by Sir George Reid, signed. Bequeathed by
             Professor Blackie 1909.
  PG 742*   Plaster bust, h. 76.5 (30⅛), by William Brodie. Executed *c.* 1863. Given by
             A. Stodart Walker 1910.
  PG 2677*   Waxed plaster bust, h. 72.5 (28½), by David Watson Stevenson. Sculpted
             1890. Purchased 1903.

BLACKLOCK, Rev. Thomas, 1721–91. *Minister of Kirkcudbright and poet*
  PG 319   Millboard, 20.7 x 17.7 (8½ x 7), by William Bonnar. Bequeathed by
             W. F. Watson 1886.
  PG 1770*   (*Burns at an evening party of Lord Monboddo's 1786.*) See GROUPS

BLACKWOOD, William, 1776–1834. *Publisher*
  PG 2748*   Canvas, 127 x 101.9 (50 x 40), by Sir William Allan, signed. Dated
             indistinctly 18[30]. Purchased 1988.

BLAIKIE, Rev. William Garden, 1820–99. *Professor of Theology*
  PG 2025   Canvas, 24 x 18.5 (9½ x 7¼), by Percival Novice. Painted 1853. Purchased
             1963.

BLAIR, Hugh, 1718–1800. *Divine and author*
  PG 134*   Paste medallion, h. 7.2 (2¹³⁄₁₆), by James Tassie. Dated 1791. Purchased
             1886.
  PG 466   Medallion (plaster replica), h. 7.6 (3), after James Tassie. Dated 1791. Cast
             from a medallion in possession of Jeffery Whitehead 1893.
  PG 1770*   (*Burns at an evening party of Lord Monboddo's 1786.*) See GROUPS.

Bellany, John,
with Alan Davie   PG 2632

Beugo, John
PG 102

Bikaner, Maharaja of
PG 1130

Black, Joseph
PG 2591

Black, Joseph
PGL 259

Black, William
PG 932

Blackadder, Colonel John
PG 1534

Blackie, Professor John Stuart
PG 676

Blackie, Professor John Stuart
PG 742

Blackie, Professor John Stuart
PG 2677

Blackwood, William
PG 2748

Blair, Hugh
PG 134

Blake, George, with Neil Gunn
and Douglas Young   PG 2586

Blyth, Robert Henderson
PG 2716

Bohemia, Queen of
PG 1053

BLAIR, Sir James Hunter, 1741–87. *Banker and Lord Provost of Edinburgh*
PG 946*   (Probably Sir James Hunter Blair, in *The Inauguration of Robert Burns as Poet Laureate of the Lodge Canongate, Kilwinning, 1787*.) See GROUPS.

BLAIR, Robert Blair, Lord, 1741–1811. *Lord President of the College of Justice*
PG 1265   Paste medallion, h. 7.5 (2¹⁵⁄₁₆), by James Tassie. Dated 1792. Purchased 1935.

BLAKE, George, 1893–1961. *Novelist*
PG 2586*   (With Neil Gunn and Douglas Young.) Ink, chalk and pencil drawing, 35 x 41.4 (13¾ x 16⁵⁄₁₆), (irregular), by Emilio Coia, signed. Executed 1957. Given by Christopher Blake 1983.

BLAKENEY, William Blakeney, Lord, 1672–1761. *The defender of Minorca*
PG 315   Canvas, 35.6 x 30.6 (14 x 12), by Sir George Chalmers. Bequeathed by W. F. Watson 1891.

BLANTYRE, , Robert Walter Stewart, 11th Lord, 1775–1830. *Soldier and Scottish Representative Peer*
PG 2170   Pencil and water-colour drawing, 11.3 x 9 (4⁷⁄₁₆ x 3⁹⁄₁₆), by Ellen Sharpe. Purchased 1969.

BLYTH, Robert Henderson, 1919–70. *Artist*
PG 2716*   Pencil drawing with chalk highlights, 27.3 x 22.9 (10¾ x 9) (irregular), self-portrait, signed. Purchased 1987.
PGL 328*   (*Gathering at 7 London Street.*) See GROUPS.

BOHEMIA, Elizabeth, Queen of, 1596–1662. *Daughter of James VI and I*
PG 1053*   Panel, 66 x 55.9 (26 x 22), from the studio of Michiel van Miereveld. Given by Arthur W. Brown 1917.
PG 1781*   (Formerly called Elizabeth, Queen of Bohemia, with Frederick, King of Bohemia.) See UNIDENTIFIED SUBJECTS.

BOHEMIA, Frederick, King of, 1596–1632. *Husband of Elizabeth, daughter of James VI and I*
PG 1781*   (Formerly called Frederick, King of Bohemia, with Elizabeth, Queen of Bohemia.) See UNIDENTIFIED SUBJECTS.

BOLD, Alan, b. 1943. *Poet and critic*
PG 2597*   (*Poets' Pub.*) See GROUPS.

BOLINGBROKE, Henry St John, 1st Viscount, 1678–1751. *Statesman*
PG 373   Medallion (plaster replica), h. 6.7 (2⅝), after unknown artist; also known in Tassie paste. Dated 1740. Cast from a medallion in the possession of W. G. Patterson 1889.

BONCLE, Sir Edward, d. 1496. *Provost of the Collegiate Church of the Holy Trinity in Edinburgh*
PG 1656   Water-colour drawing, 13.8 x 7.6 (5⅜ x 3), by unknown artist after Hugo van der Goes. Bequeathed by W. F. Watson 1886.
PG 1766   Ink and water-colour drawing, 36.5 x 19 (14¾ x 7½), by unknown artist after Hugo van der Goes. Purchased 1945.

BONE, Sir Muirhead, 1876–1953. *Artist*
PG 2057*   Ink drawing, 30.2 x 26.7 (11⅝ x 10½), by Francis Dodd, 1907, signed. Given by Sir Henry Rushbury 1966.

BONNAR, William, 1800–53. *Artist*
PGL 303*   Millboard, 35.6 x 29.9 (14 x 11¾), self-portrait. On loan from the National Gallery of Scotland.

BORDEN, Sir Robert Laird, 1854–1937. *Prime Minister of Canada*
PG 1140*   Canvas, 90 x 69.3 (35½ x 27¼), by Sir James Guthrie; study for portrait in *Statesmen of the Great War* (National Portrait Gallery, London). Given by W. G. Gardiner and Sir Frederick Gardiner 1930.

BOSWELL, James, 1740–95. *Diarist and biographer of Dr Samuel Johnson*
PG 804*   Canvas, 135.2 x 96.5 (53¼ x 38), by George Willison. Painted 1765. Bequeathed by Captain James Wood 1912.
PG 946*   (*The Inauguration of Robert Burns as Poet Laureate of the Lodge Canongate, Kilwinning, 1787.*) See GROUPS.
PG 1250*   (Boswell and his family.) See GROUPS.

BOSWELL, James, 1778–1822. *Barrister; son of James Boswell of Auchinleck*
PG 1250*   (Probably James Boswell.) See GROUPS

BOSWELL, Margaret Montgomerie, Mrs James, d. 1789. *Wife of James Boswell of Auchinleck*
PG 1250*   (With her husband and family.) See GROUPS.

BOTHA, General Louis, 1863–1919. *Soldier and statesman*
PG 1139*   Canvas, 91.4 x 71.1 (36 x 28), by Sir James Guthrie; study for portrait in *Statesmen of the Great War* (National Portrait Gallery, London). Given by W. G. Gardiner and Sir Frederick Gardiner 1930.

BOTHWELL, TENT PREACHING AT
PG 1759*   Ink and water-colour drawing, 28.3 x 40 (11⅛ x 15¾), attributed to James Howe. Given by the legatees of J. A. Gardiner.

BOTHWELL, James Hepburn, 4th Earl of, c. 1535–78. *Third husband of Mary, Queen of Scots*
PG 869*   Oil on copper, dia. 3.7 (1½), by unknown artist. Dated 1566. Purchased 1917.

BOTHWELL, James Hepburn, 4th Earl of (*continued*)
    PGL 106   Canvas, 28.7 x 27.3 (11⅜ x 10¾), by Otto Bache, 1861, signed; study of mummified head. On loan from the National Museums of Scotland.

BOTHWELL, Lady Jean Gordon, Countess of, 1544–1629. *First wife of James Hepburn, 4th Earl of Bothwell*
    PG 870*   Oil on copper, dia. 3.5 (1⅜), by unknown artist. Dated 1566. Purchased 1917.

BOUGH, Samuel, 1822–78. *Landscape painter*
    PG 673   Cameo, h. 3.8 (1½), by John Mossman. Dated 1850. Given by Henry N. Veitch 1909.
    PG 693*   Canvas, 111.8 x 85.7 (44 x 33¾), by John Phillip, 1856, signed. Bequeathed by Mr and Mrs John F. Hodgson 1909.
    PG 1080   Pencil and chalk drawing, 17.4 x 13 (6⅞ x 5⅛), by Thomas Fairbairn, 1854, signed. Given by the family of the late Lady Wingate 1928.
    PG 1809*   Bronze statuette, h. 36.8 (14½), by W. G. Stevenson. Bequeathed by R. T. G. Paterson 1955.
    PG 2030   Water-colour drawing, 15.5 x 15.2 (6⅛ x 6), by Mary Slee after William Percy. Given by Mrs M. M. Young 1963.
    PG 2053*   Millboard, 19 x 12.7 (7½ x 5), by Robert Anderson, signed. Given by A. G. B. Cameron 1965.

BOWIE, James, fl. 1899. *Of Preston Curling Club*
    PG 1856*   (*Curling at Carsebreck.*) See GROUPS.

BOYD, Sir Robert, 1710–94. *Governor of Gibraltar*
    PG 374   Medallion (plaster replica), h. 7.7 (3⅛), after William Tassie. Cast from a medallion in the possession of W. G. Patterson 1889.

BOYD ORR, John Boyd Orr, 1st Baron, 1880–1971. *Nutritional physiologist*
    PG 2698*   Bronze head, h. 30 (11¾), by Benno Schotz, signed. Sculpted 1950. Purchased 1986.

BOYLE, David Boyle, Lord, 1772–1853. *Lord President of the Court of Session*
    PG 227   (Artist's plaster.) Plaster statue, h. 215 (84⅝), by Sir John Steell. Purchased 1888.
    PG 949*   Millboard, 41.9 x 26.7 (16½ x 10½), by Sir John Watson Gordon. Purchased 1923.

BRAGANZA, Catherine of, 1638–1705. *Queen of Charles II*
    PG 760   (Marriage to Charles II 1662.) Silver medal, dia. 3.5 (1⅜), by John Roettier. Struck 1662. Purchased 1911.
    PG 1121*   Canvas, 114.3 x 92.1 (45 x 36¼), by unknown artist. Purchased 1930.
    PGL 124   Canvas, 33.6 x 26.5 (13¼ x 10⅜), by unknown artist after Dirk Stoop. On loan from the Duke of Buccleuch.

Bone, Sir Muirhead
PG 2057

Bonnar, William
PGL 303

Borden, Sir Robert Laird
PG 1140

Boswell, James
PG 804

Botha, Louis
PG 1139

Bothwell, Tent Preaching at
PG 1759

Bothwell, 4th Earl of
PG 869

Bothwell, Countess of
PG 870

Bough, Samuel
PG 693

Bough, Samuel
PG 1809

Bough, Samuel
PG 2053

Boyd Orr, 1st Baron
PG 2698

Boyle, Lord
PG 949

BRAXFIELD, Robert Macqueen, Lord, 1722–99. *Lord Justice-Clerk*
  PG 1615* Canvas, 120.6 x 100.3 (47½ x 39½), by Sir Henry Raeburn. Painted
      c. 1798. Purchased 1954.

BREADALBANE, Gavin Campbell, 1st Marquess of, 1851–1922.
  PG 1856* (*Curling at Carsebreck.*) See GROUPS.

BREADALBANE, John Campbell, 1st Earl of, 1635–1716. *Soldier and statesman*
  PG 996* Canvas, 125.1 x 99.1 (49¼ x 39), by Sir John Baptiste de Medina. Purchased
      1925.

BREADALBANE, John Campbell, 3rd Earl of, 1696–1782. *Statesman and diplomat*
  PG 993* Canvas, 127 x 101.6 (50 x 40), by Jeremiah Davison, 1730, signed.
      Purchased 1925.

BREADALBANE, John Campbell, 1st Marquess of, 1762–1834. *Soldier and statesman*
  PG 2358* Canvas, 226.1 x 150.8 (89 x 59⅜), by Sir Henry Raeburn. Purchased 1975.

BREADALBANE, John Campbell, 2nd Marquess of, 1796–1862. *Statesman*
  PG 1497* (With the Marquess of Dalhousie and Lords Cockburn and Rutherfurd.) See
      GROUPS.

BREWSTER, Sir David, 1781–1868. *Natural philosopher*
  PG 1044* Chalk drawing, 52.7 x 37.5 (20¾ x 14¾), by William Bewick, 1824, signed.
      Purchased 1927.

BRIDGEMAN, John, 1577–1652. *Bishop of Chester*
  PG 1725 Pencil drawing, 14.3 x 10.4 (5⅝ x 4⅛), by unknown artist after a painting of
      1623. Purchased 1933.

BRIDGES, David, fl. 1812.
  PG 1684 Pencil drawing, 18.4 x 13.2 (7¼ x 5¼), by W. H. Lizars. Given by Sir
      William Fettes Douglas 1885.

BRIDIE, James; see MAVOR, Osborne Henry.

BRIDPORT, Alexander Hood, 1st Viscount, 1727–1814. *Admiral*
  PG 2256 Black and white chalk drawing, 28.3 x 24.3 (11⅛ x 9⁹⁄₁₆), by Mather Brown.
      Drawn 1788/91. Provenance untraced.

BRISBANE, Sir Charles, *c.* 1769–1829. *Admiral*
  PGL 315 Canvas, 237.5 x 151.1 (93½ x 59½), by James Northcote. On loan from
      Hector Monro.

BRISBANE, General Sir Thomas Makdougall, 1773–1860. *Colonial governor and astronomer*
  PG 1075   Pencil drawing, 16.2 x 11 (6⅜ x 4⅜), by Sir John Watson Gordon. Provenance untraced.

BRISTOL, Augustus John Hervey, 3rd Earl of, 1724–79. *Admiral*
  PG 1946   Medallion (plaster replica), 6.7 (2⅝), after unknown artist. Provenance untraced.

BRISTOL, Elizabeth Chudleigh, Countess of, 1720–88. *Bigamous wife of 2nd Duke of Kingston*
  PG 1906   Medallion (plaster replica), h. 3.4 (1⁵⁄₁₆), after James Tassie. Provenance untraced.

BROADWAY; see STEVENSON, Robert Macaulay (PG 2704).

BRODIE, Sir Thomas Dawson, 1832–96. *Lawyer*
  PG 1707   Pencil drawing, 37.5 x 33.6 (14¾ x 13¼), by W. Graham Boss. Given by the artist.

BROUGH, Robert, 1872–1905. *Artist*
  PG 1228   Pencil drawing, 22.2 x 16.9 (8¾ x 6⅝), by James Cadenhead, signed. Bequeathed by Dr A. S. Walker 1934.
  PG 1477*   Bronze head, h. 49.5 (19½), by Francis Derwent Wood. Purchased 1946.

BROUGHAM, Eleanora Syme, Mrs Henry, 1752–1839. *Mother of Lord Brougham and Vaux*
  PG 350   Plaster bust, h. 65.4 (25¾), by unknown artist. Purchased 1887.

BROUGHAM AND VAUX, Henry Peter Brougham, 1st Baron, 1778–1868. *Statesman*
  PG 520   Medallion (plaster replica), h. 6.5 (2⅜), after John Henning. Cast from a medallion in possession of J. M. Gray 1894.
  PG 677   Marble bust, h. 64.8 (25½), by John Adams Acton. Sculpted 1867. Purchased 1908.
  PG 851   Bronze bust, h. 13.7 (5⁷⁄₁₆), copy by unknown artist. Dated 1831. Given by Sir J. R. Findlay 1916.
  PG 882*   Canvas, 238.7 x 146.8 (94 x 57¾), by Andrew Morton, signed. Purchased 1917.
  PG 1317   Water-colour, 22.5 x 17.2 (8⅞ x 6¹³⁄₁₆), by James Stewart after Andrew Morton. Purchased 1937.

BROWN, Alexander, fl. 1776–94. *Keeper of the Advocates' Library*
  PGL 70*   Pencil drawing, 50.3 x 35.1 (19¾ x 13¾), by John Brown. On loan from the National Museums of Scotland.

BROWN of Longformacus, Major Alexander, 1776–1858. *Of the East India Company*
PG 2622   (Formerly called William Ritchie.) Canvas, 92 x 73.8 (36¼ x 29⅛), by
            William Smellie Watson. Painted 1850. Purchased 1984.

BROWN, Andrew Betts, 1839–1906. *Engineer and inventor*
PG 658   Canvas, 76.2 x 63.5 (30 x 25), by Robert P. Bell. Given by Robert Brown
           1907.

BROWN, George Mackay, b. 1921. *Poet*
PG 2597*   (*Poets' Pub.*) See GROUPS.

BROWN, John, 1749–87. *Artist*
PG 147*   Red chalk drawing, 24.1 x 18.4 (9½ x 7¼), by William Delacour, 1766,
           signed. Given by Sir William Fettes Douglas 1886.
PGL 31*   (With Alexander Runciman.) Canvas, 63.6 x 76.5 (25 x 30⅛), by Alexander
           Runciman, 1784, signed. On loan from the National Museums of Scotland.

BROWN, Dr John, 1735–88. *Physician*
PGL 71*   Pencil drawing, 50.7 x 34.9 (20 x 13¾), by John Brown. On loan from the
           National Museums of Scotland.

BROWN, Dr John, 1810–82. *Physician and author of* Rab and his Friends
PG 275*   Chalk drawing, 66.4 x 51.4 (26⅛ x 20¼), by James Rannie Swinton. Drawn
           1874. Given by Mrs Swinton 1889.
PG 290*   Canvas, 34.9 x 29.9 (13¾ x 11¾), by Sir George Reid, 1881, signed. Given
           by J. Irvine Smith 1890.
PG 852   Panel, 22.7 x 19 (9 x 7½), by Sir William Fettes Douglas. Purchased 1916.
PG 986   Marble bust, h. 68.2 (26⅞), by Robert Cauer, 1862, signed. Given by John
           Brown 1925.
PG 1813   (Possibly Dr John Brown.) Pencil drawing, 17 x 12.1 (6¾ x 4¾), by Sir John
           Watson Gordon. Provenance untraced.

BROWN, Rev. John, 1754–1832. *Minister of the Burgher Church in Whitburn*
PGL 150   Water-colour on ivory, 7.3 x 6 (2⅞ x 2⅜), by John Pairman. On loan from
           W. B. Pairman.

BROWN, John Taylor, d. 1901. *Librarian to the Society of Antiquaries of Scotland*
PG 1712   Pencil drawing 37.5 x 33 (14¾ x 13), by W. Graham Boss. Given by the artist.

BROWN, Walter, fl. 1810–30. *Lord Provost of Edinburgh*
PG 2148*   Cut paper silhouette, h. 20.9 (8¼), by Augustin Edouart, 1830, signed.
           Given by Mrs J. H. G. Ross 1969.

BROWN, William Beattie, 1831–1909. *Landscape painter*
PG 1739   (In his studio.) Wash drawing, 38.1 x 28 (15 x 11), by J. R. Abercromby,
           signed. Drawn 1898. Purchased 1940.

Braganza, Catherine of
PG 1121

Braxfield, Lord
PG 1615

Breadalbane, 1st Earl of
PG 996

Breadalbane, 3rd Earl of
PG 993

Breadalbane, 1st Marquess
of   PG 2358

Brewster, Sir David
PG 1044

Brough, Robert
PG 1477

Brougham and Vaux,
1st Baron   PG 882

Brown, Alexander
PGL 70

Brown, John
PG 147

Brown, John, with
Alexander Runciman   PGL 31

Brown, Dr John
PGL 71

Brown, Dr John
PG 275

Brown, Dr John
PG 290

Brown, Walter
PG 2148

BROWNE, Sir George Washington, 1853–1939. *Architect*
  PG 1431* Tempera on canvas laid on board, 118.7 x 91.4 (46¾ x 36), by A. E.
            Borthwick, 1932, signed. Given by the artist 1942.
  PG 1793   Pencil drawing, 46.3 x 29.2 (18¼ x 11½), by David Foggie, 1933, signed.
            Given by Mrs M. Foggie 1955.

BRUCE, Dr Alexander, 1854–1911. *Physician*
  PG 1735   Watercolour, 33.7 x 19 (13¼ x 7½), by unknown artist signing 'A.H.'
            Purchased 1933.

BRUCE of Kinnaird, James, 1730–94. *African explorer*
  PG 141*   Canvas, 72.4 x 62.2 (28½ x 24½), by Pompeo Batoni. Painted 1762.
            Bequeathed by Lady Ruthven 1885.
  PG 1460   (Called James Bruce.) Water-colour on ivory, 4.1 x 3.5 (1⅝ x 1⅜),
            attributed to John Bogle. Bequeathed by Sir St Clair Thomson 1944.
  PG 1667   Wash drawing, 12.5 x 10.5 (4⅞ x 4⅛), by unknown artist after David
            Martin. Bequeathed by W. F. Watson 1886.

BRUCE, Jane, fl. 1798.
  PG 1876   Medallion (plaster replica), h. 7.8 (3⅛), after James Tassie. Provenance
            untraced.

BRUCE, Professor John, 1745–1826. *Historian*
  PG 1016* Canvas, 125.7 x 100.3 (49½ x 39½), by Sir Henry Raeburn. Painted
            c. 1794. Given by Mrs K. A. Hamilton Bruce 1926.

BRUCE, Sir John, 1905–75. *Regius Professor of Clinical Surgery at Edinburgh University*
  PG 2648* Bronze medal, dia. 5 (2), by Charles d'Orville Pilkington Jackson, signed in
            monogram on the obverse. Dated 1965. Given by the trustees of the artist
            1985.

BRUCE of Clackmannan, Katherine Bruce, Mrs Henry, d. 1791.
  PG 1770* (*Burns at an evening party of Lord Monboddo's 1786.*) See GROUPS.

BRUCE, Robert the; see ROBERT I

BRUCE, Thomas, 1785–1850. *Depute Clerk of Session and friend of Sir Walter Scott*
  PG 1599   Canvas, 52.1 x 38.1 (20½ x 15), attributed to Sir John Watson Gordon.
            Bequeathed by Miss Maria S. Steuart 1953.

BRUCE, Sir William, *c.* 1630–1710. *Architect*
  PG 109   Wash drawing, 16.6 x 14.3 (6⁹⁄₁₆ x 5⅝), by unknown artist after Sir John
            Baptiste de Medina. Bequeathed by W. F. Watson 1886.
  PG 894*   Canvas, 72.4 x 61 (28½ x 24), by John Michael Wright, signed. Dated
            166[ ]. Probably painted 1664. Purchased 1919.
  PG 957*   Canvas, 74.9 x 62.2 (29½ x 24½), by Sir John Baptiste de Medina, signed.
            Purchased 1923.

BRUNTON, George, fl. 1790–1830. *Merchant and banker*
   PG 2149   Cut paper silhouette, h. 20.1 (8), by Augustin Edouart, 1830, signed. Given
            by Mrs J. H. G. Ross 1969.

BRUNTON, Sir Thomas Lauder, 1844–1916. *Physician*
   PG 2353   Bronze medal, dia. 5 (2), by C. d'O. Pilkington Jackson. Dated 1923. Given
            by the artist 1956.

BRYCE, David, 1803–76. *Architect*
   PG 1090*   Marble bust, h. 59.1 (23¼), by George MacCallum, 1868, signed. Given by
            H. Johnston 1928.
   PG 1432*   Chalk drawing, 51.2 x 37.8 (20⅛ x 14⅞), by unknown artist. Given by the
            Council of the Scottish National Buildings Record 1942.

BRYCE, James Bryce, 1st Viscount, 1838–1922. *Statesman and ambassador*
   PG 878*   Chalk drawing, 47 x 34.3 (18½ x 13½), by Sir William Rothenstein.
            Purchased 1917.

BUCCLEUCH, Charlotte Anne Thynne, Duchess of, 1811–95. *Wife of the 5th Duke of*
              Buccleuch and Mistress of the Robes to Queen Victoria
   PG 2417*   (*The Visit of Queen Victoria and Prince Albert to Hawthornden.*) See
            GROUPS.

BUCCLEUCH, Walter Francis Scott, 5th Duke of, and 7th Duke of Queensberry,
              1806–84. *Lord Privy Seal*
   PG 906*   Canvas, 139.7 x 110.5 (55 x 43½), by F. R. Say. Given by the Duke of
            Buccleuch 1920.
   PG 2419   Pencil and ink drawing, 18 x 11.4 (7³⁄₃₂ x 4¹⁵⁄₃₂), by Sir Daniel Macnee.
            Given by Dr Ruth Waddell 1978.

BUCCLEUCH, William Henry Walter Montagu-Douglas-Scott, 6th Duke of, and 8th
              Duke of Queensberry, 1831–1914.
   PG 1856*   (*Curling at Carsebreck.*) See GROUPS.

BUCHAN, Agnes Stewart, Countess of, d. 1778. *Wife of the 10th Earl of Buchan*
   PG 1645   Chalk drawing, 29.5 x 26.7 (11½ x 10½), by the 11th Earl of Buchan after
            unknown artist. Bequeathed by W. F. Watson 1886.

BUCHAN, David Steuart Erskine, 11th Earl of, 1742–1829. *Antiquary*
   PG 471   Medallion (plaster replica), h. 7.8 (3⅛), after James Tassie. Dated 1783.
            Cast from a medallion in possession of R. W. Cochran Patrick 1893.
   PGL 72*   Pencil drawing, 49.8 x 35.1 (19⅝ x 13⅞), by John Brown. On loan from the
            National Museums of Scotland.

BUCHAN, James Erskine, 6th Earl of, c. 1600–40. *Lord of the Bedchamber*
>PG 1635*   Chalk drawing, 47.2 x 35 (18½ x 13¾), by the 11th Earl of Buchan, 1795,
>signed, after George Jamesone. Bequeathed by W. F. Watson 1886.
>PGL 234*   Canvas, 63.5 x 50.8 (25 x 20), by Adam de Colone. Dated 1626. On loan
>from the Earl of Mar and Kellie.

BUCHAN, John Stewart, Earl of, c. 1380–1424. *Chamberlain of Scotland; Constable of
France*
>PG 1617   Chalk drawing, 43 x 35.4 (17 x 14), by the 11th Earl of Buchan after a copy.
>Bequeathed by W. F. Watson 1886.

BUCHAN, William, 1729–1805. *Physician*
>PG 367   Wedgwood medallion, h. 7.9 (3⅛). Given by Messrs J. Wedgwood and Sons
>1889.

BUCHANAN, Sir Andrew, 1807–82. *Diplomat*
>PG 2742   Pencil drawing, 20.5 x 15 (8¹⁄₁₆ x 5⅞), by George Frederick Watts.
>Purchased 1988.

BUCHANAN, George, 1506–82. *Historian, poet and reformer*
>PG 988   Panel, 48.4 x 30.8 (19¹⁄₁₆ x 12⅛), by Archibald McGlashan after unknown
>artist. Commissioned 1925.
>PG 1506   Panel, dia. 25.4 (10), by unknown artist. Purchased 1948.
>PG 1622   Pencil and chalk drawing, 34.7 x 25.4 (13⅝ x 10), by the 11th Earl of
>Buchan, signed, after unknown artist. Bequeathed by W. F. Watson 1886.
>PG 2678*   Panel, 34.1 x 27.7 (13⁹⁄₁₆ x 10¹⁵⁄₁₆), attributed to Arnold Bronckorst. Dated
>1581. Purchased 1985.

BUCHANAN, James, d. 1793. *East India merchant*
>PG 1261   Paste medallion, h. 8.1 (3³⁄₁₆), by James Tassie. Dated 1798. Purchased 1935.

BUCHANAN, Rev. Robert, 1802–75. *Free Church leader*
>PG 1861   Chalk drawing, 45.7 x 35.4 (18 x 14), by unknown artist. Bequeathed by
>Miss Dorothy Haverfield 1959.

BUCKLITSCH, John, 1755–1831. *Gamekeeper to the Earl of Kintore*
>PGL 335*   Canvas, 232.1 x 182.3 (91⅜ x 71¾), by Sir Henry Raeburn. On loan from
>the Kintore Trust.

BULLER, Sir Francis, 1746–1800. *Judge*
>PG 357*   Chalk drawing, 35.6 x 23 (14 x 11), by Mather Brown. Drawn c. 1792.
>Given by J. M. Gray 1889.

BULSTRODE, Richard, fl. 1754.
>PG 2546   Indian ink on paper, h. 6.6 (2⅝), by James Ferguson. Drawn 1754.
>Transferred from the National Gallery of Scotland 1982.

Browne, Sir George
Washington   PG 1431

Bruce, James
PG 141

Bruce, Professor John
PG 1016

Bruce, Sir John
PG 2648

Bruce, Sir William
PG 894

Bruce, Sir William
PG 957

Bryce, David
PG 1090

Bryce, David
PG 1432

Bryce, 1st Viscount
PG 878

Buccleuch, 5th Duke of
PG 906

Buchan, 11th Earl of
PGL 72

Buchan, 6th Earl of
PGL 234

Buchan, 6th Earl of
PG 1635

Buchanan, George
PG 2678

BURGES (later BURGES-LAMB), Sir James Bland, 1752–1824. *Politician*
    PG 1877   Medallion (plaster replica), h. 5.9 (2⅜), after W. Whitley; also known in
                Tassie paste. Provenance untraced.

BURKE, Edmund, 1729–97. *Statesman, orator and author*
    PG 406   Medallion (plaster replica), h. 8 (3⅛), after William Tassie. Cast from a
                medallion in possession of the Rev. F. Vernon 1889.
    PG 1878   Medallion (plaster replica), h. 8.6 (3⅜), after a Wedgwood medallion after
                J. C. Lochee; also known in Tassie paste. Provenance untraced.
    PG 2362*   Canvas, 76.2 x 63.5 (30 x 25), by Sir Joshua Reynolds. Bequeathed
                conditionally by Miss E. Drummond to the National Gallery of Ireland 1930
                and transferred 1969.

BURKE, William, 1792–1829. *Murderer*
    PG 841*   Cut paper silhouette, h. 19.2 (7⅝), by Augustin Edouart. Purchased 1914.

BURN, John, 1802–85. *Surgeon*
    PG 1419   Canvas, 25.5 x 20.5 (10 x 8), by unknown artist. Purchased 1941.

BURNET, Gilbert, 1643–1715. *Bishop of Salisbury*
    PGL 27   Panel, 35.6 x 28.1 (14¹/₁₆ x 11¹/₁₆), by unknown artist, 1681, signed, perhaps
                'P.A.' On loan from the National Museums of Scotland.

BURNET, John, 1784–1868. *Painter, engraver and writer on art*
    PG 2*   Water-colour and charcoal drawing, 22.9 x 19.2 (9 x 7⅝), by Stephen
                Poyntz Denning. Given by William Bell Scott 1884.

BURNET, Thomas, c. 1635–1715. *Author and Master of the Charterhouse*
    PG 106   Pencil drawing, 11.3 x 9 (4½ x 3½), by unknown artist. Bequeathed by
                W. F. Watson 1886.

BURNETT, Eliza or Elizabeth, 1767–90. *Daughter of Lord Monboddo*
    PG 1770*   (*Burns at an evening party of Lord Monboddo's 1786.*) See GROUPS.

BURNETT, Thomas Stuart, 1853–88. *Sculptor*
    PG 2460*   (*Friendly Critics.*) See GROUPS.

BURNS, Sir George, 1795–1890. *Founder of the Cunard Line*
    PG 786   Cut paper silhouette, h. 20.1 (8), by Augustin Edouart. Purchased 1912.

BURNS, Jean Armour, Mrs Robert, 1768–1834. *Wife of the poet Robert Burns*
    PG 809*   Canvas, 74.9 x 62.3 (29½ x 24½), by John Alexander Gilfillan. Bequeathed
                by Mrs McDiarmid 1912.
    PGL 332*   (With her granddaughter Sarah Burns.) Canvas, 126.4 x 103.5
                (49¾ x 40¾), by Samuel Mackenzie. Painted 1824/5. On loan from
                Group Captain Richard Gowring RAF.

Bucklitsch, John
PGL 335

Buller, Sir Francis
PG 357

Burke, Edmund
PG 2362

Burke, William
PG 841

Burnet, John
PG 2

Burns, Jean
PG 809

Burns, Jean, with Sarah Burns
PGL 332

BURNS, Robert, 1759–96. *Poet*

PG 113*   Ink silhouette on paper, h. 7.3 (2⅜), by or after John Miers. Dated 1787. Bequeathed by W. F. Watson 1886.

PG 183   Plaster cast of skull, h. 17.2 (6⅞), by David Dunbar. Probably taken 1834. Given by William Calder Marshall 1887.

PG 341*   Water-colour on ivory, 7.6 x 6.3 (3 x 2½), by Alexander Reid. Painted 1795/6. Bequeathed by W. F. Watson 1892.

PG 425   Medallion (plaster replica), h. 7.5 (3), after William Tassie. Dated 1801. Bequeathed by William Tassie 1892.

PG 745*   Chalk drawing, 54.9 x 42.5 (21⅝ x 16¾), by Archibald Skirving. Drawn 1796/8. Purchased 1911.

PG 946*   (*The Inauguration of Burns as Poet Laureate of the Lodge Canongate, Kilwinning, 1787.*) See GROUPS

PG 1060   (Burns's cottage at Alloway.) Water-colour, 19.4 x 32.1 (7⅝ x 12⅝), by Hugh William Williams. Transferred from the National Gallery of Scotland.

PG 1062*   Panel, 61.1 x 44.5 (24 x 17½), by Alexander Nasmyth. Painted 1828. Bequeathed by Sir Hugh H. Campbell to the National Gallery of Scotland 1894 and transferred.

PG 1063*   Canvas, 38.4 x 32.4 (15⅛ x 12¾), by Alexander Nasmyth, 1787, signed (on reverse). Bequeathed by Colonel William Burns 1872.

PG 1085*   Panel, 22.2 x 20.3 (8¾ x 8), by Peter Taylor. Painted 1786. Given by W. A. Taylor 1928.

PG 1275   Plaster medallion, h. 4.7 (1⅞), by John Henning. Dated 1807. Purchased 1935.

PG 1356*   Canvas, 73.7 x 63.2 (29 x 24⅞), by or after Peter Taylor. Purchased 1938.

PG 1380*   Pencil drawing, 20.8 x 14.3 (8¼ x 5⅝), by Alexander Nasmyth. Transferred from the National Gallery of Scotland 1939.

PG 1381   (With Alexander Nasmyth at Roslin Castle.) Pencil drawing, 15.9 x 21 (6¼ x 8¼), by Alexander Nasmyth, 1786, signed. Transferred from the National Gallery of Scotland 1939.

PG 1770*   (*Burns at an evening party of Lord Monboddo's 1786*). See GROUPS.

PG 2325   Watercolour on ivory, oval 6.8 x 5.5 (2¹¹⁄₁₆ x 2³⁄₁₆), copy by unknown artist. Bequeathed by W. F. Watson 1886.

PGL 139*   Marble statue on plinth, overall h. 292.4 (115⅛), figure only h. 182.2 (71¾), by John Flaxman, signed. Begun 1824. On loan from the City of Edinburgh District Council.

BURR, John, 1831–93. *Artist*

PG 1319   Canvas, 45.7 x 38.1 (18 x 15), self-portrait, signed. Purchased 1937.

BURTON, John Hill, 1809–81. *Historian*

PG 148*   Marble bust, h. 62.2 (24½), by Alexander Rhind after a bust by William Brodie of 1859. Dated 1885. Given by John Ritchie Findlay 1885.

BURY, Lady Charlotte; see CAMPBELL.

Burns, Robert
PG 113

Burns, Robert
PG 341

Burns, Robert
PG 745

Burns, Robert
PG 1062

Burns, Robert
PG 1063

Burns, Robert
PG 1085

Burns, Robert
PG 1356

Burns, Robert
PG 1380

Burns, Robert
PGL 139

Burton, John Hill
PG 148

Bute, 3rd Earl of
PG 308

Byres, James
PG 2189

Byron, 6th Lord
PG 1561

BUTE, John Crichton-Stuart, 2nd Marquess of, and 6th Earl of Dumfries, 1793–1848.
    PG 2576   (When Earl of Dumfries.) Bronzed silhouette in ink on plaster, h. 8.2 (3¼),
            by or after John Miers. Drawn 1809. Transferred from the National Gallery
            of Scotland 1982.

BUTE, John Patrick Crichton-Stuart, 3rd Marquess of, 1847–1900. *Antiquary*
    PG 1710*   Pencil drawing, 37.5 x 33.7 (14¾ x 13¼), by W. Graham Boss. Given by
            the artist.

BUTE, John Stuart, 3rd Earl of, 1713–92. *Prime Minister*
    PG 308   Canvas, 76.2 x 63.5 (30 x 25), by unknown artist. Bequeathed by W. F.
            Watson 1886.

BYRES of Tonley, Family of James; see GROUPS (PG 2601).

BYRES of Tonley, James, 1734–1817. *Architect and antiquary*
    PG 368   Wedgwood medallion, h. 5.9 (2⁵⁄₁₆), after James Tassie. Given by Messrs
            J. Wedgwood and Sons 1889.
    PG 2189*   Paste medallion, h. 6.3 (2½), by James Tassie. Purchased 1971.
    PG 2601*   See GROUPS.

BYRES of Tonley, Janet Moir, Mrs Patrick, 1711–87.
    PG 2601*   See GROUPS.

BYRES of Tonley, Patrick, 1713–78. *Jacobite*
    PG 2601*   See GROUPS.

BYRON, George Gordon, 6th Lord, 1788–1824. *Poet*
    PG 1561*   Canvas, 72.4 x 62.2 (29½ x 24½), by William Edward West, 1822. Given by
            Colonel William Stirling of Keir 1951.

CADENHEAD, James, 1858–1927. *Artist*
> P G 1230   Chalk drawing, 45.1 x 30.2 (17¾ x 11⅞), by James Paterson, 1915, signed.
> Bequeathed by Dr A. Stodart Walker 1934.

CAIRNS, Rev. John, 1818–92. *United Presbyterian divine*
> P G 1389*   Millboard, 38.1 x 31.6 (15 x 12⅜), by James Edgar, 1862, signed. Purchased
> 1939.
> P G 1417   Millboard, 20.2 x 15.4 (8 x 6⅛), by unknown artist. Given by James Hutton
> 1941.

CAMERON, Sir David Young, 1865–1945. *Artist*
> P G 2193*   Canvas, 60.9 x 51.3 (24 x 20¼), by Alfred Kingsley Lawrence, signed.
> Bequeathed by Miss Margaret Anderson 1971.
> P G 2607*   Pencil drawing, 31.6 x 20.3 (12½ x 8) (irregular), by Katherine Cameron.
> Dated 1922. Purchased 1984.

CAMERON of Lochiel, Sir Ewen, 1629–1719. *Chief of Clan Cameron*
> P G L 138*   Canvas, 61.1 x 50.7 (24 x 20), by unknown artist. Provenance untraced.

CAMERON, Hugh, 1835–1918. *Artist*
> P G 1740   (In his studio.) Wash drawing, 38.7 x 52.7 (15¼ x 20¾), by J. R.
> Abercromby, signed. Drawn 1898. Purchased 1940.
> P G 1814   Pencil drawing, 35.5 x 23.7 (14 x 9¼), by Charles Matthew, 1890, signed.
> Bequeathed by J. M. Gray 1894.

CAMERON, Mary, fl. 1886–1919. *Artist*
> P G 1741*   (In her studio.) Wash drawing, 52.7 x 38.7 (20¾ x 15¼), by J. R.
> Abercromby. Drawn 1898. Purchased 1940.

CAMMELL, Charles Richard, b. 1890. *Poet and author*
> P G 2002*   Black chalk drawing, 45.7 x 28.6 (18 x 11¼), by David Foggie, 1933, signed.
> Given by Mrs M. Foggie 1962.

CAMPBELL, Archibald, 1768–1833. *Edinburgh City Officer and King's Beadle*
> P G 958*   Water-colour drawing, 23.2 x 18.6 (9⅛ x 7⁵⁄₁₆), by John Kay. Purchased
> 1923.

CAMPBELL, Colonel Archibald, 1755–96. *Soldier*
> P G 1880   Medallion (plaster replica), h. 9.2 (3⅝), after James Tassie. Dated 1797.
> Provenance untraced.

CAMPBELL, Colonel Sir Archibald, 1739–91. *Governor of Jamaica and Madras*
> P G 442   Medallion (plaster replica), h. 10.1 (4), after James Tassie. Given by the
> South Kensington Museum 1893.
> P G 2435   Paste medallion, h. 9.2 (3⅝), by James Tassie. Dated 1779. Bequeathed by
> William Tassie to the National Gallery of Scotland 1860 and transferred 1979.

CAMPBELL, Colonel Sir Archibald (*continued*)
PG 2690   Paste medallion, h. 9.2 (3⅝), by James Tassie. Purchased 1986.

CAMPBELL of Lochlane, Charles, d. 1751. *Advocate*
PG 2180*   Canvas, 126 x 99.7 (49⅝ x 39¼), by unknown artist. Purchased 1970.

CAMPBELL, Lady Charlotte, 1775–1861. *Writer and famous beauty*
PG 645*   Chalk drawing, 67.3 x 52.1 (26½ x 20½), by Alexander Blaikley, 1841,
           signed. Given by the artist's executor 1905.
PG 2275*   Canvas, 197.2 x 134 (77⅝ x 52¾), by Johann Wilhelm Tischbein, signed.
           Painted *c*. 1789. Purchased 1975.

CAMPBELL, Sir Colin, 1776–1847. *General*
PG 2178*   Water-colour drawing, 26.2 x 16.5 (10⅜ x 6½), by Robert Dighton.
           Purchased 1970.

CAMPBELL, Duncan, d. 1453. *Lord of Lochow; father of the 1st Laird of Glenorchy*
PG 2074   Wash drawing, 17.6 x 12.5 (6⅞ x 5), by Robert Johnson after 'a German
           painter', signed. Transferred from the National Gallery of Scotland 1950.

CAMPBELL of Glenorchy, Sir Duncan, 1545–1631. *Highland improver*
PG 2165*   Canvas, 88.5 x 70.9 (34⅞ x 27⅞), by unknown artist. Dated 1619.
           Purchased 1969.
PG 2364*   Panel, 113.4 x 70 (44⅝ x 27⅝), by unknown artist. Dated 1601. Purchased
           1975.

CAMPBELL, Lord Frederick, 1729–1816. *Lord Clerk Register*
PG 409   Medallion (plaster replica), h. 6.9 (2¾), after John Henning. Cast from a
           medallion in possession of Robert Dundas 1889.

CAMPBELL, Professor George, 1719–96. *Divine. Principal of Marischal College,
           Aberdeen*
PG 2727   Water-colour on ivory, h. 3.7 (1⁷⁄₁₆), by unknown artist. Purchased 1987.

CAMPBELL of Lawers and Rowallan, Sir James, 1667–1745. *General*
PG 1395   Canvas, 76.1 x 64.3 (30 x 25¼), by unknown artist. Purchased 1940.

CAMPBELL of Colgrain, Janet Miller Hamilton, Mrs Colin, d. 1863. *Wife of the Deputy
           Lieutenant of Dunbartonshire*
PG 2026*   (Study for *The Landing of Queen Victoria at Dumbarton in 1847*, in the
           collection of Dumbarton District Council.) Watercolour, 59.7 x 41.2
           (23½ x 16¼), by Hope James Stewart. Purchased 1963.

CAMPBELL, John Campbell, 1st Baron, 1779–1861. *Lord Chief Justice and Lord
           Chancellor*
PG 560   Canvas, 30.7 x 25.7 (12⅛ x 10⅛), by Sir Francis Grant. Purchased 1896.

Cairns, Rev. John
PG 1389

Cameron, Sir David Young
PG 2193

Cameron, Sir David Young
PG 2607

Cameron, Sir Ewen
PGL 138

Cameron, Mary
PG 1741

Cammell, Charles Richard
PG 2002

Campbell, Archibald
PG 958

Campbell, Charles Y
PG 2180

Campbell, Lady Charlotte
PG 645

Campbell, Lady Charlotte
PG 2275

Campbell, Sir Colin
PG 2178

Campbell, Sir Duncan
PG 2165

Campbell, Sir Duncan
PG 2364

Campbell, Janet
PG 2026

Campbell, 1st Baron
PG 912

Campbell, Captain Robert X
PG 995

CAMPBELL, John Campbell, 1st Baron (*continued*)

PG 912*   Marble bust, h. 75.7 (29¾), by Sir John Steell, 1843, signed. Given by Alice, Lady Stratheden and Campbell and Lord Stratheden and Campbell 1921.

PG 2720   Canvas, 91.5 x 71.1 (36 x 28), by unknown artist. Given by Miss Joanna Gordon 1987.

CAMPBELL, Juliana Campbell, Lady, b. 1581. *Wife of the 8th Laird of Glenorchy*

PG 2073   Wash drawing, 17 x 11.4 (6⅝ x 4½), by Robert Johnson after unknown artist. Transferred from the National Gallery of Scotland 1950.

CAMPBELL, Mariot Stewart, Lady, fl. 1400. *Daughter of Robert, Duke of Albany and wife of Duncan Campbell of Lochow*

PG 2075   Wash drawing, 16.2 x 12.1 (6⅜ x 4¾), by Robert Johnson after George Jamesone. Transferred from the National Gallery of Scotland 1950.

CAMPBELL of Ardmaddie, Neil, c. 1630–92. *Governor of Dumbarton Castle*

PG 999   Canvas, 74.6 x 66 (29⅜ x 26), by unknown artist. Purchased 1925.

CAMPBELL of Glenlyon, Captain Robert, 1632–96. *In command at Glencoe*

PG 995*   Canvas, 76.2 x 63.1 (30 x 24⅞), by unknown artist. Purchased 1925.

CAMPBELL, Rev. Robert, c. 1738–1803. *Minister of Erskine Secession Church, Stirling*

PG 1881   (Probably Rev. Robert Campbell.) Medallion (plaster replica), h. 7.5 (3), after James Tassie. Dated 1795. Provenance untraced.

CAMPBELL, Thomas, 1777–1844. *Poet and critic*

PG 11   Canvas, 76.2 x 63.5 (30 x 25), by Henry Room. Purchased 1884.

PG 825*   (*Sir Walter Scott and his friends at Abbotsford.*) See GROUPS.

PG 1034*   Pencil and watercolour drawing, 24.4 x 17.6 (9⅝ x 7), by Sir Thomas Lawrence. Purchased 1926.

CAMPBELL of Tullichewan, William, d. 1864. *Sheriff of Dunbartonshire*

PG 1163   (Study for *The Landing of Queen Victoria at Dumbarton in 1847*, in the collection of Dumbarton District Council.) Pencil and water-colour drawing, 55.3 x 42.5 (21¾ x 16¾), by Hope James Stewart. Purchased 1931.

CAMPBELL of Glenorchy Family-Tree. The Genealogy of the House of Glenorchy

PG 2167*   Canvas, 235.6 x 149.5 (92¾ x 59), by George Jamesone, 1635, signed. Purchased 1969.

CAMPBELL-BANNERMAN, Sir Henry, 1836–1908. *Statesman*

PG 775*   Canvas, 215.9 x 127 (85 x 50), by Sir James Guthrie, signed. Given by the Scottish Liberal Association 1912.

CANNING, Charlotte Stuart, Countess, 1817–61. *Wife of Earl Canning,*
            Governor-general of India
   PG 1530*   (With her sister Louisa Stuart, Marchioness of Waterford.) Water-colour
            on ivory, 50.5 x 34 (19⅞ x 13⅜), by Robert Thorburn. Purchased 1949.

CARDONNEL (later CARDONNEL-LAWSON), Adam de, d. 1820. *Surgeon and*
            antiquary
   PGL 73*   Pencil drawing, 49.7 x 34.9 (19½ x 13¾), by John Brown. On loan from the
            National Museums of Scotland.

CARDROSS, David Erskine, 2nd Lord, 1616–71. *Promoter of the Engagement in 1648*
   PG 1636   Pencil and chalk drawing, 34 x 24.3 (13⅜ x 9⅝), by the 11th Earl of Buchan
            after unknown artist. Bequeathed by W. F. Watson 1886.

CARDROSS, Henry Erskine, 3rd Lord, c. 1649–93. *Privy Councillor and General of the*
            Mint
   PG 2206*   Canvas, 121 x 96.8 (47⅝ x 38⅛), attributed to L. Schuneman. Purchased
            1972.

CARFRAE, Robert, d. 1900. *Curator of the National Museum of Antiquities of Scotland*
   PG 1704   Pencil drawing, 37.5 x 33.7 (14¾ x 13¼), by W. Graham Boss. Given by
            the artist.

CARLYLE, Rev. Alexander, 1722–1805. *Divine and pamphleteer*
   PG 155   Canvas, 76.2 x 63.5 (30 x 25), by Archibald Skirving. Purchased 1886.
   PG 245   Porcelain medallion, h. 7.3 (2⅞), by John Henning. Dated 1805. Given by
            the Duke of Buccleuch 1889.
   PG 407   Medallion (plaster replica), h. 2.8 (1⅛), after John Henning. Cast from a
            medallion in possession of Robert Dundas 1889.
   PG 1975*   Pencil drawing, 60.6 x 41.6 (23⅞ x 16⅜), by John Brown. Purchased 1961.
   PG 2724*   Canvas, 73.7 x 61 (29 x 24), by Sir Henry Raeburn. Painted 1796.
            Purchased 1987.
   PGL 154*   Chalk drawing, 53.3 x 42.2 (21 x 16⅝), by Archibald Skirving. On loan
            from the Kirk Session of Inveresk.

CARLYLE, Jane Baillie Welsh, Mrs Thomas, 1801–66. *Wife of the historian Thomas*
            Carlyle
   PG 1123*   Water-colour on ivory, 9.5 x 7.6 (3¾ x 3), by Kenneth Macleay. Painted
            1826. Given by Alexander Carlyle 1930.

CARLYLE, Thomas, 1795–1881. *Historian and essayist*
   PG 202   Plaster bust (bronzed) h. 65.2 (25⅝), by William Brodie. Dated 1879. Given
            by W. G. Patterson 1887.
   PG 240   Medallion (electrotype), dia. 10.7 (4¼), after Alphonse Legros. Given by
            H. A. Grueber 1889.

CARLYLE, Thomas (*continued*)

PG 551*   Plaster medallion, dia. 22.4 (8⅞), by Thomas Woolner. Modelled 1851 and reworked 1855. Given by Sir James L. Caw 1896.

PG 637   Copper medallion, dia. 10.9 (4⁵⁄₁₆), by Sir Joseph Edgar Boehm. Modelled 1875. Purchased 1905.

PG 803*   Canvas, 75 x 62.5 (29½ x 24½), by Robert Herdman, 1875, signed. Purchased 1912.

PG 845*   Water-colour, 19.4 x 28 (7¹¹⁄₁₆ x 11), by Mrs Helen Allingham, 1879, signed. Purchased 1915.

PG 893*   Canvas, 76.2 x 63.2 (30 x 25), by John Linnell, 1844, signed. Given by Mrs Riches 1919.

PG 898*   (View of Carlyle's house at Craigenputtock.) Water-colour, 17.6 x 25.2 (6⅞ x 9⅞), by William Young, 1883, signed. Purchased 1919.

PG 940*   Canvas, 114.3 x 88.9 (45 x 35), by Alphonse Legros, 1877, signed. Purchased 1922.

PG 982*   Panel, 62.9 x 40.6 (24¾ x 16), by Walter Greaves, signed. Painted *c.* 1879. Given by Arthur Kay 1925.

PG 1067   a. (View of Carlyle's house at Craigenputtock.) Wash drawing, 20.9 x 14.8 (5⅞ x 8⅜), by James Paterson, signed.
b. (View of the kitchen in Carlyle's house, Craigenputtock.) Wash and pencil drawing, 25.8 x 16.6 (10⅛ x 6½), by James Paterson, signed.
c. (View of Craigenputtock Moor with Carlyle's house.) Wash drawing, 15.5 x 24.2 (6⅛ x 9⅜), by James Paterson, 1882, signed. Provenance untraced.

PG 1152   Water-colour, 23.4 x 18.6 (9¼ x 7⅜), by unknown artist. Purchased 1931.

PG 1218* Marble statue, h. 162 (63¾), by Sir Joseph Edgar Boehm, 1881, signed. Transferred from the National Gallery of Scotland 1934.

PG 1348   Pencil drawing, 15.4 x 9.9 (6⅛ x 3⅞), by unknown artist. Dated 1881. Given by Walter Bennet 1937.

PG 1593* Pencil and wash drawing, 34.5 x 28 (13⅝ x 11), by Walter Greaves, 1870, signed. Purchased 1952.

CARMICHAEL of Skirling, Sir John Gibson, 6th Baronet, 1773–1803.

PGL 330* Canvas, 125.7 x 100.3 (49½ x 39½), by Sir Henry Raeburn. Painted *c.*1800. On loan from T. M. Wheeler-Carmichael.

CARNEGIE, Andrew, 1835–1919. *Iron master and philanthropist*

PG 1003* Canvas, 74.9 x 62.2 (29½ x 24½), by Catherine Ouless after W. W. Ouless. Commissioned 1925.

PG 2483   Pencil drawing, 21.5 x 13.5 (8⁷⁄₁₆ x 5⁵⁄₁₆), by Edward Arthur Walton. Given by Dr Camilla Uytman 1981.

CAROLINE of Brandenburg-Anspach, Queen, 1683–1737. *Consort of George II*

PG 278   Canvas, 100.3 x 126.4 (39½ x 49¾), attributed to Jacopo Amigoni. Purchased 1889.

PG 1058* Canvas, 241 x 149 (95 x 58⅝), by unknown artist. Bequeathed by Mrs Nisbet Hamilton Ogilvy 1921.

Campbell, Thomas
PG 1034

Campbell of Glenorchy
Family Tree   PG 2167

Campbell-Bannerman,
Sir Henry   PG 775

Canning, Countess, with
Marchioness of Waterford   PG 1530

Cardonnel, Adam de
PGL 73

Cardross, 3rd Lord
PG 2206

Carlyle, Rev. Alexander
PG 1975

Carlyle, Rev. Alexander
PG 2724

Carlyle, Rev. Alexander
PGL 154

Carlyle, Jane
PG 1123

Carlyle, Thomas
PG 551

Carlyle, Thomas
PG 803

Carlyle, Thomas
PG 845

Carlyle, Thomas
PG 893

CAROLINE, Queen; Princess Caroline Amelia Elizabeth, 1768–1821. *Daughter of Charles, Duke of Brunswick-Wolfenbüttel; Queen of George IV*

PG 234* Canvas, 91.2 x 70.5 (35⅞ x 27¾), by Samuel Lane. Purchased 1888.

PG 410 Medallion (plaster replica), h. 5 (2), after John Henning. Cast from a medallion in possession of Mrs D. Robertson 1889.

PG 2383 (When Princess of Wales). Water-colour (grisaille), 10.4 x 8 (4⅛ x 3⅛), copy by unknown artist. Given by Mrs Gore Browne Henderson to the National Gallery of Scotland 1976 and transferred 1977.

CARRINGTON, Sir Archibald Primrose, Lord, 1616–79. *Scottish official and judge*

PG 1607* Canvas, 75.6 x 63.6 (29¾ x 25), by unknown artist. Given by Ronald A. L. Boase 1954.

CARSE, Alexander, c. 1770–1843. *Artist*

PG 320* Oil on steel, 22.9 x 20.4 (9 x 8), self-portrait, 1811, signed. Bequeathed by W. F. Watson 1886.

PG 1782 Pencil drawing, 27.6 x 22 (10⅞ x 8⅝), self-portrait. Dated 1830. Transferred from the National Gallery of Scotland 1952.

PG 1841* (Probably Alexander Carse with his mother and sister.) Panel, 21.7 x 27.5 (8½ x 10⅞), self-portrait. Purchased with help from an anonymous donor 1957.

CARSEBRECK, CURLING AT; see GROUPS (PG 1856).

CARSTARES, William, 1649–1715. *Statesman and divine*

PG 933* Canvas, 76.2 x 63.5 (30 x 25), by unknown artist. Purchased 1922.

CASSILLIS, Susanna Hamilton, Countess of, 1632–94. *First wife of 7th Earl of Cassillis*

PG 2687* Canvas, 72.4 x 61 (28½ x 24), by John Michael Wright, 1662, signed. Purchased 1986.

CATHCART, Mr, fl. 1793.

PG 2553 Water-colour on ivory, h. 7.3 (2⅞) (sight), by Horace Hone, signed. Dated 1793. Transferred from the National Gallery of Scotland 1982.

CATHCART, Mrs

PG 2554 Water-colour on ivory, h. 6.6 (2⅝) (sight), by Horace Hone. Transferred from the National Gallery of Scotland 1982.

CATHCART, R., fl. 1899. *Of Abdie Curling Club*

PG 1856* (*Curling at Carsebreck.*) See GROUPS.

CATHCART, General Sir William Schaw, 10th Baron and 1st Earl of, 1755–1843. *Diplomat and soldier*

PG 835 Pencil and water-colour, 21.5 x 17.8 (8½ x 7), by Luke Clennell. Given by Sir Hew Dalrymple 1913.

Carlyle's House at Craigenputtock
PG 898

Carlyle, Thomas
PG 940

Carlyle, Thomas
PG 982

Carlyle, Thomas
PG 1218

Carlyle, Thomas
PG 1593

Carmichael, Sir John Gibson
PGL 330

Carnegie, Andrew
PG 1003

Caroline of Brandenburg-
Anspach, Queen   PG 1058

Caroline, Queen
PG 234

Carrington, Lord
PG 1607

Carse, Alexander
PG 320

Carse, Alexander
PG 1841

CATHERINE II of Russia, 1729–96. *Reigned 1762–96*
- PG 1882   Medallion (plaster replica), h. 7.5 (3), after James Tassie. Provenance untraced.
- PG 1884   Medallion (plaster replica), h. 5.6 (2¼), after James Tassie. Provenance untraced.

CATHERINE of Braganza; see BRAGANZA

CAVAN, Richard Ford William Lambart, 7th Earl of, 1763–1836. *General*
- PG 2684   d. (Study related to *The Battle of Alexandria* and *The Landing of British Troops at Aboukir.*) Water-colour and pencil drawing 14.3 x 11.5 (5⅝ x 4½), attributed to Philip James de Loutherbourg. Purchased 1986.

CAW, Sir James Lewis, 1864–1950. *First Director of the National Galleries of Scotland*
- PG 1158   Bronze medallion, dia. 14.3 (5⅝), by Robert Bryden. Dated 1928. Given by Stanley Cursiter 1931.
- PG 1570*   Bronze bust, h. 45.7 (18), by Benno Schotz. Sculpted *c.* 1928. Bequeathed by Sir James and Lady Caw 1951.

CAW, John. *Antiquary*
- PGL 84   Pencil drawing, 49.4 x 35.3 (19½ x 13⅞), by John Brown. On loan from the National Museums of Scotland.

CHALMERS, George, 1742–1825. *Author of* Caledonia
- PG 94   Canvas, 92.7 x 72.4 (36½ x 28½), by James Tannock. Painted 1824. Given by John Inglis 1885.
- PG 136*   Paste medallion, h. 8.3 (3⁵⁄₁₆), by James Tassie. Dated 1796. Purchased 1886.
- PG 2037*   Canvas, 76.2 x 63.5 (30 x 25), by Andrew Geddes. Purchased 1964.

CHALMERS, George Paul, 1836–78. *Artist*
- PG 856*   Canvas, 61.6 x 51.4 (24¼ x 20¼), by John Pettie, 1862, signed. Purchased 1916.
- PG 881   Canvas, 20.3 x 15.2 (8 x 6), by Joseph Farquharson, signed. Given by Kenneth T. McLelland 1918.
- PG 1245*   Canvas, 31.7 x 25.4 (12½ x 10), self-portrait. Purchased 1934.

CHALMERS, Rev. Hugh, 1648–1707. *Covenanting minister of Marnoch*
- PG 1418   a. Canvas, 20.3 x 15.2 (8 x 6), copy by unknown artist. Given by Thomas Gascoigne 1941.

CHALMERS, Margaret; see HAY, Mrs Lewis.

CHALMERS, Rev. Thomas, 1780–1847. *Preacher and social reformer*
- PG 175   Plaster bust, h. 52 (20½), by Sir John Steell. Dated 1846. Purchased 1886.
- PG 564   Marble bust, h. 55 (21⅝), by Sir John Steell, 1883, signed. Purchased 1897.

Carstares, William
PG 933

Cassillis, Countess of
PG 2687

Caw, Sir James Lewis
PG 1570

Chalmers, George
PG 136

Chalmers, George
PG 2037

Chalmers, George Paul
PG 856

Chalmers, George Paul
PG 1245

Chalmers, Rev. Thomas
PG 591

Chalmers, Rev. Thomas
PG 687

Chalmers, Rev. Thomas
PG 1211

Chalmers, Rev. Thomas
PG 1394

Chalmers, Rev. Thomas,
with Thomas Chalmers Hanna
PG 2365

Chambers, Sir William
PG 629

CHALMERS, Rev. Thomas (*continued*)

PG 591* Water-colour, 8.9 x 7.7 (3½ x 3) by Kenneth Macleay after a daguerreotype by Antoine Claudet, signed. Dated 1847. Given by Sir Thomas Gibson Carmichael 1900.

PG 687* Millboard, 35.4 x 30.3 (13⅞ x 11⅞), by William Bonnar. Given by James Clason Harvie 1910.

PG 836 Cut paper silhouette, h. 20.7 (8¼), by Augustin Edouart. Purchased 1914.

PG 853 Millboard, 30.2 x 22.7 (12 x 9), by Sir Daniel Macnee. Painted 1843. Purchased 1916.

PG 1094 Canvas, 98.6 x 78.9 (38¾ x 31), by Sir John Watson Gordon. Painted posthumously. Purchased 1928.

PG 1211* Cut paper silhouette on water-colour background, 27.6 x 18.7 (10⅞ x 7⅜), by Augustin Edouart. Purchased 1933.

PG 1394* Canvas, 128 x 102 (50⅜ x 40⅛), by Thomas Duncan. Given by Mrs Gilbert Hole 1940.

PG 2029 Silvered glass medallion, oval 4.3 x 3.9 (1¹¹⁄₁₆ x 1⁹⁄₁₆), by Thomas Boston. Given by Mrs R. Foskett 1963.

PG 2150 Cut paper silhouette, h. 15.3 (6¹⁄₁₆), by Augustin Edouart, 1830, signed. Given by Mrs J. H. G. Ross 1969.

PG 2282 Cut paper silhouette, h. 15.6 (6⅛), by Augustin Edouart, 1831, signed. Provenance untraced.

PG 2365* (With his grandson Thomas Chalmers Hanna.) Millboard, 40.6 x 30.5 (16 x 12), by David Octavius Hill, signed. Based on a calotype by D. O. Hill and Robert Adamson taken 1844. Purchased 1976.

CHAMBERS, Sir William, 1726–96. *Architect*

PG 365 Wedgwood medallion, h. 7.5 (3), after unknown artist. Given by Messrs J. Wedgwood and Sons 1889.

PG 629* Chalk, 63.5 x 48.2 (25 x 19), by Francis Cotes, 1764, signed. Purchased 1904.

CHANDOS, Elizabeth Major, Duchess of, c. 1731–1813. *Third wife of Henry, 2nd Duke of Chandos*

PG 507 Medallion (plaster replica), h. 7.3 (2⅞), after James Tassie. Dated 1787. Cast from a medallion in possession of Mrs Shadford Walker 1894.

CHANTREY, Sir Francis Legatt, 1781–1842. *Sculptor*

PG 182 Plaster cast of life-head, h. 26.6 (10½), by unknown artist. Given by William Calder Marshall 1887.

PG 230 Plaque (plaster replica), h. 11.4 (4½), after a self-portrait. Purchased 1888.

PG 602 Camera lucida drawing in pencil, 21.4 x 29.3 (8½ x 11⅝), by Sir Henry Raeburn. Dated 1818. Given by C. Fairfax Murray 1902.

PG 1222 Bronze plaque, dia. 39.9 (15⅝), by James Heffernan. Cast 1842. Transferred from the National Gallery of Scotland 1934.

CHAPMAN, W. W., fl. 1899. *Of New Monkland Curling Club*

PG 1856* (*Curling at Carsebreck.*) See GROUPS.

CHARLES I, 1600–49. *Reigned 1625–49*

PG 306   Canvas, 74.3 x 62.2 (29¼ x 24½), by unknown artist. Bequeathed by W. F. Watson 1886.

PG 763   (Memorial of the king 1649.) Copper medal, dia. 5 (2) by John Roettier. Purchased 1911.

PG 815*   Canvas, 127.6 x 102.2 (50¼ x 40¼), by or after Edward Bower. Given by Mrs Andrew Lang 1913.

PG 858   (With James, Duke of York.) Canvas, 103.5 x 140.3 (40¾ x 55¼), by unknown artist (perhaps Henry Stone) after Sir Peter Lely. Original painted 1647. Purchased 1916.

PG 916   (Commemorates the king's return to London from Edinburgh.) Silver medal, dia. 4 (1⅝), by Nicolas Briot. Dated 1633.

PG 951   Canvas, 247.8 x 151.2 (97½ x 59½), by the studio of Sir Anthony Van Dyck. Purchased 1923.

PG 1454   Panel, 35.2 x 26 (13⅞ x 10¼), by unknown artist. Bequeathed by Miss Adeline Edwards 1944.

PG 1659   Pencil drawing, 41.6 x 27.3 (16⅜ x 10¾), by Sir Robert Strange after Sir Anthony Van Dyck. Bequeathed by W. F. Watson 1886.

PG 2093   Wash drawing, 18.8 x 13.1 (7½ x 5⅛), copy by unknown artist after Daniel Mytens. Transferred from the National Gallery of Scotland 1950.

PG 2212*   Canvas, 127 x 85.7 (50 x 33¾), by or after Robert Peake. Bequeathed by 13th Baron Elibank 1973.

PG 2762   (Coronation in Scotland 1633.) Silver medal, dia. 3 (1³⁄₁₆), by Nicolas Briot. Purchased 1989.

PGL 156   Canvas, 61 x 48.3 (24 x 19), by unknown artist. On loan from the National Museums of Scotland.

PGL 184   (Commemorates the marriage of the king with Henrietta Maria.) Silver medal, dia. 2.3 (⅞), by unknown artist. Dated 1625. On loan from the National Museums of Scotland.

PGL 193   Water-colour on ivory, 0.9 x 0.8 (⅜ x ¼), by unknown artist. On loan from the National Museums of Scotland.

PGL 208*   (The Execution of Charles I.) Canvas, 163.2 x 296.8 (64¼ x 116¾), by unknown artist. On loan from the Earl of Rosebery.

PGL 239*   Canvas, 206 x 137.2 (81⅛ x 54), by Daniel Mytens. On loan from the Earl of Mar and Kellie.

CHARLES II, 1630–85. *King of Scots 1649–85, King of England and Ireland 1660–85*

PG 96   (With James, Duke of York and Princess Mary.) Canvas, 121.9 x 139.7 (48 x 55), by Henry Stone or Simon Stone after Sir Anthony Van Dyck. Purchased 1886.

PG 97   Canvas, 126.4 x 103.5 (49¾ x 40¾), by unknown artist. Purchased 1899.

PG 751*   (Commemorates the king's departure from Scheveningen.) Silver medal, dia. 7 (2¾), by Pieter van Abeele. Dated 1660. Purchased 1910.

PG 760   Silver medal, dia. 3.5 (1⅜), by John Roettier. Struck 1662 at or soon after the marriage to Catherine of Braganza. Purchased 1911.

CHARLES II (*continued*)

PG 762 (Commemorates the Restoration.) Silver medal, dia. 6.3 (2½), by John Roettier. Struck 1660. Purchased 1911.

PG 1244* (When Prince of Wales, with a page.) Canvas, 153.6 x 129.8 (60½ x 51⅛), by William Dobson. Purchased 1935.

PG 1430 Water-colour on ivory, 2.3 x 2 (⅞ x ¾), by unknown artist. Given by Miss Maria Steuart 1942.

PG 2764 (Commemorates the Restoration.) Silver medal, dia. 3.5 (1⅜), by George Bower. Purchased 1989.

CHARLOTTE, Queen; Princess Sophia Charlotte of Mecklenburg-Strelitz, 1744–1818. *Queen of George III*

PG 217* Canvas, 249.5 x 163.3 (98¼ x 64¼), by the studio of Allan Ramsay. Purchased 1888.

PG 398 Medallion (plaster replica), h. 2.9 (1⅛), after James Tassie. Cast from a medallion in possession of J. R. Findlay 1889.

PG 1372 Paste medallion, h. 4 (1⁹⁄₁₆), by James Tassie. Purchased 1938.

PGL 274 Chalk drawing, 35.2 x 27 (13⅞ x 10⅝), by Allan Ramsay. On loan from the National Gallery of Scotland.

CHARLOTTE Augusta, Princess, 1796–1817. *Only child of George IV*

PG 535 Plaster medallion, h. 2.5 (1), by John Henning, 1813. Given by Miss Brown 1894.

PG 536 Plaster medallion, h. 4.4 (1¾), by John Henning, 1813. Given by Miss Brown 1894.

PG 730 Pencil drawing, 25.5 x 19.4 (10 x 7⅝), attributed to G. L. Saunders. Given by the Royal Scottish Academy 1910.

PG 1726 Wash drawing, 22.2 x 18.1 (8¾ x 7⅛), by unknown artist. Purchased 1933.

PG 2499 Paste plaque, h. 9.5 (3¾), by John Henning. Dated 1812. Purchased 1981.

CHATHAM, William Pitt, 1st Earl of, 1708–78. *Statesman*

PG 1493* Marble bust, h. 76.2 (30), by Joseph Wilton, *c.* 1759, signed. Given by Lady Sybil Grant 1947.

CHATTERTON, Thomas, 1752–70. *Poet*

PG 1274 (Doubtful identification.) Paste medallion, h. 7.9 (3⅛), by James Tassie. Purchased 1935.

CHAUNCEY, Charles, 1706–77. *Physician and antiquary*

PG 488 Medallion (plaster replica), h. 7.3 (2⅞), after James Tassie. Cast from a medallion in possession of Jeffery Whitehead 1894.

CHELSUM, Rev. James, *c.* 1740–1801. *Author*

PG 375 Medallion (plaster replica), h. 7.3 (2⅞), after James Tassie. Dated 1788. Cast from a medallion in possession of W. G. Patterson 1889.

PG 469 Medallion (plaster replica), h. 7 (2¾), after James Tassie. Dated 1788. Cast from a medallion in possession of R. W. Cochran Patrick 1893.

Charles I
PG 815

Charles I
PG 2212

Execution of Charles I
PGL 208

Charles I
PGL 239

Charles II
PG 751

Charles II
PG 1244

Charlotte, Queen
PG 217

Chatham, 1st Earl of
PG 1493

Churchill, Sir Winston
PG 1131

Clapperton, Captain Hugh
PG 5

Clapperton, Captain Hugh
PG 1114

Clark, Arthur Melville
PG 1854

Clark, Sir James
PG 1168

Clerk, Sir Dugald
PG 1224

Clerk, John
PGL 30

CHESTERFIELD, Philip Dormer Stanhope, 4th Earl of, 1694–1773. *Statesman and letter-writer*

PG 521   Medallion (plaster replica), h. 8.5 (3⅜), after Isaac Gosset; also known in Tassie paste. Cast from a medallion in possession of J. M. Gray 1894.

CHRISTIE, Charles, fl. 1899. *Of Dunkeld Curling Club*

PG 1856*   (*Curling at Carsebreck*) See GROUPS.

CHRISTIE, George, fl. 1844.

PG 1812   Bronzed cut paper silhouette on water-colour background, h. 24.9 (9⅞), by Frederick Frith, 1844, signed. Given by Mrs J. M. Fleming 1945.

CHRISTISON, David, 1831–1912. *Secretary to the Society of Antiquaries of Scotland*

PG 1693   Pencil drawing, 37.5 x 33 (14¾ x 13), by W. Graham Boss. Given by the artist.

CHURCHILL, Sir Winston, 1874–1965. *Statesman*

PG 1131*   Canvas, 91.5 x 71.1 (36 x 28), by Sir James Guthrie; study for portrait in *Statesmen of the Great War* (National Portrait Gallery, London). Given by W. G. Gardiner and Sir Frederick C. Gardiner 1930.

CLANN-FHEARGHUIS of Strachur, Sheamais, Chief of, 1879–1961. *Director of the Explorers Club*

PG 1777   Chalk drawing, 38.1 x 27.3 (15 x 10¾), by Graham Glen, 1905, signed. Given by D. Dunn 1950.

CLAPPERTON, Captain Hugh, 1788–1827. *African explorer*

PG 5*   Water-colour, 17.2 x 14.3 (6¾ x 5⅝), by unknown artist. Given by James M. Gow 1884.

PG 1114*   Canvas, 76.2 x 63.5 (30 x 25), by G. Manton. Purchased 1929.

CLARINA, Eyre Massey, 1st Baron, 1719–1804. *General*

PG 495   Medallion (plaster replica), h. 6.7 (2¹¹⁄₁₆), after James Tassie. Cast from a medallion in possession of R. W. Cochran Patrick 1894.

CLARK, Arthur Melville, b. 1895. *Author*

PG 1854*   Black chalk, 43.8 x 28 (17¼ x 11), by David Foggie, 1932, signed. Given by the sitter 1959.

CLARK, Sir James, 1788–1870. *Court physician*

PG 1168*   (Study for *The Landing of Queen Victoria at Dumbarton in 1847*, in the collection of Dumbarton District Council.) Pencil and water-colour, 68.6 x 50.8 (27 x 20), by Hope James Stewart. Dated 1849. Purchased 1931.

CLARKE, Edward Daniel, 1769–1822, *Traveller and mineralogist*

PG 376   Medallion (plaster replica), h. 6 (2⅜), after unknown artist. Cast from a medallion in possession of W. G. Patterson 1889.

CLARKSON, Thomas, 1760–1846. *Anti-slavery agitator*
PG 496   Medallion (plaster replica), 6 (2⅜), after Catherine Andras. Cast from a medallion in possession of R. W. Cochran Patrick 1894.

CLASON, Rev. Dr Patrick, 1789–1867. *Minister in Buccleuch Parish Church, Edinburgh*
PG 689   Millboard, 30 x 24.8 (11¾ x 9¾), by William Bonnar. Given by James Harvie 1910.
PG 1749   Water-colour, 16.5 x 17.8 (6½ x 7), attributed to James Howe. Given by the legatees of J. A. Gardiner.

CLASON, Rev. Robert, 1746–1831. *Minister of Logie*
PG 1750   Water-colour, 20.7 x 14.7 (8⅛ x 5¾), attributed to James Howe. Given by the legatees of J. A. Gardiner.

CLEMENTINA, Princess; see SOBIESKA

CLERK, Sir Dugald, 1854–1932. *Engineer*
PG 1224*   Pencil, crayon and water-colour drawing, 26.7 x 40.3 (10½ x 15⅞), by A. S. Hartrick, 1906, signed. Given by the executors of the sitter 1934.

CLERK of Eldin, John, 1728–1812. *Author of* Essay on Naval Tactics
PGL 30*   Canvas, 125.7 x 101 (49½ x 39¾), by James Saxon. On loan from the National Museums of Scotland.

CLERK of Penicuik, Sir John, 1676–1755. *Judge of the Exchequer Court in Scotland*
PG 1355   Canvas, 127 x 101.6 (50 x 40), by unknown artist after William Aikman. Purchased 1937.

CLOUGH, Charles Thomas, 1852–1916. *Geologist*
PG 2354   Silver medal, dia. 5.1 (2), by C. d'O. Pilkington Jackson. Dated 1935. Given by the artist 1956.

CLYDE, Colin Campbell, 1st Baron, 1792–1863. *Field-Marshal*
PG 284*   Millboard, 62.2 x 45.1 (24½ x 17¾), by Thomas Jones Barker, 1860, signed. Given by the Earl of Rosebery 1890.
PG 597   Plaster bust, h. 63.5 (25), by George Gamon Adams. Dated 1861. Purchased 1901.
PG 1976   (With 1st Baron Sandhurst.) Chalk drawing, 25.7 x 34 (10⅛ x 13⅜), by T. Blake Wirgman after a photograph by Felice Beato taken 1857. Given by Aberdeen University 1961.

COCHRAN-PATRICK, R.W., d. 1897. *Antiquary*
PG 1708*   Pencil drawing, 37.5 x 33.7 (14¾ x 13¼), by W. Graham Boss. Given by the artist.

COCHRANE, Admiral Sir Alexander Forrester Inglis, 1758–1832. *Governor of Guadeloupe*

PG 1578*   Canvas, 76.2 x 63.5 (30 x 25), by Robert Field, 1809, signed. Purchased 1951.

COCKBURN, Elizabeth Macdowall, Lady, fl. 1830. *Wife of Lord Cockburn*

PG 1175*   (Lord Cockburn with his family.) see GROUPS.

COCKBURN, Henry Thomas, Lord, 1779–1854. *Judge and author*

PG 173   (Artist's plaster.) Plaster bust, h. 73 (28¾), by Sir John Steell. Purchased 1887.

PG 709   Canvas, 240.6 x 148.6 (94¾ x 58½), by Sir John Watson Gordon. Given by the Royal Scottish Academy 1910.

PG 1175*   (With his family.) See GROUPS.

PG 1392*   Marble bust, h. 60.6 (23⅞), by William Brodie, 1855, signed. Given by Mrs Cockburn 1939.

PG 1497*   (With the Marquess of Breadalbane, the Marquess of Dalhousie and Lord Rutherfurd.) See GROUPS.

PG 2281   Cut paper silhouette, h. 19.3 (7⅝), by Augustin Edouart, 1831, signed. Provenance untraced.

PG 2306   (Crombie Sketchbook, fo. 10. Study for *Modern Athenians*, Pl. 14.) Pencil drawing, 15.6 x 20 (6⅛ x 7⅞), by Benjamin William Crombie. Purchased 1938.

COCKBURN of Ormiston, John, d. 1758. *Member of the Scottish Parliament*

PG 99   Wash drawing, 10.2 x 7.5 (4 x 3), by unknown artist. Bequeathed by W. F. Watson 1886.

PG 574*   Canvas 73.2 x 61 (28⅞ x 24), by unknown artist. Given by Miss Cornelia Dick Lauder 1898.

COKE, William, d. 1819. *Bookseller*

PG 1787*   Water-colour and pencil drawing, 39.2 x 28 (15½ x 11), by William Nicholson. Painted 1815. Purchased 1955.

COLERAINE, Lucy Montagu, Lady, d. 1682. *Wife of the 1st Baron Coleraine*

PG 2072   Wash drawing, 13.1 x 9.5 (5⅛ x 3¾), copy by unknown artist. Transferred from the National Gallery of Scotland 1950.

COLONSAY, Duncan MacNeill, Lord, 1793–1874. *Judge*

PG 171   (Artist's plaster.) Plaster bust, h. 83.8 (33), by Sir John Steell. Purchased 1887.

PG 249   Canvas, 118.7 x 89.6 (46¾ x 35¼), by Thomas Duncan. Transferred from the National Gallery of Scotland 1889.

COLQUHOUN, Robert, 1914–62. *Artist*

PG 2220*   Black chalk drawing, 27.3 x 15.7 (10¾ x 6³⁄₁₆), by Robert MacBryde, signed. Dated 1939. Given by an anonymous donor 1973.

Clyde, 1st Baron
PG 284

Cochran-Patrick, R. W.
PG 1708

Cochrane, Sir Alexander
PG 1578

Cockburn, Lord
PG 1392

Cockburn, John
PG 574

Coke, William
PG 1787

Colquhoun, Robert
PG 2220

Colquhoun, Robert,
with Robert MacBryde   PG 2487

Combe, Andrew
PG 555

Combe, George
PG 167

Combe, George
PG 556

Connery, Sean
PG 2700

Constable, Archibald
PG 609

Conti, Tom
PG 2685

Cook, Sir Joseph
PG 1136

COLQUHOUN, Robert (*continued*)
PG 2487* (With Robert MacBryde.) Pencil and chalk drawing, 26.2 x 38.9 (10³⁄₁₆ x 15⁵⁄₁₆), by John Laurie. Dated 1939. Purchased 1981.

COLVILLE, Sir Charles, 1770–1843. *General*
PG 630 Chalk drawing, 38.1 x 30.5 (15 x 12), by Alexander Blaikley. Dated 1849. Purchased 1904.

COMBE, Andrew, 1797–1847. *Physiologist*
PG 555* Marble bust, h. 70.2 (27⅝), by John Hutchison, 1889, signed. Given by Robert Cox 1895.

COMBE, George, 1788–1858. *Phrenologist*
PG 167* Plaster medallion, h 18.4 (7¼), by Shakspere Wood. Dated 1849. Given by John D. Michie 1886.
PG 542 Plaster medallion, h. 28.5 (11¼), by William Brodie. Given by Mrs Hodgson 1894.
PG 556* Marble bust, h. 69.4 (27⅜), by Lawrence Macdonald. Given by Robert Cox 1895.

CONNERY, Sean, b. 1930. *Actor*
PG 2700* Canvas, 152.5 x 122.3 (60 x 48⅛), by John Bellany, signed. Purchased 1986.
PG 2701 Conté drawing, 75.6 x 55.5 (29¾ x 21⅞), by John Bellany, 1986, signed. Given by the artist 1986.

CONOLLY, Captain Arthur, 1807–42. *Asiatic traveller*
PG 1298 Water-colour on ivory, 10.5 x 8.1 (4⅛ x 3¼), by Robert Thorburn. Bequeathed by Edward Thorburn 1936.

CONSTABLE, Archibald, 1774–1827. *Publisher*
PG 609* Panel, 58.9 x 42 (23⅛ x 16½), by Andrew Geddes. Painted 1813. Purchased 1902.
PG 825* (*Sir Walter Scott and his friends at Abbotsford.*) See GROUPS.

CONSTABLE, Thomas, 1812–81. *Printer and publisher*
PG 1612 Marble bust, h. 79.5 (31¼), by William Brodie, 1870, signed. Given by Mrs Katherine Burn-Murdoch 1954.

CONSTABLE, William, fl. 1791. *Collector of gems*
PG 1885 Medallion (plaster replica), h. 8.1 (3¼), after James Tassie. Cast from a medallion in possession of R. W. Cochran Patrick 1894.

CONSTANTINE, Grand Duke, 1779–1831. *Brother of Alexander I of Russia*
PG 1928 (With Alexander I.) Medallion (plaster replica), h. 5.1 (2), after James Tassie. Modelled by the Empress Maria Feodorovna 1791. Provenance untraced.

CONTI, Tom, b. 1942. *Actor*
  PG 2685*   Water-colour, 69.8 x 49.9 (27½ x 19⅝), by Ishbel McWhirter, signed.
             Purchased 1986.

COOK, Captain James, 1728–1779. *Circumnavigator*
  PG 487   Medallion (plaster replica), h. 9.4 (3¾), after James Tassie. Cast from a
            medallion in possession of Jeffery Whitehead 1894.

COOK, Sir Joseph, 1860–1947. *Prime Minister of Australia*
  PG 1136*   Canvas, 91 x 71 (35⅞ x 28), by Sir James Guthrie; study for portrait in
             Statesmen of the Great War (National Portrait Gallery, London). Given by
             W. G. Gardiner and Sir Frederick Gardiner 1930.

COOK, Robert, 1795–*c.* 1876. *Engineer*
  PG 2367   Canvas, 91.7 x 71.2 (36⅛ x 28), by Robert Harvey. Given by Mrs L. A.
             Gordon, 1976.

COOPER, Richard, d. 1764. *Engraver*
  PG 728*   Canvas, 58.4 x 50.8 (23 x 20), by Jeremiah Davison. Given by the Royal
             Scottish Academy 1910.

COOPER, Richard, *c.* 1740–*c.* 1814. *Painter and engraver*
  PG 1869   Chalk drawing, 29.7 x 23.5 (11½ x 9¼), by John Hoppner. Given by Miss
             Eyre to the National Gallery of Scotland and transferred 1959.

COOPER, Thomas, fl. 1794. 'Of America'
  PG 1886   Medallion (plaster replica), h. 7.5 (3), after James Tassie. Dated 1794.
             Provenance untraced.

COOTE, Sir Eyre, 1762–1823. *General*
  PG 2681*   (*The Landing of British Troops at Aboukir, 8 March 1801.*) See GROUPS.

COREHOUSE, George Cranstoun, Lord, d. 1850. *Judge.*
  PG 100*   Pencil drawing, 6.8 x 5.6 (2¹¹⁄₁₆ x 2¼), by Benjamin William Crombie.
             Bequeathed by W. F. Watson 1886.

CORSE (or CROSS), Jean Irvine, Mrs Hugh, fl. 1801. *Daughter-in-law of the Rev. John
             Corse*
  PG 1887   Medallion (plaster replica), h. 8.2 (3¼), after William Tassie. Dated 1801.
             Provenance untraced.

CORSE (or CROSS), Rev. John, 1713/14–82. *Minister of the Tron Church, Glasgow*
  PG 501   Medallion (plaster replica), h. 7.5 (3), after William Tassie. Dated 1800.
             Cast from a medallion in possession of R. W. Cochrain Patrick 1894.

COURLAND AND SEMGALLEN, Peter, Duke of.
>   PG 451   Medal (plaster replica), dia. 4.3 (1¹¹⁄₁₆), after Karl von Leberecht. Given by the South Kensington Museum 1893.

COVENTRY, Andrew, 1764–1832. *Agriculturist*
>   PG 431   Paste medallion, h. 8.2 (3¼), by James Tassie. Dated 1794. Purchased 1893.

COWAN, Alexander, 1775–1859. *Paper-maker and philanthropist*
>   PG 2470   Canvas, 128.2 x 102.2 (50⅜ x 40¼), by Colvin Smith. Painted *c.* 1836. Given by Reed Paper & Board (UK) Ltd. 1980.

COWAN, Charles, 1735–1805. *Merchant and paper-maker*
>   PG 2469   Canvas, 75 x 63.3 (29½ x 25), by unknown artist. Given by Reed Paper & Board (UK) Ltd. 1980.

COWELL, , Thomas, fl. *c.* 1720.
>   PG 2097   Ink drawing, 13.1 x 9.7 (5⅛ x 3⅞), copy by unknown artist. Transferred from the National Gallery of Scotland 1950.

COWIE, James, 1886–1956. *Artist*
>   PG 2210*   Pastel, 76.5 x 55.9 (30⅛ x 22), by John Laurie, 1947, signed. Purchased 1973.

COX, David, 1783–1859. *Landscape painter*
>   PG 554   Millboard, 35.4 x 26.7 (13⅞ x 10½), by Sir John Watson Gordon. Purchased 1896.

CRABBE, Rev. George, 1754–1832. *Poet*
>   PG 825*   (*Sir Walter Scott and his friends at Abbotsford.*) See GROUPS.

CRAIG, James, 1744–95. *Architect*
>   PG 729*   Canvas, 76.7 x 60.8 (30³⁄₁₆ x 23¹⁵⁄₁₆), by David Allan. Given by the Royal Scottish Academy 1910.

CRAIG, Sir James Gibson, 1765–1850. *Politician*
>   PG 351   Plaster bust, h. 64.2 (25¼), by Thomas Campbell. Purchased 1887.
>   PG 2306   (Crombie Sketchbook, fo. 7v.) Pencil, ink and watercolour drawing, 15.6 x 20 (6⅛ x 7⅞), by Benjamin William Crombie.
>   (Crombie Sketchbook, fo. 8r. Study for *Modern Athenians*, Pl. 15.) Pencil, ink and watercolour drawing, 15.6 x 20 (6⅛ x 7⅞), by Benjamin William Crombie.
>   (Crombie Sketchbook, fo. 8v. Study for *Modern Athenians*, Pl. 15.) Pencil drawing, 15.6 x 20 (6⅛ x 7⅞), by Benjamin William Crombie. Purchased 1938.

CRAIG, Sir James Henry Gibson, 3rd Baronet, 1841–1908. *Advocate*
>   PG 1856*   (*Curling at Carsebreck.*) See GROUPS.

Cooper, Richard
PG 728

Corehouse, Lord
PG 100

Cowie, James
PG 2210

Craig, James
PG 729

Craig, Robert
PG 326

Craig, Lord
PGL 279

Craig, Sir William
Gibson   PG 711

Craigmyle, 1st Baron
PG 2130

Crawford, 28th Earl of
PG 2778

Crawford, Hugh Adam
PG 2520

Crawford, 17th Earl of
PG 817

Crawhall, Joseph
PG 971

Crawhall, Joseph
PG 2136

Crawhall, Joseph
PG 2650

Creech, William
PG 1041

CRAIG, John, d. 1655. *Physician to James VI and Charles I*
 PG 2143   Canvas, 68.8 x 59.7 (27⅛ x 23½), by unknown artist. Purchased 1968.

CRAIG, John, fl. 1899. *Of Blantyre Curling Club*
 PG 1856*   (*Curling at Carsebreck.*) See GROUPS.

CRAIG, Robert, b. 1718/19.
 PG 2446   Paste medallion, h. 7.6 (3), by William Tassie. Dated 1800. Bequeathed by William Tassie to the National Gallery of Scotland 1860 and transferred 1979.

CRAIG of Riccarton, Robert, 1730–1823. *Advocate and political writer*
 PG 326*   Canvas, 91.7 x 71.6 (36⅛ x 28⅛), by Andreas van der Mijn, 1765, signed. Bequeathed by W. F. Watson 1886.

CRAIG, William Craig, Lord, 1745–1813. *Scottish Judge*
 PGL 279*   Pastel, 68.8 x 55.9 (27¹⁄₁₆ x 22), by Archibald Skirving. On loan from Sir Edward Playfair.

CRAIG, Sir William Gibson, 1797–1878. *Lord Clerk Register*
 PG 711*   Canvas, 238.4 x 148 (93⅞ x 58¼), by Sir John Watson Gordon. Given by the Royal Scottish Academy 1910.

CRAIGENPUTTOCK
 PG 898   (View of Carlyle's house at Craigenputtock.) See CARLYLE, Thomas.
 PG 1067   a. (View of Carlyle's house at Craigenputtock).
          b. (View of the kitchen in Carlyle's house at Craigenputtock).
          c. (View of Craigenputtock Moor with Carlyle's house.) See CARLYLE, Thomas.

CRAIGHALL, Sir John Hope, Lord, *c.* 1605–54. *Judge*
 PGL 94   Canvas, 74.2 x 61.7 (29¼ x 24¼), by George Jamesone. On loan from Mrs J. R. B. Lennox and Dr T. S. B. Crawshaw.

CRAIGMYLE, Thomas Shaw, 1st Baron, 1850–1937. *Lawyer and politician*
 PG 2130*   Canvas, 95.5 x 75.2 (37½ x 29⅝), by George Fiddes Watt. Given by the sitter's son 1968.

CRAWFORD, David Alexander Robert Lindsay, 28th Earl of, and 11th Earl of Balcarres, 1900–75.
 PG 2502   Ink drawing, 53.5 x 32 (21 x 12⅝), by Emilio Coia, signed. Purchased 1981.
 PG 2778*   Canvas, 40.5 x 50.5 (16 x 20), by Derek Hill. Purchased 1989.

CRAWFORD, Hugh Adam, 1898–1982. *Artist*
 PG 2520*   Plywood panel, 124.6 x 88.6 (49 x 34⅞), self-portrait. Purchased 1982.

CRAWFORD, John Lindsay, 17th Earl of, 1596–1678. *Statesman*
  PG 817*   Canvas, 76.2 x 62.6 (30 x 24⅝), by unknown artist. Dated 1663. Purchased
             1913.

CRAWFURD of Cartsburn, Thomas, 1746–91.
  PG 2436   Paste medallion, h. 8.1 (3³⁄₁₆), by James Tassie. Dated 1795. Bequeathed by
             William Tassie to the National Gallery of Scotland 1860 and transferred 1979.

CRAWHALL, Joseph, 1821–96. *Writer and amateur artist*
  PG 2480   Pencil drawing, 11.2 x 7 (4⅜ x 2¾), by Joseph Crawhall. Given by Dr
             Camilla Uytman 1981.

CRAWHALL, Joseph, 1861–1913. *Artist*
  PG 971*   Canvas, 74.3 x 36.8 (29¼ x 14½), by Edward Arthur Walton, 1884, signed.
             Given by Mrs E. A. Walton 1924.
  PG 2136*   Ink drawing (caricature), 18.1 x 11.4 (7⅛ x 4½), by Sir James Guthrie.
             Given by A. J. Mackenzie Stuart 1968.
  PG 2484   (With Sir James Guthrie and E. A. Walton.) Ink drawing (caricature), 9 x
             11.3 (3½ x 4⁷⁄₁₆), by Sir James Guthrie. Given by Dr Camilla Uytman to the
             National Gallery of Scotland and transferred 1981.
  PG 2650*   Bronze tondo plaque, dia. 30.5 (12), by James Pittendrigh Macgillivray.
             Dated 1881. Purchased 1985.

CREECH, William, 1745–1815. *Publisher and Lord Provost of Edinburgh*
  PG 1041*   Canvas, 127 x 101.6 (50 x 40), by Sir Henry Raeburn. Painted 1806. Given
             by the family of the Rev. Robert Watson 1928.

CRICHTON, James (the Admirable), 1560–c. 1585. *Scholar and adventurer*
  PG 1623*   Pencil and chalk drawing, 30.4 x 25.9 (12 x 10⅛), by the 11th Earl of
             Buchan after unknown artist. Bequeathed by W. F. Watson 1886.

CROMARTY, George Mackenzie, 1st Earl of, 1630–1714. *Statesman*
  PG 304   Canvas, 70.5 x 62.4 (27¾ x 24⅝), after Sir John Baptiste de Medina.
             Bequeathed by W. F. Watson 1886.

CROMBIE PORTRAIT AND CARICATURE SKETCHES
  PG 2305   29 miscellaneous unidentified portrait and caricature sketches attributed to
             Benjamin William Crombie. Purchased 1938.

CROMBIE SKETCHBOOK
  PG 2306   Portrait and caricature sketches, including studies for *Modern Athenians*,
             by Benjamin William Crombie. Purchased 1938.

CROMWELL, Oliver, 1599–1658. *Lord Protector*
  PG 178   Canvas, 75.9 x 62.9 (29⅞ x 24¾), by unknown artist after Robert Walker.
             Purchased 1886.

CROMWELL, Oliver (*continued*)

PG 740 (Commemorates the battle of Dunbar.) Silver medal, oval 2.4 x 2 ($^{15}/_{16}$ x $^{13}/_{16}$), by Thomas Simon. Dated 1650. Purchased 1910.

PGL 187 Medallion (gutta-percha replica), h. 11.3 (4½), after unknown artist. On loan from the National Museums of Scotland.

PGL 188 Brass medallion, h. 8.5 (3⅜), by unknown artist. On loan from the National Museums of Scotland.

CROOKS of Leven, Miss.

PG 2543 Water-colour on ivory, 9 x 7 (3½ x 2¾) (sight), by unknown artist. Transferred from the National Gallery of Scotland 1982.

CROOKS of Leven, Adam, fl. 1805.

PG 2530 Water-colour on ivory, h. 7.3 (2⅞), by Peter Paillou, signed. Dated 1805. Transferred from the National Gallery of Scotland 1982.

CROZIER, William, 1877–1930. *Artist*

PG 2494 Canvas board, 55.5 x 45.1 (21$^{13}/_{16}$ x 17¾), by Sir William MacTaggart. Signed on the reverse. Given by the executors of the artist 1981.

PG 2587* Water-colour with some pencil, 51.3 x 39.8 (20$^{3}/_{16}$ x 15¾) (irregular), self-portrait. Purchased 1983.

CRUIKSHANK, William Cumberland, 1745–1800. *Anatomist*

PG 377 Medallion (plaster replica), h. 7.9 (3⅛), after James Tassie. Dated 1795. Cast from a medallion in possession of W. G. Patterson 1889.

CULLEN, Sir Francis Grant, Lord, 1658–1726. *Judge*

PG 1521* Canvas, 76.5 x 63.5 (30⅛ x 25), by John Smibert. Purchased 1949.

CULLEN, William, 1710–1790. *Chemist and physician*

PG 98 Pencil and water-colour drawing, 8 x 7 (3⅛ x 2¾), by David Allan. Dated 1774. Bequeathed by W. F. Watson 1886.

PG 268 Paste medallion, h. 7 (2$^{13}/_{16}$), by James Tassie. Dated 1786. Transferred from the National Gallery of Scotland 1889.

PG 1479 Canvas, 81.2 x 69.2 (32 x 27¼), by William Cochrane. Purchased 1946.

PGL 260* Canvas, 127 x 101.9 (50 x 40⅛), by David Martin, 1776, signed. On loan from the Royal Medical Society.

CUMBERLAND, William Augustus, Duke of, 1721–65. *Youngest son of George II*

PG 415 Medallion (plaster replica), h. 9 (3½), after unknown artist; also known in Tassie paste. Cast from a medallion in possession of the British Museum 1892.

PG 705 (Commemorates the battle of Culloden.) Silver medal, dia. 5 (2), by Richard Yeo. Dated 1746. Purchased 1910.

PG 706 (Commemorates the capture of Carlisle.) Silver medal, dia. 3.3 (1$^{5}/_{16}$), by Thomas Pingo. Dated 1745. Purchased 1910.

Crichton, James
PG 1623

Crozier, William
PG 2587

Cullen, Lord
PG 1521

Cullen, William
PGL 260

Cumberland, Duke of
PG 910

Cummyng, James
PGL 86

Cunningham, Allan
PG 276

Cunningham, Allan
PG 1494

Cunningham, Francis
PG 1495

Cunningham, William
PG 1839

Cunningham, Rev. William
PG 688

Currie, Sir Donald
PG 2064

Cursiter, Stanley, with Phyllis Cursiter and Poppy Low
PG 2451

CUMBERLAND, William Augustus, Duke of (*continued*)

PG 910*   Canvas, 76.2 x 63.5 (30 x 25), after Sir Joshua Reynolds. Purchased 1920.

PG 1334   (Commemorates the capture of Carlisle.) Copper medal, dia. 3.6 (1⁷⁄₁₆), by Johann Henrik Wolff. Dated 1745. Purchased 1937.

PG 1335   (Commemorates the capture of Carlisle.) Copper medal, dia. 3.5 (1⅜), after Johann Henrik Wolff. Dated 1745. Purchased 1937.

PG 1336   (Commemorates the capture of Carlisle.) Copper medal, dia. 3.6 (1⁷⁄₁₆), by unknown artist. Dated 1745. Purchased 1937.

PG 1337   (Commemorates the capture of Carlisle.) Brass medal, dia 3.4 (1⅜), by unknown artist. Dated 1745. Purchased 1937.

PG 1338   (Commemorates the defeat of the rebels.) Copper medal, dia. 3.4 (1⅜), by A. Kirk and John Kirk. Dated 1745. Purchased 1937.

PG 1339   (Commemorates the battle of Culloden.) Copper medal, dia. 3.6 (1⁷⁄₁₆), by unknown artist. Dated 1745. Purchased 1937.

PG 1340   (Commemorates the battle of Culloden.) Brass medal, dia. 4.2 (1⅝), by unknown artist. Dated 1746.

PG 1341   (Commemorates the battle of Culloden.) Brass medal, dia. 4.2 (1¹¹⁄₁₆), by unknown artist. Dated 1746. Purchased 1937.

PG 1342   (Commemorates the battle of Culloden.) Brass medal, dia. 3.4 (1⅜), by unknown artist. Dated 1746. Purchased 1937.

PG 1343   (Commemorates the battle of Culloden.) Copper medal, dia. 3.6 (1⁷⁄₁₆), by A. Kirk and John Kirk. Dated 1746. Purchased 1937.

PG 1344   (Commemorates the defeat of the rebels.) Brass medal, dia. 3.1 (1¼), by unknown artist. Dated 1746. Purchased 1937.

PG 1345   (Commemorates the defeat of the rebels.) Brass medal, dia. 3.3 (1⁵⁄₁₆), by unknown artist after Thomas Pingo. Dated 1746. Purchased 1937.

PG 1952   Wedgwood medallion, h. 7.3 (2⅞), after unknown artist. Provenance untraced.

PG 2773   (Commemorates the battle of Culloden.) Silver medal, dia. 4.1 (1⅝), by Johann Henrik Wolff, 1746. Purchased 1989.

CUMMING, Alastair S., b. 1890. *Of Logie*

PG 1978   Chalk drawing, 56.2 x 44 (22⅛ x 17¼), by unknown artist signing 'F.L.R.' Dated 1901. Given by Aberdeen University 1961.

CUMMYNG, James, 1732–93. *First secretary to the Society of Antiquaries of Scotland*

PGL 86*   Pencil drawing, 51.2 x 36.6 (20³⁄₁₆ x 14½), by John Brown. On loan from the National Museums of Scotland.

CUNNINGHAM, Allan, 1784–1842. *Poet and critic*

PG 276*   Plaster bust, h. 68 (26¾), by Sir Francis Legatt Chantrey. Purchased 1889.

PG 659   Wash drawing, 10.6 x 8.2 (4⅛ x 3¼), by J. J. Penstone. Given by W. Skeoch Cumming 1907.

PG 1490   Canvas, 77.1 x 67 (30⅜ x 26⅜), by Henry William Pickersgill. Purchased 1947.

PG 1494*   Marble bust, h. 73 (28¾), by Henry Weekes, 1842, signed. Given by an anonymous donor 1947.

CUNNINGHAM, Francis, 1820–75. *Author and critic*
  PG 1495* Marble bust, h. 64 (25¼), by Sir Francis Legatt Chantrey. Given by an
            anonymous donor 1947.

CUNNINGHAM, Laurence, fl. 1899. *Of Currie Curling Club*
  PG 1856* (*Curling at Carsebreck.*) See GROUPS.

CUNNINGHAM, , William, 1849–1919. *Economic historian*
  PG 1839* Chalk and water-colour drawing, 41.9 x 27.3 (16½ x 10¾), by William
            Strang, 1908, signed. Purchased 1957.

CUNNINGHAM, Rev. William, 1805–61. *Theologian*
  PG 617   Canvas, 91.5 x 71.1 (36 x 28), by Sir John Watson Gordon. Given by Miss
            Cunningham 1904.
  PG 688*   Millboard, 35.5 x 30.5 (14 x 12), by William Bonnar. Given by James
            Clason Harvie 1910.

CURRIE, , Sir Donald, 1825–1909. *Shipping magnate and educational benefactor*
  PG 2064* Canvas, 127 x 101.6 (50 x 40), by Walter W. Ouless, 1908, signed. Given by
            Major Wisely and Mrs Wisely 1967.

CURSITER, Stanley, 1887–1976. *Artist; Director of the National Galleries of Scotland*
  PG 2451* (With his wife Phyllis Eda Hourston and his model Poppy Low. Exhibited as
            Chez Nous.) Canvas, 101.3 x 152.5 (39⅞ x 60), self-portrait, 1925, signed.

DAER, Basil William Douglas, styled Lord, 1763–94. *Politician*

PG 1263   Paste medallion, h. 7.7 (3¹⁄₁₆), by James Tassie. Dated 1794. Purchased 1935.

PG 1685   Pencil drawing, 5.5 x 4.8 (2⅛ x 1⅞), by John Brown, 1784, signed. Bequeathed by W. F. Watson 1886.

DALE, David, 1739–1806. *Manufacturer and philanthropist*

PG 2219*   Paste medallion, h. 7 (2¾), by James Tassie. Dated 1791. Given by the Royal Bank of Scotland 1973.

DALGLISH, 'Steenie'.

PG 2017   Pencil drawing, 13.7 x 10.2 (5⅜ x 4), by unknown artist. Given by E. Kersley 1962.

DALHOUSIE, Fox Maule, 11th Earl of, 1801–74. *Parliamentarian*

PG 2139*   Canvas, 76.6 x 63.9 (30⅛ x 25⅛), by Sir John Watson Gordon. Purchased 1968.

DALHOUSIE, James Andrew Ramsay, 10th Earl and 1st Marquess of, 1812–60. *Governor-General of India*

PG 177   (Artist's plaster.) Plaster statue, h. 206.7 (81⅜), by Sir John Steell. Purchased 1887.

PG 1078   Pencil drawing, 18.2 x 10.8 (7¼ x 4¼), by Sir John Watson Gordon. Acquired 1927.

PG 1119*   Millboard, 59.7 x 38.7 (23½ x 15¼), by Sir John Watson Gordon. Purchased 1929.

PG 1497*   (As Lord Panmure, with the Marquess of Breadalbane and Lords Cockburn and Rutherfurd.) See GROUPS.

DALKEITH, Caroline Campbell, Countess of (later Baroness Greenwich), 1717–94. *Wife of Francis Scott, Earl of Dalkeith*

PG 2374   Varnished pencil drawing on semi-transparent paper, 34.4 x 23.6 (13⁹⁄₁₆ x 9⁵⁄₁₆), by Thomas Bardwell. Provenance untraced.

DALKEITH, Francis Scott, Earl of, 1721–50. *Eldest son of the 2nd Duke of Buccleuch*

PG 2375   Varnished pencil drawing on semi-transparent paper, 37.8 x 28 (14⅞ x 11), by Thomas Bardwell. Provenance untraced.

DALRYMPLE of High Mark, Sir Adolphus John, 2nd Baronet, 1784–1866.

PG 2562   Water-colour on ivory, 6.2 x 5.7 (2⁷⁄₁₆ x 2¼) (octagonal), by Anthony Stewart. Transferred from the National Gallery of Scotland 1982.

DALRYMPLE of Dalmahoy, George, 1680–1745. *Baron of Exchequer*

PG 945*   Canvas, 126.9 x 100.8 (50 x 39⅝), by Sir John Baptiste de Medina. Purchased 1923.

DALRYMPLE, Sir Hew, 1652–1737. *Lord President and politician*
 PG 621*   Canvas, 76.2 x 64.2 (30 x 25¼), attributed to Sir John Baptiste de Medina.
                Purchased 1903.

DALRYMPLE of High Mark, Sir Hew Whitefoord, 1st Baronet, 1750–1830. *General*
 PG 2561   Water-colour on ivory, 7.8 x 6.5 (3⅛ x 2⁹/₁₆), by Anthony Stewart.
                Transferred from the National Gallery of Scotland 1982.

DALRYMPLE of Orangefield, James, fl. 1787.
 PG 946*   (*The Inauguration of Robert Burns as Poet Laureate of the Lodge
                Canongate, Kilwinning, 1787.*) See GROUPS.

DALRYMPLE, Sir John, 1726–1810. *Judge and author*
 PGL 74*   Pencil drawing, 52.2 x 36.1 (20⁹/₁₆ x 14³/₁₆), by John Brown. On loan from
                the National Museums of Scotland.

DALRYMPLE, Colonel Samuel, fl. 1801. *Soldier*
 PG 2681*   (*The Landing of British Troops at Aboukir, 8 March 1801.*) See GROUPS.

DALTON, John, 1766–1844. *Chemist and natural philosopher*
 PG 145   Water-colour drawing, 15.7 x 12.5 (6³/₁₆ x 5), by unknown artist.
                Bequeathed by W. F. Watson 1886.

DALYELL of Lingo, John, d. 1843. *Soldier*
 PGL 337*   (*A Meet of the Fife Hounds.*) See GROUPS.

DALYELL, Sir John Graham, 1775–1851. *Antiquary and naturalist*
 PG 2581   Plaster bust, h. 70.5 (27¾), by unknown sculptor. Provenance untraced.

DALYELL, General Thomas, *c.* 1599–1685. *Soldier in Russia and Commander-in-Chief
                in Scotland*
 PG 2129*   Canvas, 124.4 x 101.6 (49 x 40), by L. Schuneman. Purchased 1967.

DALZEL, Professor Andrew, 1742–1806. *Classical scholar*
 PG 199*   Canvas, 127.4 x 100.9 (50⅛ x 39¾), by Sir Henry Raeburn. Purchased
                1887.

DAMER, Anne Seymour, 1749–1828. *Sculptress*
 PG 2125   Water-colour, 21.6 x 16.5 (8½ x 6½), by Henry Carr, 1788, signed.
                Transferred from the National Gallery of Scotland 1950.

DARLING, Sir William Young, 1885–1962. *Businessman and author; Lord Provost of
                Edinburgh*
 PG 2010*   Black chalk drawing, 46.7 x 29.2 (18⅜ x 11½), by David Foggie, 1939,
                signed. Given by Mrs M. Foggie 1962.

DARNLEY, Henry Stewart, Lord, 1545–67. *Consort of Mary, Queen of Scots*

PG 752   a. (With Mary, Queen of Scots. Commemorates the marriage of Mary and Lord Darnley.) Silver medal, dia. 4.4 (1¾), by unknown artist. Dated 1565. Purchased 1910.

b. (With Mary, Queen of Scots. Commemorates the marriage of Mary and Lord Darnley.) Silver medal (electrotype replica), dia. 4.3 (1¹¹⁄₁₆), after unknown artist. Dated 1565. Provenance untraced.

PG 1087   (Plaster cast of effigy on tomb of Lady Margaret Lennox in Westminster Abbey.) h. 72.1 (28⅜), after unknown artist. Purchased 1928.

PG 2279*   Panel, 76.2 x 58.4 (30 x 23), by unknown artist. Purchased 1975.

PG 2314   Panel, 12.1 x 9.4 (4¾ x 3¹¹⁄₁₆), copy by unknown artist. Bequeathed by W. F. Watson 1886.

PG 2461   a. Pencil and grey ink drawing, 23.7 x 14.5 (9⁵⁄₁₆ x 5¾). Copy by David Allan. Purchased 1980.

PG 2471*   Panel, 70.4 x 55.2 (27¾ x 21¾), by Hans Eworth, signed in monogram. Painted 1555. Purchased 1980.

DAVIDSON, J. Scott, fl. 1899. *Of Colinsburgh Curling Club*

PG 1856*   (*Curling at Carsebreck.*) See GROUPS.

DAVIDSON, Randall Thomas Davidson, 1st Baron, 1848–1930. *Archbishop of Canterbury*

PG 2059*   Water-colour, 34.3 x 26.7 (13½ x 10½), by Lucy Graham Smith, 1893, signed. Bequeathed by Mrs J. L. Lindsay 1966.

DAVIDSON of Curriehill, Sir William, 1615/16–89. *Conservator of the Staple at Veere*

PG 2462*   (With his son Charles.) Canvas, 140 x 108 (55⅛ x 42½), attributed to Simon Luttichuys. Painted c. 1664. Purchased 1980.

DAVIE, Alan, b. 1920. *Artist*

PG 2632*   (With John Bellany.) Canvas, 213.3 x 165 (84 x 65), by John Bellany, signed. Dated 1983. Purchased 1984.

DAVY, Sir Humphry, 1778–1829. *Chemist*

PG 825*   (*Sir Walter Scott and his friends at Abbotsford.*) See GROUPS.

DAWSON of Asterley, Sir William, fl. 1680. *Recorder of Ripon*

PG 2114   Pencil drawing, 10.5 x 8.5 (4⅛ x 3⅜), by unknown artist. Transferred from the National Gallery of Scotland 1950.

DEAN, Stansmore; see STEVENSON.

DELACOUR, William, d. 1767. *First Master of the Trustees' Academy*

PG 1844*   Panel, 37.5 x 28.6 (14¾ x 11¼), self-portrait, 1765, signed. Purchased 1957.

Dale, David
PG 2219

Dalhousie, 11th Earl of
PG 2139

Dalhousie, 1st Marquess
of   PG 1119

Dalrymple, George
PG 945

Dalrymple, Sir Hew
PG 621

Dalrymple, Sir John
PG L 74

Dalyell, General Thomas
PG 2129

Dalzel, Professor Andrew
PG 199

Darling, Sir William
Young   PG 2010

Darnley, Lord
PG 2279

Darnley, Lord
PG 2471

Davidson, 1st Baron
PG 2059

Davidson, Sir William, with
Charles Davidson   PG 2462

Delacour, William
PG 1844

De Quincey, Thomas
PG 581

De Quincey, Thomas
PG 1116

DEMPSTER of Dunnichen, George, 1732–1818. *Agriculturist and Member of Parliament*
    PG 138   Canvas, 76.2 x 63.5 (30 x 25), by J. T. Nairn. Given by George Dempster of Tranent 1885.
    PG 257   Paste medallion, h. 7.6 (3), by James Tassie. Transferred from the National Gallery of Scotland 1889.
    PG 2510   Canvas, 76.2 x 63.5 (30 x 25), by John Opie. Purchased 1982.

DENNISTOUN, James, 1803–55. *Antiquary*
    PG 795   Cut paper silhouette, h. 19.9 (7⅞), by Augustin Edouart. Purchased 1912.

DE QUINCEY, Thomas, 1785–1859. *Author and essayist*
    PG 220   Plaster medallion, dia. 21.4 (8½), by Shakspere Wood. Given by John Ritchie Findlay 1888.
    PG 553   Millboard, 35.6 x 28.6 (14 x 11¼), by Sir John Watson Gordon, signed. Purchased 1896.
    PG 581*   Marble bust, h. 67.6 (26⅝), by Sir John Steell, 1875, signed. Bequeathed by John Ritchie Findlay 1899.
    PG 1116*   Canvas, 76.2 x 63.5 (30 x 25), by Sir John Watson Gordon. Dated 1846. Purchased 1929.

DERRY, Tom, fl. 1614. *Jester to Anne of Denmark*
    PG 1111*   (Previously called 1st Viscount Stormont.) Panel, 71.4 x 57.9 (28⅛ x 22¾), attributed to Marcus Gheeraerts the younger. Dated 1614. Bequeathed by A. W. Inglis.

DETHICK, John, 1567–1657.
    PG 2083   Wash drawing, 15.3 x 12.6 (6 x 5), copy attributed to George Perfect Harding after engraving by Pierre Lombard. Transferred from the National Gallery of Scotland 1950.

DEUCHAR, David, 1743–1808. *Seal engraver*
    PG 980*   Pencil drawing, 5.3 x 4.6 (2⅛ x 1⅞), by John Brown. Dated (on reverse) 1787. Bequeathed by Miss Jane Deuchar 1925.
    PGL 75*   Pencil drawing, 49 x 33.5 (19⁵⁄₁₆ x 13³⁄₁₆), by John Brown. On loan from the National Museums of Scotland.

DEVONSHIRE, Georgiana Spencer, Duchess of; see UNIDENTIFIED (PG 2246)

DEWAR, Professor Sir James, 1842–1923. *Chemist*
    PG 603   Canvas, 56 x 66 (22 x 26), by Thomas W. Dewar. Dated 1900. Given by the artist 1902.
    PG 1089*   Canvas, 83.8 x 111.7 (33 x 44), by Edmund Dyer after Sir William Quiller Orchardson, signed. Given by Lady Dewar 1928.

DICK, Sir Alexander, 1703–85. *Physician and antiquary*
    PGL 83*   Pencil drawing, 50.2 x 36.5 (19¾ x 14⅜), by John Brown. On loan from the National Museums of Scotland.

DICK, Thomas, 1774–1857. *Populariser of astronomy and science*
   PG 2137   Water-colour, 21.8 x 18.9 (8⅜ x 7½), by unknown artist. Purchased 1968.

DICK, Professor William, 1793–1866. *Founder of the Dick Veterinary College*
   PG 663*   Water-colour, 26.5 x 22 (10⅜ x 8⅝), by Elizabeth Olden, 1853, signed.
              Purchased 1907.

DICK, Sir William Reid, 1879–1961. *Sculptor*
   PG 2449*   Canvas, 61 x 50.8 (24 x 20), by Richard Grenville Eves, signed. Dated 1933.
              Given by Lady Catherine Reid Dick 1979.

DICKSON, Thomas, d. 1904. *Antiquary*
   PG 1705   Pencil drawing, 37.5 x 33 (14¾ x 13), by W. Graham Boss. Given by the
              artist.

DISRUPTION OF THE CHURCH OF SCOTLAND 1843, THE
   PG 1154   (Drawing for the engraved key to the painting in the collection of the Free
              Church, entitled *The First General Assembly of the Free Church signing the
              Act of Separation and Deed of Demission, Tanfield, Edinburgh, 23 May
              1843.*) Ink drawing, 19 x 40.6 (7½ x 16), by David Octavius Hill, 1866,
              signed. Purchased 1931.

DIXON, William, 1788–1859. *Ironmaster*
   PG 787   Cut paper silhouette, h. 15.3 (6¹⁄₁₆), by Augustin Edouart. Purchased 1912.

DOBSON, Henry John, 1858–1928. *Artist*
   PG 2509*   Canvas, 137.8 x 91.7 (54¼ x 36), by Cowan Dobson, 1923, signed. Given by
              Mrs L. R. Morpeth 1982.

DODS, Rev. Marcus, 1834–1909. *Presbyterian minister and Biblical scholar*
   PG 1207   Bronze medallion, dia. 14.5 (5¾), by John Stevenson Rhind. Given by Dr
              R. Cochrane Buist 1933.

DOLBEN, Sir John English, c. 1750–1837. *4th Baronet of Finedon*
   PG 1282   Paste medallion, h. 8.1 (3³⁄₁₆), by James Tassie. Acquired 1935.

DONALD, John Milne, 1819–66. *Artist*
   PG 746   Canvas, 53.1 x 43 (20⅞ x 16⅞), by James Stewart, signed. Purchased 1910.
   PG 867*   Chalk drawing, 37 x 27.1 (14⅝ x 10¾), by Alexander Duff Robertson.
              Purchased 1916.

DONALDSON, James, d. 1797. *Merchant in Glasgow*
   PG 1269   Paste medallion, h. 7.6 (3), by James Tassie. Dated 1796. Purchased 1935.
   PG 2437   Paste medallion, h. 7.5 (2¹⁵⁄₁₆), by James Tassie. Dated 1796. Bequeathed by
              William Tassie to the National Gallery of Scotland 1860 and transferred
              1979.

DONALDSON, James, 1751–1830. *Founder of Donaldson's Hospital*
  PG 1176   Cut paper silhouette, h. 15.7 (6¼), by Augustin Edouart. Purchased 1932.

DONOUGHMORE, John Hely-Hutchinson, Baron Hutchinson of Alexandria and 2nd
        Earl of, 1757–1832.
  PG 2584   (Probably the 2nd Earl of Donoughmore. Silhouette album, no. 14. See
        GROUPS.) Printed (?) silhouette, h. 6 (2⅜), by unknown artist. Acquired
        c. 1951.
  PG 2680*   (*The Battle of Alexandria, 21 March 1801.*) See GROUPS.

DOTT, Aitken, 1815–*c*. 1880. *Art dealer*
  PG 2514*   Canvas, 44.6 x 35.5 (17⁹⁄₁₆ x 14), by Robert McGregor, 1891, signed.
        Painted from a photograph taken 1878. Given by William C. Jackson 1982.

DOTT, Jean Morton, b. 1896. *Artist*
  PG 2605   Pencil drawing, 10.8 x 13.6 (5⅜ x 4¼) (irregular), self-portrait. Executed
        1917/18. Given by Dr Eric Dott 1984.

DOTT, Peter McOmish, 1856–1934. *Art dealer and critic*
  PG 2602*   Canvas, 64.2 x 80.9 (25⅜ x 31⅞), by Jean Morton Dott, signed. Dated
        1916. Given by William C. Jackson 1983.

DOUGLAS, Arthur Henry Johnstone, 1846–1923. *Of Ruthwell Curling Club*
  PG 1856*   (*Curling at Carsebreck.*) See GROUPS.

DOUGLAS, George Norman, 1868–1952. *Writer*
  PG 2489*   Bronze head, h. 32.8 (12⅞), by George Havard Thomas, signed. Dated
        indistinctly 193[0]. Purchased 1981.

DOUGLAS, James, fl. 1850. *Accountant and amateur artist; father of the artist*
  PG 1284   Water-colour, 15.2 x 11.4 (6 x 4½), by Sir William Fettes Douglas. Dated
        1845/50. Given by J. Kent Richardson 1935.

DOUGLAS, James, d. 1869. *Accountant of the Commercial Bank*
  PG 2151   Cut paper silhouette, h. 20.6 (8³⁄₁₆), by Augustin Edouart, 1830, signed.
        Given by Mrs J. H. G. Ross 1969.

DOUGLAS, General Sir Neil, 1779–1853. *Soldier*
  PG 1866*   Canvas, 241.2 x 147.2 (95 x 58), by Sir John Watson Gordon. Given by
        Major A. J. A. Douglas 1959.

DOUGLAS, Sir William Fettes, 1822–91. *Artist*
  PG 1589*   (With James Ballantyne and Thomas Faed.) Wash drawing, 16.2 x 20.2
        (6⅜ x 8), by John Faed, signed. Given by J. A. Faed 1952.
  PG 1700   Pencil drawing, 37.5 x 33.7 (14¾ x 13¼), by W. Graham Boss. Given by
        the artist.

Derry, Tom
PG 1111

Deuchar, David
PG 980

Deuchar, David
PGL 75

Dewar, Professor Sir James
PG 1089

Dick, Sir Alexander
PGL 83

Dick, Professor William
PG 663

Dick, Sir William Reid
PG 2449

Dobson, Henry John
PG 2509

Donald, John Milne
PG 867

Dott, Aitken
PG 2514

Dott, Peter McOmish
PG 2602

Douglas, George Norman
PG 2489

Douglas, Sir Neil
PG 1866

Drummond, Alexander
PGL 76

DOUGLAS, Sir William Fettes (*continued*)
    PG 2626   Water-colour with some pencil, 10.3 x 10.5 (4¹⁄₁₆ x 4⅛), by John Faed,
           signed. Provenance untraced.

DOUGLASS, Major-General Robert, 1727–1809. *Commander at Bois-le-duc*
    PG 1666   Wash drawing, 8.5 x 6.6 (3⅜ x 2⅝), by —de Brauw. Drawn *c.* 1790. Given
           by T. H. Douglas 1885.

DOYLE, General Sir John, *c.* 1750–1834. *Soldier*
    PG 2683   a. (Study related to *The Battle of Alexandria* and *The Landing of British
           Troops at Aboukir.*) Water-colour and pencil drawing, 14.3 x 11.6
           (5⅝ x 4⁹⁄₁₆) (irregular), attributed to Philip James de Loutherbourg.
           Purchased 1986.

DRUMMOND, Alexander, fl. 1758–1815. *Teacher of French and French Secretary to the
           Society of Antiquaries of Scotland*
    PGL 76*   Pencil drawing, 50.5 x 35.5 (19⅞ x 14), by John Brown. On loan from the
           National Museums of Scotland.

DRUMMOND, Flora, 1879–1949. *Suffragette*
    PG 2229*   Canvas, 112 x 86.3 (44⅛ x 34), by Flora Lion, 1936, signed. Purchased 1974.

DRUMMOND, Sir George, 1687–1766. *Lord Provost of Edinburgh*
    PG 829*   Canvas, 124.5 x 99.1 (49 x 39), by Sir George Chalmers, 1764, signed.
           Purchased 1913.

DRUMMOND of Blair Drummond, Lieutenant-Colonel Henry Edward Home,
           1846–1911. *Of Blair Drummond Curling Club*
    PG 1856*   (*Curling at Carsebreck.*) See GROUPS.

DRUMMOND, Mary Barbara Drummond, Mrs William Abernethy, 1721/2–89. *Wife of
           the Bishop of Edinburgh*
    PG 2408*   Canvas, 76.2 x 63.5 (30 x 25), by David Martin, 1788, signed. Purchased 1977.

DRUMMOND, Robert Hay, 1711–76. *Archbishop of York*
    PG 903*   Canvas, 127 x 101.6 (50 x 40), by Sir Joshua Reynolds. Purchased 1919.

DRUMMOND, Thomas, 1797–1840. *Irish administrator*
    PG 2363*   Canvas, 143.5 x 111.7 (56½ x 44), by Henry William Pickersgill.
           Bequeathed conditionally by Miss E. Drummond to the National Gallery of
           Ireland 1930 and transferred 1969.

DRUMMOND of Hawthornden, William, 1585–1649. *Poet*
    PG 810   Panel, 50.7 x 37.5 (20 x 14¾), by unknown artist. Dated 1609. Purchased
           1912.
    PG 1013*   Panel, 50.8 x 43.2 (20 x 17), by unknown artist. Purchased 1925.

PG 1096*   Panel, 60.4 x 48.5 (23¾ x 19⅛), by unknown artist. Dated 1612. Purchased
           1928.

DRUMMOND, William Abernethy, 1719/20–1809. *Bishop of Edinburgh*
      PG 2407*   Canvas, 76.2 x 63.5 (30 x 25), by David Martin, 1788, signed. Purchased 1977.

DRUMMORE, Hew Dalrymple, Lord, 1690–1755. *Scottish judge*
      PGL 287*   Canvas, 76.5 x 63.8 (30⅛ x 25⅛), by John Alexander, 175[ ], signed.
                 On loan from Dr E. H. D. Phillips.

DRYANDER, Jonas, 1748–1810. *Botanist and librarian to the Royal Society*
      PG 2274   Pen and wash drawing, 35.5 x 24.8 (14 x 9¾), by unknown artist after
                 engraving by George Dance. Original dated 1796. Purchased 1936.

DUFF, Rev. Alexander, 1806–78. *Missionary and educationalist*
      PG 640   (Probably the artist's plaster.) Plaster bust, h. 81 (32), by John Hutchison.
                 Purchased 1905.

DUFFUS, Kenneth Sutherland, 3rd Lord, d. 1732. *Jacobite*
      PG 1095*   Canvas, 203.2 x 140.6 (80 x 55⅜), by Richard Waitt. Purchased 1928.

DUMERGUE, Miss Sophia, fl. 1797–1814. *Friend of Sir Walter and Lady Scott*
      PG 1462*   Water-colour on ivory, 7.6 x 5.7 (3 x 2¼), by unknown artist. Purchased 1944.

DUN, Alexander, fl. 1899. *Of Buchlyvie Curling Club*
      PG 1856*   (*Curling at Carsebreck.*) See GROUPS.

DUNBAR, Sir George Home, Earl of, d. 1611. *Lord High Treasurer of Scotland*
      PG 816   Canvas, 128.3 x 102.2 (50½ x 40¼), by unknown artist. Purchased 1913.

DUNBAR of Boath, William, fl. 1787. *Writer to the Signet*
      PG 946*   (As Senior Warden, in *The Inauguration of Robert Burns as Poet Laureate
                 of the Lodge Canongate, Kilwinning. 1787.*) See GROUPS.

DUNCAN of Camperdown, Adam Duncan, 1st Viscount, 1731–1804. *Admiral*
      PG 264   Paste medallion, h. 7.4 (2⅞), by William Tassie after James Tassie. Dated
                 1798. Transferred from the National Gallery of Scotland 1889.
      PG 270   Medallion (plaster replica), h. 9.4 (3¾), after James Tassie. Given by
                 A. C. Lamb 1889.
      PG 271   Paste medallion, h. 2.4 (¹⁵⁄₁₆), by James Tassie. Transferred from the
                 National Gallery of Scotland 1889.
      PG 366   Wedgwood medallion, 7.4 (2⅞), after unknown artist. Given by Messrs
                 J. Wedgwood and Sons 1889.
      PG 1065*   Canvas, 269 x 195.8 (105½ x 76½), by Henri-Pierre Danloux, signed. Dated
                 1798. Bequeathed by the Earl of Camperdown to the National Gallery of
                 Scotland in 1919 and transferred.

DUNCAN of Camperdown, Adam Duncan, 1st Viscount (*continued*)

PG 1199   Water-colour, 19.5 x 15.4 (7⅝ x 6⅛), by William Derby after John
           Hoppner. Dated (on reverse) 1835. Bequeathed by Mrs Anstruther-Duncan
           1933.

PG 2640*   Paste medallion, h. 9.5 (3¾), by James Tassie. Dated 1797. Purchased 1985.

DUNCAN, Andrew, 1744–1828. *President of the Royal Medical Society and of the Royal
           College of Physicians*

PG 165   Canvas, 76.2 x 62.9 (30 x 24¾), copy by unknown artist. Bequeathed by
           Mrs Elizabeth Bevan 1886.

PG 238   Porcelain bust, h. 15.2 (6), by Peter Slater after Benjamin Cheverton. Given
           by Miss Duncan 1888.

PGL 77*   Pencil drawing, 50.3 x 36.4 (19¾ x 14⁵⁄₁₆), by John Brown. On loan from
           the National Museums of Scotland.

PGL 258*   Canvas, 240 x 151.1 (94½ x 59½), by Sir John Watson Gordon. On loan
           from the Royal Medical Society.

DUNCAN, Elizabeth Knox, Mrs Andrew, d. 1839. *Wife of Andrew Duncan, the physician*

PG 166*   Canvas, 74.8 x 63 (29½ x 24¾), by David Martin. Bequeathed by Mrs
           Elizabeth Bevan 1886.

DUNCAN, Lieutenant-Colonel J., fl. 1801. *Soldier*

PG 2681*   (*The Landing of British Troops at Aboukir, 8 March 1801.*) See GROUPS.

PG 2683   d. (Study related to *The Battle of Alexandria* and *The Landing of British
           Troops at Aboukir.*) Water-colour, 10.6 x 7.6 (3⁹⁄₁₆ x 3), attributed to Philip
           James de Loutherbourg. Purchased 1986.

DUNCAN, Thomas, 1807–45. *Artist*

PG 292*   Canvas, 71.1 x 53.3 (28 x 21), by Robert Scott Lauder. Painted *c.* 1839.
           Given by Mrs Thomson 1890.

PG 1289   Canvas, 76.2 x 63.5 (30 x 24¾), by Sir Daniel Macnee. Bequeathed by Mrs
           Jane Fraser 1935.

DUNCAN, Lieutenant-Colonel William, fl. 1774–97. *Soldier*

PG 2584   (Silhouette album no. 38. See GROUPS.) Printed (?) silhouette, h. 6 (2⅜),
           by unknown artist. Acquired *c.* 1951.

DUNDAS, Sir David, 1735–1820. *General*

PG 1281   Canvas, 75.9 x 63.3 (29⅞ x 24⅞), by Samuel Drummond. Purchased 1935.

DUNDAS, Henry; see MELVILLE.

DUNDAS of Arniston, Robert, 1713–87. *Judge; Lord President of the Court of Session*

PG 1770*   (*Burns at an evening party of Lord Monboddo's 1786.*) See GROUPS.

Drummond, Flora
PG 2229

Drummond, Sir George
PG 829

Drummond, Mary Barbara
PG 2408

Drummond, Robert Hay
PG 903

Drummond, Thomas
PG 2363

Drummond of Hawthornden,
William   PG 1013

Drummond of Hawthornden,
William   PG 1096

Drummond, William Abernethy
PG 2407

Drummore, Lord
PGL 287

Duffus, 3rd Lord
PG 1095

Dumergue, Sophia
PG 1462

Duncan, 1st Viscount
PG 1065

Duncan, 1st Viscount
PG 2640

Duncan, Andrew
PGL 77

DUNDAS of Arniston, Robert, 1758–1819. *Judge and chief baron of the exchequer in Scotland*
PG 408   Medallion (plaster replica), h. 6.2 (2½), after John Henning. Cast from a medallion in possession of Robert Dundas 1889.

DUNDAS, Sir Robert, 1761–1835. *Clerk of the Court of Session*
PG 796   Cut paper silhouette, h. 19.9 (7⅞), by Augustin Edouart. Purchased 1912.

DUNDAS, William, 1762–1845. *Politician*
PG 289*   Canvas, 76.2 x 63.5 (30 x 25), by John Hoppner. Given by Robert Dundas 1890.

DUNDEE, John Graham of Claverhouse, Viscount, c. 1649–89. *Jacobite leader*
PG 588*   Ink drawing, 10.5 x 8.3 (4⅛ x 3¼), by David Paton. Given by A. Sholto Douglas 1900.
PG 979   Canvas, 76.5 x 63.5 (30⅛ x 25), by William Hastie Geissler after unknown artist. Commissioned and purchased 1924.
PG 1318   Ink drawing, 12.4 x 9.8 (4⅞ x 3⅞), by unknown artist. Purchased 1937.
PG 1390   Red chalk drawing, 28.9 x 20.2 (11⅜ x 8), by David Allan after unknown artist. Given by Kenneth Sanderson 1939.
PG 2183   Canvas, 74.3 x 62 (29¼ x 24⅜), copy by unknown artist. Purchased 1970.

DUNDONALD, Thomas Cochrane, 10th Earl of, 1775–1860. *Admiral*
PG 2734* Marble bust, h. 78.4 (30⅞), by Patric Park, 1847, signed. Purchased 1988.

DUNFERMLINE, Alexander Seton, 1st Earl of, 1555–1622. *Lord Chancellor of Scotland*
PG 1020   (As a youth, with his father, 5th Lord Seton, his brothers and sister.) See GROUPS.
PG 2176* Canvas, 115.5 x 88.2 (45½ x 34¾), by Marcus Gheeraerts the younger. Dated 1610. Purchased 1970.
PGL 312* (As a youth, with his father, 5th Lord Seton, his brothers and sister.) See GROUPS.

DUNFERMLINE, Charles Seton, 2nd Earl of, 1608–72. *Lord Privy Seal*
PG 2222* Canvas, 220.7 x 134 (87 x 52¾), by Sir Anthony Van Dyck. Purchased with assistance from The National Art-Collections Fund 1973.

DUNFERMLINE, James Abercromby, 1st Baron, 1776–1858. *Speaker of the House of Commons*
PG 330*   Marble bust, h. 60.9 (24), by William Brodie, 1858, signed. Given by Mrs Mary Trotter 1891.
PG 990   Canvas, 127 x 101.6 (50 x 40), by Sir John Watson Gordon. Bequeathed by A. Abercromby Trotter 1925.

Duncan, Andrew
PGL 258

Duncan, Elizabeth
PG 166

Duncan, Thomas
PG 292

Dundas, William
PG 289

Dundee, Viscount
PG 588

Dundonald, 10th Earl of
PG 2734

Dunfermline, 1st Earl of
PG 2176

Dunfermline, 2nd Earl
of   PG 222

Dunfermline, 1st Baron
PG 330

Dunlop, Frances
PG 1208

Dunlop, Sir Thomas
PG 2744

Dunmore, 1st Earl of
PGL 224

Dunmore, 4th Earl of
PGL 163

Durham, Sir Philip
PG 1605

Dyce, William
PG 208

Dysart, Countess of
PG 954

DUNLOP of Dunlop, Frances Anna Wallace, Mrs John, 1730–1815. *Friend of Robert Burns*
PG 1208* Water-colour drawing, 32 x 23.4 (12⅝ x 9¼), by unknown artist signing 'A.C.' Purchased 1933.
PG 1770* (*Burns at an evening party of Lord Monboddo's 1786.*) See GROUPS.

DUNLOP, Sir Thomas, 1st Baronet (1855–1938). *Shipowner and Lord Provost of Glasgow*
PG 2744* Bronze bust, h. 37.5 (14¾), by Benno Schotz. Sculpted 1935. Given by Sir Thomas Dunlop 1988.

DUNLOP, William, d. 1811. *Surgeon*
PG 1945 Medallion (plaster replica), h. 5.3 (2⅛), after John Henning. Provenance untraced.

DUNMORE, Lord Charles Murray, 1st Earl of, 1661–1710. *Soldier*
PGL 224* Canvas, 127.3 x 102 (50⅛ x 40⅛), by Sir Godfrey Kneller, 1683, signed. On loan from Mrs Elizabeth Murray.

DUNMORE CHILDREN
PG 1889 See GROUPS.

DUNMORE, Janet Napier, Mrs Robert fl. 1791. *Wife of Robert Dunmore of Kelvinside*
PG 2438 Paste medallion, h. 7.5 (2¹⁵⁄₁₆), by James Tassie. Dated 1791. Bequeathed by William Tassie to the National Gallery of Scotland 1860 and transferred 1979.

DUNMORE, John Murray, 4th Earl of, 1732–1809. *Governor of New York and Virginia*
PGL 163* Canvas, 238.1 x 146.2 (93¾ x 57¾), by Sir Joshua Reynolds. Dated 1765. On loan from Mrs Elizabeth Murray.

DUNMORE of Kelvinside, Robert, 1744–99. *Merchant in Glasgow*
PG 1888 Medallion (plaster replica), h. 7.5 (3), after James Tassie. Dated 1797. Cast from a medallion in possession of R. W. Cochran Patrick.

DUNS, Professor John, 1820–1909. *Divine and antiquary*
PG 1694 Pencil drawing, 37.5 x 33 (14¾ x 13), by W. Graham Boss. Given by the artist.

DURHAM, Janetta McCulloch, Mrs Thomas Maxwell, fl. 1899. *Of Boghead Ladies Curling Club*
PG 1856* (*Curling at Carsebreck.*) See GROUPS.

DURHAM, Sir Philip Charles, 1763–1845. *Admiral*
PG 1605* Canvas, 127 x 101.6 (50 x 40), by Sir Francis Grant. On loan from the Earl of Buckinghamshire.

DUTENS, Rev. Louis, 1730–1812. *Diplomatist and man of letters*
    PG 513   Medallion (plaster replica), h. 8.9 (3⅝), after James Tassie. Cast from a
                medallion in possession of Mrs Shadford Walker 1894.

DYCE, William, 1806–64. *Artist*
    PG 208*   Watercolour, 24.2 x 22.8 (9⅝ x 9), by David Scott, 1832, signed. Given by
                W. Bell Scott 1887.
    PG 797   Cut paper silhouette, h. 20.5 (8⅛), by Augustin Edouart. Purchased 1912.

DYER of Tottenham, Sir Thomas, 7th Baronet, *c.* 1770–1838. *Soldier*
    PG 2680*   (*The Battle of Alexandria, 21 March 1801*). See GROUPS.
    PG 2684   a. (*Study for The Battle of Alexandria.*) Water-colour, 22.8 x 14 (9 x 5½),
                attributed to Philip James de Loutherbourg. Purchased 1986.

DYMOCK, Wilhelmina Sheriff, Mrs James, fl. 1833.
    PG 2551   Water-colour on ivory, 7.5 x 6 (3 x 2⅜) (sight), by Kenneth Macleay.
                Painted 1833. Transferred from the National Gallery of Scotland 1982.

DYSART, Katherine Bruce, Countess of, d. 1649. *Wife of the 1st Earl of Dysart*
    PG 954*   Canvas, 127 x 107 (50 x 42⅛), by unknown artist. Purchased 1923.

EASTON, Rev. Alexander, fl. 1792–1808. *Secession minister*
  PG 2595   Paste medallion, h. 8 (3⅛), by James Tassie. Dated 1794. Purchased 1982.

EBSWORTH, Joseph, 1788–1868. *Musician and dramatist*
  PG 1118*   Water-colour drawing, 22.4 x 18 (8⅞ x 7), by J. W. Ebsworth, 1848, signed. Purchased 1929.

EDGEWORTH, Richard Lovell, 1744–1817. *Author*
  PG 2135   Paste medallion, h. 7.6 (3), by John Henning. Dated 1803. Purchased 1968.

EDINBURGH, Alfred Ernest Albert, Duke of, 1844–1900. *Second son of Queen Victoria and Prince Albert*
  PG 170   (Artist's plaster.) Plaster bust, h. 69.9 (27½), by Sir John Steell. Purchased 1887.

EDINBURGH, His Royal Highness, The Prince Philip, Duke of, b. 1921.
  PG 2394   Pencil drawing, 37.4 x 27.2 (14¾ x 10¹¹⁄₁₆), by Sir William Oliphant Hutchison. Given by the executors of Margery, Lady Hutchison 1977.

EDINBURGH
  PG 1664   b. (View of Lord Arniston's House in Adam Square.) See ARNISTON, Lord
  PG 1663   b. (View of Lord Milton's house.) See MILTON, Lord
  PG 2295   a. (Birthplace of Sir Walter Scott in College Wynd.) See SCOTT, Sir Walter

EDINBURGH FROM CANONMILLS
  PG 2619*   Canvas, 90.8 x 128 (35¾ x 50⅜), attributed to John Knox. Painted *c.* 1820/5. Purchased 1984.

EDINBURGH FROM THE WEST
  PG 1112*   Canvas, 59.2 x 126.6 (23⅜ x 49⅞), by unknown artist. Bequeathed by A. W. Inglis 1929.

EDWARD VII, 1841–1910. *Reigned 1901–10*
  PG 169   Plaster bust, h. 71.4 (28⅛), by Sir John Steell. Purchased 1887.
  PG 664   Colour print, 32.3 x 25.2 (12¾ x 9¹⁵⁄₁₆), by Joseph Simpson. Purchased 1907.
  PG 1169   (As Prince of Wales, with Queen Victoria, Prince Albert and the Princess Royal.) See GROUPS.
  PG 1562   (Coronation 9 August 1902.) Bronze medal, dia. 5.4 (2⅛), by G. W. de Saulles. Dated 1902. Given by Mrs Stewart 1951.
  PG 2066   (Artist's plaster.) Plaster bust, h. 33 (13), by Henry Snell Gamley. Dated 1916. Given by Miss Mary E. Mackenzie 1966.

EDWARD, Thomas, 1814–86. *Naturalist*
PG 163*   Ink drawing, 23.9 x 18.1 (9½ x 7⅛), by Sir George Reid, signed. Given by
            the artist 1886.

EGLINTON, Archibald Montgomerie, 11th Earl of Eglinton, 1726–96. *General;*
            Representative Peer of Scotland
PG 946*   (*The Inauguration of Robert Burns as Poet Laureate of the Lodge*
            Canongate, Kilwinning, 1787). See GROUPS.

EGLINTON, Hugh Montgomerie, 12th Earl of, 1739–1819. *Soldier; Lord Lieutenant of*
            Ayrshire
PG 1516*   Canvas, 226.3 x 148.9 (89⅛ x 58⅝), by John Singleton Copley. Purchased 1949.

EGLINTON, Susanna Kennedy, Countess of, 1689–1780. *Third wife of the 9th Earl of*
            Eglinton; patroness of letters
PG 942   Canvas, 230.2 x 147.7 (90⅝ x 58⅛), by William Aikman. Purchased 1922.

ELCHIES, Patrick Grant, Lord, 1690–1754. *Judge*
PG 152*   Canvas, 75.6 x 63.1 (29¾ x 24⅞), by Allan Ramsay, 1749, signed. Given by
            D. Pringle 1885.

ELCHO, Francis Charteris, Lord, 1749–1808. *Agriculturist*
PG 946*   (Probably Lord Elcho, as Grand-Master Mason, in *The Inauguration of*
            Robert Burns as Poet Laureate of the Lodge Canongate, Kilwinning, 1787.)
            See GROUPS.

ELDER, Thomas, 1737–99. *Lord Provost of Edinburgh*
PG 1271   Paste medallion, h. 7.6 (3), by James Tassie. Dated 1795. Purchased 1935.

ELDIN, John Clerk, Lord, 1757–1832. *Judge*
PG 346   Plaster bust, h. 40 (15¾), by Samuel Joseph. Purchased 1887.
PG 625   Canvas, 41 x 33.4 (16⅛ x 13⅛), by Andrew Geddes. Purchased 1903.
PG 1052*   Chalk drawing, 51.5 x 41.5 (20¼ x 16⅜), by William Bewick, 1824, signed.
            Purchased 1927.
PG 1491*   Canvas, 128.2 x 101.6 (50½ x 40), by Sir Henry Raeburn. Painted *c.* 1815.
            Purchased 1947.

ELGIN, Victor Alexander Bruce, 9th Earl of, and 13th Earl of Kincardine, 1849–1917.
            Statesman and Viceroy of India
PG 871*   Canvas, 40.5 x 30.5 (16 x 12), by Charles Martin Hardie, 1899, signed.
            Purchased 1917.
PG 1856*   (*Curling at Carsebreck.*) See GROUPS.

ELIZABETH, Queen of England, 1533–1603. *Reigned 1558–1603*
PG 162   Medal (electrotype), dia. 6.2 (2½), after Jacopo Primavera. Original cast
            1572. Given by J. M. Gray 1886.

ELIZABETH, Queen of Bohemia; see BOHEMIA.

ELIZABETH, QUEEN OF THE UNITED KINGDOM OF GREAT BRITAIN
AND NORTHERN IRELAND, b. 1926.
PG 2168*   Canvas, 76.2 x 63.5 (30 x 25), by Sir William Oliphant Hutchison. Painted
1956. Given by the artist 1969.

ELIZABETH, The Queen Mother, b. 1900. *Queen of George VI*
PG 2598*   Canvas, 49.7 x 50.3 (19⁹⁄₁₆ x 19¹³⁄₁₆), by Avigdor Arikha, 1983, signed.
Purchased by commission 1983.

ELLESMERE, Francis Egerton, 1st Earl of, 1800–57. *Statesman and poet*
PG 1040*   (As Lord Leveson-Gower, in *The Entrance of George V at Holyroodhouse*.)
See GROUPS.
PG 1299   Water-colour on ivory, 14 x 18.8 (5½ x 7⅜), by Robert Thorburn.
Bequeathed by Edward Thorburn 1936.

ELLIOT, Jane (or Jean), 1727–1805. *Poetess*
PG 1672   Wash drawing, 13.7 x 9.6 (5⅜ x 6¹³⁄₁₆), by unknown artist. Bequeathed by
W. F. Watson 1886.

ELLIOT, Walter Elliot, 1888–1958. *Politician*
PG 2395   Charcoal and white chalk drawing, 54.8 x 37.8 (21⁹⁄₁₆ x 14⅞), by Sir
William Oliphant Hutchison. Given by the executors of Margery, Lady
Hutchison 1977.

ELPHINSTONE, John Elphinstone, 13th Baron, 1807–60. *Governor of Madras and
Bombay*
PG 1974   Water-colour drawing, 23.2 x 17.8 (9⅛ x 7), by unknown artist. Purchased
1961.

ELPHINSTONE, William, 1431–1514. *Bishop of Aberdeen and founder of King's
College*
PG 1619   Pencil and chalk drawing, 39.7 x 30.3 (15⅝ x 12), by the 11th Earl of
Buchan, signed, after unknown artist. Bequeathed by W. F. Watson 1886.

ERSKINE, Alexander, 1598–1656. *Swedish plenipotentiary at Munster, 1648*
PG 1634   Pencil and chalk drawing, 30.9 x 24.3 (12³⁄₁₆ x 9⁹⁄₁₆), by the 11th Earl of
Buchan, 1795, signed, after Anselm van Hulle. Original painted 1649.
Bequeathed by W. F. Watson 1886.

ERSKINE of Gogar, Sir Alexander, c. 1521–c. 1592. *Guardian of James VI*
PG 1625   Pencil and chalk drawing, 33.1 x 26.3 (13 x 10⅜), by the 11th Earl of
Buchan after unknown artist. Bequeathed by W. F. Watson 1886.

Ebsworth, Joseph
PG 1118

Edinburgh from Canonmills
PG 2619

Edinburgh from the West
PG 1112

Edward, Thomas
PG 163

Eglinton, 12th Earl of
PG 1516

Elchies, Lord
PG 152

Eldin, Lord
PG 1052

Eldin, Lord
PG 1491

Elgin, 9th Earl of
PG 871

Elizabeth, Queen of the
United Kingdom   PG 2168

Elizabeth, The Queen Mother
PG 2598

Erskine, Rev. Henry
PG 1240

Erskine, Henry
PG 1582

ERSKINE, Rev. Ebenezer, 1680–1754. *Secession leader*
> PG 1238   Canvas, 76.2 x 63.2 (30 x 24⅞), by unknown artist. Given by the family of the late Walter Wardlaw 1934.

ERSKINE, Rev. Henry, 1624–96. *Covenanting minister*
> PG 1240*   Canvas, 76.2 x 62.9 (30 x 24¾), attributed to Sir John Medina. Given by the family of the late Walter Wardlaw 1934.

ERSKINE, Henry, 1746–1817. *Lord Advocate*
> PG 121   Pencil and water-colour drawing, 9.2 x 7 (3⅝ x 2¾), by John Bogle. Bequeathed by W. F. Watson 1886.
> PG 265   Paste medallion, h. 7.5 (3), by James Tassie. Dated 1791. Transferred from the National Gallery of Scotland 1889.
> PG 1582*   Marble relief monument, h. 74.7 (27⅜), by Mary Grant. Given by the Earl of Buchan 1952.
> PG 2047   Canvas, 42.1 x 34.2 (16⁹⁄₁₆ x 13⁷⁄₁₆), attributed to William Yellowlees after Sir Henry Raeburn. Given by James Anderson Yellowlees 1964.

ERSKINE of Torrie, Sir James, 3rd Baronet, 1772–1825.
> PGL 333*   See GROUPS.

ERSKINE of Cambus, John, 1758–92. *Advocate and antiquary*
> PGL 78*   Pencil drawing, 50.7 x 35.4 (19¹⁵⁄₁₆ x 13¹⁵⁄₁₆), by John Brown. On loan from the National Museums of Scotland.

ERSKINE, Rev. Dr John, 1721–1803. *Theologian*
> PG 2382*   Canvas, 76.2 x 63.2 (30 x 24⅞), attributed to Sir Henry Raeburn. Painted *c.* 1804. Purchased 1977.
> PG 2642   Paste medallion, h. 7.7 (3), by William Tassie. Dated 1801. Purchased 1985.

ERSKINE of Torrie, Sir John Drummond, 4th and last Baronet, 1776–1836.
> PGL 333*   See GROUPS.

ERSKINE, Rev. Ralph, 1685–1752. *Secession leader and poet*
> PG 1239*   Canvas, 75.9 x 63.5 (29⅞ x 25), by Richard Waitt, 1712, signed. Given by the family of the late Walter Wardlaw 1934.

ERSKINE, Thomas Erskine, Lord, *c.* 1705–66. *Son of 6th Earl of Mar; Member of Parliament*
> PGL 237*   (With 6th Earl of Mar.) Canvas, 232.7 x 140.7 (91⅝ x 55⅜), by Sir Godfrey Kneller, signed. Painted *c.* 1715. On loan from the Earl of Mar and Kellie.

ERSKINE of Linlathen, Thomas, 1788–1870. *Advocate and theologian*
> PG 2709*   Charcoal drawing heightened with white, 22.7 x 19.3 (8⅞ x 7⅝), attributed to Charles Baillod. Purchased 1986.

Erskine, John
PGL 78

Erskine, Rev. Dr John
PG 2382

Erskine, Rev. Ralph
PG 1239

Erskine, Thomas
PG 2709

Etty, William
PG 1236

Ewart, David
PG 2614

ERSKINE of Torrie, Sir William, Family of; See GROUPS (PGL 333).

ERSKINE of Torrie, Sir William, 1st Baronet, 1728–95. *Soldier*
   PGL 333* See GROUPS.

ERSKINE of Torrie, Sir William, 2nd Baronet, 1770–1813.
   PGL 333* See GROUPS.

ESKGROVE, Sir David Rae, Lord, 1724–1804. *Lord Justice-Clerk*
   PG 1198   Water-colour on ivory, 6.5 x 5.2 (2⅝ x 2), by unknown artist. Purchased
          1933.

ETTY, William, 1787–1849. *Artist*
   PG 1236*   Pencil and water-colour drawing, 27.7 x 23 (10⅞ x 9⅛), by William
          Nicholson. Purchased 1934.

EWART, David, 1901–65. *Artist*
   PG 2614*   Canvas, 91.5 x 81.3 (36 x 32), self-portrait. Given by Mrs Eve Binnie 1984.

EWEN, John, 1741–1821. *Merchant and poet*
   PG 1290   Panel, 11.1 x 8.2 (4⅜ x 3¼), by unknown artist. Given by Dr David Rorie
          1935.

FAED, James, 1856–1920. *Artist*
  PG 1590*   (As a boy.) Panel, 30.5 x 22.9 (12 x 9), by James Faed. Given by J. A. Faed 1952.

FAED, Thomas, 1826–1900. *Artist*
  PG 674*   Canvas, 86 x 73.6 (33⅞ x 29), by Sir William Fettes Douglas. Given by
             Alfred Jones 1908.
  PG 962   (In his studio.) Canvas, 63.5 x 76.2 (25 x 30), by John Ballantyne, signed.
             Purchased 1923.
  PG 1589*   (With John Ballantyne and Sir William Fettes Douglas.) Wash drawing,
             16.2 x 20.2 (6⅜ x 8), by John Faed, signed. Given by J. A. Faed 1952.
  PG 1591*   Water-colour, 55.2 x 42.4 (21¾ x 16¾), by John Faed. Given by J. A. Faed
             1952.
  PG 1772   Pencil drawing, 17.5 x 13.8 (6⅞ x 5⅜), by George Faed, 1852, signed.
             Provenance untraced.

FAIRLEY, Alexander, fl. 1899. *Of Holyrood Curling Club*
  PG 1856*   (*Curling at Carsebreck.*) See GROUPS.

FALKIRK
  PG 1680   b. (Birthplace of Sir Charles Napier at Falkirk.) See NAPIER, Sir Charles.

FALKLAND PALACE AND THE HOWE OF FIFE
  PG 2409*   Panel, 45.6 x 68.6 (17¹⁵⁄₁₆ x 27), by Alexander Keirincx, signed in
             monogram. Painted *c.* 1635–40. Purchased 1979.

FANSHAWE, Sir Edward, 1785–1858. *General*
  PG 2563   Water-colour on ivory, 8.3 x 6.4 (3¼ x 2½), by Anthony Stewart.
             Transferred from the National Gallery of Scotland 1982.

FANSHAWE, Sir Edward Gennys, 1814–1906. *Admiral*
  PG 2565   Water-colour on ivory, dia. 4.8 (1⅞), by Anthony Stewart. Transferred
             from the National Gallery of Scotland 1982.

FANSHAWE, Frances Mary Dalrymple, Lady, 1790–1865. *Wife of Sir Edward Fanshawe*
  PG 2564   Water-colour on ivory, 7.5 x 6.2 (3 x 2⁷⁄₁₆), by Anthony Stewart.
             Transferred from the National Gallery of Scotland 1982.

FARQUHAR, Sir Arthur, 1772–1843. *Rear-Admiral*
  PG 1595   Canvas, 91.4 x 71.1 (36 x 28), by Sir John Watson Gordon. Bequeathed by
             Miss Lillie M. McRae 1953.

FAUCIT, Helen, (subsequently Lady Martin), 1817–98. *Actress*
  PG 649   Water-colour, 23.8 x 17.5 (9⅜ x 7), by Kenneth Macleay, signed. Painted
             c. 1844. Purchased 1906.
  PG 695*   Water-colour, 91.5 x 58.4 (36 x 23), by Sir Frederick William Burton,
             Bequeathed by Sir Theodore Martin 1909.

FENTON, Sir John Charles, 1880–1951. *Sheriff of the Lothians and Peebles*
PG 1802   Crayon drawing, 47 x 29.2 (18½ x 11½), by David Foggie, 1933, signed.
Given by Mrs M. Foggie 1955.

FERGUSON, Professor Adam, 1723–1816. *Philosopher and author*
PG 463   Plaster medallion (replica), h. 7.5 (3¹⁄₁₆), after James Tassie. Dated 1791.
Cast from a medallion in possession of Jeffery Whitehead 1893.
PG 541*   Canvas on panel, 34.9 x 28 (13¾ x 11), by unknown artist after Sir Henry
Raeburn. Given by Mrs Alexander Leslie 1894.
PG 1492   Pencil and wash drawing, 30.5 x 24.8 (12 x 9¾), by William Evans after Sir
Henry Raeburn. Purchased 1947.
PG 1770*   (*Burns at an evening party of Lord Monboddo's 1786.*) See GROUPS.

FERGUSON, Sir Adam, 1771–1855. *Soldier; friend of Sir Walter Scott*
PG 4*   Canvas, 76.2 x 63.5 (30 x 25), by William Nicholson. Purchased 1884.
PG 825*   (*Sir Walter Scott and his friends at Abbotsford.*) See GROUPS.
PG 1303*   (*The Abbotsford Family.*) See GROUPS.
PG 1304   Millboard, 25.4 x 20.4 (10 x 8), by Charles Lees. Given by T. L. Galloway
1936.
PG 1517*   (With Lady Ferguson.) Canvas, 57.1 x 66.7 (22½ x 26¼), by David Cooke
Gibson. Painted *c.* 1847/51. Purchased 1949.

FERGUSON of Craigdarroch, Alexander, d. 1796. *Advocate*
PG 946*   (As Master of the Lodge Canongate, in *The Inauguration of Robert Burns as
Poet Laureate of the Lodge Canongate, Kilwinning, 1787.*) See GROUPS.

FERGUSON, James.
PG 2541   Water-colour on ivory, h. 6.6 (2⅝) (sight), by 'J.B.', signed in monogram.
Transferred from the National Gallery of Scotland 1982.

FERGUSON, James, 1710–76. *Mathematician, astronomer and miniature painter*
PG 91*   Chalk drawing, 55.9 x 47 (22 x 18½), by unknown artist. Purchased 1885.

FERGUSSON, John Duncan, 1874–1961. *Artist*
PG 2515*   Canvas, 50.8 x 56.4 (20 x 22¼), self-portrait. Painted *c.* 1902. Purchased 1982.
PG 2699   Wash and charcoal drawing, 19.3 x 13.3 (7⅝ x 5¼), by Hamish Lawrie,
1960, signed. Purchased 1986.

FERGUSSON, Robert, 1750–74. *Poet*
PG 895   Canvas, 39.4 x 31.7 (15½ x 12½), by unknown artist. Purchased 1920.
PG 1863*   Paper on millboard, 26.7 x 21.3 (10½ x 8⅜), by Alexander Runciman.
Purchased 1959.

FERGUSSON, Robert Cutlar, 1768–1838. *Judge; advocate-general*
PG 1824   Pencil drawing, 16.9 x 12.5 (6⅝ x 4⅞), by Alfred, Count d'Orsay, 1832,
signed. Purchased 1955.

FERGUSSON, W. S. fl. 1899. *Of Scone and Perth Curling Club*
  PG 1856* (*Curling at Carsebreck.*) See GROUPS.

FERGUSSON, Sir William, 1808–77. *Surgeon*
  PG 565* Canvas, 76.2 x 63.5 (30 x 25), by Sir John Watson Gordon. Given by Lady McLeod 1897.

FERRIER, Susan Edmonstone, 1782–1854. *Novelist*
  PG 830 (Called Susan Ferrier.) Cut paper silhouette, h. 19.9 (7¹⁵⁄₁₆), by Augustin Edouart. Purchased 1913.

FETTES, Sir William, 1750–1836. *Lord Provost of Edinburgh and founder of Fettes College*
  PG 334* Plaster bust, h. 72 (28⅜), by Samuel Joseph. Given by Lady Fettes Douglas 1892.
  PG 779 Cut paper silhouette, h. 15.2 (6), by Augustin Edouart. Purchased 1912.

FIFE HOUNDS, A MEET OF THE; see GROUPS (PGL 337).

FINCH, General Edward, 1756–1843. *Soldier*
  PG 2683 b. (Study related to *The Battle of Alexandria* and *The Landing of British Troops at Aboukir.*) Water-colour, 10.7 x 8.9 (4³⁄₁₆ x 3½), attributed to Philip James de Loutherbourg. Purchased 1986.

FINDLAY, Harriet Jane Backhouse, Lady, 1880–1954. *Wife of Sir John Findlay of Aberlour*
  PG 1805 Black chalk drawing, 46 x 28.3 (18⅛ x 11⅛), by David Foggie, 1933, signed. Given by Mrs M. Foggie 1955.

FINDLAY of Aberlour, John Ritchie, 1824–98. *Proprietor of* The Scotsman; *founder of the Scottish National Portrait Gallery*
  PG 590* Canvas, 76.2 x 61 (30 x 24), by Sir George Reid. Painted 1899. Given by a number of subscribers 1900.
  PG 1702* Pencil drawing, 37.5 x 33.7 (14¾ x 13¼), by W. Graham Boss. Given by the artist.

FLATTELY, Alastair, b. 1922. *Artist*
  PGL 328* (*Gathering at 7 London Street.*) See GROUPS.

FLAXMAN, John, 1755–1826. *Sculptor and draughtsman*
  PG 144 Pencil drawing, 20.5 x 16.8 (8¹⁄₁₆ x 6⅝), by William Home Lizars. Drawn 1815. Bequeathed by W. F. Watson 1886.
  PG 205 Plaster medallion, h. 12.6 (5), self-portrait. Possibly a cast from PG 231. Given by William Calder Marshall 1887.
  PG 231 Intaglio version of PG 205. Purchased 1888.

Faed, James
PG 1590

Faed, Thomas
PG 674

Faed, Thomas
PG 1591

Falkland Palace
PG 2409

Faucit, Helen
PG 695

Ferguson, Professor Adam
PG 541

Ferguson, Sir Adam
PG 4

Ferguson, Sir Adam, with
Lady Ferguson   PG 1517

Ferguson, James
PG 91

Fergusson, John Duncan
PG 2515

Fergusson, Robert
PG 1863

Fergusson, Sir William
PG 565

FLEMING, Miss. *Daughter of Elizabeth Veralt and John Fleming*
    PG 2371   (Called a daughter of Elizabeth Veralt and John Fleming, perhaps Mrs
               MacNaughton.) Chalk drawing, 32.9 x 28.1 (12¹⁵⁄₁₆ x 11¹⁄₁₆), attributed to
               Bernard Vaillant. Given by R. P. F. Donald 1976.

FLEMING, Miss. *Daughter of Elizabeth Veralt and John Fleming*
    PG 2372   (Called a daughter of Elizabeth Veralt and John Fleming, perhaps Mrs
               MacNaughton.) Chalk drawing, 33.2 x 27.7 (13¹⁄₁₆ x 10⅞), attributed to
               Bernard Vaillant. Given by R. P. F. Donald 1976.

FLEMING, Sir Alexander, 1881–1955. *Discoverer of penicillin*
    PG 1835*   Bronze bust, h. 28.9 (11⅜), by E. Roland Bevan. Dated 1948. Purchased
               1956.

FLEMING, Elizabeth Veralt, Mrs John, fl. 1663. *Wife of John Fleming, merchant in
               Greenock*
    PG 2369   (Called Elizabeth Veralt.) Chalk drawing, 33.1 x 28.1 (13 x 11¹⁄₁₆),
               attributed to Bernard Vaillant. Given by R. P. F. Donald 1976.

FLEMING, Sir Sandford, 1827–1915. *Railway engineer; chief engineer of the Canadian
               Pacific Railway*
    PG 2621*   Terracotta bust, h. 28.5 (11¼), by Edouard Lantéri, signed. Dated 1887.
               Purchased 1984.

FLEMING, Thomas, d. 1724. *Merchant in Greenock and governor to the Marquis of
               Tullibardine*
    PG 2370*   (Called Thomas Fleming.) Chalk drawing, 33.4 x 27.9 (13⅛ x 11),
               attributed to Bernard Vaillant. Given by R. P. F. Donald 1976.

FLETCHER of Saltoun, Andrew, 1655–1716. *Scottish patriot*
    PG 890   Canvas, 76.2 x 63.5 (30 x 25), by unknown artist after William Aikman.
               Purchased 1918.
    PG 1642   Pencil and chalk drawing, 26.2 x 20.8 (10⅜ x 8⅛), by the 11th Earl of
               Buchan, 1794, signed, after unknown artist. Bequeathed by W. F. Watson
               1886.
    PGL 262   Canvas, 76.2 x 63.5 (30 x 25), by unknown artist after William Aikman.
               On loan from J. T. Fletcher.

FLETCHER, Eliza Dawson, Mrs Archibald, 1770–1858. *Authoress*
    PG 418   Medallion (plaster replica), h. 3.9 (1⁹⁄₁₆), after John Henning. Cast from a
               medallion in possession of Montgomery Bell 1892.
    PG 696   Porcelain medallion, h. 3.7 (1½), by John Henning. Dated 1802. Given by
               Montgomery Bell 1910.
    PG 1004*   Pencil drawing, 59.6 x 47.3 (23½ x 18⅝), by George Richmond, 1850,
               signed. Given by Sir Humphrey Rolleston 1925.

Fettes, Sir William
PG 334

Findlay, John Ritchie
PG 590

Findlay, John Ritchie
PG 1702

Fleming, Sir Alexander
PG 1835

Fleming, Sir Sandford
PG 2621

Fleming, Thomas
PG 2370

Fletcher, Eliza
PG 1004

Fletcher, General Henry
PGL 265

Foggie, David
PG 2311

Forbes, Anne
PG 191

Forbes, Duncan
PG 545

Forbes, James David
PG 1079

Forbes, John
PG 1550

Forbes, William
PGL 327

Forbes, Sir William
PG 1296

FLETCHER, General Henry, 1734–1803. *Soldier*
  PGL 265* Canvas, 126 x 101 (49⅝ x 39¾), by David Martin. On loan from J. T. T.
      Fletcher.

FLETCHER-CAMPBELL, General John, 1727–1806. *Soldier*
  PGL 266 Canvas, 76.4 x 63.1 (30⅛ x 24⅞), by unknown artist after Sir Joshua
      Reynolds. On loan from J. T. T. Fletcher.

FLOCKHART, Robert, 1778–1857. *Street preacher*
  PG 2297 Cut paper silhouette and pencil drawing, 30 x 30.5 (11¹³⁄₁₆ x 12), by
      unknown artist after Edmund Holt. Provenance untraced.

FOGGIE, David, 1878–1948. *Artist*
  PG 2311* Canvas, 45.9 x 35.7 (18 x 14), self-portrait, 1945, signed. Given by
      A. Foggie 1975.

FOLLETT, Sir William Webb, 1798–1845. *Attorney general*
  PG 146 Pencil and chalk drawing, 32.8 x 25.6 (12¹⁵⁄₁₆ x 9⅞), by Frank Stone.
      Bequeathed by W. F. Watson 1886.

FOOT, Victorine Anne, b. 1920. *Artist*
  PGL 328* (*Gathering at 7 London Street.*) See GROUPS.

FORBES, Anne, 1745–1834. *Artist*
  PG 191* Canvas, 38.3 x 32 (15⅛ x 12⅛), by David Allan. Dated 1781 (on reverse).
      Purchased 1887.

FORBES of Culloden, Duncan, 1685–1747. *Lord President of the Court of Session*
  PG 111 Water-colour, 17.9 x 10.6 (7 x 4⅛), by John Campbell, 1746, signed.
      Bequeathed by W. F. Watson 1886.
  PG 545* Canvas, 76.2 x 63.3 (30 x 24⅞), attributed to Jeremiah Davison. Bequeathed
      by Dr Robert A. Goodsir 1895.

FORBES, Professor Edward, 1815–54. *Naturalist*
  PG 174 (Artist's plaster.) Plaster bust, h. 58.7 (23⅛), by Sir John Steell. Purchased
      1887.
  PG 919 Silvered glass medal, dia. 5.1 (2), by Leonard Charles Wyon after J. G.
      Lough. Purchased 1920.

FORBES, James, 1749–1819. *Author and antiquary*
  PG 1891 Medallion (plaster replica), h. 7.2 (2⅞), after James Tassie. Provenance
      untraced.

FORBES, James David, 1809–68. *Scientist and Principal of the University of Edinburgh*
  PG 1079* Wash drawing, 13.4 x 10.2 (5¼ x 4), by Thomas Faed, signed. Acquired
      1928.

FORBES of Culloden, John, 1672–1734. *Member of Parliament; elder brother of Duncan Forbes*
  PG 1550* Canvas, 91 x 70.8 (35⅞ x 27⅞), by unknown artist. Purchased 1950.

FORBES, Bishop William, 1585–1634. *First Protestant Bishop of Edinburgh*
  PG 773   Canvas, 37 x 31.7 (14½ x 12½), copy by unknown artist. Purchased 1912.
  PG 1629 Pencil and chalk drawing, 32.6 x 27.5 (12¾ x 10¾), by the 11th Earl of Buchan, signed, after George Jamesone. Bequeathed by W. F. Watson 1886.

FORBES of Callendar, William, 1756–1823. *Coppersmith and landowner*
  PGL 327* Canvas, 236.8 x 150.5 (93¼ x 59¼), by Sir Henry Raeburn. Painted 1798. On loan from Captain W. F. E. Forbes.

FORBES of Pitsligo, Sir William, 1739–1806. *Banker and author*
  PG 142   Porcelain medallion, h. 6 (2⁵⁄₁₆), by John Henning. Dated 1802. Given by William Lyon 1886.
  PG 380   Paste medallion, h. 8 (3¹⁄₁₆), by James Tassie. Dated 1791. Purchased 1889.
  PG 946* (*The Inauguration of Robert Burns as Poet Laureate of the Lodge Canongate, Kilwinning, 1787.*) See GROUPS.
  PG 1296* Canvas, 76.2 x 63.5 (30 x 25), by Sir Joshua Reynolds. Bequeathed by John Houblon Forbes 1936.

FORBES, Williamina Belsches, Lady; see BELSCHES.

FORBES-ROBERTSON, Sir Johnston, 1853–1937. *Actor-manager*
  PG 1981* Canvas, 61 x 50.8 (24 x 20), self-portrait. Given by Mrs F. G. Miles 1961.

FORD, Sir Patrick Johnston, 1880–1945. *Advocate and Member of Parliament*
  PG 1801 Black chalk drawing, 46.4 x 29.2 (18¼ x 11½), by David Foggie, 1933, signed. Given by Mrs M. Foggie 1955.

FORDYCE, Rev. James, 1720–96. *Presbyterian divine and poet*
  PG 2468 Paste medallion, h. 8.4 (3⁵⁄₁₆), by James Tassie, signed. Purchased 1980.

FOULIS, Robert, 1707–76. *Publisher and patron of the arts*
  PG 137* Paste medallion, h. 4.1 (1¹¹⁄₁₆), by James Tassie. Purchased 1886.
  PG 296   Medallion (plaster replica), h. 6.6 (2⅝), after James Tassie. Cast from a medallion in possession of W. G. Patterson 1891.
  PG 1892 Medallion (plaster replica), h. 6.6 (2⅝), after James Tassie. Provenance untraced.

FOWLER, Sir John, 1817–98. *Designer of the Forth Railway Bridge*
  PG 612   (Artist's plaster.) Plaster bust, h. 73.5 (29), by David Watson Stevenson. Modelled 1889. Purchased 1903.

FOX, Charles James, 1749–1806. *Statesman*
  PG 298   Medallion (plaster replica), h. 7.5 (3), after W. Whitley; also known in
              Tassie paste. Cast from a medallion in possession of W. G. Patterson 1891.
  PG 344   Bust (plaster replica), h. 68 (26¾), after Joseph Nollekens. Purchased 1887.
  PG 2387   Sepia wash, 15.5 x 11.8 (6¼ x 4⅝), copy by unknown artist. Given by Mrs
              Gore Browne Henderson to the National Gallery of Scotland 1976 and
              transferred 1977.

FRANCIS II, 1544–60. *King of France*
  PG 733   (With Mary, Queen of Scots. Commemorates the marriage of Mary and the
              Dauphin.) Silver medal, dia. 5.1 (2), by unknown artist. Dated 1558.
              Purchased 1910.

FRANKLIN, Benjamin, 1706–90. *American statesman, philosopher and author*
  PG 300   Medallion (plaster replica), h. 7.4 (2¹⁵⁄₁₆), after unknown artist; also known
              in Tassie paste. Cast from a medallion in possession of W. G. Patterson
              1891.
  PG 547   Medallion (plaster replica), h. 8.1 (3¼), after Jean Baptiste Nini. Dated
              1777. Cast from a medallion in possession of Mr Butti 1895.
  PG 2341   Oil on paper, 6.3 x 5.3 (2⁷⁄₁₆ x 2¹⁄₁₆), by unknown artist. Bequeathed by
              W. F. Watson 1886.

FRANKLIN, Sir John, 1786–1847. *Arctic explorer*
  PG 546   Medallion (plaster replica), h. 10.4 (4⅛), after David d'Angers. Dated 1829.
              Cast from a medallion in possession of Sir F. L. McClintock 1895.

FRASER, Sir Alexander, c. 1536–1623. *Founder of Fraserburgh*
  PG 1627   Pencil drawing, 35 x 23.6 (13¾ x 9¼), by the 11th Earl of Buchan after
              unknown artist. Bequeathed by W. F. Watson 1886.

FRASER, Alexander, 1827–99. *Artist*
  PG 1081   Pencil and chalk drawing, 22.2 x 18.8 (8¾ x 7⅜), by Thomas Fairbairn,
              1858, signed. Given by the family of the late Lady Wingate 1928.

FRASER, Colonel Archibald Campbell, 1736–1815. *British Consul at Tripoli and Algiers*
  PG 2414   Paste medallion, h. 7.4 (2⅞), by James Tassie. Dated 1795. Purchased 1977.
  PG 2439   Paste medallion, h. 7.4 (2⅞), by James Tassie. Dated 1795. Bequeathed by
              William Tassie to the National Gallery of Scotland 1860 and transferred 1979.

FRASER of Allander, Hugh Fraser, 1st Baron, 1903–66. *Businessman and philanthropist*
  PG 2695*   Canvas, 127 x 101.6 (50 x 40), by Sir Herbert James Gunn, 1964, signed.
              Given by Sir Hugh Fraser and Lady K. Fraser 1986.

FRASER of Castle Leathers, Major James, 1670–1760. *Hanoverian supporter*
  PGL 276*   Canvas, 220.5 x 134.7 (87 x 53), by unknown artist. On loan from Mrs
              R. Townshend.

Forbes-Robertson, Sir Johnston
PG 1981

Foulis, Robert
PG 137

Fraser, 1st Baron
PG 2695

Fraser, Major James
PGL 276

Fraser, Marjory Kennedy
PG 2304

Frazer, Lady
PG 1183

Frazer, Sir James George
PG 1182

FRASER, Sir John, 1885–1947. *Surgeon and Vice-Chancellor of the University of Edinburgh*
   PG 1806   Black chalk drawing, 45.7 x 28.9 (18 x 11⅜), by David Foggie, 1933, signed. Given by Mrs M. Foggie 1955.

FRASER, John Simpson, fl. 1879–83. *Artist*
   PG 2460*   (*Friendly Critics.*) See GROUPS.

FRASER, Marjory Kennedy, Mrs A. Y., 1857–1930. *Musician and collector of Hebridean songs*
   PG 1155   Canvas, 61 x 50.8 (24 x 20), by John Duncan, signed. Painted 1931. Purchased 1931.
   PG 2304*   Canvas, 61 x 50.8 (24 x 20), by John Duncan, signed. Given by Mrs A. W. Dawson 1975.

FRASER, Sir William, d. 1818. *First baronet of Ledeclune*
  PG 1893   Medallion (plaster replica), h. 7.9 (3⅛), after William Tassie. Provenance untraced.

FRAZER, Elizabeth Adelsdorfer, Lady, d. 1941. *Wife of Sir James George Frazer*
  PG 1183*   Crayon drawing, 57.1 x 45.1 (22½ x 17¾), by Lucien Hector Monod, 1907, signed. Given by Sir James and Lady Frazer 1932.

FRAZER, Sir James George, 1854–1941. *Social anthropologist*
  PG 1182*   Crayon drawing, 59.5 x 44.6 (23⅜ x 17½), by Lucien Hector Monod, 1907, signed. Given by Sir James and Lady Frazer 1932.

FRAZER, William Miller, 1864–1961. *Artist*
  PG 2737*   (*The Smoking Room, the Scottish Arts Club.*) See GROUPS.

FREDERICK II (the Great), 1712–86. *King of Prussia*
  PG 448   Medallion (plaster replica), h. 9.9 (3¹⁵⁄₁₆), after James Tassie. Given by the South Kensington Museum 1893.

FREER, Robert, 1745–1827. *Professor of the Practice of Medicine in Glasgow University*
  PG 2644   Paste medallion, h. 7.7 (3), by William Tassie. Dated 1800. Purchased 1985.

FREIND, Rev. Robert, 1667–1751. *Headmaster of Westminster School*
  PG 491   Medallion (plaster replica), h. 6.9 (2¾), after James Tassie. Cast from a medallion in possession of Jeffery Whitehead 1894.

FRENCH, Rev. James, 1761–1835. *Tutor of Sir Walter Scott and Minister at East Kilbride*
  PG 1758   Water-colour, 26.1 x 18.8 (10¼ x 7⅜), attributed to James Howe. Given by the legatees of J. A. Gardiner.

FRIENDLY CRITICS; see GROUPS (PG 2460).

FULLERTON, John Fullerton, Lord, 1775–1853. *Judge*
  PG 172   (Artist's plaster.) Plaster bust, h. 71 (27⅞), by Sir John Steell. Purchased 1887.

GALLOWAY, Alan Plantagenet Stewart, 10th Earl of, 1835–1901. *Member of Parliament*
 PG 1764   Ink drawing, 25.7 x 10.3 (10⅛ x 4⅛), by Sir Francis Lockwood. Purchased
             1945.

GALT, John, 1779–1839. *Novelist*
 PG 1144*   Canvas, 74.9 x 62.5 (29½ x 24⅝), by Charles Grey, signed. Dated 1835.
             Purchased 1930.
 PG 1823*   Pencil drawing, 14.7 x 12.2 (5¾ x 4¾), by Alfred, Count d'Orsay, signed.
             Purchased 1955.

GAMLEY, Andrew, 1869–1949. *Artist*
 PG 1807   Black chalk drawing, 45.1 x 28 (17¾ x 11), by David Foggie, 1929, signed.
             Given by Mrs M. Foggie 1955.

GAMMON, Leonard, fl. *c.* 1650.
 PG 2084   Wash drawing, 21.2 x 15.3 (8¼ x 6¼), copy attributed to George Perfect
             Harding after engraving by William Faithorne. Transferred from the
             National Gallery of Scotland 1950.

GARDEN, Mary, 1874–1967. *Opera singer*
 PG 2133*   Chalk drawing, 63.2 x 47.4 (24⅞ x 18⅝), by Mark Tobey, 1918, signed.
             Purchased 1968.

GARDNER, Alexander, 1748–1818. *Of the Exchequer*
 PG 880   Chalk drawing, 21.5 x 18.3 (8½ x 7¼), by Sir William Allan. Bequeathed
             by the Misses G. and E. Gibson 1918.

GARIOCH, Robert, 1909–81. *Poet*
 PG 2597*   (*Poets' Pub.*) See GROUPS.

GARRICK, David, 1717–79. *Actor and dramatist*
 PG 474   Medallion (plaster replica), h 9.7 (3⅞), after James Tassie after a painting by
             Benjamin Vandergucht. Dated 1780. Cast from a medallion in possession of
             Jeffery Whitehead 1894.
 PG 1449   Painted silhouette, dia. 9.9 (3⅞), by unknown artist. Bequeathed by
             Kenneth Sanderson 1944.
 PG 1903   Medallion (plaster replica), h. 7.2 (2⅞), after James Tassie. Provenance untraced.

GAY, John, 1685–1732. *Poet and dramatist*
 PG 718   Canvas, 48.9 x 36.8 (19¼ x 14½), by William Aikman. Given by the Royal
             Scottish Academy 1910.

GEDDES, Andrew, 1783–1844. *Artist*
 PG 577*   Canvas, 76.2 x 62.9 (30 x 24¾), self-portrait. Painted *c.* 1815. Bequeathed
             by the artist's widow to the National Gallery of Scotland in 1877 and
             transferred 1898.

GEDDES, Andrew (*continued*)
> PGL 42*   Panel, 34 x 28 (13⅜ x 11), self-portrait. Dated 1812. On loan from the
>   National Museums of Scotland.

GEDDES, Sir Eric Campbell, 1875–1931. *Statesman*
> PG 1129*   Canvas, 91.8 x 71.4 (36⅛ x 28⅛), by Sir James Guthrie; study for portrait
>   in *Statesmen of the Great War* (National Portrait Gallery, London). Given
>   by W. G. Gardiner and Sir Frederick C. Gardiner 1930

GEDDES, Sir Patrick, 1854–1932. *Sociologist and town planner*
> PG 1305*   Bronze head, h 31.1 (12¼), by Charles James Pibworth. Modelled 1907.
>   Cast 1936. Purchased 1936.
> PG 2028   Board, 40.9 x 33 (16⅛ x 13), by unknown artist, signed with indecipherable
>   monogram. Painted *c*. 1930. Given by Lady Mears 1963.
> PG 2044*   Pencil drawing, 33.4 x 23.7 (13⅛ x 9⅜), by Desmond Chute, 1930, signed.
>   Given by Colin McFadyean 1964.

GEIKIE, Sir Archibald, 1835–1924. *Geologist*
> PG 1422   Pencil drawing, 30.4 x 22.8 (12 x 9), by R. G. Eves, signed. Purchased 1941.

GEORGE I, 1660–1727. *Reigned 1714–27*
> PG 484   Medallion (plaster replica), h. 8.5 (3⅜), after James Tassie. Cast from a
>   medallion in possession of Jeffery Whitehead 1894.
> PG 918   (Commemorates the rebels taken at Preston.) Silver medal, dia. 4.6 (1¹³⁄₁₆),
>   by John Croker. Dated 1715. Purchased 1920.
> PG 1059*   Canvas, 238.4 x 147.3 (93⅞ x 58), by unknown artist. Bequeathed by Mrs
>   Nisbet Hamilton Ogilvy 1921.
> PG 2770   (Battle of Sheriffmuir 1715.) Bronze medal, dia. 4.5 (1¾), by John Croker.
>   Purchased 1989.
> PG 2771   (Commemorates the rebels taken at Preston 1715.) Copper medal, dia. 4.5
>   (1¾), by John Croker. Purchased 1989.

GEORGE II, 1683–1760. *Reigned 1727–60*
> PG 221*   Canvas, 240 x 148 (94½ x 58¼), by John Shackleton, 1755, signed.
>   Purchased 1888.
> PG 381   Medallion (plaster replica), h. 8.7 (3½), after James Tassie. Cast from a
>   medallion in possession of W. G. Patterson 1889.
> PG 2774   (The rebels repulsed December 1745.) Copper medal, dia. 2.9 (1⅛), by John
>   Kirk. Purchased 1989.
> PG 2775   (The rebels repulsed December 1745.) Copper medal, dia. 2.9 (1⅛), by John
>   Kirk. Purchased 1989.

GEORGE III, 1738–1820. *Reigned 1760–1820*
> PG 216*   Canvas, 249.7 x 163 (98¼ x 64⅛), from the studio of Allan Ramsay.
>   Purchased 1888.

Galt, John
PG 1144

Galt, John
PG 1823

Garden, Mary
PG 2133

Geddes, Andrew
PG 577

Geddes, Andrew
PGL 42

Geddes, Sir Eric Campbell
PG 1129

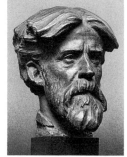

Geddes, Sir Patrick
PG 1305

Geddes, Sir Patrick
PG 2044

Geddes, Andrew
PGL 42

George I
PG 1059

George II
PG 221

George III
PG 216

George IV
PG 139

George IV at Portobello
PG 2458

George V
PG 974

German Fleet after Surrender
PG 2733

GEORGE III (*continued*)

PG 400   Medallion (plaster replica), h. 2.9 (1⅛), after James Tassie. Cast from a medallion in possession of John Ritchie Findlay 1889.

PG 485   Medallion (plaster replica), h. 5.9 (2⅜), after James Tassie. Cast from a medallion in possession of Jeffery Whitehead 1894.

PG 1371   Paste medallion, h. 4.1 (1⅝), by James Tassie. Purchased 1938.

PG 1904   Medallion (plaster replica), h. 2.9 (1⅛), after James Tassie. Provenance untraced.

GEORGE IV, 1762–1830. *Reigned as Regent 1811–20, as King 1820–30*

PG 139*   Canvas, 91.4 x 71.1 (36 x 28), by Sir Thomas Lawrence. Purchased 1885.

PG 206   Plaque (plaster replica), h. 41.6 (16⅜), after Sir Francis Legatt Chantrey. Dated 1829. Given by William Calder Marshall 1887.

PG 701   (Commemorates the foundation of the National Monument.) Copper medal, dia. 4.5 (1¾), by W. Bain. Dated 1822. Purchased 1910.

PG 767   (Commemorates the King's visit to Edinburgh.) Pewter medal, dia. 4.5 (1¾), by unknown artist. Dated 1822. Purchased 1911.

PG 1040* (*The Entrance of George IV at Holyroodhouse.*) See GROUPS

PG 1983   (Commemorates the King's visit to Edinburgh.) Bronze medal, dia. 4.5 (1¾), by W. Bain. Dated 1822. Given by W. H. H. Bayne 1961.

PG 2218* (*An incident during the visit of George IV to Edinburgh, 1822.*) See GROUPS.

PG 2384   (When Prince of Wales.) Watercolour (grisaille), 15 x 12.5 (5⅞ x 4¹⁵⁄₁₆), copy by unknown artist. Given by Mrs Gore Browne Henderson to the National Gallery of Scotland 1976 and transferred 1977.

PG 2458* (At a military review on Portobello Sands 23 August 1822.) Canvas, 66.1 x 91.1 (26 x 35⅞), by William Turner 'de Lond', signed. Dated indistinctly 182[8]. Purchased 1980.

PGL 326   (At a review of cavalry on Portobello Sands 1822.) Water-colour with some pencil, 54.5 x 75 (21⁷⁄₁₆ x 29⅝) (irregular), by Denis Dighton. On loan from Lothians and Borders Regimental Club.

GEORGE V, 1865–1936. *Reigned 1910–36*

PG 974*   (Study for a portrait exhibited 1924 and now destroyed.) Canvas, 101.6 x 70.8 (40 x 27⅞), by Charles Sims, signed. Purchased 1924.

GERBIER, Sir Balthazar, c. 1591–1667. *Artist and diplomat*

PG 2087   Wash drawing, 11.6 x 8.7 (4½ x 3⅜), by Edward Harding, signed, after unknown artist. Transferred from the National Gallery of Scotland 1950.

THE GERMAN FLEET AFTER SURRENDER, FIRTH OF FORTH, 21 NOVEMBER 1918

PG 2733* Canvas, 71.3 x 91.5 (28 x 36), by James Paterson, 1918, signed. Purchased 1988.

GIBB, Robert, 1845–1932. *Artist*
PG 1742   (In his studio.) Wash drawing, 38.6 x 50.7 (15⅛ x 20), by J. R. Abercromby, signed. Drawn 1898. Purchased 1940.

GIBBONS, Grinling, 1648–1720. *Wood-carver and sculptor*
PG 358   (With his wife.) Chalk drawing, 27.2 x 34 (10¾ x 13⅜), by unknown artist. Bequeathed by W. F. Watson 1886.

GIBSON, Sir Alexander, b. 1926. *Conductor*
PG 2676*   Canvas, 152.7 x 127.3 (60⅛ x 50⅛), by John Houston, 1984/5, signed. Purchased by commission 1986.
PG 2691*   Canvas, 127 x 101.6 (50 x 40), by John Houston, 1985, signed. Given by the artist 1986.
PG 2692   Pencil drawing, 41.9 x 29.5 (16½ x 11⅝), by John Houston, 1985, signed. Purchased 1986.
PG 2693   Pencil drawing, 44.5 x 33 (17½ x 13), by John Houston, 1985, signed. Purchased 1986.

GIBSON, David, fl. 1810. *Stockbroker*
PG 1853*   Pencil drawing, 38.1 x 27.3 (15 x 10¾), by unknown artist. Provenance untraced.

GIBSON, Jemima Wilkie, Mrs David, fl. *c.* 1820.
PG 2294   Pencil drawing, 25.9 x 19.4 (10³⁄₁₆ x 7⅝), by unknown artist. Bequeathed to the Royal Museum of Science and Art, Edinburgh, by E. and C. Gibson and transferred.

GIBSON, John, d. 1852. *Artist*
PG 1428   Painted silhouette, 11.1 x 8.3 (4⅜ x 3¼), by unknown artist. Bequeathed by Mrs Louisa Wallace James 1942.

GIBSON, Patrick, *c.* 1782–1829. *Artist and writer on art*
PG 118   Water-colour drawing, 22.4 x 17.2 (8⅞ x 6¹³⁄₁₆), self-portrait. Bequeathed by W. F. Watson 1886.

GILFILLAN, Robert, 1798–1850. *Poet*
PG 772   Painted silhouette, 11.5 x 7.5 (4½ x 3), by unknown artist. Purchased 1912.

GILLESPIE, Very Rev. Dr John, 1836–1912. *Minister and agriculturalist*
PG 873   Canvas, 40.3 x 30.5 (15⅞ x 12), by Charles Martin Hardie, 1899, signed. Purchased 1917.
PG 1856*   (*Curling at Carsebreck.*) See GROUPS.

GILLESPIE, William, *c.* 1743–1807. *Spinner and calico printer*
PG 1895   Medallion (plaster replica), h. 7.5 (3), after James Tassie. Dated 1791. Provenance untraced.

GILLESPIE of Clearburn, William. *Brother of Rev. Thomas Gillespie, founder of the
          Presbytery of Relief*
PG 1579   Chalk drawing, 56.8 x 43.5 (22⅜ x 17⅛), attributed to Archibald Skirving.
          Bequeathed by Sir John Douglas Don Wauchope 1951.

GILLIES, John, 1747–1836. *Historiographer Royal of Scotland*
PG 1397*   Canvas, 76.2 x 63.5 (30 x 25), by John Opie. Given by George Gillies
          Mennell through the National Art-Collections Fund in memory of Mrs Jane
          Lilias Hudson Mennell 1939.

GILLIES, Sir William George, 1898–1973. *Artist*
PG 2355*   Bronze head, h. 27.4 (10¾), by Eric Schilsky. Purchased 1976.
PG 2448*   Canvas, 86.9 x 71.4 (34¼ x 28⅛), self-portrait, signed. Dated 1940 (on the
          reverse). Purchased 1979.
PGL 328*   (*Gathering at 7 London Street.*) See GROUPS.

GILMOUR of Lundin and Montrave, Henrietta Gilmour, Lady, fl. 1899. *Of Lundin and
          Montrave Curling Club*
PG 1856*   (*Curling at Carsebreck.*) See GROUPS.

GILMOUR, Hugh, fl. 1899. *Of Waverley Curling Club*
PG 1856*   (*Curling at Carsebreck.*) See GROUPS.

GLADSTONE, William Ewart, 1809–98. *Liberal statesman and author*
PG 670*   Canvas, 73.6 x 66 (29 x 26), by Prince Pierre Troubetskoy. Purchased 1908.
PG 753   Charcoal drawing, 68 x 54 (26¾ x 21¼), by Sir William Quiller
          Orchardson. Purchased 1910.
PG 837*   Canvas, 108.6 x 86.4 (42¾ x 34), by Franz-Seraph von Lenbach, signed.
          Purchased 1914.

GLENBERVIE, Sylvester Douglas, Lord, 1743–1823. *Barrister and politician*
PG 1276   Porcelain medallion, h. 5.4 (2⅛), by John Henning. Dated 1808. Purchased
          1935.
PG 2032*   Chalk drawing, 52.6 x 44.2 (20¾ x 17⅜), by John Henning, 1805, signed.
          Purchased 1963.

GLENCAIRN, Elizabeth Macguire, Countess, of 1724–1801.
PG 359*   Pencil drawing, 56.3 x 40.7 (22⅛ x 16), by John Brown. Purchased 1889.

GLENCAIRN, James Cunningham, 13th Earl of, 1749–91. *Patron of Robert Burns*
PG 1770*   (*Burns at an evening party of Lord Monboddo's 1786.*) See GROUPS.

GLENCAIRN, William Cunningham, 8th Earl of, c. 1610–64. *Lord Chancellor of
          Scotland*
PG 661*   Canvas, 127 x 102.2 (50 x 40¼), by John Michael Wright. Probably painted
          1661. Purchased 1907.

Gibson, Sir Alexander
PG 2676

Gibson, Sir Alexander
PG 2691

Gibson, David
PG 1853

Gillies, John
PG 1397

Gillies, Sir William
PG 2355

Gillies, Sir William
PG 2448

Gladstone, William Ewart
PG 670

Gladstone, William Ewart
PG 837

Glenbervie, Lord
PG 2032

Glencairn, Countess ot
PG 359

Glencairn, 8th Earl of
PG 661

Glenorchy, Viscountess
PG 2476

Golf Match
PG 2019

Good, Thomas Sword
PG 1829

Gordon, Lord Adam
PG 192

GLENCORSE, John Inglis, Lord, 1810–91. *Lord Justice General*
    PG 1106   Chalk drawing, 60.3 x 48.9 (22¾ x 19¼), by John Faed. Given by A. W. Inglis 1929.
    PG 1314   Ink drawing, 28 x 17.7 (11 x 7), by Sir George Reid, 1882, signed. Purchased 1937.
    PG 1315   Cut paper silhouette, h. 27 (10⅝), by Ernst Ljungh, 1888, signed. Purchased 1937.

GLENLEE, Sir Thomas Miller, Lord, 1717–89. *Lord President of the Court of Session*
    PG 131   Paste medallion, h. 7.9 (3⅛), by James Tassie. Purchased 1885.

GLENORCHY Family-Tree; see CAMPBELL of Glenorchy

GLENORCHY, Willielma Campbell, Viscountess, 1741–1786. *Religious enthusiast and benefactor of the Society for Promoting Christian Knowledge*
    PG 2476*   Canvas, 126.5 x 100.2 (49¹³⁄₁₆ x 39½), by David Martin. Purchased 1981.

GLENSHIEL, THE BATTLE OF, 1719
    PG 2635*   See GROUPS.
    PGL 334   (Plan of the Battle of Glenshiel 1719.) Water-colour and Indian ink, 43 x 47.8 (17 x 18¹³⁄₁₆) (irregular), by John Ross probably after Lieutenant John Bastide. On loan from Mrs E. C. Mackenzie.

GOLF. A Golf Match.
    PG 2019*   Millboard, 22.9 x 30.5 (9 x 12), by Charles Lees. Provenance untraced.

GOOD, , Thomas Sword, 1789–1872. *Painter in Berwick*
    PG 1829*   Panel, 21.2 x 17.8 (8⅜ x 7), self-portrait. Painted c. 1816. Purchased 1956.

GORDON, Mr, fl. 1800. *Of Edinburgh*
    PG 1756   Water-colour, 21.6 x 13.5 (8½ x 5¼), attributed to James Howe. Given by the legatees of J. A. Gardiner.

GORDON, Lord Adam, *c.* 1726–1801. *General; Commander of forces in Scotland 1782–98*
    PG 192*   Canvas, 27 x 22 (10⅝ x 8⅝), by Henri-Pierre Danloux. Dated 1799 (on reverse). Purchased 1887.

GORDON, Alexander Gordon, 4th Duke of, 1743–1827. *Keeper of the Great Seal of Scotland*
    PG 207*   Canvas, 76.2 x 63.5 (30 x 25), by John Moir, 1817, signed. Purchased 1887.
    PG 1194   Paste medallion, h. 2.8 (1⅛), by James Tassie. Purchased 1932.

GORDON, Rev. Alexander, fl. 1780. *Principal of the Scots College, Douai*
    PGL 79*   Pencil drawing, 50.8 x 34.6 (20 x 13⅝), by John Brown. On loan from the National Museums of Scotland.

GORDON, Alexander ('Picture'), fl. 1796. *Connoisseur*
PG 2440   Paste medallion, h. 8.1 (3³⁄₁₆), by James Tassie. Dated 1796. Bequeathed by
           William Tassie to the National Gallery of Scotland 1860 and transferred
           1979.

GORDON, Alexander Esmé, b. 1910. *Architect*
PG 2777   (As a child.) Canvas, 41 x 35.8 (16⅛ x 14⅛), by Stanley Cursiter, 1915,
           signed in monogram. Given by the sitter 1989.

GORDON, General Sir Alexander Hamilton, 1817–90. *Equerry to the Prince Consort and*
           Member of Parliament
PG 1568*   (Study for *The Landing of Queen Victoria at Dumbarton in 1847*, in the
           collection of Dumbarton District Council.) Water-colour, 69.8 x 46.7 (27½
           x 18⅜), by Hope James Stewart. Dated 1849. Bequeathed by Major-General
           Granville Egerton 1951.

GORDON, General Charles George, 1833–85. *Soldier in China and Egypt*
PG 1972   Terracotta bust, h. 28 (11), by William Frederick Woodington, 1885, signed.
           Given by Ernest Galinsky 1961.

GORDON, Elizabeth, fl. 1795. *Probably the wife of Alexander ('Picture') Gordon*
PG 2441   Paste medallion, h. 7.9 (3⅛), by James Tassie. Dated 1795. Bequeathed by
           William Tassie to the National Gallery of Scotland 1860 and transferred 1979.

GORDON, Lord George, 1751–93. *Political agitator*
PG 465   Medallion (plaster replica), h. 6.7 (2¾), after James Tassie. Dated 1781.
           Cast from a medallion in possession of Jeffery Whitehead 1893.

GORDON, George Gordon, 5th Duke of Gordon, 1770–1836. *General*
PG 2208   (As Marquess of Huntly, with his mother Jane Maxwell, Duchess of
           Gordon.) Canvas, 126.4 x 102.5 (49¾ x 40⅜), by George Romney. Painted
           1778. Purchased with assistance from the Pilgrim Trust 1972.

GORDON, Jane Maxwell, Duchess of, *c.* 1749–1812. *Wife of the 4th Duke of Gordon*
PG 927*   (With Lady Wallace.) Pencil drawing, 7 x 9.5 (2¾ x 3¾), by John Brown.
           Purchased 1921.
PG 1153*   Pencil drawing, 13 x 8.2 (5⅛ x 3¼), by John Brown. Drawn 1786.
           Purchased 1931.
PG 1770*   (*Burns at an evening party of Lord Monboddo's 1786.*) See GROUPS.
PG 2208*   (With her son the Marquess of Huntly, later 5th Duke of Gordon.) Canvas,
           126.4 x 102.5 (49¾ x 40⅜), by George Romney. Painted 1778. Purchased
           with assistance from the Pilgrim Trust 1972.

GORDON, Sir John Watson, 1788–1864. *Artist*
PG 715*   Canvas, 238.8 x 148.6 (94 x 58½), by John Graham Gilbert, 1854, signed.
           Given by the Royal Scottish Academy 1910.

GORDON, Sir John Watson (*continued*)

PG 1771   Pencil, chalk and wash drawing, 13.5 x 12.1 (5⅜ x 4¾), self-portrait. Provenance untraced.

GORDON, R., fl. 1899. *Of Bathgate Curling Club*

PG 1856*   (*Curling at Carsebreck.*) See GROUPS.

GORDON, Rev. Robert, 1786–1853. *Professor of Divinity in the Free Church College*

PG 1213   Cut paper silhouette with water-colour background, 28 x 11.9 (11 x 7½), by Augustin Edouart. Purchased 1933.

PG 2152*   Cut paper silhouette, h. 15.4 (6⅛), by Augustin Edouart, 1830, signed. Given by Mrs J. H. G. Ross 1969.

GORDON, Sir Robert, 1580–1656. *Courtier at the courts of James VI and I, and Charles I*

PG 1513   Canvas, 59 x 46.4 (23¼ x 18¼), by unknown artist. Dated 1621. Purchased 1948.

GORDON of Gordonstoun, Sir Robert, 1647–1704. *Man of science*

PG 1512*   Canvas, oval 73.7 x 62.9 (29 x 24¾), by unknown artist. Dated 1692. Purchased 1948.

GORDON of Straloch, Robert, 1580–1661. *Geographer*

PG 1632   Pencil drawing, 34.8 x 24 (13⅝ x 9½), by the 11th Earl of Buchan after George Jamesone. Bequeathed by W. F. Watson 1886.

PG 1633   Pencil drawing, 43 x 33.4 (17 x 13⅛), by the 11th Earl of Buchan after George Jamesone. Bequeathed by W. F. Watson 1886.

GOSFORD, Sir Peter Wedderburn, Lord, *c.* 1616–79. *Judge*

PG 1583*   Canvas, 77.4 x 64.8 (30¼ x 25¼), by David Scougall. Purchased 1951.

GOUDIE, Gilbert, d. 1918. *Author and Treasurer to the Society of Antiquaries of Scotland*

PG 1711   Pencil drawing, 37.5 x 33 (14¾ x 13), by W. Graham Boss. Given by the artist.

GOW, Donald, fl. *c.* 1780. *Cellist; brother of Niel Gow*

PG 2126*   (With his brother Niel Gow.) Canvas, 58.8 x 45.6 (23⅛ x 18), by David Allan. Painted *c.* 1780. Purchased 1967.

GOW, Niel, 1727–1807. *Violinist and composer*

PG 160*   Canvas, 123.2 x 97.8 (48½ x 38½), by Sir Henry Raeburn. Painted 1787. Purchased 1886.

PG 2126*   (With his brother Donald Gow.) Canvas, 58.8 x 45.6 (23⅛ x 18), by David Allan. Painted *c.* 1780. Purchased 1967.

GRAHAM of Duntrune, Clementina Stirling, 1782–1877. *Authoress and song writer*

PG 1252*   Water-colour, 21.3 x 16.2 (8⅜ x 6⅜), by unknown artist. Purchased 1935.

Gordon, Rev. Alexander
PGL 79

Gordon, 4th Duke of
PG 207

Gordon, Sir Alexander
Hamilton   PG 1568

Gordon, Duchess of, with Lady Wallace
PG 927

Gordon, Duchess of
PG 1153

Gordon, Duchess of, with
Marquess of Huntly   PG 2208

Gordon, Sir John Watson
PG 715

Gordon, Rev. Robert
PG 2152

Gordon, Sir Robert
PG 1512

Gosford, Lord
PG 1583

Gow, Niel, with Donald Gow
PG 2126

Gow, Niel
PG 160

Graham, Clementina Stirling
PG 1252

Graham, Robert Bontine
Cunninghame   PG 1363

Graham, Robert Bontine
Cunninghame   PG 1468

GRAHAM, Sir James Robert George, 1792–1861. *Statesman*
 PG 2306 (Crombie Sketchbook, fo. 5.) Pencil drawing, 15.6 x 20 (6⅛ x 7⅞), by
         Benjamin William Crombie. Purchased 1938.

GRAHAM, John; see GRAHAM-GILBERT (PG 789)

GRAHAM, Mary (later Mrs Davidson), fl. 1844.
 PG 1811 Bronzed cut paper silhouette, h. 21.3 (8¼), by Frederick Frith, 1844, signed.
         Given by Mrs J. M. Fleming 1945.

GRAHAM, Robert Bontine Cunninghame, 1852–1936. *Writer and traveller*
 PG 1363* Bronze head, h. 35 (13¾), by Sir Jacob Epstein. Sculpted 1923. Purchased
          1938.
 PG 1468* Bronze bust, h. 68.5 (27), by Albert Toft. Dated 1891. Given by
          Rear-Admiral A. B. Cunninghame Graham 1945.
 PG 2124* (Riding in Rotten Row.) Crayon and wash drawing, 36.4 x 45.1
          (14⁵⁄₁₆ x 17¾), by Leslie Hunter, signed. Bequeathed by R. C. Roy 1967.

GRAHAM of Gartmore, Robert Cunninghame, d. 1797. *Poet and politician*
 PG 885* Canvas, 127 x 101.6 (50 x 40), attributed to Sir Henry Raeburn. Given by
         R. B. Cunninghame Graham 1919.
 PG 2620* Canvas, 128.5 x 103.5 (50⅝ x 40¾), by Sir Henry Raeburn. Painted
          c. 1794. Bequeathed by Mrs E. M. F. Landale 1984.

GRAHAM, Thomas Alexander, 1840–1906. *Artist*
 PG 721 Millboard, 19.5 x 14.7 (7⅝ x 5⅞), by James Archer. Given by the Royal
        Scottish Academy 1910.
 PG 827 Canvas, 40.6 x 33 (16 x 13), by Sir William Quiller Orchardson. Purchased
        1913.

GRAHAM-GILBERT, John, 1794–1866. *Artist*
 PG 789* Cut paper silhouette, h. 20.9 (8¼), by Augustin Edouart. Purchased 1912.

GRAHAME, Rev. James, 1765–1811. *Advocate, clergyman and poet*
 PG 526 Porcelain medallion, 5.4 (2⅛), by John Henning. Given by Miss Brown
        1894.
 PG 1541 Porcelain medallion, 5.5 (2³⁄₁₆), by John Henning. Dated 1810. Purchased
         1949.

GRAHAME, Jane, 1773–1850. *Wife of Archibald Grahame, writer in Glasgow*
 PG 1894 Medallion (plaster replica), h. 7.8 (3⅛), after James Tassie. Provenance
         untraced.

GRANGE, James Erskine, Lord, 1679–1754. *Judge*
 PGL 236* Canvas, 241 x 149.6 (94⅞ x 58⅞), attributed to William Aikman. Painted
          c. 1720. On loan from the Earl of Mar and Kellie.

Graham, Robert Bontine
Cunninghame   PG 2124

Graham, Robert Cunninghame
PG 885

Graham, Robert Cunninghame
PG 2620

Graham-Gilbert, John
PG 789

Grange, Lord
PGL 236

Grange, Lady
PGL 235

Grant, Anne
PG 274

Grant, Anne
PG 1046

Grant, Anne
PG 1177

Grant, Duncan
PG 2459

Grant, Sir Francis
PG 6

Grant, Sir Francis
PG 2732

Grant, Sir James Hope
PG 343

Granton, Lord
PGL 215

GRANGE, Rachel Chiesley, Lady, d. 1749. *Wife of James Erskine, Lord Grange*
  PGL 235*   Canvas, 76.8 x 62.4 (30¼ x 24⅝), attributed to Sir John Baptiste de Medina.
           On loan from the Earl of Mar and Kellie.

GRANT of Laggan, Anne MacVicar, Mrs James, 1755–1838. *Writer*
  PG 274*   Canvas, 80.3 x 65.4 (31⅝ x 25¾), by James Tannock. Given by Mrs Jane
           Grant 1889.
  PG 1046*   Chalk drawing, 52.4 x 37.2 (20½ x 14⅝), by William Bewick. Dated 1824.
           Purchased 1927.
  PG 1177*   Cut paper silhouette, h. 16.5 (6½), by Augustin Edouart. Cut 1831.
           Purchased 1932.
  PG 2474   Wax medallion, h. 7 (2¾), by John Henning, signed. Dated 1810. Purchased
           1981.
  PG 2615   Water-colour, 40.3 x 31.1 (15⅞ x 12¼), by unknown artist. Executed 1810.
           Given by Bernard Babington Smith 1984.

GRANT, Duncan James Corrowr, 1885–1978. *Artist*
  PG 2459*   Canvas, 61 x 45.8 (24 x 18), self-portrait. Painted *c.* 1920. Purchased 1980.

GRANT, Sir Francis, 1803–78. *Artist*
  PG 6*   Canvas, 76.2 x 63.5 (30 x 25), by John Prescott Knight. Purchased 1884.
  PG 2732*   Pencil drawing, 17.2 x 11.9 (6¾ x 4¾), by John Landseer. Purchased 1988.

GRANT, Sir James, 1738–1811. *Member of Parliament*
  PG 1956   Panel, 20.4 x 16.8 (8 x 6⅝), by William Staveley. Painted 1797. Purchased
           1960.

GRANT, General Sir James Hope, 1808–75. *Soldier*
  PG 343*   (As Colonel of the 9th Lancers.) Canvas, 223.4 x 132.1 (88 x 52), by Sir
           Francis Grant. Painted 1853. Bequeathed by Lady Hope Grant 1892.

GRANT of Congalton, Captain John, fl. 1848. *Factor to the Earl of Seafield*
  PG 1734   Pencil drawing, 25.4 x 19.1 (10 x 7¼), by G. R. Halkett from a mezzotint
           after Colvin Smith. Purchased 1935.

GRANT of Kilgraston, John, 1798–1873. *Brother of Sir Francis Grant*
  PGL 337*   (*A Meet of the Fife Hounds.*) See GROUPS.

GRANTON, Charles Hope, Lord, 1763–1851. *Lord President of the Court of Session*
  PGL 215*   Canvas, 126 x 100.3 (49⅝ x 39½), by Sir Henry Raeburn: On loan from
           Henry J. D. Cook.

GRAY of Teasses, Jane, d. 1792. *Philanthropist*
  PG 1270   Paste medallion, h. 7.6 (3¹⁄₁₆), by James Tassie. Purchased 1935.

GRAY, John Miller, 1850–94. *Art critic and first curator of the Scottish National Portrait Gallery*
    PG 1072   Pencil drawing, 10.7 x 7.6 (4⅛ x 3), by Charles Matthew, 1888, signed. Provenance untraced (probably bequeathed by the sitter 1894).
    PG 1077   Pencil drawing, 7.6 x 6.6 (3 x 2⅝), by Charles Matthew. Provenance untraced (probably bequeathed by the sitter 1894).
    PG 1226*   Canvas board, 30.3 x 25.1 (11⅞ x 9⅞), by Patrick William Adam, 1885, signed. Bequeathed by the sitter 1894.
    PG 1729   Pencil drawing, 16 x 10.1 (6¼ x 4), by W. G. Burn Murdoch, 1889, signed. Bequeathed by the sitter 1894.
    PG 2070   Bronze medallion, dia. 13.3 (5¼), by Charles Matthew. Dated 1886. Bequeathed by the sitter 1894.
    PG 2071   Water-colour, 18 x 10.3 (7 x 4), by G. R. Halkett, signed. Dated 1881. Bequeathed by the sitter 1894.

GREEN, Charles Edward, 1866–1920. *Publisher*
    PG 1870*   Chalk drawing, 36.8 x 27 (14½ x 10⅝), by James Paterson, 1917, signed. Bequeathed by Mrs M. A. Green 1960.

GREGORY, Professor James, 1638–75. *Mathematician*
    PG 1637   Pencil and chalk drawing, 32.7 x 27.5 (12⅞ x 10⅞), by the 11th Earl of Buchan after John Scougall. Bequeathed by W. F. Watson 1886.
    PG 1640*   Chalk drawing, 44 x 33.6 (17¼ x 13¼), by the 11th Earl of Buchan after unknown artist. Bequeathed by W. F. Watson 1886.

GREGORY, Professor James, 1753–1821. *Physician and author*
    PG 287*   Plaster bust, h. 73.7 (29), by Samuel Joseph. Dated 1821. Given by Mrs General Birch 1890.
    PG 1262   Paste medallion, h. 7.6 (3¹⁄₁₆), by James Tassie. Dated 1791. Purchased 1935.

GREVILLE, Robert Kaye, 1794–1866. *Botanist*
    PG 1045   Chalk drawing, 51.8 x 37.2 (20⅜ x 14⅝), by William Bewick. Purchased 1927.

GREY of Fallodon, Edward Grey, Viscount, 1862–1933. *Statesman*
    PG 1133*   Canvas, 91.5 x 71.5 (36 x 28⅛), by Sir James Guthrie; study for portrait in *Statesmen of the Great War* (National Portrait Gallery, London). Given by W. G. Gardiner and Sir Frederick C. Gardiner 1930.

GRIEVE, Christopher Murray (nom de plume, 'Hugh MacDiarmid'), 1892–1978. *Poet*
    PG 2434*   Bronze head, h. 39.4 (15½), by Benno Schotz, signed. Sculpted 1958. Purchased 1979.
    PG 2597*   (*Poets' Pub.*) See GROUPS.
    PG 2604*   Canvas, 112.3 x 86.7 (44³⁄₁₆ x 34⅛), by Robert Heriot Westwater, signed. Dated 1962. Acquired from the estate of Christopher Murray Grieve 1978.

GRIEVE, Christopher Murray (nom de plume, 'Hugh MacDiarmid') (*continued*)
  PG 2618*   Pencil drawing, 25.6 x 18.2 (10¹⁄₁₆ x 7⅛), by William Johnstone, signed.
         Dated 1936. Purchased 1984.
  PG 2637*   (Artist's plaster.) Bronzed plaster head, h. 37.5 (14¾), by Laurence
         Henderson Bradshaw. Sculpted 1956. Given by Mrs Eileen Bradshaw 1985.

GRIEVE, James, 1841–1924. *Horticulturist*
  PG 1990*   Water-colour, 79.4 x 56.5 (31¼ x 22¼), by Henry Wright Kerr. Given by
         Ian Scott 1962.

GRIFFITH, Sir Richard John Waldie-, 3rd Baronet, 1850–1933. *Of Kelso Curling Club*
  PG 1856*   (*Curling at Carsebreck.*) See GROUPS.

GRIMOND, Joseph Grimond, 1st Baron, b. 1913. *Liberal statesman and theorist*
  PG 2717*   Canvas, 121 x 91.5 (47⅝ x 36), by Patrick Heron. Purchased by commission
         1987.

GROSE, Captain Francis, *c.* 1731–91. *Antiquary*
  PG 116*   Chalk drawing, 22.1 x 13.5 (8¹¹⁄₁₆ x 5¼), by Nathaniel Dance. Bequeathed
         by W. F. Watson 1886.
  PG 891*   Canvas, 69.9 x 58.4 (28½ x 23), by unknown artist. Purchased 1918.
  PG 946*   (*The Inauguration of Robert Burns as Poet Laureate of the Lodge
         Canongate, Kilwinning, 1787.*) See GROUPS.
  PG 1770*   (*Burns at an evening party of Lord Monboddo's 1786.*) See GROUPS.
  PG 2654   Sepia and pencil drawing, 20.4 x 12.5 (8 x 4¹⁵⁄₁₆), by unknown artist.
         Provenance untraced.

GUNN, Sir Herbert James, 1893–1964. *Artist*
  PG 2378*   Canvas board, 33.1 x 26.4 (13 x 10⅜), by Sir William Oliphant Hutchison.
         Painted 1911. Given by the executors of Margery, Lady Hutchison 1977.

GUNN, Neil, 1891–1973. *Novelist*
  PG 2586*   (With George Blake and Douglas Young.) Ink chalk, and pencil drawing,
         35 x 41.4 (13¾ x 16⁵⁄₁₆) (irregular), by Emilio Coia, signed. Executed 1957.
         Given by Christopher Blake 1983.

GUNNING, Elizabeth; see HAMILTON and ARGYLL

GUTHRIE, Sir James, 1859–1930. *Artist and President of the Royal Scottish Academy*
  PG 1150*   Pencil drawing, 27 x 19.9 (10⅝ x 7⅞), by Edward Arthur Walton, 1888,
         signed. Purchased 1931.
  PG 1867*   Canvas on board, 35.3 x 25.3 (13⅞ x 10), self-portrait. Purchased 1959.
  PG 2484   (With Joseph Crawhall and E. A. Walton.) Ink drawing (caricature),
         9 x 11.3 (3½ x 4⁷⁄₁₆), by Sir James Guthrie. Given by Dr Camilla Uytman
         to the National Gallery of Scotland and transferred 1981.

Gray, John Miller
PG 1226

Green, Charles Edward
PG 1870

Gregory, Professor James
PG 1640

Gregory, Professor James
PG 287

Grey, Viscount
PG 1133

Grieve, Christopher Murray
PG 2434

Grieve, Christopher Murray
PG 2604

Grieve, Christopher Murray
PG 2618

Grieve, Christopher Murray
PG 2637

Grieve, James
PG 1990

Grimond, 1st Baron
PG 2717

Grose, Francis
PG 116

Grose, Francis
PG 891

Gunn, Sir Herbert James
PG 2378

Guthrie, Sir James
PG 1150

GUTHRIE, John, d. 1834. *Merchant and Glasgow Dean of Guild in 1814*
  PG 1965   Paste medallion, h. 8 (3³⁄₁₆), by James Tassie. Transferred from the National
           Gallery of Scotland 1960.

GUTHRIE, Rev. Thomas, 1803–73. *Preacher and philanthropist*
  PG 805*   Bronze bust, h. 49.5 (19½), by Sir John Steell. Given by Lord Guthrie 1912.
  PG 1502*   (With his children, Patrick and Anne, fishing on Lochlee.) Millboard,
           46.3 x 60.3 (18¼ x 23¾), by Sir George Harvey, 1855, signed. Given by
           Mrs Ethel M. Pearse 1947.
  PG 1592   Millboard, 31.4 x 24.1 (12³⁄₈ x 9½), by unknown artist. Given by J. Robb
           Knox 1952.
  PG 1845*   Water-colour, 32.5 x 23.4 (12⅞ x 9³⁄₁₆), by Kenneth Macleay. Purchased
           1957.
  PG 2633*   (Exhibited as *Dr Guthrie on a mission of mercy*.) Millboard, 54.7 x 45.7
           (21¼ x 18), by James Edgar, 1862, signed. Purchased 1984.

Guthrie, Sir James
PG 1867

Guthrie, Rev. Thomas
PG 805

Guthrie, Rev. Thomas,
Anne and Patrick Guthrie   PG 1502

Guthrie, Rev. Thomas
PG 1845

Guthrie, Rev. Thomas
PG 2633

HADDINGTON, Thomas Hamilton, 1st Earl of, 1563–1637. *Advocate and statesman*
  PG 818*   Canvas, 114.3 x 91.4 (45 x 36), by unknown artist after Adam de Colone.
            Purchased 1913.

HADDINGTON, Thomas Hamilton, 6th Earl of, 1680–1735. *Supporter of the Union*
  PG 1610*   Canvas, 127 x 101.6 (50 x 40), by Sir John Baptiste de Medina. Purchased 1954.

HAIG, , Douglas Haig, 1st Earl, 1861–1928. *Soldier*
  PG 1010*   (Study for portrait in *General Officers of World War I, 1914–18*, in the
            National Portrait Gallery, London.) Canvas, 56 x 41 (22 x 16⅛), by John
            Singer Sargent. Purchased 1925.

HALDANE, Professor John Scott, 1860–1936. *Physiologist*
  PGL 269*   Canvas, 117.1 x 89.2 (46⅛ x 35⅛), by Philip Alexius de Laszlo, 1933,
            signed. On loan from Dr D. A. Michison.

HALDANE, Mary Elizabeth Burdon-Sanderson, Mrs Robert, d. 1925. *Mother of
            Viscount Haldane of Cloan*
  PG 2022   Chalk drawing, 36.8 x 27 (14½ x 10⅜), by James Paterson, 1914, signed.
            Given by Miss Naomi Mitchison 1962.

HALDANE of Cloan, Richard Burdon Haldane, 1st Viscount, 1856–1928. *Statesman*
  PG 877*   Chalk drawing, 39.7 x 37.8 (15⅝ x 14⅞), by Sir William Rothenstein, 1916,
            signed. Purchased 1917.
  PG 1401*   Canvas, 75.9 x 63.1 (29⅞ x 24⅞), by George Fiddes Watt. Purchased 1940.
  PG 2755   Pencil drawing, 27.7 x 30.4 (10⅞ x 11¹⁵⁄₁₆) (slightly irregular), by Edward
            Tennyson Reed, signed. Drawn 1908. Purchased 1988.

HALKETT, Samuel, 1814–71. *Librarian*
  PGL 47   Water-colour, 9.6 x 7.7 (3¾ x 3), by unknown artist. On loan from G. R.
            Halkett.

HALL, Agnes and Isabella, fl. 1795. *Daughters of the Rev. James Hall*
  PG 1897   Medallion (plaster replica), h. 6.3 (2½), after James Tassie. Provenance untraced.

HALL, Rev. James, 1755–1826. *Secession minister*
  PG 522   Medallion (plaster replica), h. 8 (3⅛), after James Tassie. Dated 1794. Cast
            from a medallion in possession of J. M. Gray 1894.

HALL, John, 1739–97. *Line engraver*
  PG 445   Medallion (plaster replica), h. 2.8 (1⅛), after James Tassie. Given by the
            South Kensington Museum 1893.

HALL, John, fl. 1796–1807. *Teacher in Glasgow*
  PG 492   Medallion (plaster replica), h. 7.1 (2¹³⁄₁₆), after James Tassie. Dated 1796.
            Cast from a medallion in possession of Jeffery Whitehead 1894.

HALL, Mary Maxwell, Mrs James, *c.* 1756–1829. *Wife of the Rev. James Hall*
  PG 1899   Medallion (plaster replica), h. 8.2 (3¼), after James Tassie. Dated 1795.
             Provenance untraced.

HAMILTON, Alexander Douglas-Hamilton, 10th Duke of, and 7th Duke of Brandon,
             1767–1852. *Art collector; Lord-Lieutenant of Lanarkshire*
  PG 1040*   (*The Entrance of George IV at Holyroodhouse.*) See GROUPS.
  PG 2062*   Pencil drawing, 21.1 x 12.7 (8⅜ x 5), by unknown artist. Purchased 1967.

HAMILTON, David, 1768–1843. *Architect*
  PG 788   Cut paper silhouette, h. 20.8 (8³⁄₁₆), by Augustin Edouart. Purchased 1912.

HAMILTON, Douglas Douglas-Hamilton, 14th Duke of, and 11th Duke of Brandon,
             1903–73. *Aviator*
  PG 2723   (With Elizabeth, Duchess of Hamilton.) Canvas, 89.8 x 129.8 (35⅜ x 51⅛),
             by Oskar Kokoschka, signed. Painted 1969. Purchased with assistance from
             the National Art-Collections Fund, the National Heritage Memorial Fund
             and the Pilgrim Trust 1987.

HAMILTON, Elizabeth, 1757–1816. *Writer and educationist*
  PG 1486*   Canvas, 88.9 x 69.8 (35 x 27½), by Sir Henry Raeburn. Purchased with
             assistance from the National Art-Collections Fund 1947.

HAMILTON, Elizabeth Gunning, Duchess of (later Duchess of Argyll), 1734–90.
             Famous beauty
  PG 814*   Canvas, 67.3 x 55 (26½ x 21⅝), by Gavin Hamilton. Purchased 1913.
  PG 1444*   Canvas, 67.5 x 55.5 (26⅝ x 21⅞), by Gavin Hamilton. Bequeathed by
             Kenneth Sanderson 1944.

HAMILTON, Elizabeth Ivy Percy, Duchess of, b. 1916. *Wife of the 14th Duke of
             Hamilton*
  PG 2723*   (With 14th Duke of Hamilton.) Canvas, 89.8 x 129.8 (35⅜ x 51⅛), by
             Oskar Kokoschka, signed. Painted 1969. Purchased with assistance from the
             National Art-Collections Fund, the National Heritage Memorial Fund and
             the Pilgrim Trust 1987.

HAMILTON, Gavin, 1723–98. *Artist*
  PG 198*   Pencil drawing, 53.1 x 43.1 (20⅞ x 17), self-portrait, 1767, signed. Given by
             the Earl of Stair 1887.
  PG 2472*   Pastel, 61 x 48.7 (24 x 19³⁄₁₆), by Archibald Skirving. Given by Mrs Leila
             Hoskins 1981.

HAMILTON, Gilbert, 1744–1808. *Provost of Glasgow*
  PG 502   Medallion (plaster replica), h. 8.2 (3¼), after James Tassie. Dated 1796.
             Cast from a medallion in possession of R. W. Cochran Patrick 1894.

HAMILTON, Colonel Henry, fl. 1786. *Soldier*
    PG 1264   Paste medallion, h. 8.5 (3⅜), by James Tassie. Dated 1786. Purchased 1935.

HAMILTON, General Sir Ian Standish Monteith, 1853–1947. *Soldier*
    PG 1406*   (As Commander of the 3rd Brigade, Tirah Field Force.) Canvas, 71.8 x 54
        (28¼ x 21¼), by John Singer Sargent, signed. Given by Lady Hamilton
        1941.

HAMILTON, James Hamilton, 2nd Marquess of, 1589–1625. *Statesman*
    PG 1056*   Canvas, 206.4 x 129.5 (81¼ x 51), by unknown artist after Daniel Mytens.
        Bequeathed by Mrs Nisbet Hamilton Ogilvy 1920.

HAMILTON, James Hamilton, 1st Duke of, 1606–49. *Royalist*
    PG 777   Canvas, 216.5 x 132.7 (85¼ x 52¼), by unknown artist after Sir Anthony
        van Dyck. Dated 1640. Purchased 1912.
    PG 1055   Canvas, 65.4 x 47.7 (25¾ x 18¾), by unknown artist after Daniel Mytens.
        Bequeathed by Mrs Nisbet Hamilton Ogilvy 1920.
    PG 2722*   Canvas, 221 x 139.7 (87 x 55), by Daniel Mytens, 1629, signed. Purchased
        with assistance from the National Art-Collections Fund, the National
        Heritage Memorial Fund and the Pilgrim Trust 1987.

HAMILTON, James Douglas, 4th Duke of, 1658–1712. *Statesman*
    PG 840   Canvas, oval 76 x 62.6 (29⅞ x 24¾), by unknown artist after Sir Godfrey
        Kneller. Purchased 1914.
    PGL 12*   Canvas, 239.8 x 158.1 (94⅜ x 58¼), by Sir Godfrey Kneller, signed. Painted
        c. 1715. On loan from the Duke of Hamilton.

HAMILTON, James, 1749–1835. *Physician*
    PG 799   Cut paper silhouette, h. 18.8 (7⅜), by Augustin Edouart. Purchased 1912.
    PG 1070   Canvas, 240 x 148 (94½ x 58¼), by William Dyce. Painted 1832. Given by
        the Governors of Heriot's Hospital to the National Gallery of Scotland in
        1870 and transferred.

HAMILTON, James Hamilton, 5th Duke of, 1703–43. *Lord of the Bedchamber*
            to George II
    PGL 281*   Canvas, 239 x 147.3 (94⅛ x 58), by William Aikman. On loan from the
        Duke of Hamilton.

HAMILTON, Margaret; see BELHAVEN.

HAMILTON, Dr R., 1721–93. *Physician*
    PG 798   Cut paper silhouette, h. 20.5 (8⅛), by Augustin Edouart. Purchased 1912.

HAMILTON, Captain Thomas, 1789–1842. *Soldier and writer*
    PG 2750*   Canvas, 127.4 x 101.9 (50³⁄₁₆ x 40), by Sir John Watson Gordon. Purchased
        1988.

Haddington, 1st Earl of
PG 818

Haddington, 6th Earl of
PG 1610

Haig, 1st Earl
PG 1010

Haldane, Professor John Scott
PGL 269

Haldane, 1st Viscount
PG 877

Haldane, 1st Viscount
PG 1401

Hamilton, 10th Duke of
PG 2062

Hamilton, Elizabeth
PG 1486

Hamilton, Duchess of
PG 814

Hamilton, Duchess of
PG 1444

Hamilton, 14th Duke of, with
Duchess of Hamilton   PG 2723

Hamilton, Gavin
PG 198

Hamilton, Gavin
PG 2472

Hamilton, Sir Ian
PG 1406

Hamilton, 2nd Marquess
of   PG 1056

HAMILTON, William Hamilton, 2nd Duke of, 1616–51. *Soldier*
  PG 859   Canvas, 104.5 x 87.6 (41⅛ x 34½), by unknown artist after Cornelius
            Johnson. Purchased 1916.

HAMILTON, William Douglas, 3rd Duke of, 1634–94. *Statesman*
  PGL 166* Canvas, 128.6 x 103.8 (50⅝ x 40⅞), by Sir Godfrey Kneller. On loan from
            the Duke of Hamilton.

HAMILTON of Bangour, William, 1704–54. *Poet*
  PG 310*   Canvas, 91.6 x 71.2 (36¹/₁₆ x 28), by Gavin Hamilton. Bequeathed by W. F.
            Watson 1886.

HAMILTON, Sir William, 1730–1803. *Diplomat, archaeologist and art patron*
  PG 133*   Paste medallion, h. 7.3 (2⅞), by James Tassie. Dated 1784. Purchased 1885.
  PG 210   Wedgwood medallion, h. 11.1 (4⅜), by Joachim Smith. Given by
            J. Maxtone Graham 1889.
  PG 269   Wedgwood medallion, h. 9 (3½), by Joachim Smith. Given by J. Maxtone
            Graham 1889.
  PG 486   Medallion (plaster replica), h. 9.5 (3¾), after James Tassie. Dated 1784.
            Cast from a medallion in possession of Jeffery Whitehead 1894.
  PG 2611* (*Kenneth Mackenzie, 1st Earl of Seaforth, at home in Naples: concert
            party.*) See GROUPS.

HAMILTON, Professor Sir William, 1788–1856. *Metaphysician*
  PG 717   Canvas, 91.1 x 71.2 (35⅞ x 28), by John Ballantyne. Given by the Royal
            Scottish Academy 1910.
  PGL 43*   Water-colour, 52 x 44.5 (20½ x 17½), by Hope James Stewart, 1845,
            signed. On loan from Mrs J. F. Hope Stewart.

HANDYSIDE, Andrew, fl. 1877. *Civil engineer*
  PG 1862   Charcoal drawing, 47.6 x 39.1 (18¾ x 15⅜), by unknown artist. Bequeathed
            by Miss Dorothy Haverfield 1959.
  PG 1865   Chalk drawing, 41 x 33.3 (16⅛ x 13⅛), by unknown artist. Bequeathed by
            Miss Dorothy Haverfield 1959.

HARCARSE, Sir Roger Hog, Lord, 1635–1700. *Judge*
  PG 2138* Canvas, 76.2 x 63.5 (30 x 25), attributed to John Scougall. Given by Mrs
            Edna M. Hogg 1968.

HARDIE, Charles Martin, 1858–1916. *Artist*
  PG 1745   (In his studio.) Wash drawing, 39 x 50.2 (15⅜ x 19¾), by J. R.
            Abercromby, signed. Drawn 1898. Purchased 1940.
  PG 2460* (*Friendly Critics.*) See GROUPS.

HARDIE, James Keir, 1856–1915. *Labour leader*
  PG 1580* Canvas, 127 x 101.6 (50 x 40), by H. J. Dobson, 1893, signed. Given by
            Emrys Hughes 1952.

Hamilton, 1st Duke of
PG 2722

Hamilton, 4th Duke of
PGL 12

Hamilton, 5th Duke of
PGL 281

Hamilton, Captain Thomas
PG 2750

Hamilton, 3rd Duke of
PGL 166

Hamilton, William
PG 310

Hamilton, Sir William
PG 133

Hamilton, Professor Sir William
PGL 43

Harcarse, Lord
PG 2138

Hardie, James Keir
PG 1580

Hardie, Matthew
PG 1955

Harker, Robert
PG 1900

Harvey, Sir George
PG 277

Harvey, Sir George
PG 848

HARDIE, Matthew, 1755–1826. *Violin maker*
 PG 1955* Panel, 26.7 x 22.9 (10½ x 9), by Sir William Allan. Purchased 1960.

HARE, Hugh, 1668–1707. *Translator*
 PG 2120 Oil on paper, 34.6 x 24 (13¾ x 9½), by unknown artist after Sir Godfrey Kneller. Transferred from the National Gallery of Scotland 1950.

HARE, James, fl. 1804. *Doctor*
 PG 1898 Medallion (plaster replica), h. 7.6 (3), after William Tassie. Dated 1804. Provenance untraced.

HARKER, Robert, fl. 1777.
 PG 1900* Wax medallion, h. 9 (3⅝), by James Tassie, 1777, signed. Provenance untraced.

HARRISON, John, 1693–1776. *Horologist*
 PG 299 Medallion (plaster replica), h. 7.8 (3¹⁄₁₆), after James Tassie. Cast from a medallion in possession of W. G. Patterson 1891.

HART, Jessie Berry, fl. 1934.
 PG 1999 Black chalk drawing, 42.9 x 28.9 (16⅞ x 11⅜), by David Foggie, 1934, signed. Given by Mrs M. Foggie 1962.

HARTMAN, Adam Samuel, fl. 1680. *Divine*
 PG 2096 Ink drawing, 18 x 14.4 (7 x 5⅝), by George Perfect Harding after unknown artist. Transferred from the National Gallery of Scotland 1950.

HARTRICK, Archibald Standish, 1864–1950. *Artist*
 PG 1200 Chalk drawing, 33 x 27 (13 x 10⅝), self-portrait, signed. Given by the artist 1933.

HARVEY, Sir George, 1806–76. *Artist*
 PG 277* (In his studio.) Canvas, 71.4 x 92 (28⅛ x 36¼), by John Ballantyne, signed. Given by William Ford 1889.
 PG 848* Canvas, 71.1 x 61 (28 x 24), by Robert Herdman, 1874, signed. Bequeathed by Miss Ellen Harvey 1915.

HARVIE-BROWN, John Alexander, 1844–1916. *Naturalist*
 PGL 149 Water-colour, 23 x 19.5 (9 x 7¾), by John Pedder, signed. On loan from the Trustees of the British Museum.

HASTINGS, Francis Rawdon-Hastings, 2nd Earl of Moira and 1st Marquess of, 1754–1826. *Soldier and Governor General of India*
 PG 2385 Water-colour (grisaille), 15 x 12.5 (5⅞ x 4¹⁵⁄₁₆), copy by unknown artist. Given by Mrs Gore Browne Henderson to the National Gallery of Scotland 1976 and transferred 1977.
 PGL 39 Water-colour on ivory, 17.3 x 13.4 (6¾ x 5¼), by J. S. Harvie. On loan from the National Museums of Scotland.

HAWTHORNDEN
   PG 2417*   (*The Visit of Queen Victoria and Prince Albert to Hawthornden,
              14 September 1842.*) See GROUPS.

HAY of Smithfield, Sir James, 1652–c. 1683
   PG 2461   b. (Called Sir James Hay of Smithfield.) Pencil, grey ink and wash drawing,
              18.8 x 15.5 (7⅜ x 6⅛), copy by David Allan. Purchased 1980.

HAY, Brigadier-General Lord John, d. 1706. *Soldier*
   PG 2223*   Canvas, 126 x 100.5 (49⅝ x 39⁹⁄₁₆), by Sir John Baptiste de Medina.
              Purchased with assistance from the National Art-Collections Fund 1973.

HAY, Mrs Katherine, fl. 1756.
   PG 1669   Water-colour, 21.7 x 14.1 (8½ x 5½), by John Collie, 1756, signed.
              Bequeathed by W. F. Watson 1886.

HAY, Margaret Chalmers, Mrs Lewis, d. 1843. *Friend and correspondent of Robert Burns*
   PG 317*   Canvas, 33 x 28 (13 x 11), by John Irvine. Bequeathed by W. F. Watson
              1886.

HAY of Edington, Captain William, 1706–60. *Adherent of the Stewarts*
   PG 1565*   Canvas, 62 x 48 (24½ x 18⅞), by Domenico Dupra. Dated 1739. Purchased
              1951.

HAYDN, Joseph, 1732–1809. *Composer*
   PG 1901   Medallion (plaster replica), h. 7.8 (3¹⁄₁₆), after James Tassie. Dated 1792.
              Provenance untraced.

HEATHFIELD, George Augustus Eliott, Baron, 1717–90. *General; defender of Gibraltar*
   PG 2048*   Chalk drawing, 15.8 x 12.9 (6¼ x 5¹⁄₁₆), by Antonio Poggi. Purchased 1964.

HENDERSON, Alexander, c. 1583–1646. *Presbyterian divine and diplomatist*
   PG 862   Canvas, 39.1 x 31.1 (15⅜ x 12¼), copy by unknown artist. Purchased 1917.
   PG 983   Panel, 39.1 x 31.1 (15⅜ x 12¼), by unknown artist. Purchased 1924.
   PG 2227*   Canvas, 127 x 105.4 (50 x 41½), attributed to Sir Anthony Van Dyck.
              Purchased with assistance from the National Art-Collections Fund and the
              Pilgrim Trust 1974.

HENDERSON of Fordell, Sir Francis, d. 1622. *Governor of Namur*
   PG 1603   Canvas, 120.4 x 97 (47⅜ x 38¼), by unknown artist. Dated 1616. On loan
              from the Earl of Buckinghamshire.

HENDERSON, Rev. James, 1797–1874. *Minister of St Enoch's Church, Glasgow*
   PG 1212   (With Rev. James Martin.) Cut paper silhouette, h. 21.2 (8⁵⁄₁₆), by
              Augustin Edouart, signed. Purchased 1933.

HENDERSON of Fordell, Sir James, fl. 1600–16. *Colonel in the French Army*
   PG 1602   Canvas, 120 x 97.2 (47¼ x 38¼), by unknown artist. Dated 1616. On loan from the Earl of Buckinghamshire.

HENDERSON, John, d. 1829. *Collector of coins and medals*
   PG 652   Paste medallion, h. 7.4 (2⅞), by James Tassie. Dated 1787. Purchased 1905.

HENDERSON of Fordell, Sir John, c. 1600–50. *Soldier and traveller*
   PG 1600*   Canvas, 63.5 x 57.8 (25 x 22¾), by George Jamesone. On loan from the Earl of Buckinghamshire.

HENDERSON of Fordell, Sir John, 1752–1817. *Advocate and antiquary*
   PGL 80*   Pencil drawing, 50.8 x 35 (20 x 13¾), by John Brown. On loan from the National Museums of Scotland.

HENDERSON, Joseph Morris, 1863–1936. *Artist*
   PGL 323   Canvas, 76.3 x 63.8 (30 x 25⅛), self-portrait. On loan from P. R. Prenter.

HENDERSON of Fordell, Sir Robert, fl. 1579–1616. *Colonel under Gustavus Adolphus*
   PG 1601*   Canvas, 120 x 97 (47¼ x 38¼), by unknown artist. Dated 1616. On loan from the Earl of Buckinghamshire.

HENDERSON of Fordell, 'Wife' of Sir John; see ARAB PRINCESS.

HENDERSON, William, fl. 1811–30. *Director of the Commercial Bank*
   PG 2153   Cut paper silhouette, h. 20.7 (8⅛), by Augustin Edouart, 1830, signed. Given by Mrs J. H. G. Ross 1969.

HENLEY, William Ernest, 1849–1903. *Poet and essayist*
   PG 838*   Bronze head, h. 55.9 (22) by Auguste Rodin. Modelled 1882. Cast 1914. Purchased from the artist 1914.

HENNIKER, Sir Brydges Trecothick, 1767–1816. *Captain in the 1st Horse-Grenadier Guards*
   PG 1902   Medallion (plaster replica), h. 7.6 (3), after James Tassie. Dated 1788. Provenance untraced.

HENNING, John, 1771–1851. *Sculptor*
   PG 411   Medallion (plaster replica), h. 6.1 (2⁷⁄₁₆), after a self-portrait. Cast from a medallion in possession of Mrs D. Robertson 1889.
   PG 1375*   Canvas, 23.5 x 19.7 (9¼ x 7¾), by Robert Scott Lauder. Purchased 1938.
   PG 1498   Medallion (cement replica), h. 6 (2⅜), after a self-portrait. Given by Dr T. Lauder Thomson 1947.

HENRIETTA MARIA, Queen, 1609–69. *Queen of Charles I*
   PG 952*   Canvas, 247 x 150 (97¼ x 59⅛), by unknown artist after Sir Anthony van Dyck. Purchased 1923.

Hay, Lord John
PG 2223

Hay, Margaret
PG 317

Hay, Captain William
PG 1565

Heathfield, Baron
PG 2048

Henderson, Alexander
PG 2227

Henderson, Sir John
PG 1600

Henderson, Sir John
PGL 80

Henderson, Sir Robert
PG 1601

Henley, William Ernest
PG 838

Henning, John
PG 1375

Henrietta Maria, Queen
PG 952

Henry, George
PG 1984

Henry, Rev. Robert
PGL 37

HENRIETTA MARIA, Queen (*continued*)

PGL 184 (Commemorates the marriage of the King with Henrietta Maria.) Silver medal, dia. 2.3 (⅞), by unknown artist. Dated 1625. On loan from the National Museums of Scotland.

HENRIETTA, Princess; see ORLEANS

HENRY, Prince of Wales; see WALES

HENRY, George, 1858–1943. *Artist*

PG 1984* Canvas, 76.2 x 63.5 (30 x 25), by T. C. Dugdale, signed. Purchased 1961.

HENRY, Rev. Robert, 1718–90. *Historian*

PGL 37* Canvas, 76.5 x 63.5 (30⅛ x 25), by David Martin. On loan from the National Museums of Scotland.

HENSCHEL, Sir George, 1850–1934, *Musician*

PG 1474 Bronze bust, h. 61 (24), by Edward Onslow Ford. Dated 1895. Given by Mrs Helen Claughton 1945.

HERDMAN, Robert, 1829–88. *Artist*

PGL 229* Canvas, 39.4 x 48.2 (15½ x 19), by Robert Duddingstone Herdman, 1886, signed. On loan from the Royal Scottish Academy.

HERSCHEL, Sir Frederick William, 1738–1822. *Astronomer*

PG 511 Medallion (plaster replica), h 5.4 (2⅛), after William Tassie. Cast from a medallion in possession of Mrs Shadford Walker 1894.

HERZFELD, Gertrude, 1890–1981. *Surgeon*

PG 1996* Black chalk drawing, 46.7 x 29.2 (18⅜ x 11½), by David Foggie, 1933, signed. Given by Mrs M. Foggie 1962.

HIGHLAND CHIEFTAIN; see MURRAY, Sir Mungo (PG 997)

HIGHLAND OFFICERS (Black Watch), *c*. 1743.

PG 2302 (Two studies.) Pen and wash drawing, 22.9 x 16.5 (9 x 6½), copy by unknown artist after engraving by G. or J. Van der Gucht. Original drawn 1743. Provenance untraced.

HILL, Amelia Robertson Paton, Mrs D.O., 1820–1904. *Sculptress*

PG 632 Chalk drawing, 39.9 x 28 (15¹¹⁄₁₆ x 11), by Alexander Blaikley, signed. Given by the executors of the artist 1904.

HILL, David Octavius, 1802–70. *Artist and pioneer photographer*

PG 620* Marble bust, h. 81 (31⅞), by Amelia Robertson Hill, 1868, signed. Given by the artist 1904.

PG 969   Marble bust, h. 81.3 (32), by Patric Park. Transferred from the National
          Gallery of Scotland 1924.
PG 1954   Canvas, 76.2 x 63.5 (30 x 25), by John Maclaren Barclay. Given by Norman
          Hill 1960.
PG 2067   Plaster medallion, h. 10.8 (4¼), by Amelia Robertson Hill, signed. Executed
          c. 1851. Given by A. R. Cross 1967.
PG 2182* Wax medallion, h. 10.8 (4¼), by Amelia Robertson Hill, signed. Executed
          c. 1851. Purchased 1970.

HISLOP, Joseph, 1884–1977. *Singer*
PG 2688* Bronze head, h. 32.4 (12¾), by Gloria Loring, 1972. Purchased 1986.

HOBBES, Thomas, 1588–1679. *Philosopher*
PG 188   Canvas, 56.5 x 47.2 (22¼ x 18⅝), attributed to David Beck. Purchased 1887.

HODDER, Charles, 1835–1926. *Artist*
PG 1441   Canvas, 76.5 x 63.8 (30⅛ x 25⅛), self-portrait. Given by Miss A. L. J.
          Hodder 1943.

HODGSON, Rev. Dr John, 1781–1832. *Minister at Blantyre*
PG 1757   a. Water-colour, 17.7 x 12.7 (7 x 5), attributed to James Howe.
          b. Water-colour, h. 8.7 (3⁷⁄₁₆) (trimmed to image), attributed to James
          Howe. Given by the legatees of J. A. Gardiner.

HOGG, James, 1770–1835. *Poet; 'The Ettrick Shepherd'*
PG 825*   (*Sir Walter Scott and his friends at Abbotsford.*) See GROUPS.
PG 1320* Chalk drawing, 56 x 42.8 (22 x 16⅞), by William Bewick. Dated 1824.
          Purchased 1937.
PG 2718* Canvas, 127 x 101.6 (50 x 40), by Sir John Watson Gordon. Painted 1830.
          Purchased 1987.
PGL 15*   Panel, 27.1 x 23.7 (10⅝ x 9⅜), by William Nicholson. Painted c. 1817.
          On loan from Mrs Catriona White.

HOLE, William, 1846–1917. *Artist*
PG 2058* Chalk drawing, 36.2 x 25.7 (14¼ x 10⅛), by James Paterson, 1917, signed.
          Given by Miss Dora Hole 1966.
PG 2131   Pencil drawing, 26.5 x 18.9 (10⅜ x 7½), by Dora Hole. Given by the artist
          1968.

HOLLES, Sir Frescheville, 1641–72. *Sailor*
PG 2080   Wash drawing, 13.8 x 12.8 (5⅝ x 5), copy attributed to Edward Harding
          after Sir Peter Lely. Transferred from the National Gallery of Scotland 1950.

HOME of the Hirsel, Alexander Frederick Douglas-Home, Baron, b. 1903. *Prime Minister*
PG 2736* Canvas, 91.5 x 71.3 (36 x 28), by Avigdor Arikha, 1988, signed. Purchased
          by commission 1988.

HOME of Wedderburn and Paxton, George, d. 1820. *Principal Clerk to the Court of Session*

PG 1266   Paste medallion, h. 7.9 (3³⁄₁₆), by James Tassie. Dated 1791. Purchased 1935.

HOME, Rev. John, 1722–1808. *Historian and author of* Douglas

PG 1209   Water-colour on ivory, 10.2 x 7.6 (4 x 3), by unknown artist. Purchased 1933.

PG 1253*   Paste medallion, h. 7.9 (3⅛), by James Tassie. Dated 1791. Purchased 1935.

PG 1378*   Canvas, 76.2 x 63.5 (30 x 25), by unknown artist. Purchased 1939.

PG 1564   Canvas, 76.2 x 63.5 (30 x 25), by William Millar, 1762, signed. Purchased 1951.

HOME GUARD; see RANKIN, Walter (PG 2719).

HONYMAN, Lady, Family of; see GROUPS (PG 2303).

HONYMAN, Mary McQueen, Lady, d. 1846. *Wife of Lord Armadale*

PG 2303*   See GROUPS.

HONYMAN, Sir Richard Bemptde Johnstone, 2nd Baronet, 1787–1842. *Member of Parliament*

PG 2303*   (As a child.) See GROUPS.

HONYMAN, Lieutenant-Colonel Robert, c. 1782–1809. *Soldier*

PG 2303*   (As a child.) See GROUPS.

HOOD, Samuel Hood, 1st Viscount, 1724–1816. *Admiral*

PG 1195   Paste medallion, h. 9.2 (3⅝), by James Tassie. Purchased 1932.

HOPE, George, 1811–76. *Agriculturist*

PG 1028*   (Cut down on acquisition.) Canvas, 64.8 x 49.5 (25½ x 19½), by Sir George Reid. Given by A. P. Hope and the trustees of A. M. Roberts 1926.

HOPE of Hopetoun, Sir James, 1614–61. *Lawyer*

PG 655*   Canvas, 78.1 x 65.4 (30¾ x 25¾), by unknown artist. Purchased 1907.

HOPE, John, 1794–1858. *Lord Justice-Clerk*

PG 101   Water-colour drawing, 5.4 x 3.8 (2⅛ x 1½), attributed to Benjamin William Crombie. Bequeathed by W. F. Watson 1886.

PG 712*   Canvas, 76.2 x 63.5 (30 x 25), by Colvin Smith. Given by the Royal Scottish Academy 1910.

HOPE, Margaret Murray, Lady. *Wife of Sir John Hope, Lord Craighall*

PGL 95   Canvas, 72.4 x 61.6 (28½ x 24¼), by George Jamesone. On loan from Mrs J. R. B. Lennox and Dr T. S. B. Crawshaw.

Herdman, Robert
PGL 229

Herzfeld, Gertrude
PG 1996

Hill, David Octavius
PG 620

Hill, David Octavius
PG 2182

Hislop, Joseph
PG 2688

Hogg, James
PG 1320

Hogg, James
PG 2718

Hogg, James
PGL 15

Hole, William
PG 2058

Home, Baron
PG 2736

Home, Rev. John
PG 1253

Home, Rev. John
PG 1378

Hope, George
PG 1028

Hope, Sir James
PG 655

Hope, John
PG 712

HOPE, Sir Thomas, d. 1646. *Lord Advocate of Scotland*
> PG 953*   Canvas, 123.2 x 94 (48½ x 37), by George Jamesone. Dated 1627. Purchased
> 1923.
> PG 1526   Pencil and chalk drawing, 37.5 x 31.8 (14¾ x 12½), by the 11th Earl of
> Buchan after George Jamesone. Given by an anonymous donor 1949.

HOPE-SCOTT of Abbotsford, James Robert, 1812–1873. *Parliamentary barrister*
> PG 1467*   Water-colour. 39.1 x 28.9 (15⅜ x 11⅜), by George Richmond. Purchased 1945.

HOPETOUN, Elizabeth Carnegie, Countess of, 1750–93. *Wife of the 3rd Earl of*
> *Hopetoun*
> PG 2779   Paste medallion, h. 7.6 (3), by James Tassie, 1791. Purchased 1989.

HOPETOUN, John Hope, 4th Earl of, 1765–1823. *General*
> PG 1040*   (As Captain-General of the Royal Company of Archers, in *The Entrance of*
> *George IV at Holyroodhouse.*) See GROUPS.
> PG 2680*   (*The Battle of Alexandria, 21 March 1801.*) See GROUPS.

HORNE, General Henry Sinclair, Baron, 1861–1929. *Soldier*
> PG 1011*   (Study for portrait in *General Officers of World War I, 1914–18*, in the
> National Portrait Gallery, London.) Canvas, 56 x 41 (22 x 16⅛), by John
> Singer Sargent. Purchased 1925.

HORNE, Robert Stevenson Horne, Viscount, 1871–1940. *Statesman*
> PG 1548*   Canvas, 91.4 x 71.1 (36 x 28), by Herbert James Gunn, signed. Given by
> Mrs J. Ferguson 1950.

HORNEL, Edward Atkinson, 1864–1933. *Artist*
> PG 2757   Cut paper silhouette, h. 20.2 (7 ⁹⁄₁₀), by James Gunyeon Jeffs. Cut 1932.
> Signed on the mount by the sitter and the artist. Purchased 1989.

HORNER, Francis, 1778–1817. *Political economist*
> PG 253*   Canvas, 76.2 x 63.5 (30 x 25), by Sir Henry Raeburn. Bequeathed by Lady
> Murray to the National Gallery of Scotland and transferred 1889.
> PG 533   Plaster medallion, h. 6 (2⅜), by John Henning. Given by Miss Brown 1894.
> PG 1221*   Marble bust, h. 61 (24), by Sir Francis Legatt Chantrey, 1818, signed. Based
> on a drawing by John Henning *c.* 1802. Bequeathed by Lady Murray to the
> National Gallery of Scotland and transferred 1934.
> PG 1537   Porcelain medallion, h. 5.7 (2¼), by John Henning. Dated 1806. Purchased
> 1949.

HORSMAN, Katie. *Potter*
> PGL 328*   (*Gathering at 7 London Street.*) See GROUPS.

HOUSTON, Sir William, 1766–1842. *Soldier*
> PG 2680*   (*The Battle of Alexandria, 21 March 1801.*) See GROUPS.

HOWARD of Escrick, William Howard, 3rd Baron, *c.* 1630–94. *Member of the Convention Parliament*
    PG 2085   Wash drawing, 19.9 x 15 (7¾ x 5⅞), by George Perfect Harding, signed, after unknown artist. Transferred from the National Gallery of Scotland 1950.

HOWDEN, John Francis Cradock or Caradoc, 1st Baron, 1762–1839. *Soldier*
    PG 2680*   (*The Battle of Alexandria, 21 March 1801.*) See GROUPS.

HOWE, James, 1780–1836. *Animal painter*
    PG 1828   Panel, 26.3 x 21 (10⅜ x 8¼), by Thomas Sword Good. Purchased 1956.
    PG 2171   Pencil drawing, 23.8 x 17.2 (9¾ x 6¹³⁄₁₆), self-portrait. Provenance untraced.

HOWE, Richard Howe, 1st Earl, 1726–99. *Admiral*
    PG 476   Medallion (plaster replica), h. 9.2 (3⅝), after James Tassie. Dated 1798. Cast from a medallion in possession of Jeffery Whitehead 1894.
    PG 477   Medallion (plaster replica), dia. 5.5 (2³⁄₁₆), after James Tassie. Dated 1799. Cast from a medallion in possession of Jeffery Whitehead 1894.
    PG 1950   Wedgwood medallion, h. 7.3 (2⅞), after unknown artist. Provenance untraced.

HOWLEY, William, 1766–1848. *Archbishop of Canterbury*
    PG 1784   Pencil and ink drawing, 34.9 x 25.5 (13¾ x 10¹⁄₁₆), by Samuel Friedrich Diez, 1841, signed. Transferred from the National Gallery of Scotland 1952.

HUGHES, William Morris, 1862–1952. *Prime Minister of Australia*
    PG 1137*   Canvas, 91.5 x 71.1 (36 x 28), by Sir James Guthrie; study for portrait in *Statesmen of the Great War* (National Portrait Gallery, London). Given by W. G. Gardiner and Sir Frederick C. Gardiner 1930.

HUME, David, 1711–76. *Historian and philosopher*
    PG 578   (Doubtful identification.) Tin-plate, oval 16.8 x 12.7 (6⅝ x 5), by unknown artist. Given by Robert Chambers to the National Gallery of Scotland and transferred 1898.
    PG 615   Paste medallion, h. 7.5 (2¹⁵⁄₁₆), by James Tassie. Purchased 1903.
    PG 1057*   Canvas, 76.2 x 63.5 (30 x 25), by Allan Ramsay. Painted 1766. Bequeathed by Mrs Macdonald Hume to the National Gallery of Scotland 1858 and transferred.
    PG 1196   Paste medallion, h. 7.3 (2⅞), by James Tassie. Purchased 1932.
    PG 2238*   Pencil, red chalk, and water-colour drawing, 30 x 17.3 (11¹³⁄₁₆ x 6¹³⁄₁₆), by Louis Carrogis. Purchased 1974.

HUME of Ninewells, John, 1709–86. *Brother of David Hume*
    PG 1382   Canvas, 76.2 x 63.5 (30 x 25), by David Martin. Bequeathed by Miss E. K. H. Scott 1939.

HUME, Joseph, 1777–1855. *Political Economist*
 PG 698*   Canvas, 142.2 x 113 (56 x 44½), by John Graham Gilbert. Purchased 1910.

HUNTER, Rev. Andrew, 1743–1809. *Professor of Divinity in the University of Edinburgh*
 PG 462   Medallion (plaster replica), h. 7.3 (2⅞), after James Tassie. Dated 1791.
            Cast from a medallion in possession of Jeffery Whitehead 1893.

HUNTER, Rev. Dr Henry, 1741–1802. *Divine and author*
 PG 2506   Paste medallion, h. 8 (3³⁄₁₆), by James Tassie. Dated 1795. Purchased 1981.

HUNTER, John, 1728–93. *Surgeon and anatomist*
 PG 263   Paste medallion, h. 7.1 (2¹³⁄₁₆), by James Tassie. Dated 1791. Transferred
            from the National Gallery of Scotland 1889.

HUNTER, John, 1745–1837. *Classical scholar*
 PG 218   Pencil drawing, 50.7 x 36.8 (20 x 14½), by John Brown. Given by James
            Leslie 1888.

HUNTER, Mollie, b. 1922. *Writer*
 PG 2735*   Canvas, 76.5 x 101.6 (30⅛ x 40), by Elizabeth Blackadder, 1988, signed.
            Purchased by commission 1988.
 PG 2758   Pencil drawing, 41.9 x 59.2 (16½ x 23⁵⁄₁₆), by Elizabeth Blackadder, 1987,
            signed. Purchased 1989.

HUNTER, Oswald, d. 1820. *Physician*
 PG 2557   Water-colour on ivory, h. 9 (3½) (sight), by George Sanders. Transferred
            from the National Gallery of Scotland 1982.

HUNTER, William, 1718–83. *Anatomist*
 PG 2647*   Copper medal, dia. 8 (3³⁄₁₆), by Edward Burch, signed. Purchased 1985.

HUNTLY, George Gordon, 1st Marquess of, 1562–1636. *Catholic leader*
 PG 1374   (Previously called 1st Marquess of Huntly.) See MAURICE of
            Orange-Nassau.
 PG 1737   (With his wife Lady Henrietta Stewart.) Pencil and wash drawing,
            21.8 x 25.3 (8½ x 10), by C. K. Sharpe after unknown artist. Given by
            Mrs N. G. Beadnell.

HUNTLY, George Gordon, 2nd Marquess of, d. 1649. *Royalist*
 PG 902   Canvas, 58.3 x 44.5 (23 x 17½), by unknown artist. Purchased 1919.
 PG 2079   Chalk drawing, 29.8 x 25.1 (11⅝ x 10), copy by unknown artist.
            Transferred from the National Gallery of Scotland 1950.

HUTCHESON, Professor Francis, 1694–1746. *Metaphysician*
 PG 297   Plaster medallion (replica), h. 9.2 (3⅝), from a James Tassie cast after Isaac
            Gosset. Dated 1746. Purchased 1890.

Hope, Sir Thomas
PG 953

Hope-Scott, James
PG 1467

Horne, Baron
PG 1011

Horne, Viscount
PG 1548

Horner, Francis
PG 253

Horner, Francis
PG 1221

Hughes, William Morris
PG 1137

Hume, David
PG 1057

Hume, David
PG 2238

Hume, Joseph
PG 698

Hunter, Mollie
PG 2735

Hunter, William
PG 2647

Hutcheson, Professor Francis
PG 699

Hutchison, Isobel Wylie
PG 2005

HUTCHESON, Professor Francis (*continued*)
PG 699*   Bronze medal, dia. 10.5 (4⅛), cast by Antonio Selvi after Isaac Gosset. Dated 1746. Purchased 1910.

HUTCHISON SKETCHBOOKS
PG 2665   Portrait and other sketches by Sir William Oliphant Hutchison. Dated 1952. Given by the executors of Margery, Lady Hutchison 1977.
PG 2666   Portrait and other sketches by Sir William Oliphant Hutchison. Dated 1957. Given by the executors of Margery, Lady Hutchison 1977.
PG 2667   Portrait and other sketches by Sir William Oliphant Hutchison. Dated 1966. Given by the executors of Margery, Lady Hutchison 1977.

HUTCHISON, Rev. Alexander, 1734–1821. *Minister at Hamilton*
PG 1754   Water-colour, 18.8 x 12.4 (7⅜ x 4⅞), attributed to James Howe. Given by the legatees of J. A. Gardiner.

HUTCHISON, Isobel Wylie, b. 1889. *Author and horticulturist*
PG 2005*   Black chalk drawing, 46.7 x 29.5 (18⅜ x 11⅝), by David Foggie, 1935, signed. Given by Mrs M. Foggie 1962.

HUTCHISON, John, 1833–1910. *Sculptor*
PG 1376   Canvas, 22.7 x 17.8 (9 x 7), by George Paul Chalmers. Purchased 1938.

HUTCHISON, Margery Walton, Lady, d. 1977. *Wife of Sir William Oliphant Hutchison*
PG 2670   (With her sons Henry Peter Hutchison and Robert Edward Hutchison.) Four pencil sketches on a single sheet, 38.3 x 56 (15¹⁄₁₆ x 22¹⁄₁₆), by Sir William Oliphant Hutchison. Given by the executors of Margery, Lady Hutchison 1977.

HUTCHISON, Robert Edward, b. 1922. *Keeper of the Scottish National Portrait Gallery 1953–82*
PG 2670   (As a child, with his mother Margery Walton, Lady Hutchison, and his brother Henry Peter Hutchison.) Four pencil sketches on a single sheet, 38.3 x 56 (15¹⁄₁₆ x 22¹⁄₁₆), by Sir William Oliphant Hutchison. Given by the executors of Margery, Lady Hutchison 1977.

HUTCHISON, Robert Gemmell, 1855–1936. *Artist*
PG 2234   Water-colour drawing, 20.2 x 15.2 (7¹⁵⁄₁₆ x 6), by Henry Wright Kerr, 1886, signed. Given by Mrs Ann Laidlaw 1974.

HUTCHISON, Sir William Oliphant, 1889–1970. *Artist*
PG 2379*   Canvas board, 26.4 x 34.6 (10⅜ x 13⅝), by Sir Herbert James Gunn, 1911, signed. Given by the executors of Margery, Lady Hutchison 1977.
PG 2668   Pencil drawing, 38.4 x 28.3 (15⅛ x 11⅛) (irregular), self-portrait. Given by the executors of Margery, Lady Hutchison 1977.
PG 2669   Pencil drawing, 38.4 x 28.3 (15⅛ x 11⅛), self-portrait. Given by the executors of Margery, Lady Hutchison 1977.

Hutchison, Sir William Oliphant
PG 2379

Hutton, James
PG 267

Hutton, James
PG 2686

Hyndford, 3rd Earl of
PG 1556

HUTTON, Dr Isabel Emslie, Lady, d. 1960. *Psychiatrist*

PG 2478   Pastel, 52 x 34.8 (20½ x 13¹¹⁄₁₆) (irregular), by Henry Charles Bevan
Petman, signed. Dated 1946. Bequeathed by Lieutenant-General Sir
Thomas Jacomb Hutton 1981.

PG 2479   Pencil and chalk drawing, 24.5 x 20.2 (9⅝ x 8), by S. Corbian or Corbiau,
signed. Dated indistinctly 194[3]. Bequeathed by Lieutenant-General Sir
Thomas Jacomb Hutton 1981.

HUTTON, James, 1726–97. *Geologist*

PG 115   Wash drawing, 13.3 x 10.8 (5¼ x 4¼), by unknown artist. Bequeathed by
W. F. Watson 1886.

PG 267*   Paste medallion, h. 7.7 (3¹⁄₁₆), by James Tassie. Dated 1792. Transferred
from the National Gallery of Scotland 1889.

PG 2686*   Canvas, 125.1 x 104.8 (49¼ x 41¼), by Sir Henry Raeburn. Painted
c. 1776. Purchased with assistance from the National Art-Collections Fund
and the National Heritage Memorial Fund 1986.

HYNDFORD, John Carmichael, 3rd Earl of, 1701–67. *Diplomat*

PG 1556*   Canvas 140.3 x 113.7 (55¼ x 44¾), by Jonathan Richardson, 1726, signed.
Given by Mrs A. N. S. Carmichael 1950.

I'ANSON, William J., fl. 1899. *Of Malton Curling Club*
  PG 1856* (*Curling at Carsebreck.*) See GROUPS.

INGLIS, Rear-Admiral Charles, c. 1731–91. *Sailor*
  PG 1567* Canvas, 125.7 x 104.1 (49½ x 41), by Sir Henry Raeburn. Painted c. 1783
         and re-touched c. 1795. Bequeathed by Sir John Wauchope 1951.

INGLIS, Dr Elsie Maud, 1864–1917. *Physician and surgeon*
  PG 1825* Bronze bust, h. 66 (26), by Ivan Mestrovic. Modelled and cast 1918. Given
         by the people of Serbia to the National Gallery of Scotland 1918 and
         transferred 1955.

INGLIS, Esther; see KELLO

INGLIS, Rev. John, 1762–1834. *Church leader and Minister at Old Greyfriars, Edinburgh*
  PG 215   Canvas, 76.2 x 63.5 (30 x 25), by unknown artist. Given by John Inglis
         1888.
  PG 832   Cut paper silhouette, h. 22.5 (8⅞), by Augustin Edouart. Purchased 1913.
  PG 2154* Cut paper silhouette, h. 22.5 (8⅞), by Augustin Edouart, 1830, signed.
         Given by Mrs J. H. G. Ross 1969.

INGLIS, William, c. 1712–92. *Surgeon and Captain of the Honourable Company of*
                   Edinburgh Golfers
  PG 1971* Canvas, 129.5 x 105.1 (51 x 41⅜), by David Allan, 1787, signed (on
         reverse). Purchased 1961.

INNES, Alexander, fl. 1756–84. *Admiral*
  PG 494   Medallion (plaster replica), h. 9.4 (3¹¹⁄₁₆), after James Tassie. Purchased
         1894.

INNES, Cosmo, 1798–1874. *Antiquary*
  PG 780   Cut paper silhouette, h. 21.2 (8⅜), by Augustin Edouart. Purchased 1912.

'INNES, George.' *A fictitious 15th-century Cardinal of the Scottish Trinitarian Order*
  PGL 155 Canvas, 104.1 x 84.5 (41 x 33¼), by unknown artist. On loan from the
         National Museums of Scotland.

INNES of Stow, Gilbert, d. 1832. *Depute-Governor of the Bank of Scotland; patron of*
                   Thomas Campbell
  PG 2582 Plaster bust (replica), h. 50.8 (20), after Thomas Campbell. Provenance
         untraced.

IRONSIDE, William Edmund Ironside, 1st Baron, 1880–1959. *Field-Marshal*
  PG 2396 Pencil drawing, 36.7 x 25.4 (14⁷⁄₁₆ x 10), by Sir William Oliphant
         Hutchison. Given by the executors of Margery, Lady Hutchison 1977.

Inglis, Rear-Admiral Charles
PG 1567

Inglis, Dr Elsie
PG 1825

Inglis, Rev. John
PG 2154

Inglis, William
PG 1971

Irving, Rev. Edward
PG 1035

Irwin, Dr John
PG 1598

Jacob, Violet
PG 2381

IRVING, Rev. Edward, 1792–1834. *Founder of the Catholic Apostolic Church*

PG 360   Pencil and ink drawing, 20.7 x 13.4 (8 x 5¼), by James Atkinson. Dated
            1825. Given by the Rev. Canon Atkinson 1889.

PG 820   Canvas, 121.9 x 83.4 (48 x 32¾), by unknown artist. Purchased 1913.

PG 868   Canvas, 39.2 x 31.8 (15⁷⁄₁₆ x 12½), by John Allan. Given by J. Carlyle
            Johnstone 1917.

PG 1035*   Marble bust, h. 68.6 (27), by Hamilton W. MacCarthy, 1867, signed.
            Bequeathed by Miss E. M. Fergusson 1927.

IRVING, Washington, 1783–1859. *Statesman and author*

PG 2340   Canvas, 11.2 x 8.6 (4⁷⁄₁₆ x 3⅜), by unknown artist. Bequeathed by
            W. F. Watson 1886.

IRWIN, Dr John, d. 1759. *Physician to the Stewarts at Rome*

PG 1598*   Canvas, 62.9 x 48.5 (24¾ x 19⅛), by Domenico Dupra, 1739, signed
            (on reverse). Purchased 1953.

JACOB, Violet Kennedy-Erskine, Mrs Arthur, 1863–1946. *Author*
  PG 2381* Chalk drawing, 56.1 x 38.3 (22$\frac{1}{16}$ x 15$\frac{1}{8}$), by unknown artist. Purchased
        1977.

JACQUIN, Nicolaus Joseph von, 1727–1817. *Botanist*
  PG 1874 Medallion (plaster replica), h. 6.2 (2$\frac{1}{2}$), after Leonhard Posch. Original cast
        1792. Provenance untraced.

JAMES I, 1394–1437. *Reigned 1406–37*
  PG 337   Panel, 37.5 x 24.7 (14$\frac{3}{4}$ x 9$\frac{3}{4}$), by unknown artist. Bequeathed by
        W. F. Watson 1886.
  PG 682* Panel, 41.2 x 33 (16$\frac{1}{4}$ x 13), by unknown artist. Purchased 1909.
  PG 1646 Water-colour, 9.1 x 5.9 (3$\frac{5}{8}$ x 2$\frac{1}{4}$), copy by unknown artist. Bequeathed by
        W. F. Watson 1886.
  PG 1650 Water-colour, 35.4 x 23.2 (13$\frac{7}{8}$ x 9$\frac{1}{8}$), copy by unknown artist. Bequeathed
        by W. F. Watson 1886.

JAMES II, 1430–60. *Reigned 1437–60*
  PG 683* Panel, 41.3 x 32.9 (16$\frac{1}{4}$ x 13), by unknown artist. Purchased 1909.
  PG 1618 Pencil and chalk drawing, 39.1 x 29 (15$\frac{3}{8}$ x 11$\frac{3}{8}$), by the 11th Earl of
        Buchan, 1794, signed, after unknown artist. Bequeathed by W. F. Watson
        1886.
  PG 1733 Water-colour, 23.7 x 16.5 (9$\frac{1}{4}$ x 6$\frac{1}{2}$), copy by unknown artist. Purchased
        1932.

JAMES III, 1451–88. *Reigned 1460–88*
  PG 684* Panel, 40.8 x 32.7 (16$\frac{1}{16}$ x 12$\frac{7}{8}$), by unknown artist. Purchased 1909.
  PG 1654 Water-colour, 13.9 x 7.7 (5$\frac{1}{2}$ x 3), by unknown artist after Hugo van der
        Goes. Bequeathed by W. F. Watson 1886.
  PG 1657 Water-colour, 46.1 x 32.1 (18$\frac{1}{8}$ x 12$\frac{5}{8}$), after Hugo van der Goes.
        Bequeathed by W. F. Watson 1886.
  PG 1732 Water-colour, 23.6 x 16.2 (9$\frac{1}{4}$ x 6$\frac{3}{8}$), copy by unknown artist. Purchased
        1932.

JAMES IV, 1473–1513. *Reigned 1488–1513*
  PG 685* Panel, 41.2 x 33 (16$\frac{1}{4}$ x 13), by unknown artist. Purchased 1909.

JAMES V, 1512–42. *Father of Mary, Queen of Scots. Reigned 1513–42*
  PG 338   Panel, 49.5 x 31.1 (19$\frac{1}{2}$ x 12$\frac{1}{4}$), by unknown artist. Bequeathed by
        W. F. Watson 1886.
  PG 361   Panel, 92.7 x 64.2 (36$\frac{1}{2}$ x 25$\frac{1}{4}$), by unknown artist. Purchased 1890.
  PG 686* Panel, 41.3 x 33 (16$\frac{1}{4}$ x 13), by unknown artist. Purchased 1909.
  PG 1038 Canvas, 76.8 x 63.8 (30$\frac{1}{4}$ x 25$\frac{1}{8}$), by unknown artist. Given by
        A. W. Inglis 1927.
  PG 1458 Enamel miniature, 7.6 x 5.8 (3 x 2$\frac{1}{4}$), by William Essex after unknown
        artist. Dated 1847. Bequeathed by Sir St Clair Thomson 1944.

PG 1647   Water-colour, 9.1 x 6 (3⅝ x 2⅜), copy by unknown artist. Bequeathed by
           W. F. Watson 1886.
PG 1651   Water-colour, 45.8 x 30.3 (18 x 11⅞), copy by unknown artist. Bequeathed
           by W. F. Watson 1886.
PG 2077   Water-colour, 13.8 x 11.2 (5⅜ x 4⅜), copy by unknown artist. Transferred
           from the National Gallery of Scotland 1950.

JAMES VI AND I, 1566–1625. *King of Scotland 1567–1625. King of England and Ireland*
           1603–25
PG 156*   Panel, 72.9 x 62.3 (28¹¹⁄₁₆ x 24½), attributed to Adrian Vanson. Dated 1595.
           Purchased 1886.
PG 339   Panel, 45.8 x 31 (18 x 12⅛), by unknown artist. Bequeathed by
           W. F. Watson 1886.
PG 561*   Canvas, 82.9 x 61.9 (32⅜ x 24⅜), by unknown artist. Dated 1604.
           Bequeathed by Sir James Naesmyth 1897.
PG 759   Pewter badge, h. 4.9 (2), after unknown artist. Purchased 1911.
PG 959   (Commemorates the king's coronation) Silver medal, dia. 2.9 (1⅛), by
           unknown artist. Struck 1603. Purchased 1923.
PG 992*   (As a boy.) Panel, 45.7 x 30.6 (18 x 12¹⁄₁₆), by Arnold Bronckorst. Painted
           c. 1580. Purchased 1925.
PG 1109*   Panel, dia. 11.9 (4¹¹⁄₁₆), attributed to Adrian Vanson. Dated 1595.
           Bequeathed by A. W. Inglis 1929.
PG 1648   Water-colour, 9 x 6 (3½ x 2⅜), copy by unknown artist. Bequeathed by
           W. F. Watson 1886.
PG 1652   Water-colour, 44.4 x 32.3 (17½ x 12¾), copy by unknown artist.
           Bequeathed by W. F. Watson 1886.
PG 2172*   Canvas, 109.3 x 83.5 (43 x 32⅞), by Adam de Colone. Bequeathed by Sir
           Theophilus Biddulph 1969.
PGL 17   Panel, 26.8 x 20 (10⅝ x 7⅞), by unknown artist. On loan from the National
           Museums of Scotland.
PGL 153*   Water-colour on vellum, oval 5.2 x 4.3 (2¹⁄₁₆ x 1¹¹⁄₁₆), by Isaac Oliver,
           signed. On loan from the Buchanan Society.

JAMES VII AND II, 1633–1701. *Reigned 1685–88*
PG 96   (With Charles II and Princess Mary.) Canvas, 121.9 x 139.7 (48 x 55), by
           Henry Stone or Simon Stone after Sir Anthony Van Dyck. Purchased 1886.
PG 744   Silver gilt medal, dia. 3.6 (1⁷⁄₁₆), by Norbert Roettier. Dated 1699. Reverse:
           Prince James Francis Edward Stewart. Purchased 1910.
PG 858   (As Duke of York, with Charles I.) Canvas, 103.5 x 140.3 (40¾ x 55¼), by
           unknown artist (perhaps Henry Stone) after Sir Peter Lely. Original painted
           1647. Purchased 1916.
PG 901*   (As Duke of York.) Canvas, 182.5 x 143.3 (71⅞ x 56⅜), by Sir Peter Lely.
           Purchased 1919.
PG 922   (Commemorates the birth of Prince James.) Pewter medal, dia. 6 (2⅜), by
           Jan Smeltzing. Dated 1688. Purchased 1920.

JAMES VII AND II (*continued*)

PG 1321   (Commemorates Louis XIV receiving James after the Revolution.) Copper medal, dia. 4.1 (1⅝), after Sébastien Le Clerc. Dated 1689. Purchased 1937.

PG 2052*   Terracotta bust, h. 99.1 (39), by unknown artist. Bequeathed by Mrs Dora Constantino 1965.

PG 2765   (Execution of the Duke of Monmouth and the 9th Earl of Argyll 1685.) Obverse: James VII and II. Silver medal, dia. 6.2 (2⁷⁄₁₆), by Regnier Arondeaux. Purchased 1989.

JAMESON, John Gordon, 1878–1955. *Advocate*

PG 1804   Black chalk drawing, 46.7 x 29.2 (18⅜ x 11½), by David Foggie, 1933, signed. Given by Mrs M. Foggie 1955.

JAMESON, Robert, 1774–1854. *Mineralogist*

PG 2054   Canvas, 76.2 x 63.5 (30 x 25), by George Watson. Given by Mrs Dickson 1965.

JAMESONE, George, 1589/90–1644. *Portrait painter*

PG 592*   Canvas, 28.9 x 23.2 (11⅜ x 9⅛), self-portrait. Given by the Hon. Hew Dalrymple 1900.

PG 2361*   Canvas, 72 x 87.4 (28⅜ x 34⅜), self-portrait. Purchased 1976.

JAMIESON, Alexander, 1873–1937. *Artist*

PG 1476*   Bronze bust, h. 63.5 (25), by Francis Derwent Wood. Dated 1902. Given by Mrs Wood 1946.

JAMIESON, Rev. John, 1759–1838. *Antiquary and philologist*

PG 10*   Canvas mounted on millboard, 24.1 x 19.9 (9½ x 7⅞), by William Yellowlees. Purchased 1884.

JARDINE, James, 1776–1858. *Engineer*

PG 1203*   Marble bust, h. 73.6 (29), by Patric Park, 1842, signed. Given by Mrs J. F. K. Branford and Mrs A. W. Peck 1933.

PG 1384   Water-colour, 16 x 12.8 (6⁵⁄₁₆ x 5¹⁄₁₆), by unknown artist. Purchased 1939.

JARDINE, Sir William, 1800–74. *Naturalist*

PG 1683   Pencil drawing, 11.8 x 17.6 (4⅝ x 7), by William Home Lizars, signed. Given by Sir William Fettes Douglas 1885.

PG 2192*   Canvas, 75.8 x 63.9 (29⅞ x 25⅛), by unknown artist. Purchased 1971.

JEANS, William, fl. 1769–84. *Sculptor*

PGL 82*   Pencil drawing, 50.5 x 34.4 (19⅞ x 13½), by John Brown. On loan from the National Museums of Scotland.

James I
PG 682

James II
PG 683

James III
PG 684

James IV
PG 685

James V
PG 686

James VI and I
PG 156

James VI and I
PG 561

James VI and I
PG 992

James VI and I
PG 1109

James VI and I
PG 2172

James VI and I
PGL 153

James VII and II
PG 901

James VII and II
PG 2052

Jamesone, George
PG 592

JEFFREY, Francis Jeffrey, Lord, 1773–1850. *Judge and critic*
    PG 229   Plaster bust, h. 71.4 (28½), by Samuel Joseph. Dated 1822. Purchased 1888.
    PG 280   Canvas, 27.7 x 23 (10⅞ x 9¹/₁₆), by John Pairman, 1823, signed. Given by J. M. Gray 1889.
    PG 345   Plaster bust, h. 77.2 (30⅜), by Sir John Steell. Dated 1852. Purchased 1887.
    PG 532   Wax medallion, h. 6.9 (2¾), by John Henning, 1801, signed. Given by Miss Brown 1894.
    PG 569*   Canvas, 91.4 x 72.4 (36 x 28½), by Colvin Smith. Bequeathed by Miss Brown of Waterhaughs 1897.
    PG 608   Plaster bust, h. 77.8 (30⅝), by Patric Park. Given by A. W. Inglis 1903.
    PG 667*   Chalk drawing, 48.6 x 38.7 (19⅛ x 15¼), by William Bewick, signed. Purchased through the Gray Bequest 1908.
    PG 825*   (*Sir Walter Scott and his friends at Abbotsford.*) See GROUPS.
    PG 1539   Porcelain medallion, h. 5.4 (2⅛), by John Henning. Dated 1807. Purchased 1949.
    PG 2043   Chalk drawing, 44.5 x 38.3 (17½ x 15⅛), by John Henning, 1806, signed. Provenance untraced.
    PG 2306   (Crombie Sketchbook, fo. 6v. Study for *Modern Athenians*, Pl. 25.) Pencil and water-colour drawing, 15.6 x 20 (6⅛ x 7⅞), by Benjamin William Crombie.
        (Crombie Sketchbook, fo. 8r. Study for *Modern Athenians*, Pl. 25.) Pencil drawing, 15.6 x 20 (6⅛ x 7⅞), by Benjamin William Crombie. Purchased 1938.

JEFFREY, George, fl. 1773–1808. *Depute Clerk of Session*
    PG 530   Porcelain medallion, h. 7.4 (2¹⁵/₁₆), by John Henning. Dated 1801. Given by Miss Brown 1894.
    PG 1947   Medallion (plaster replica), h. 7.4 (2¹⁵/₁₆), after John Henning. Provenance untraced.

JEFFREY, Rev. Robert, 1786–1844. *Minister of Girthon and Anworth Free Church*
    PG 2547*   Water-colour on ivory, 9.2 x 7 (3⅝ x 2¾), by John Faed, signed. Transferred from the National Gallery of Scotland 1982.

JEWEL, John, 1522–71. *Bishop of Salisbury*
    PG 2088   Water-colour, 11.1 x 8.6 (4⅜ x 3⅜), copy by unknown artist. Transferred from the National Gallery of Scotland 1950.

JOCELYN, Frances Elizabeth Cowper, Viscountess, d. 1880. *Lady of the Bedchamber to Queen Victoria*
    PG 1164   (Study for *The Landing of Queen Victoria at Dumbarton in 1847*, in the collection of Dumbarton District Council.) Water-colour, 63.2 x 41 (24⅞ x 16⅛), by Hope James Stewart. Purchased 1931.

JOHNSTON, Archibald; see WARRISTON

Jamesone, George
PG 2361

Jamieson, Alexander
PG 1476

Jamieson, Rev. John
PG 10

Jardine, James
PG 1203

Jardine, Sir William
PG 2192

Jeans, William
PGL 82

Jeffrey, Lord
PG 569

Jeffrey, Lord
PG 667

Jeffrey, Rev. Robert
PG 2547

Johnston, Arthur
PG 1014

Johnston, Thomas
PG 2056

Johnstone, Commodore George
PG 2523

Johnstone, William Borthwick
PG 2040

Jones, John Paul
PG 669

JOHNSTON, Arthur, c. 1577–1641. *Poet and physician*

PG 329   Canvas, 34.9 x 29.1 (13¾ x 11½), by James Wales after George Jamesone. Bequeathed by W. F. Watson 1886.

PG 1014*   Terracotta bust, h. 59.4 (23⅜), by John Michael Rysbrack, 1739, signed. Purchased 1925.

PG 1630   Pencil and chalk drawing, 30.1 x 28.2 (11⅞ x 11), by the 11th Earl of Buchan, 1794, signed, after George Jamesone. Bequeathed by W. F. Watson 1886.

JOHNSTON, Rev. John, 1780–1833. *Minister at Roxburgh Place Chapel, Edinburgh*

PG 1768   Cut paper silhouette, h. 20.1 (7⅞), by Augustin Edouart, 1831, signed. Given by the Royal Scottish Museum 1947.

JOHNSTON, Thomas, 1881–1965. *Statesman*

PG 2056*   Canvas, 127 x 101.6 (50 x 40), by Sir James Gunn, signed. Bequeathed by the sitter 1965.

JOHNSTON, Rev. Thomas Peter, 1836–1932. *Minister at Carnbee*

PG 1006   Bronze medallion, dia. 12.3 (4⅞), by Charles Matthew. Dated 1886. Bequeathed by Mr and Mrs W. R. Macdonald 1925.

JOHNSTONE, Dorothy; see SUTHERLAND.

JOHNSTONE, Commodore George, 1730–87. *Naval commander and Governor of Western Florida*

PG 2523*   Water-colour on ivory, h. 9.9 (3⅞), by John Bogle, signed. Painted c. 1767/74. Purchased 1982.

JOHNSTONE, George Whitton, 1849–1901. *Artist*

PG 2460*   (*Friendly Critics.*) See GROUPS.

JOHNSTONE, William Borthwick, 1804–68. *Artist*

PG 1682   Wash drawing, 13.9 x 8.9 (5⅛ x 3½), by Thomas Frank Heaphy, signed. Bequeathed by W. F. Watson 1886.

PG 1783   (With Horatio McCulloch.) Ink drawing, 25.2 x 17.5 (9⅞ x 6⅞), by Thomas Frank Heaphy, signed. Transferred from the National Gallery of Scotland 1952.

PG 2040*   Canvas, 49.8 x 60.3 (19⅝ x 23¾), by John Phillip, 1861, signed. Given by Mrs Johnstone to the National Gallery of Scotland in 1868 and transferred 1964.

JONES, John Paul, 1747–92. *Naval adventurer*

PG 669*   Bust (plaster replica), h. 72.1 (28⅜), after Jean Antoine Houdon. Dated 1780. Given by Augustus Biesel 1908.

PG 758   (Capture of the frigate Serapis by Jones.) Copper medal, dia. 5.6 (2¼), by Augustin Dupré. Portrait on obverse after a bust by Jean Antoine Houdon. Dated 1779. Purchased 1911.

PGL 104   Wax medallion, h. 4.6 (1¹³⁄₁₆), attributed to Jean Martin Renaud. On loan
           from the National Museums of Scotland.

JOSEPH II, 1741–90. *Emperor of Austria. Reigned 1765–90*
    PG 935   Electrotype medallion, dia. 8.9 (3½), by unknown artist. Dated 1782.
              Purchased 1922.

JOSEPH II, 1741–90. *Emperor of Austria. Reigned 1765–90*
    PG 2100   (Probably Joseph II.) Chalk drawing, 23.3 x 22.4 (11 x 8⅞), copy by
               unknown artist. Transferred from the National Gallery of Scotland 1950.

JUSTAMOND, John Obadiah, 1737–86. *Surgeon*
    PG 383   Medallion (plaster replica), h. 7.4 (3), after James Tassie. Dated 1786. Cast
              from a medallion in possession of W. G. Patterson 1889.

KAMES, Henry Home, Lord, 1696–1782. *Scottish judge and author*
- PG 822*   Canvas, 126.6 x 101 (49⅞ x 39¾), by David Martin, 1794, signed. Purchased 1913.
- PG 2344   Water-colour, 7.8 x 6.9 (3⅛ x 2¾), by unknown artist after David Martin. Bequeathed by W. F. Watson 1886.

KAY, Arthur, 1860–1939. *Collector and critic*
- PG 2187*   Canvas board, 35.2 x 30.2 (13⅞ x 11⅞), by Sir James Gunn. Painted 1930. Purchased 1970.

KAY, John, 1742–1826. *Caricaturist*
- PG 892*   Canvas, 26 x 20.6 (10¼ x 8⅛), self-portrait. Purchased 1918.

KEATS, John, 1795–1821. *Poet*
- PG 127   Wash drawing, 23.3 x 21.4 (9¼ x 8½), copy by unknown artist after Joseph Severn. Given by John Ritchie Findlay 1885.

KEDERMISTER of Langley, Sir John, 1576–1631.
- PG 2086   Ink drawing, 13 x 10.1 (5⅛ x 4), by George Perfect Harding, 1801, signed, after engraving by Thomas Cecill. Transferred from the National Gallery of Scotland 1950.

KEITH of Ravelston and Dunnottar, Sir Alexander, d. 1832. *Knight Marischal of Scotland*
- PG 1040*   (*The entrance of George IV at Holyroodhouse.*) See GROUPS.

KEITH, George Keith Elphinstone, Viscount, 1746–1823. *Admiral*
- PG 1030   Canvas, 76.2 x 63.5 (30 x 25), by William Stavely after G. L. Saunders. Purchased 1926.

KEITH, George Skene, 1819–1910. *Physician*
- PG 1566   Water-colour and gouache, 29.1 x 23.1 (11½ x 9⅛), by Erskine Nicol, 1892. signed. Given by Mrs Violet C. Keith 1951.

KEITH, Field Marshal James Francis Edward, 1696–1758. *Soldier in Russian and Prussian service*
- PG 813*   Canvas, 142.2 x 110.5 (56 x 43½), by Antoine Pesne. Purchased 1913.

KEITH, Dr Thomas, 1827–95. *Surgeon*
- PG 549   a. Water-colour, 28.9 x 23.8 (11⅜ x 9⅜), by W. Skeoch Cumming, 1893, signed. Based on PG 549b. and a photograph.
- *   b. Water-colour, 29.4 x 24.1 (11⅝ x 9), by W. Skeoch Cumming, 1893, signed. Bequeathed by J. M. Gray 1894.

KELLIE, Thomas Alexander Erskine, 6th Earl of, 1732–81. *Dilettante musician*
- PGL 241*   Canvas, 92 x 71.8 (36¼ x 28¼), by Robert Home. On loan from the Earl of Mar and Kellie.

KELLO, Mrs Esther or Hesther (née Inglis or Langlois), 1571–1624. *Calligrapher and miniaturist*
PGL 18*   Panel, 74.6 x 63.2 (29⅜ x 24⅞), by unknown artist. Dated 1595. On loan from the National Museums of Scotland.

KELVIN, Sir William Thomson, Baron, 1824–1907. *Scientist*
PG 681*   Bronze bust, h. 72.4 (28½), by Archibald McFarlane Shannan. Dated 1896. Purchased 1909.
PG 743*   Pastel drawing, 24 x 19.7 (9⁷⁄₁₆ x 7¾), by Sir William Rothenstein, 1904, signed. Purchased 1910.
PG 884   Charcoal drawing, 55.9 x 34.3 (22 x 13½), by Sir William Quiller Orchardson. Given by R. E. Miller 1917.
PG 926   Canvas, 42.2 x 29.6 (16⅝ x 11⅝), by Elizabeth Thomson King. Given by Miss A. G. King 1921.

KEMP, George Meikle, 1795–1844. *Architect and designer of the Scott Monument*
PG 239*   Plaster bust, h. 75.9 (29⅞), by Alexander Handyside Ritchie. Given by Thomas Bonnar 1888.
PG 246*   Panel, 34.3 x 28 (13½ x 11), by William Bonnar. Given by Thomas Bonnar to the National Gallery of Scotland and transferred 1889.

KENNEDY, David, 1825–86. *Singer*
PG 1581   Canvas, 76.2 x 63.5 (30 x 25), by unknown artist. Given by Mr Kennedy-Fraser 1952.

KENNEDY, Thomas Francis, 1788–1879. *Liberal politician*
PG 1295   Millboard, 35.5 x 30.1 (13¹⁵⁄₁₆ x 11⅞), by Sir George Hayter. Purchased 1936.

KENT, H. R. H. Victoria Mary Louisa, Duchess of, 1786–1861. *Mother of Queen Victoria*
PG 1001*   Water-colour drawing, 43.5 x 30 (17⅛ x 11⅞), by Alfred Edward Chalon, 1838, signed. Purchased 1925.

KENT and STRATHERN, H. R. H. Edward Augustus, Duke of, 1767–1820. *Fourth son of George III and father of Queen Victoria*
PG 241   Marble bust, h. 79.4 (31¼), by Peter Turnerelli, signed. Given by W. G. Patterson 1889.

KEPPEL, Augustus Keppel, Viscount, 1725–86. *Admiral*
PG 414   Medallion (plaster replica), h. 8.3 (3¼), after James Tassie. Cast from a medallion in the British Museum 1892.
PG 505   Medallion (plaster replica), h. 6.6 (2⅝), after James Tassie. Dated 1779. Cast from a medallion in possession of Mrs Shadford Walker 1894.
PG 519   Medallion (plaster replica), h. 5.7 (2¼), after James Tassie. Cast from a medallion in possession of J. M. Gray 1894.

KER, Mark, c. 1511–84. *Abbot of Newbattle*
    PGL 305   (Called Mark Ker.) Panel, 39.2 x 29 (15⁷/₁₆ x 11⁷/₁₆), attributed to Willem
                Key. Dated 1551. On loan from the National Gallery of Scotland.

KERR of Buchtrigg and Calderbank, Captain Charles, 1753–1813. *Soldier*
    PG 2533   Water-colour on ivory, h. 5 (2), by John Bogle, signed. Dated 1802.
                Transferred from the National Gallery of Scotland 1982.

KERR, Rev. John, 1852–1920. *Minister of Dirleton*
    PG 1856*   (*Curling at Carsebreck.*) See GROUPS.

KERSHAW, James, c. 1730–97. *Methodist preacher*
    PG 1905   Medallion (plaster replica), h. 8.2 (3¼), after James Tassie. Dated 1795.
                Provenance untraced.

KILPATRICK, Lieut.-General John; see KIRKPATRICK

KIMMERGHAME, Andrew Hume, Lord, d. 1730. *Judge*
    PG 1554*   Canvas, 76.2 x 63.5 (30 x 25), by John Medina after William Aikman. Dated
                1753. Purchased 1950.

KINEDDER, William Erskine, Lord. 1769–1822. *Judge*
    PG 1100   Water-colour, 27.8 x 22.6 (11 x 8⅞), by William Nicholson. Purchased
                1928.

KING, Sir George, 1840–1909. *Indian botanist*
    PG 748   Bronze medallion, dia. 42.6 (16¾), by Frank Bowcher. Dated 1899.
              Bequeathed by Sir George King 1910.

KING, Jessie Marion; see TAYLOR

KING, Sir Richard, 1730–1806. *Admiral*
    PG 470   Medallion (plaster replica), h. 7.9 (3⅛), after William Tassie. Dated 1804.
              Cast from medallion in possession of R. W. Cochran Patrick 1893.

KINGSTON, Alexander Seton, 1st Viscount 1620–91. *Royalist*
    PGL 336*   (With his father, the 3rd Earl of Winton, and his brother Lord Seton.)
               Canvas, 113 x 83.8 (44½ x 33), by Adam de Colone, 1625. On loan from the
               Kintore Trust 1988.

KINGSTON, Elizabeth Chudleigh, Duchess of; see BRISTOL

KINNOULL, George Hay, 1st Earl of, c. 1572–1634. *Lord High Chancellor of Scotland*
    PGL 189*   Canvas, 215.4 x 134.3 (84¾ x 52⅞), by Daniel Mytens, 1633, signed.
               On loan from the Earl of Kinnoull.

Kames, Lord
PG 822

Kay, Arthur
PG 2187

Kay, John
PG 892

Keith, James
PG 813

Keith, Dr Thomas
PG 549b

Kellie, 6th Earl of
PGL 241

Kello, Esther
PGL 18

Kelvin, Baron
PG 681

Kelvin, Baron
PG 743

Kemp, George Meikle
PG 239

Kemp, George Meikle
PG 246

Kent, Duchess of
PG 1001

Kimmerghame, Lord
PG 1554

Kinnoull, 1st Earl of
PGL 189

Kinross, 1st Baron
PG 1396

KINNOULL, Thomas Hay, 9th Earl of, 1710–87. *Statesman*
> PG 2276   Canvas, 127 x 101.5 (50 x 40), by David Martin. Purchased 1975.

KINROSS, John, 1855–1931. *Architect*
> PG 2694*   Bronze bust, h. 64.2 (25¼), by William Birnie Rhind, 1922, signed. Given
> by John B. Kinross 1986.

KINROSS of Glasclune, John Blair Balfour, 1st Baron, 1837–1905. *Lord President of the
> Court of Session*
> PG 1396*   Canvas, 116.2 x 78.7 (45¾ x 31), by Sir George Reid, signed. Given by Lady
> Kinross 1940.

KINTORE, Algernon Hawkins Thomond Keith-Falconer, 9th Earl of, 1852–1930.
> PG 1856*   (*Curling at Carsebreck.*) See GROUPS.

KINTORE, Mary Erskine, Countess of, 1714–72. *Wife of the 3rd Earl of Kintore*
> PGL 338*   Canvas, 30 x 25 (76.2 x 63.5), by John Alexander. Painted 1731. On loan
> from the Kintore Trust.

KINTORE, William Keith, 4th Earl of, d. 1761.
> PGL 339*   Canvas, 76.2 x 63.5 (30 x 25), by John Alexander. On loan from the Kintore
> Trust.

KIRKPATRICK, Lieut.-General John, d. 1681. *Governor of Bois-le-Duc*
> PG 2061*   Canvas, 154 x 113 (60⅝ x 44½), attributed to Adriaen Hanneman and
> studio. Purchased 1966.

KIRKWALL
> PG 1675   b. (View of Malcolm Laing's tomb in Kirkwall Cathedral.)
> c. (View of Kirkwall.) See LAING, Malcolm.

KITCHENER of Khartoum, Horatio Herbert Kitchener, 1st Earl, 1850–1916.
> *Field-Marshal*
> PG 1466*   (*Some Statesmen of the Great War.*) See GROUPS.

KNOX, John, 1505–72. *Reformer and historian*
> PG 1658   Water-colour, 47.1 x 37.1 (18½ x 14⅝), copy by unknown artist.
> Bequeathed by W. F. Watson 1886.
> PGE 27*   Wood engraving, 13 x 10 (5⅛ x 4⅛), from Theodore Beza's *Icones*, after
> Adrian Vanson. Published 1580. Bequeathed by W. F. Watson 1886.

KNOX, John, *c.* 1555–1623. *Divine*
> PG 1620   Pencil and chalk drawing, 32.2 x 22 (12⅝ x 8⅝), by the 11th Earl of Buchan,
> 1794, signed, after unknown artist. Bequeathed by W. F. Watson 1886.

Kinross, John
PG 2694

Kintore, Countess of
PGL 338

Kintore, 4th Earl of
PGL 339

Kirkpatrick, John
PG 2061

Knox, John
PGE 27

Knox, John
PG 2689

Knox, Dr Robert
PG 831

KNOX, John ('Jack'), b. 1936. *Artist*
  PG 2689*   Canvas, 111.8 x 97.2 (44 x 38¼), self-portrait, signed. Commissioned by
          the Gallery and given by the artist 1986.

KNOX, R., fl. 1899. *Of Alloa Curling Club*
  PG 1856*   (*Curling at Carsebreck*.) See GROUPS.

KNOX, Dr Robert, 1791–1862. *Anatomist*
  PG 831*   Cut paper silhouette, h. 18.6 (7⁵⁄₁₆), by Augustin Edouart. Purchased 1913.

LAIDLAW, William, 1780–1845. *Steward to Sir Walter Scott and writer*
  PG 104   Chalk drawing, 8.5 x 8.3 (3⅜ x 3¼), by Sir William Allan. Given by
             Gourlay Steell 1885.

LAING, David, 1793–1878. *Antiquary*
  PG 349   Plaster bust, h. 67.6 (26⅝), by David Watson Stevenson. Dated 1880.
             Purchased 1887.
  PG 2041* Canvas, 25.5 x 63.5 (14 x 25), by Sir William Fettes Douglas. Painted 1862.
             Transferred from the National Gallery of Scotland 1964.
  PGL 45*   Canvas, 127 x 101.6 (50 x 40), by Robert Herdman, 1874, signed. On loan
             from the National Museums of Scotland.

LAING, Henry, 1741–1820. *Medallist*
  PG 1907   Medallion (plaster replica), h. 6.5 (2⁹⁄₁₆), after William Tassie. Dated 1793.
             Provenance untraced.

LAING, Malcolm, 1762–1818. *Historian*
  PG 1675   a. Wash drawing, 9.7 x 8.1 (3¾ x 3⅛), by unknown artist.
             b. (View of the sitter's tomb in Kirkwall Cathedral.)
             Wash drawing, 13.4 x 18 (5½ x 7¹⁄₁₆), by unknown artist.
             c. (View of Kirkwall.) Wash drawing, 8.8 x 22.5 (3⁷⁄₁₆ x 8⅞), by Samuel
             Laing, 1804, signed. Bequeathed by W. F. Watson 1886.

LAING, Ronald David, 1927–1989. *Psychiatrist*
  PG 2616* Oil on hardboard over acrylic underpainting, 91.4 x 71.1 (36 x 28), by
             Victoria Crowe, signed. Dated 1984. Purchased by commission 1984.

LAING, William, 1764–1832. *Bookseller*
  PG 2149   Cut paper silhouette, h. 20 (7¹⁵⁄₁₆), by Augustin Edouart, 1830, signed.
             Given by Mrs J. H. G. Ross 1969.

LAMBALLE, Marie Thérèse, Princesse de, 1749–92. *Confidante of Marie Antoinette*
  PG 1908   Medallion (plaster replica), h. 8.6 (3⅜), after James Tassie (original
             modelled by John Charles Lochee). Provenance untraced.

LAMOND, Frederic, 1868–1948. *Pianist and composer*
  PG 1504   Bronze bust, h. 56.5 (22¼), by Alexander Proudfoot. Dated 1941.
             Purchased 1948.
  PG 2049   Charcoal drawing, 57.5 x 46.7 (22⅝ x 18⅜), by Howard Somerville, signed.
             Given by Miss Mabel Adamson 1965.
  PG 2493* Chalk drawing, 44.8 x 39.7 (17⅝ x 15⅝), by unknown artist. Dated 1909.
             Purchased 1981.

LANG, Andrew, 1844–1912. *Poet and writer*
  PG 1206* Canvas, 111.8 x 86.3 (44 x 34), by Sir William Blake Richmond. Bequeathed
             by Mrs Andrew Lang 1933.

LANGLOIS, Esther; see KELLO

LAUD, William, 1573–1645. *Archbishop of Canterbury*
    PG 2106   Chalk drawing, 28.8 x 20.7 (11¼ x 8¼), by unknown artist after Sir
                Anthony Van Dyck. Transferred from the National Gallery of Scotland
                1950.

LAUDER, Sir Harry, 1870–1950. *Comedian*
    PG 1552*   Canvas board, 30.3 x 25.2 (11⅞ x 9⅞), by Theodora Roscoe, 1936, signed.
                Given by the artist 1950.
    PG 2202*   Pencil, ink and water-colour (caricature), 29.1 x 30.2 (11⁷⁄₁₆ x 11⅞), by
                Henry Mayo Bateman, 1915, signed. Purchased 1972.

LAUDER, James Eckford, 1811–69. *Artist*
    PG 675   Canvas, 61 x 50.8 (24 x 19⅞), by Robert Innes. Given by Mrs Lauder
                Thomson 1908.
    PG 2027*   Millboard, 45.7 x 35.6 (18 x 14), self-portrait. Given by Mrs Lauder
                Thomson 1963.

LAUDER, Robert Scott, 1803–69. *Artist*
    PG 593   Millboard, 18.7 x 15.3 (7⅜ x 6), self-portrait. Probably painted in the mid
                1820s. Purchased 1900.
    PG 970*   Marble bust, h. 82.5 (32½), by John Hutchison, 1861, signed. Transferred
                from the National Gallery of Scotland 1924.
    PG 1425*   Canvas (oval), 60 x 50.8 (23⅝ x 20), by Thomas Duncan, signed (on
                reverse). Given by James Brown 1942.
    PG 2301   Pencil and chalk drawing, 24.8 x 17.9 (9¾ x 7¹⁄₁₆), self-portrait. Dated 1823.
                Provenance untraced.

LAUDER, Sir Thomas Dick, 1774–1848. *Author; Secretary to the Board of Trustees for
                Manufactures in Scotland*
    PG 226   Plaster bust, h. 65.4 (25¾), by Sir John Steell. Purchased 1888.

LAUDERDALE, James Maitland, 8th Earl of, 1759–1839. *Statesman*
    PG 119*   Pencil drawing, 19.2 x 16.6 (7⁹⁄₁₆ x 6½), by John Henning, signed.
                Bequeathed by W. F. Watson 1886.
    PG 212   Paste medallion, h. 4.4 (1¾), by John Henning. Dated 1806. Given by John
                Ritchie Findlay 1887.
    PG 348   Plaster bust, h. 54.9 (21⅝), by unknown artist after Joseph Nollekens.
                Purchased 1887.
    PG 397   Pencil drawing, 15.8 x 12.4 (6¼ x 4⅞), by John Henning, 1806. Given by
                John Ritchie Findlay 1889.
    PG 756   Canvas, 72.4 x 59.7 (28½ x 23½), by Thomas Phillips, 1806, signed.
                Purchased 1911.
    PG 1364*   Marble bust, h. 54.5 (21⁷⁄₁₆), by Joseph Nollekens, 1803, signed. Purchased
                1938.
    PG 1538   Porcelain medallion, h. 4.6 (1⅞), by John Henning. Dated 1806. Purchased
                1949.

LAUDERDALE, John Maitland, 1st Duke of, 1616–82. *Statesman*
PG 734   Silver medal, dia. 6.2 (2⁷⁄₁₆), by John Roettier. Dated 1672. Purchased 1910.
PG 2128*   Canvas, 124.4 x 101.6 (49 x 40), by Sir Peter Lely. Painted *c.* 1665.
          Purchased 1967.

LAVERY, Sir John, 1856–1941. *Artist*
PG 1436*   Pencil drawing, 50.8 x 38.3 (20 x 15⅛), by James Kerr-Lawson. Purchased 1943.

LAW, Andrew Bonar, 1858–1923. *Statesman*
PG 1127*   Canvas, 91.1 x 71.1 (35⁷⁄₈ x 28), by Sir James Guthrie; study for portrait in
          Statesmen of the Great War (National Portrait Gallery, London). Given by
          W. G. Gardiner and Sir Frederick C. Gardiner 1930.

LAW, David, 1831–1901. *Engraver and etcher*
PG 1440   Paper mounted on canvas, 29.4 x 21.5 (11½ x 8½), by George Paul
          Chalmers, 1878, signed. Given by Ralph Houlder 1943.

LAW, James, fl. 1899. *Of Waverley Curling Club*
PG 1856*   (*Curling at Carsebreck.*) See GROUPS.

LAWSON, Rev. George, 1749–1820. *Theologian*
PG 457   Medallion (plaster replica), h. 8 (3⅛), after James Tassie. Dated 1794. Given
          by J. M. Gray 1893.
PG 1469   Wax medallion, h. 7.6 (3), by James Tassie. Dated 1794. Given by Miss
          Brown Johnstone 1945.

LAWSON, George Anderson, 1832–1904. *Sculptor*
PG 724   Canvas on millboard, 19.4 x 14.6 (7⅝ x 5¾), by James Archer. Given by the
          Royal Scottish Academy 1910.

LEE, Sir James Lockhart, Lord, 1595–1674. *Scottish judge*
PGL 291   Canvas, 76.5 x 64 (30⅛ x 25³⁄₁₆), attributed to Robert Walker. On loan from
          Major S. F. Macdonald Lockhart.

LEE, Professor John, 1779–1859. *Professor of Divinity and Principal of Edinburgh
          University*
PG 781   Cut paper silhouette, h. 16 (6⁵⁄₁₆), by Augustin Edouart. Purchased 1912.
PG 2410   Pencil, chalk and wash drawing, 16.7 x 11.4 (6⁹⁄₁₆ x 4½), by Sir John Watson
          Gordon. Given by Miss Helen W. Thornton 1977.

LEE, R. A., fl. 1894.
PG 2664   Cut paper silhouette, 59.5 x 45.6 (23⁷⁄₁₆ x 17¹⁵⁄₁₆), by unknown artist. Dated
          1894. Provenance untraced.

LEE, Rev. Robert, 1804–68. *Regius Professor of Biblical Criticism*
PG 285*   Canvas, 128.2 x 101.6 (50½ x 40), by James Edgar, 1853, signed. Given by
          Lockhart Thomson 1890.

Laing, David
PG 2041

Laing, David
PGL 45

Laing, Ronald David
PG 2616

Lamond, Frederic
PG 2493

Lang, Andrew
PG 1206

Lauder, Sir Harry
PG 1552

Lauder, Sir Harry
PG 2202

Lauder, James Eckford
PG 2027

Lauder, Robert Scott
PG 970

Lauder, Robert Scott
PG 1425

Lauderdale, 8th Earl of
PG 119

Lauderdale, 8th Earl of
PG 1364

Lauderdale, 1st Duke of
PG 2128

LEES, James, fl. 1798. *Soldier*
>   PG 450   Medallion (plaster replica), h. 8.6 (3⅜), after James Tassie. Dated 1798. Given by the South Kensington Museum 1893.

LEFEVRE, Sir John Shaw, 1797–1879. *Clerk of the Parliaments*
>   PG 732   Canvas, 127 x 107.8 (50 x 40), by Sir John Watson Gordon. Given by the Royal Scottish Academy 1910.

LEITCH, William Leighton, 1804–83. *Water-colour painter*
>   PG 650   Chalk drawing, 45.9 x 36.2 (18⅛ x 14¼), by E. F. Bridell-Fox, 1861, signed. Purchased 1906.

LEITH, Sir James, 1763–1816. *Governor of the Leeward Islands*
>   PG 122   Pencil, chalk and water-colour drawing, 22.2 x 17.6 (8¾ x 6⅞), by Benjamin Burrell, signed. Bequeathed by W. F. Watson 1886.

LENNOX, Esme Stewart, 1st Duke of, c. 1542–83. *Favourite of James VI and I*
>   PG 1624   Pencil and chalk drawing, 34.5 x 26.7 (13½ x 10½), by the 11th Earl of Buchan, signed, after unknown artist. Bequeathed by W. F. Watson 1886.
>   PG 2213   Panel, 56.8 x 47.2 (22⅜ x 18⁹⁄₁₆), by unknown artist. Dated 1590. Bequeathed by 13th Baron Elibank 1973.

LENNOX, James Stuart, 4th Duke of (later 1st Duke of Richmond), 1612–55. *Royalist*
>   PG 1420   Panel, 39.3 x 31 (15½ x 12³⁄₁₆), by unknown artist after Sir Anthony Van Dyck. Purchased 1941.

LENNOX, Ludovic Stuart, 2nd Duke of, 1574–1624. *Statesman*
>   PG 864*   Canvas, 68.9 x 63.8 (27⅛ x 25⅛), by unknown artist. Dated 1623. Purchased 1916.

LENNOX, Lady Margaret Douglas, Countess of, 1515–78. *Mother of Lord Darnley*
>   PG 1088   Bust (plaster cast of tomb effigy in Westminster Abbey), h. 51.4 (20¼), after unknown artist. Purchased 1928.

LESLIE, Lieutenant-General Alexander, 1731–94. *Soldier*
>   PG 2442   Paste medallion, h. 7.5 (2¹⁵⁄₁₆), by James Tassie. Bequeathed by William Tassie to the National Gallery of Scotland 1860 and transferred 1979.

LESLIE, Ann, fl. 1806. *Step-daughter of Sir Henry Raeburn*
>   PG 1246*   Pencil drawing, 23.2 x 19.1 (9⅛ x 7½), by unknown artist. Bequeathed by Miss Alice Leslie Inglis 1934.

LESLIE, Charles ('Mussel Mou'd Charlie'), c. 1677–1782. *Jacobite ballad-singer*
>   PG 2624   Canvas, 55.3 x 43.6 (21³⁄₁₆ x 17³⁄₁₆), by James Wales. Provenance untraced.

Lavery, Sir John
PG 1436

Law, Andrew Bonar
PG 1127

Lee, Rev. Professor Robert
PG 285

Lennox, 2nd Duke of
PG 864

Leslie, Ann
PG 1246

Leslie, Professor Sir John
PG 291

Leslie, Professor Sir John
PG 660

Leven, 1st Earl of
PG 1411

Leven, 3rd Earl of
PG 1528

Liebenthal, Tertia
PG 2184

Lindsay, Sir Patrick
PG 1

Liston, Robert
PG 920

Liston, Sir Robert
PG 1313

Little, William Charles
PG L 85

Littlejohn, Sir Henry Duncan
PG 1042

LESLIE, Lady Helen, d. 1594. *Wife of Mark Ker of Newbattle*
  PGL 306 (Called Lady Helen Leslie.) Panel, 39.4 x 28.9 (15½ x 11⅜), attributed to Willem Key, 1551, signed (on reverse). On loan from the National Gallery of Scotland.

LESLIE, John, 1527–96. *Bishop of Ross*
  PG 943 Canvas, 66.7 x 56.5 (26¼ x 22¼), by unknown artist. Purchased 1922.
  PG 1626 Pencil drawing, 47.4 x 36 (18⅝ x 14¼), by the 11th Earl of Buchan after unknown artist. Bequeathed by W. F. Watson 1886.

LESLIE, Professor Sir John, 1766–1832. *Natural philosopher*
  PG 291* Marble bust, h. 54 (21¼), by John Rhind after Samuel Joseph. Given by the representatives of James Leslie 1890.
  PG 660* Chalk drawing, 44.6 x 38.2 (17½ x 15), by John Henning. Purchased 1907.

LESLIE, Lady Margaret, 1621–88. *Wife of the 2nd Earl of Wemyss*
  PG 2456 (As a child, with her mother, the Countess of Rothes, and her sister, Lady Mary Leslie.) Canvas, 219.4 x 135.3 (86⅜ x 53¼), by George Jamesone, signed. Dated 1626. Purchased 1980.

LESLIE, Lady Mary, b. 1620. *Wife of 7th Earl of Eglinton*
  PG 2456 (As a child, with her mother, the Countess of Rothes, and her sister, Lady Margaret Leslie.) Canvas, 219.4 x 135.3 (86⅜ x 53¼), by George Jamesone, signed. Dated 1626. Purchased 1980.

LETHIEULLIER, Catherine, b. 1587. *Wife of Jacob Desbouverie of Hilleghorn*
  PG 2089 Ink drawing, 15.6 x 11.7 (6⅛ x 4⅝), copy by unknown artist. Transferred from the National Gallery of Scotland 1950.

LEVEN, Alexander Leslie, 1st Earl of, c. 1580–1661. *Soldier*
  PG 1411* Canvas, 69.1 x 59.6 (27³⁄₁₆ x 23½), attributed to George Jamesone. Bequeathed by the Marquess of Lothian 1941.

LEVEN, David Melville, 3rd Earl of, and 2nd Earl of Melville, 1660–1728. *Statesman and soldier*
  PG 1528* Canvas, 127 x 101.7 (50 x 40), by Sir John Baptiste de Medina, 1691, signed. Purchased 1949.

LEYDEN, John, 1775–1811. *Physician and poet*
  PG 1686 Ink drawing, 10.2 x 7.7 (4 x 3), by unknown artist. Bequeathed by W. F. Watson 1886.

LIEBENTHAL, Tertia, 1889–1970. *Concert organiser and musician*
  PG 2184* Bronze bust, h. 45 (17¾), after Diona Murray. Dated 1962. Cast from a plaster bust in possession of Miss I. Dunlop 1970.

LIEVEN, Dorothea Christopherovna von Benckendorff, Princess, 1784–1857.
  PG 2525   Water-colour on ivory, 6.8 (2¹¹⁄₁₆), by Andrew Robertson, signed. Dated
            1806. Transferred from the National Gallery of Scotland 1982.

LINDSAY, Lady Anne, 1750–1825. *Author*
  PG 1674   Wash drawing, 11 x 7.6 (4⅜ x 3), by unknown artist. Bequeathed by W. F.
            Watson 1886.

LINDSAY, Rear-Admiral Sir John, 1737–88. *Sailor*
  PG 440   Medallion (plaster replica), 9.2 (3⅝), after James Tassie. Original modelled
            1779. Given by the South Kensington Museum 1893.

LINDSAY, Major-General Sir Patrick, 1778–1839. *Soldier*
  PG 1*   Canvas, 76.2 x 63.5 (30 x 25), by Sir John Watson Gordon. Given by the
            Rev. H. B. Sands 1884.

LINLITHGOW, John Hope, 1st Marquess of, 1860–1908. *Statesman and Governor
            of Australia*
  PG 614   (Probably the artist's plaster.) Plaster bust, h. 74.2 (29½), by David Watson
            Stevenson, signed. Purchased 1903.
  PG 1856* (*Curling at Carsebreck.*) See GROUPS.

LINNAEUS, Sir Charles, 1707–78. *Naturalist*
  PG 1909   Medallion (plaster replica), h. 6.2 (2⁷⁄₁₆), after James Tassie. Provenance
            untraced.

LISTON, Robert, 1794–1847. *Surgeon*
  PG 920*   Silvered glass medal, dia. 4.3 (1¹¹⁄₁₆), by Leonard Charles Wyon. Purchased
            1920.

LISTON, Sir Robert, 1742–1836. *Diplomat*
  PG 1313* Panel, 30.5 x 25.4 (12 x 10), by Sir David Wilkie, 1811, signed. Purchased
            1937.

LITTLE of Liberton, William Charles, fl. c. 1780. *Advocate and antiquary*
  PGL 85*   Pencil drawing, 51 x 35.1 (20⅛ x 13¹³⁄₁₆), by John Brown. On loan from the
            National Museums of Scotland.

LITTLEJOHN, Sir Henry Duncan, 1828–1914. *President of the Royal College of
            Surgeons, Edinburgh*
  PG 1042* Canvas, 102.2 x 76.2 (40¼ x 30), by Sir George Reid, signed. Bequeathed by
            Professor Harvey Littlejohn 1927.

LIVINGSTON, Rev. Archibald, 1776–1852. *Minister of Cambusnethan*
  PG 1755   Water-colour, 19.8 x 13.5 (7¾ x 5⅜), attributed to James Howe. Given by
            the legatees of J. A. Gardiner.

LIVINGSTONE, David, 1813–73. *Missionary and explorer*
PG 844   Plaster statuette, h. 64.8 (25½), by Amelia Robertson Hill. Dated 1868. Purchased 1915.
PG 1500*   Chalk drawing, 39.7 x 30.3 (15⅝ x 11¹⁵⁄₁₆), by Edward Grimston, 1857, signed. Purchased 1947.

LIZARS, William Home, 1788–1859. *Artist*
PG 2175   Chalk drawing, 43 x 35.7 (16¹⁵⁄₁₆ x 14¹⁄₁₆), self-portrait. Given by R. K. Sanderson 1970.

LLOYD-GEORGE of Dwyfor, David Lloyd George, 1st Earl, 1863–1945. *Statesman*
PG 1126*   Canvas, 101.6 x 76.2 (40 x 30), by Sir James Guthrie; study for portrait in *Statesmen of the Great War* (National Portrait Gallery, London). Given by W. G. Gardiner and Sir Frederick C. Gardiner 1930.
PG 1466*   (*Some Statesmen of the Great War.*) See GROUPS.

LOCK, Mabel, fl. *c.* 1930.
PG 1995   Black chalk drawing, 45.4 x 28.6 (17⅞ x 11¼), by David Foggie, 1927, signed. Given by Mrs M. Foggie 1962.

LOCKHART, Charlotte Sophia Scott, Mrs John Gibson, 1799–1837. *Daughter of Sir Walter Scott*
PG 1297*   Water-colour on ivory, 10.5 x 8.2 (4⅛ x 3¼), by Robert Thorburn. Bequeathed by Edward Thorburn 1936.
PG 1303*   (*The Abbotsford Family.*) See GROUPS.
PG 2672*   (With her husband John Gibson Lockhart.) Canvas, 76.8 x 64.8 (30¼ x 25½), by Robert Scott Lauder. Posthumous likeness, painted after 1838. Purchased 1985.

LOCKHART of Carnwath, George, 1673–1731. *Jacobite*
PGL 293   Canvas, 126.8 x 103 (49⅞ x 40½), by Sir John Baptiste de Medina. Dated 1707. On loan from Major S. F. Macdonald Lockhart.

LOCKHART, Sir George, *c.* 1630–89. *Lord President of the Court of Session*
PGL 23   Canvas, 76.2 x 64.5 (30 x 25⅜), by unknown artist. On loan from the National Museums of Scotland.
PGL 292   Canvas, oval 76.2 x 64 (30 x 25⅛), attributed to Sir John Baptiste de Medina. On loan from Major S. F. Macdonald Lockhart.

LOCKHART, Rev. Dr John, 1761–1842. *Minister of the College Church, Glasgow*
PG 1751   Water-colour, 17.7 x 14.6 (7 x 5¾), attributed to James Howe. Given by the legatees of J. A. Gardiner.

LOCKHART, John Gibson, 1794–1854. *Son-in-law and biographer of Scott*
PG 825*   (*Sir Walter Scott and his friends at Abbotsford.*) See GROUPS.
PG 1588*   Canvas, 32.3 x 25.4 (12¾ x 10), by Sir Francis Grant. Purchased 1952.

Livingstone, David
PG 1500

Lloyd-George, 1st Earl
PG 1126

Lockhart, Charlotte Sophia
PG 1297

Lockhart, John Gibson, with
Charlotte Sophia Lockhart   PG 2672

Lockhart, John Gibson
PG 1588

Lockhart, Sir William
PG 941

Lockhart, William Ewart
PG 2743

Logan, Rev. John
PG 154

Lorimer, James
PG 1347

Lorimer, Sir Robert Stodart
PG 1353

Lothian, Marchioness of
PG 1415

Lothian, 1st Marquess of
PG 1410

Lothian, 1st Marquess of
PG 1414

Lothian, 1st Marquess of
PGL 211

Lothian, 4th Marquess of
PG 1436

LOCKHART, John Gibson (*continued*)

PG 1821   Pencil and chalk drawing, 19.5 x 15.8 (7¾ x 6¼), by Sir John Watson
Gordon. Given by Mrs Gore-Browne Henderson 1955.

PG 2672*   (With his wife Charlotte Sophia Scott.) Canvas, 76.8 x 64.8 (30¼ x 25½),
by Robert Scott Lauder. Painted after 1838. Purchased 1985.

PG 2711   Cut paper silhouette, h. 15.7 (6³⁄₁₆), by Augustin Edouart, 1830, signed.
Purchased 1986.

PG 2749   Canvas, 104.8 x 79.7 (41¼ x 31⅜), by Robert Scott Lauder. Painted 1841/2.
Purchased 1988.

LOCKHART of Lee, Sir William, 1621–76. *Soldier and diplomat*

PG 941*   Canvas, 76.5 x 63.5 (30⅛ x 25), by unknown artist. Purchased 1922.

PGL 290   Canvas, oval 76.2 x 63.5 (30 x 25), by unknown artist. On loan from Major
S. F. Macdonald Lockhart.

LOCKHART, William Ewart, 1846–1900. *Artist*

PG 723   Millboard, 19.4 x 14.7 (7⅝ x 5⅞), by James Archer. Given by the Royal
Scottish Academy 1910.

PG 2743*   Pencil and wash drawing, 34.5 x 28.2 (13⅝ x 11⅛), by Walker Hodgson,
1891, signed. Purchased 1988.

LODDER, Charles, fl. 1899. *Of Largs Curling Club*

PG 1856*   (*Curling at Carsebreck.*) See GROUPS.

LOGAN, Rev. George, 1759–1843. *Minister at Eastwood*

PG 1753   Water-colour, 9.9 x 7.1 (3⅞ x 2¾), attributed to James Howe. Given by the
legatees of J. A. Gardiner.

LOGAN, Rev. John, 1748–88. *Poet*

PG 154*   Pencil drawing, 54.8 x 41.6 (21⁹⁄₁₆ x 16⅜), by John Brown. Purchased 1886.

LOGAN, William, fl. 1899. *Of Lochwinnoch Garthland Curling Club*

PG 1856*   (*Curling at Carsebreck.*) See GROUPS.

LONSDALE, Henry Lowther, 3rd Viscount, 1694–1751. *Lord Lieutenant of Cumberland
and Westmorland*

PG 2109   Water-colour, 14.6 x 10.9 (5¾ x 4¼), copy by unknown artist. Transferred
from the National Gallery of Scotland 1950.

LORIMER, James, 1818–90. *Jurist and political philosopher*

PG 1347*   Canvas, 128 x 102.2 (50⅜ x 40¼), by John Henry Lorimer, 1890, signed.
Bequeathed by the artist 1937.

LORIMER, Sir Robert Stodart, 1864–1929. *Architect*

PG 1353*   Canvas, 25.4 x 35.5 (10 x 14), by John Henry Lorimer, 1886, signed. Given
by the Royal Institute of British Architects 1938.

LOTHIAN, Lady Jean Campbell, Marchioness of, d. 1700. *Wife of the 1st Marquess of Lothian*
   PG 1415* Panel, 21.6 x 17.4 (8½ x 6⅞), by unknown artist. Dated 1654. Bequeathed by the Marquess of Lothian 1941.

LOTHIAN, Robert Kerr, 1st Marquess of, 1636–1703. *Statesman*
   PG 1410* Canvas, 74.9 x 63.5 (29½ x 25), by Simon Verelst, signed. Bequeathed by the Marquess of Lothian 1941.
   PG 1414* Panel, 22.5 x 18.1 (8⅞ x 7⅛), by unknown artist, 1654. Bequeathed by the Marquess of Lothian 1941.
   PGL 211* Canvas, 73.7 x 63.5 (29 x 25), attributed to David Scougall. On loan from the Marquess of Lothian.

LOTHIAN, Schomberg Henry Kerr, 9th Marquess of Lothian, 1833–1900. *Diplomat*
   PG 1714 Pencil drawing, 37.5 x 33.7 (14¾ x 13¼), by W. Graham Boss. Given by the artist.

LOTHIAN, William Henry Kerr, 4th Marquess of, 1710–75. *General*
   PG 1426* Canvas, 50.7 x 40.7 (20 x 16), by David Morier. Purchased 1942.

LOUDOUN, Field-Marshal Gideon Ernest, 1716–90. *Soldier in Austrian service*
   PG 934 Electrotype medallion, dia. 9 (3½), by unknown artist. Purchased 1922.

LOUDOUN, John Campbell, 4th Earl of, 1705–82. *Soldier*
   PG 2190* Canvas, 76.8 x 64 (30¼ x 25³⁄₁₆), by Allan Ramsay. Purchased 1971.

LOUIS XIV, 1638–1715. *King of France*
   PG 1321 (Commemorates Louis XIV receiving James VII and II after the Revolution.) Copper medal, dia. 4.1 (1⅝), by Jean Mauger. Dated 1689. Purchased 1937.

LOUIS XVI, 1754–93. *King of France*
   PG 1910 Medallion (plaster replica), h. 6.7 (2⅝), after James Tassie. Provenance untraced.

LOUIS XVIII, 1755–1824. *King of France*
   PG 493 Medallion (plaster replica), h. 7.5 (2¹⁵⁄₁₆), after James Tassie. Original modelled by Raymond Gayrard 1814. Cast from a medallion in possession of Jeffery Whitehead 1894.

LOUISE Caroline Alberta, Princess, 1848–1939. *Duchess of Argyll*
   PG 1738 Pencil drawing, 13.2 x 9.2 (5¼ x 3⅝), by Louis Béroud, signed. Given by John Grant 1941.

LOW, William, fl. *c.* 1790. *Portrait painter*
   PGL 226 Water-colour on ivory, 5.7 x 4.5 (2¼ x 1¾), by John Kay. On loan from the National Museums of Scotland.

LUCY, Mrs, fl. *c.* 1800.
  PG 2015   Pencil drawing, 10.9 x 8.1 (4¼ x 3¼), by unknown artist. Given by
             E. Kersley 1962.

LUDLOW, George James Ludlow, 3rd and last Earl, 1758–1842. *General*
  PG 2684   c. (Study probably related to *The Landing of British Troops at Aboukir.*)
             Water-colour, 10.8 x 8.5 (4¼ x 3⅜), attributed to Philip James de
             Loutherbourg. Purchased 1986.
  PG 2681*   (*The Landing of British Troops at Aboukir, 8 March 1801.*) See GROUPS.

LUMISDEN, Andrew, 1720–1801. *Secretary to Prince Charles Edward Stewart*
  PG 135*   Paste medallion, h. 6.7 (2⅝), by James Tassie. Dated 1784. Purchased 1886.
  PG 1586   Paste medallion, h. 6.7 (2⅝), by James Tassie. Dated 1784. Purchased 1952.

LUMSDEN, Christina. *Daughter of Hugh Lumsden, 1783–1859, Sheriff of Sutherland*
  PG 1871   Cut paper silhouette, h. 21.3 (8⅜), by Augustin Edouart. Dated 1831.
             Given by Miss W. A. Willis 1960.

LUMSDEN, Ernest Stephen, 1883–1943. *Painter and etcher*
  PG 2454*   Pencil drawing, 28.5 x 21.8 (11¼ x 8⁹⁄₁₆), by Edgar Holloway, signed. Dated
             1938. Purchased 1980.

LUMSDEN, General Sir James, *c.* 1598–*c.* 1660. *Soldier*
  PGL 275*   Canvas, 127.3 x 102 (50⅛ x 40⅛), by unknown artist. On loan from Miss
             Sandys-Lumsdaine.

LUSK, Sir Andrew, 1st Baronet, 1810–1909. *Businessman and Lord Mayor of London*
  PG 2761*   Canvas, 83.5 x 65.7 (32⅞ x 25⅞), by Thomas McKinlay, 1862. Given by
             Rev. John Lusk 1989.

LYALL, C. A., fl. *c.* 1930. *Well-known Edinburgh character*
  PG 2271   Pencil and crayon drawing, 20.3 x 12.3 (8 x 4⅞), by J. Nisbet. Provenance
             untraced.

LYNEDOCH of Balgowan, Thomas Graham, 1st Baron, 1748–1843. *General*
  PG 2432*   Canvas, 91.4 x 71.6 (36 x 27³⁄₁₆), by Sir George Hayter, 1822, signed.
             Purchased 1979.
  PG 2728   (Capture of St Sebastian 1813). Copper medal, dia. 4.1 (1⅝), by Thomas
             Webb and George Mills after Peter Rouw junior. Struck 1820. Purchased
             1987.

Loudoun, 4th Earl of
PG 2190

Lumisden, Andrew
PG 135

Lumsden, Ernest Stephen
PG 2454

Lumsden, Sir James
PGL 275

Lusk, Sir Andrew
PG 2761

Lynedoch, 1st Baron
PG 2432

McADAM, John Loudoun, 1756–1836. *Road engineer*
  PG 823*   Cut paper silhouette, h. 26.9 (10⅝), by Augustin Edouart. Cut 1827.
             Purchased 1913.

MACALISTER, Major Matthew, fl. 1794–97. *Major in the Glengarry Fencibles*
  PG 1960   Paste medallion, h. 8.3 (3³⁄₁₆), by James Tassie. Dated 1796. Transferred
             from the National Gallery of Scotland 1960.

MACARTHUR, Lieut-Colonel Archibald, fl. 1781–90. *Soldier*
  PG 1912   Medallion (plaster replica), h. 9 (3⁹⁄₁₆), after James Tassie. Dated 1790.
             Provenance untraced.

McARTHUR, John, 1755–1840. *Writer on naval topics*
  PG 1584*   Canvas, 76.2 x 63.5 (30 x 25), by George Romney. Painted 1795. Purchased
             1951.

MACARTNEY, Alexander, d. 1838. *Manager of the Commercial Bank*
  PG 2156   Cut paper silhouette, h. 15.2 (6), by Augustin Edouart, 1830, signed. Given
             by Mrs J. H. G. Ross 1969.

MACAULAY, Thomas Babington, 1st Baron, 1800–59. *Historian and statesman*
  PG 559   a. Plaster plaque, dia. 25 (9¾) by Baron Carlo Marochetti, signed with
             initials. Dated 1848. Given by James L. Caw 1896.
             b. Bronze plaque, dia. 25 (9¾), after Baron Carlo Marochetti. Presumably
             cast from PG 599a. at an unknown date between 1909 and 1951. Provenance
             untraced.
             c. Plaster intaglio, dia. 25 (9¾), after Baron Carlo Marochetti. Presumably
             used for casting PG 559b. Provenance untraced.
  PG 1585*   Canvas, 44.5 x 34.9 (17½ x 13¾), by Sir John Watson Gordon, 1850,
             signed. Purchased 1951.

McBRIDE, James A., fl. 1933. *Chairman of the Scottish Artists Benevolent Fund*
  PG 1820   Black chalk drawing, 45.7 x 28 (18 x 11), by David Foggie, 1933, signed.
             Given by Mrs M. Foggie 1955.

MacBRYDE, Robert, 1913–66. *Artist*
  PG 2221*   Pen and sepia drawing, 28.5 x 22.5 (11¼ x 8⅞), by Robert Colquhoun,
             1939, signed. Given by an anonymous donor 1973.
  PG 2487*   (With Robert Colquhoun.) Pencil and chalk drawing, 26.2 x 38.9
             (10³⁄₁₆ x 15⁵⁄₁₆), by John Laurie. Dated 1939. Purchased 1981.

MacCAIG, Norman, b. 1910. *Poet*
  PG 2231*   Panel, 121.8 x 91.4 (48 x 36), by Alexander Moffat, signed. Painted 1968.
             Purchased 1973.
  PG 2597*   (*Poets' Pub.*) See GROUPS.

McAdam, John
Loudoun   PG 823

McArthur, John
PG 1584

Macaulay, 1st Baron
PG 1585

MacBryde, Robert
PG 2221

MacCaig, Norman
PG 2231

MacCallum, George
PG 1029

McCance, William
PG 2429

MacColl, Dugald Sutherland
PG 1151

McCulloch, Horatio
PG 233

McCulloch, Horatio
PG 356

McDiarmid, John
PG 2200

Macdonald, Sir Alexander,
with Sir James Macdonald
PG 2127

Macdonald, Sir Alexander
PG 2609

Macdonald, Flora
PG 1162

Macdonald, George
PG 665

MacCALLUM, George, 1840–68. *Sculptor*
> PG 1029*   Canvas, 76.2 x 63.5 (30 x 25), by unknown artist. Given by William
> Denholm 1926.

McCANCE, William, 1894–1970. *Artist, illustrator and typographer*
> PG 2429*   Canvas, 50.8 x 40.6 (20 x 16), self-portrait. Painted 1916. Purchased 1978.

McCLURE, David, b. 1926. *Artist*
> PGL 328*   (*Gathering at 7 London Street.*) See GROUPS.

McCLYMONT, W., fl. 1899. *Of Manchester Curling Club*
> PG 1856*   (*Curling at Carsebreck.*) See GROUPS.

MacCOLL, Dugald Sutherland, 1886–1948. *Artist and critic*
> PG 1151*   Pencil drawing, 25.4 x 20.2 (10 x 8), by Donald MacLaren. Purchased 1931.

McCREADY, Mr Daly, fl. *c.* 1835.
> PG 2016   Pencil drawing, 11.2 x 8.4 (4⅜ x 3⅜), by unknown artist. Given by
> E. Kersley 1962.

McCRIE, Rev. Thomas, 1772–1835. *Seceding divine and ecclesiastical historian*
> PG 197   Canvas, 91.4 x 71.1 (36 x 28), by Sir John Watson Gordon. Given by the
> sitter's representatives 1887.

McCULLOCH, Horatio, 1805–67. *Landscape painter*
> PG 233*   Canvas, 50.8 x 43.2 (20 x 17), by Sir Daniel Macnee. Purchased 1888.
> PG 356*   Chalk drawing, 40.6 x 33 (16 x 13), by Sir Daniel Macnee, 1828, signed.
> Given by T. Richardson and Co. 1889.
> PG 1783   (With William Borthwick Johnstone.) Ink drawing, 25.2 x 17.5 (9⅞ x 6⅞),
> by Thomas Frank Heaphy, signed. Transferred from the National Gallery of
> Scotland 1952.

McCULLOCH, John Ramsay, 1789–1864. *Political economist*
> PG 543   Chalk drawing, 36.2 x 28 (14¼ x 11), by William Bewick. Given by
> H. G. Reid 1895.

MacCUNN, Hamish, 1868–1916. *Musician and composer*
> PG 874   Plaster bust, h. 64.3 (25⁵⁄₁₆), by David Watson Stevenson. Purchased 1917.

MacDIARMID, Hugh; see GRIEVE, Christopher Murray.

McDIARMID, John, 1790–1852. *Journalist*
> PG 2200*   Canvas, 127.2 x 102.3 (50¹⁄₁₆ x 40¼), by William Menzies Tweedie, 1852,
> signed (on reverse). Purchased 1971.

MACDONALD, Sir Alexander, *c. 1745–95. 9th Baronet of Sleat and 1st Baron Macdonald of Slate*
PG 2127*   (With Sir James Macdonald.) Canvas, 176.5 x 147.3 (69½ x 58), by Jeremiah Davison. Purchased 1967.
PGL 2609* Canvas, 240 x 148.6 (94½ x 58½), by unknown artist (perhaps John Singleton Copley). Purchased 1984.

MACDONALD, Flora, 1722–90. *Jacobite heroine*
PG 947   Canvas, 76.7 x 64.2 (30¼ x 25¼), by unknown artist after Allan Ramsay. Purchased 1923.
PG 1162*   Canvas, 76.4 x 58.7 (30⅛ x 23⅛), by Richard Wilson, 1747, signed. Purchased 1931.
PG 1665   Chalk drawing, 35.5 x 25.4 (14 x 10), by Allan Ramsay. Bequeathed by W. F. Watson 1886.

MACDONALD, George, 1824–1905. *Poet and novelist*
PG 665*   Canvas, 75.4 x 54.8 (29⅝ x 21½), by Cecilia Harrison, 1897, signed. Purchased 1907.
PG 972*   Bronze medallion, h. 34.3 (13½), by Alexander Munro. Given by Dr Greville Macdonald 1924.
PGL 108   Copper bust, h. 27 (10⅝), by George Anderson Lawson. Dated 187[ ]. On loan from the Royal Scottish Academy.

MACDONALD, Sir George, 1862–1940. *Archaeologist*
PG 1484   Canvas, 108 x 89.3 (42½ x 35⅛), by Maurice Greiffenhagen, 1929, signed. Given by a presentation committee 1941.
PGL 171*   Canvas, 107.3 x 88.9 (42¼ x 35), by Maurice Greiffenhagen, 1929, signed. On loan from Lady Macdonald.

MACDONALD, Professor Hector Monro, 1865–1935. *Mathematician*
PG 1421   Canvas, 49.5 x 39.4 (19½ x 15½), by Richard Grenville Eves, 1933, signed. Purchased 1941.

MACDONALD, James, d. 1900. *Lawyer and antiquary*
PG 1696   Pencil drawing, 37.5 x 33.7 (14¾ x 13¼), by W. Graham Boss. Given by the artist.

MACDONALD, Sir James, 1742–66. *Scholar and 8th Baronet of Sleat*
PG 2127*   (With Sir Alexander Macdonald.) Canvas, 176.5 x 147.3 (69½ x 58), by Jeremiah Davison. Purchased 1967.

MACDONALD, James Ramsay, 1866–1937. *Prime Minister*
PG 1351*   Canvas, 99.1 x 78.7 (39 x 31), by Ambrose McEvoy, signed. Completed 1926. Given by Sir Alexander Grant through the Scottish Modern Arts Association 1938.

MACDONALD, James Ramsay (*continued*)
PG 1352*   Bronze bust, h. 48.2 (19), by Sir Jacob Epstein. Given by Sir Alexander
Grant through the Scottish Modern Arts Association 1938.
PG 1778*   a. Pencil drawing, 22.1 x 13.8 (8⅝ x 5⅜), by William Small, 1889, signed.
b. Pencil drawing, 22.5 x 13.8 (8⅞ x 5⅜), by William Small, 1889, signed.
Given by Robert Small 1951.

McDONALD, John Blake, 1829–1901. *Artist*
PG 1743   (In his studio.) Wash drawing, 53.7 x 38.4 (21⅛ x 15⅛), by J. R.
Abercromby, signed. Drawn 1898. Purchased 1940.

MACDONALD, Rev. Patrick, 1729–1824. *Collector of Gaelic music*
PG 1429   Cut paper silhouette, h. 7.5 (2⅞), by unknown artist. Bequeathed by
Mrs L. W. James 1942.

MACDONALD of Powderhall, Colonel William, fl. 1830. *Director of the Commercial
Bank*
PG 2157*   Cut paper silhouette, h. 21.6 (8½), by Augustin Edouart, 1830, signed.
Given by Mrs J. H. G. Ross 1969.

MACDONALD, William Rae, 1844–1924. *Actuary and antiquary*
PG 1009   Medallion (plaster replica), h. 7.3 (2⅞), after Charles Matthew. Bequeathed
by Mr and Mrs W. R. Macdonald 1925.

MACDONELL, General Sir James, d. 1857. *Soldier*
PG 1465*   Canvas, 142.5 x 112.5 (56⅛ x 44¼), attributed to Frederick Richard Say.
Bequeathed by Francis S. F. Traill 1945.

MACEWEN, Sir William, 1848–1924. *Surgeon*
PG 1101*   Marble bust, h. 58.4 (23), by George Paulin, 1925, signed. Given by James
Macfarlane 1928.

MACFARLAN of Macfarlan, Walter, d. 1767. *Antiquary*
PGL 34*   Canvas, 77.4 x 64.2 (30½ x 25¼), by John Thomas Seton. Dated 1757 (on
reverse). On loan from the National Museums of Scotland.

McGAHEY, Michael, b. 1925. *Mining trade unionist*
PG 2747*   Canvas, 122 x 96.5 (48 x 38), by Maggi Hambling. Painted 1988. Purchased
by commission 1988.

MacGEORGE, , William Stewart, 1861–1931. *Artist*
PG 1181   Watercolour, 50.2 x 40 (19¾ x 15¾), by Charles Oppenheimer, 1913,
signed. Given by the artist 1932.

Macdonald, George
PG 972

Macdonald, Sir George
PGL 171

Macdonald, James Ramsay
PG 1351

Macdonald, James Ramsay
PG 1352

Macdonald, James Ramsay
PG 1778a

Macdonald, William
PG 2157

Macdonell, Sir James
PG   1465

Macewen, Sir William
PG 1101

Macfarlan, Walter
PGL 34

McGahey, Michael
PG 2747

Macgillivray, James Pittendrigh
PG 1402

McGlashan, Archibald
PG 2606

Macgoun, Hannah
PG 1481

Macgregor, Alasdair Alpin
PGL 324

MacGregor, John
PG 2675

MACGILLIVRAY, James Pittendrigh, 1856–1939. *Sculptor*
  PG 1402* Bronze bust, h. 65.4 (25¾), by Benno Schotz. Modelled 1923/4. Purchased 1940.
  PG 1819 Pencil drawing, 44.8 x 32.9 (17⅝ x 12⅞), by David Foggie, signed. Dated 1917. Given by Mrs M. Foggie 1955.
  PG 1982 Pencil drawing, 18.4 x 15.3 (7¼ x 6), by Joyce W. Thompson. Drawn 1932. Given by the artist 1961.

McGLASHAN, Archibald, 1888–1980. *Artist*
  PG 2501 Ink and pencil drawing, 49 x 23.8 (19¼ x 9⅜) (irregular), by Emilio Coia, signed. Drawn *c*. 1954. Purchased 1981.
  PG 2606* Bronze head, h. 28 (11), by Alexander Goudie. Cast 1984. Purchased 1984.

MACGOUN, Hannah Clarke Preston, *c*. 1867–1913. *Artist*
  PG 1481* Water-colour, 18.8 x 14.9 (7⅛ x 5⅞), self-portrait, 1887, signed. Given by Mrs R. T. Rose 1946.

MACGOWAN, John, d. *c*. 1804. *Collector of gems*
  PG 1913 Medallion (plaster replica), h. 7.3 (2⅞), after James Tassie. Dated 1777. Provenance untraced.

MACGREGOR, Alasdair Alpin, 1898–1970. *Writer*
  PGL 324* Canvas, 76.2 x 63.5 (30 x 25), by Henry Raeburn Dobson, signed. On loan from the National Library of Scotland.

McGREGOR, Gregor, 1786–11845. *Adventurer*
  PG 2201 Canvas, 76 x 63.5 (29¹⁵⁄₁₆ x 25), by George Watson. Purchased 1972.

MACGREGOR, John, d. 1847. *Cashier of the Commercial Bank*
  PG 2158 Cut paper silhouette, h. 20.5 (8¹⁄₁₆), by Augustin Edouart, 1830, signed. Given by Mrs J. H. G. Ross 1969.

MacGREGOR, John, 1791–1870. *Piper to the Campbells of Breadalbane*
  PG 2675* (Probably John MacGregor.) Canvas, 90.2 x 70.5 (35½ x 37¾), by Alexander Johnston, signed. Dated 1840. Purchased 1985.

MACGREGOR, Rob Roy, 1671–1734. *Freebooter*
  PG 2635* (*The Battle of Glenshiel 1719*.) See GROUPS.

MACGREGOR, William York, 1855–1923. *Artist*
  PG 1159* Chalk drawing, 38.7 x 30.8 (15¼ x 12⅛), by William Strang, 1904, signed. Given by Mrs MacGregor 1931.

McGRIGOR, Sir James, 1771–1858. *Army surgeon*
  PG 1310 Plaster bust, h. 66.7 (26¼), by unknown artist. Dated 1858. Given by Mrs and Miss M. A. B. McGrigor 1936.

McIAN, Robert Ranald, 1803–56. *Actor and artist*
    PG 2033*   (In character as The Fighting Smith of Perth.) Canvas, 76.2 x 63.5 (30 x 25) by John Stone. Given by Ronald E. Whitaker 1964.
    PG 2034   Chalk drawing, 18.1 x 13.5 (7⅛ x 5¼), by Fanny McIan. Given by Ronald E. Whitaker 1964.

MACINTOSH, George, fl. 1795.
    PG 2443   Paste medallion h. 7.4 (2⅞), by James Tassie. Dated 1795. Bequeathed by William Tassie to the National Gallery of Scotland 1860 and transferred 1979.

MACKAY, Aeneas James George, 1839–1911. *Historian*
    PG 1354*   Pencil drawing, 32.8 x 24 (13 x 9½), by John Henry Lorimer, 1890, signed. Given by the artist's trustees 1938.
    PG 1698   Pencil drawing, 37.5 x 33.7 (14¾ x 13¼), by W. Graham Boss. Given by the artist.

MACKAY, Charles, 1787–1857. *Actor*
    PG 582*   Canvas, 76.2 x 63.5 (30 x 25), by Sir Daniel Macnee. Purchased 1899.

MACKAY, Fulton, 1922–87. *Actor*
    PG 2730*   Bronze head, h. 29.2 (11½), by Archibald Forrest, signed. Purchased 1988.

McKAY, William Darling, 1844–1924. *Artist*
    PG 1084   Chalk drawing, 37.2 x 26.7 (14⅝ x 10½), by James Paterson, 1918, signed. Purchased 1928.
    PG 1223*   Canvas, 111.7 x 86.3 (44 x 34), self-portrait. Given by the artist's executors 1934.
    PG 1744   (In his studio.) Wash drawing, 55.2 x 39.1 (21¾ x 15⅜), by J. R. Abercromby, signed. Drawn 1898. Purchased 1940.

McKECHNIE, Sir William Wallace, 1872–1947. *Educationalist*
    PG 1796   Black chalk drawing, 46.7 x 29.2 (18⅜ x 11½), by David Foggie, 1933, signed. Given by Mrs M. Foggie 1955.

MACKENZIE of Delvine, Sir Alexander Muir, 1st Baronet, 1764–1835.
    PG 2584   (Silhouette album no. 219. See GROUPS.) Printed (?) silhouette, h. 6.5 (2⁹⁄₁₆), by unknown artist. Acquired *c.* 1951.

MACKENZIE of Kintail, Sir Allan Russell, 2nd Baronet, 1850–1916. *Of Ballater Curling Club*
    PG 1856*   *(Curling at Carsebreck.)* See GROUPS.

MACKENZIE, Sir Compton, 1883–1972. *Author*
    PG 2003*   Black chalk drawing, 45.1 x 28.3 (17¾ x 11⅛), by David Foggie, 1933, signed. Given by Mrs M. Foggie 1962.

MACKENZIE, Sir Compton (*continued*)
  PG 2377*   Plywood panel, 30.4 x 23.2 (12 x 9⅛), by Sir William Oliphant Hutchison.
             Given by the executors of Margery, Lady Hutchison 1977.
  PG 2505*   Canvas, 111.7 x 86.3 (44 x 34), by Robert Heriot Westwater, 1962, signed.
             Given by Lady Mackenzie 1981.

MACKENZIE, , Sir George, 1636–1691. *Founder of the Advocates Library*
  PG 107   Wash drawing, 17 x 14.3 (6⅝ x 5⅝), by John Beugo after Sir Godfrey
            Kneller. Bequeathed by W. F. Watson 1886.
  PG 328   Canvas, 35.5 x 30.5 (14 x 12), by unknown artist after Sir Godfrey Kneller.
            Bequeathed by W. F. Watson 1886.
  PG 834*   Canvas, oval 76.5 x 64.8 (30⅛ x 25½), by unknown artist after Sir Godfrey
            Kneller. Purchased 1913.

MACKENZIE, Henry, 1745–1831. *Novelist and essayist*
  PG 254*   Marble bust, h. 55.2 (21¾), by Samuel Joseph. Presented by John Ritchie
            Findlay to the National Gallery of Scotland and transferred 1889.
  PG 318   Panel, 20.2 x 16.9 (7¹⁵⁄₁₆ x 6⅝), by William Stavely, 1795, signed (on
            reverse). Bequeathed by W. F. Watson 1886.
  PG 825*   (*Sir Walter Scott and his friends at Abbotsford.*) See GROUPS.
  PG 1032* Canvas, 127 x 101.6 (50 x 40), by Colvin Smith. Painted c. 1827. Purchased
            1926.
  PG 1047   Chalk drawing, 54.7 x 42.5 (21½ x 16¾), by William Bewick, 1824.
            Purchased 1927.

MACKENZIE of Delvine, Jane Murray, Lady. *Wife of Sir Alexander Muir Mackenzie*
  PG 2584   (Silhouette album no. 218. See GROUPS.) Printed (?) silhouette, h. 6.2
            (2⁷⁄₁₆), by unknown artist. Acquired c. 1951.

MACKENZIE, William Forbes, 1807–62. *Politician*
  PG 833   Cut paper silhouette, h. 22.5 (8⅞), by Augustin Edouart. Cut 1830.
            Purchased 1913.

MACKENZIE, William Mackay, 1872–1952. *Historian*
  PG 2312   Canvas, 61 x 50.8 (24 x 20), by David Foggie, 1914, signed. Given by
            A. Foggie 1975.

MACKINTOSH, Charles Rennie, 1868–1928. *Architect*
  PG 1205* (Study for group portrait *The Building Committee of the Glasgow School of
            Art*, painted 1914, in the collection of Glasgow School of Art.) Canvas,
            110.5 x 61.4 (43½ x 24³⁄₁₆), by Francis Henry Newbery, signed. Purchased
            1933.

MACKINTOSH, Sir James, 1765–1832. *Philosopher*
  PG 248   Canvas, 127 x 105.4 (50 x 41½), by Colvin Smith. Given by Mrs Mary
            Erskine to the National Gallery of Scotland in 1881 and transferred 1889.

Macgregor, William York
PG 1159

McIan, Robert Ranald
PG 2033

Mackay, Aeneas
PG 1354

Mackay, Charles
PG 582

Mackay, Fulton
PG 2730

McKay, William Darling
PG 1223

Mackenzie, Sir Compton
PG 2003

Mackenzie, Sir Compton
PG 2377

Mackenzie, Sir Compton
PG 2505

Mackenzie, Sir George
PG 834

Mackenzie, Henry
PG 254

Mackenzie, Henry
PG 1032

Mackintosh, Charles
Rennie   PG 1205

Mackintosh, Sir James
PG 938

Maclaren, Charles
PG 281

McLaren, Duncan
PG 333

MACKINTOSH, Sir James (*continued*)
    PG 938*   Chalk drawing, 83.8 x 68.3 (33 x 26⅞), by F. W. Wilkin, 1824, signed.
                Given by Brigadier-General Archibald Stirling of Keir 1923.

MACLAE, Walter Ewing, 1745–1814. *Glasgow merchant*
    PG 1915   Medallion (plaster replica), h. 6.7 (2⅝), after James Tassie. Dated 1791.
                Provenance untraced.

MACLAREN, Charles, 1782–1866. *Editor of* The Scotsman *and geologist*
    PG 281*   Marble bust, h. 72.1 (28⅜), by John Hutchison, 1889, signed, after William
                Brodie. Original executed 1861. Given by John Ritchie Findlay 1889.

McLAREN, Duncan, 1800–86. *Lord Provost of Edinburgh*
    PG 303   Ink drawing, 14 x 11.4 (5½ x 4½), by Sir George Reid, signed. Copied from
                a portrait painted 1882. Given by G. R. Halkett 1891.
    PG 333*   Canvas, 72.4 x 59.7 (28½ x 23½), by Edward John Gregory, signed. Painted
                1891 from a portrait dated 1880. Given by Lord McLaren and his brothers
                1891.

McLAREN, John McLaren, Lord, 1831–1910. *Judge*
    PG 2464*   Canvas, 58.3 x 41.5 (23 x 16⅜), by Sir John Lavery, signed. Purchased
                1980.

MACLAURIN, Colin, 1698–1746. *Mathematician*
    PG 1643   Pencil and chalk drawing, 31.1 x 26.5 (12¼ x 10⅜), by the 11th Earl of
                Buchan, signed, after James Ferguson. Bequeathed by W. F. Watson 1886.

MACLEAN, Archibald, 1733–1812. *Baptist minister*
    PG 1993   Canvas, 76.8 x 63.8 (30⅛ x 25⅛), by George Watson, signed. Painted
                c. 1810. Given by Dr C. W. Graham 1962.

MACLEAN of Duart and Morvern, Charles Hector Fitzroy Maclean, Baron, 1916–90.
                Chief Scout
    PG 2400   Pencil drawing, 36.4 x 25.3 (14⁵⁄₁₆ x 9⁵⁄₁₆), by Sir William Oliphant
                Hutchison. Given by the executors of Margery, Lady Hutchison 1977.

MACLEAN, Sir Harry, 1848–1920. *Military adviser in Morocco*
    PG 2196*   Pencil drawing, 26 x 18.1 (10¼ x 7⅛), by unknown artist. Given by
                K. M. Guichard 1971.

MacLEAN, Sorley, b. 1911. *Poet*
    PG 2597*   (*Poets' Pub.*) See GROUPS.

MACLEAY, Kenneth, 1802–78. *Miniature painter*
    PG 1427*   Canvas, 76.2 x 63.5 (30 x 25), by John Gibson. Bequeathed by Mrs Wallace
                James 1942.

MACLEHOSE, Mrs Agnes, 'Clarinda', 1759–1841. *Friend and correspondent of Burns*
   PG 567*   Silhouette on plaster, h. 6.3 (2½), by John Miers. Dated 1788. Given by
              W. G. Campbell 1897.

MACLEOD, Rev. Norman, 1812–72. *Divine and author*
   PG 633*   Millboard, 40.5 x 30.3 (16 x 11¹⁵⁄₁₆), by Tavernor Knott. Dated 1848. Given
              by Mrs John Moffat 1905.

MACLEOD, Sir Reginald, 1847–1935. *27th Chief of the Clan*
   PG 1697   Pencil drawing, 37.5 x 33.7 (14¾ x 13¼), by W. Graham Boss. Given by
              the artist.

MACNAB, Archibald, 1777–1860. *13th and Last Laird of MacNab*
   PG 1514*   Canvas, 76.2 x 61.7 (30 x 24¼), by unknown artist. Painted *c.* 1830.
              Purchased 1948.

MACNEE, Sir Daniel, 1806–82. *Artist*
   PG 741*   Canvas, 61 x 55.9 (24 x 22), by James Macbeth. Purchased 1910.

MACNEIL, Hector, 1746–1818. *Poet*
   PG 387   Medallion (plaster replica), h. 6.7 (2⅝), after John Henning. Dated 1802.
              Cast from a medallion in possession of W. G. Patterson 1889.
   PG 2357   Porcelain medallion, h. 6.7 (2⅝), by John Henning. Dated 1802. Purchased
              1976.

McNEILL of Colonsay and Oronsay, John, 1767–1846. *Agriculturist*
   PG 247*   Canvas, 104.1 x 79.4 (41 x 31¼), by Thomas Duncan. Bequeathed by Lord
              Colonsay to the National Gallery of Scotland and transferred in 1889.

McNEILL, Sir John, 1795–1883. *Diplomat*
   PG 149*   Marble bust, h. 87.8 (34⁹⁄₁₆), by Sir John Steell, 1859, signed. Bequeathed
              by Lord Colonsay 1886.
   PG 1503   Canvas, 23.9 x 19 (9½ x 7½), by unknown artist. Purchased 1947.

MACOME of Paisley, Ebenezer, b. 1738. *Writing master in Paisley*
   PG 1358   Paste medallion, h. 6.4 (2½), by John Henning. Dated 1801. Purchased
              1938.

MACPHERSON of Cluny, Andrew, 1640–66. *15th Chief*
   PG 1546*   Canvas, 76.2 x 64.1 (30 x 25¼), by Richard Waitt. Given by J. A. Pearson
              1950.

MACPHERSON, James, 1736–96. *Compiler of the poems of Ossian*
   PG 1439   Canvas, 75.5 x 63.2 (29¾ x 24⅞), by unknown artist after Sir Joshua
              Reynolds. Purchased 1943.

MACPHERSON, Sir John, 1745–1821. *Governor-General of India*
    PG 647*   Canvas, 76.2 x 63.5 (30 x 25), by Sir Joshua Reynolds. Painted 1779.
        Purchased 1906.

McPHERSON, Malcolm, d. 1743. *Army deserter*
    PG 2298   Ink drawing, 19.3 x 11.8 (7⁹⁄₁₆ x 4⅝), copy by unknown artist after
        anonymous engraving. Provenance untraced.

MACRAE, Duncan, 1905–67. *Actor*
    PG 2593*   (In character as Harry McGog.) Bronze statuette, h. 3.5 (21), by Benno
        Schotz, signed. Executed 1949. Purchased 1983.

MacTAGGART, Sir William, 1903–81. *Artist*
    PG 2495   Oil on cardboard, 50.4 x 40.5 (19⅞ x 15⅞), self-portrait, signed on the
        reverse. Given by the executors of the artist 1981.
    PG 2496*   Canvas, 51.2 x 40.6 (20⅛ x 16), by Sir William Gillies. Painted *c.* 1935.
        Given by the executors of the sitter 1981.
    PG 2588*   Pencil and chalk drawing, 56.2 x 40.6 (22⅛ x 16), by Donald Moodie,
        signed. Dated 1956. Purchased 1983.

MacWHIRTER, John, 1839–1911. *Landscape painter*
    PG 722   Millboard, 19.3 x 14.7 (7⅝ x 5¾), by James Archer. Given by the Royal
        Scottish Academy 1910.
    PG 1511*   Water-colour, 17.8 x 12.6 (7 x 5), by Sir Hubert von Herkomer, 1892,
        signed. Given by Mrs Helen Baird 1948.

MACCLESFIELD, Charles Gerard, 1st Earl of, 1618–94. *Royalist general*
    PG 1108   Canvas, 124.4 x 101.9 (49 x 40⅛), studio of Sir Peter Lely. Bequeathed by
        the Earl of Rosebery 1930.

MAGUIRE, William, fl. 1841.
    PG 1722   Water-colour and pencil, 23.3 x 16.7 (9¼ x 6½), by unknown artist.
        Provenance untraced.

MAIDMENT, James, *c.* 1795–1879. *Antiquary*
    PG 754   Water-colour, 27.8 x 22.1 (10¹⁵⁄₁₆ x 8¹¹⁄₁₆), by William Greenlees, 1850,
        signed. Given by William Steele as executor for Miss Margaret Stewart 1892.

MAIR, John, d. 1824. *Glasgow merchant*
    PG 2759   Paste medallion, h. 8.3 (3¼), by James Tassie. Dated 1797. Purchased 1989.

MAIR, Margaret Thompson, Mrs John, d. 1807. *Wife of John Mair, Glasgow merchant*
    PG 2760   Paste medallion, h. 8 (3⅛), by James Tassie. Dated 1797. Purchased 1989.

MAITLAND of Lethington, William, *c.* 1528–73. *Secretary to Mary, Queen of Scots*
    PG 1621   Chalk drawing, 35.2 x 28.3 (13⅞ x 11⅛), by the 11th Earl of Buchan, 1790,
        signed, after unknown artist. Bequeathed by W. F. Watson 1886.

McLaren, Lord
PG 2464

Maclean, Sir Harry
PG 2196

Macleay, Kenneth
PG 1427

Maclehose, Agnes
PG 567

Macleod, Rev. Norman
PG 633

Macnab, Archibald
PG 1514

Macnee, Sir Daniel
PG 741

McNeill, John
PG 247

McNeill, Sir John
PG 149

Macpherson, Andrew
PG 1546

Macpherson, Sir John
PG 647

Macrae, Duncan
PG 2593

MacTaggart, Sir William
PG 2496

MacTaggart, Sir William
PG 2588

MacWhirter, John
PG 1511

Malcolm, Sir John
PG 439

MALCOLM, Sir John, 1769–1833. *Indian administrator and diplomat*
- PG 439* Canvas, 75.8 x 62.8 (29¾ x 24¾), by Samuel Lane. Given by W. E. Malcolm 1893.
- PG 1051* Chalk drawing, 54 x 39.7 (21¼ x 15⅝), by William Bewick. Dated 1824. Purchased 1927.
- PGL 321* Canvas, 142.3 x 111.7 (56 x 44), by Sir George Hayter. Painted 1826. On loan from Sir David Malcolm.

MALCOLM, Admiral Sir Pulteney, 1768–1838. *Sailor*
- PG 2050* Canvas, 76.2 x 63.5 (30 x 25), by Samuel Lane. Purchased with assistance from the National Art-Collections Fund (London Scot Bequest) 1965.

MANN, Harrington, 1864–1937. *Artist*
- PG 1391* Canvas, 76.2 x 63.5 (30 x 25), self-portrait. Given by the artist's executor 1939.

MANN, Ludovic MacLellan, 1869–1955. *Actuary and prehistorian*
- PG 2232* Canvas, 76.2 x 63.4 (30 x 24⅞), by Cathleen Mann, 1944, signed. Given by T. Norman Frizzell 1974.

MANSFIELD, William Murray, 1st Earl of, 1705–93. *Lord Chief Justice*
- PG 312 Panel, 26.2 x 21.2 (10⅜ x 8⅜), by —— Mason after Sir Joshua Reynolds. Dated 1866. Bequeathed by W. F. Watson 1886.
- PG 369 Wedgwood medallion, h. 8.6 (3½), after James Tassie. Dated 1779. Given by Messrs J. Wedgwood and Sons 1889.
- PG 413 Medallion (plaster replica), h. 9.7 (3¹³⁄₁₆), after James Tassie. Cast from a medallion in possession of Commander C. M. Dundas 1892.
- PG 598* Canvas, 120.7 x 92.1 (47½ x 36¼), by David Martin, 1777, signed. Purchased 1901.
- PG 1445 Red chalk drawing, oval, 24.7 x 19.7 (9¾ x 7¾), by David Martin. Bequeathed by Kenneth Sanderson 1944.
- PG 2589* Paste medallion, h. 9.4 (3¾), by James Tassie. Dated 1779. Purchased 1983.

MANSFIELD, William David Murray, 4th Earl of, and 9th Viscount Stormont, 1806–93.
- PG 1856* (*Curling at Carsebreck.*) See GROUPS.

MANSON, George, 1850–76. *Artist*
- PG 672* Water-colour, 14.7 x 10.9 (5⅞ x 4¼), self-portrait. Purchased 1908.
- PG 1446 Water-colour, 11.5 x 9.2 (4½ x 3⅜), self-portrait. Bequeathed by Kenneth Sanderson 1944.
- PG 1501 Millboard, 20.7 x 17.6 (8⅛ x 6⅞), by George Paul Chalmers. Given by J. Kent Richardson 1947.

MANSON, James Bolivar, 1820–68. *Journalist and art critic*
- PG 2679 Bronze bust, h. 30.5 (12), by George MacCallum, 1866, signed. Given by Miss Mary Manson and Mrs Jean Goullet 1986.

MAR, Frances Floyer, Countess of, d. 1798. *Wife of 7th Earl of Mar*
    PGL 243*   (*With 7th Earl of Mar and their family.*) See GROUPS.

MAR, Frances Pierrepont, Countess of, d. 1761. *Wife of John Erskine, 6th Earl of Mar*
    PGL 238*   Canvas, 240 x 146.6 (93 x 57¾), by Sir Godfrey Kneller. Painted *c.* 1715.
          On loan from the Earl of Mar and Kellie.

MAR, John Erskine, 1st Earl, d. 1572. *Regent of Scotland*
    PG 653   Canvas, 73.7 x 60.7 (29 x 23⅞), copy by John Scougall after unknown artist.
          Purchased 1906.

MAR, John Erskine, 2nd Earl of, *c.* 1562–1634. *Lord High Treasurer of Scotland*
    PG 1628*   Pencil and chalk drawing, 43.6 x 35.7 (17⅛ x 14), by the 11th Earl of
          Buchan, 179–, signed, after unknown artist. Bequeathed by W. F. Watson
          1886.
    PG 2211*   Canvas, 62.9 x 53.5 (24¾ x 21), attributed to Adam de Colone. Dated 1626.
          Bequeathed by 13th Baron Elibank 1973.

MAR, John Erskine, 6th Earl of, 1675–1732. *Leader of the Jacobite Rising of 1715*
    PG 110   Pen and wash drawing, 26.1 x 20.8 (10¼ x 8⅛), studio of Sir Godfrey
          Kneller. Bequeathed by W. F. Watson 1886.
    PGL 237*   (*With his son Thomas Erskine, Lord Erskine.*) Canvas, 232.7 x 140.7
          (91⅝ x 55⅜), by Sir Godfrey Kneller, signed. Painted *c.* 1715. On loan from
          the Earl of Mar and Kellie.

MAR, Marie Stewart, Countess of, d. 1644. *Second wife of the 2nd Earl of Mar*
    PG 1631   Chalk drawing, 46.4 x 32.4 (18¼ x 12¾), by the 11th Earl of Buchan after
          unknown artist. Bequeathed by W. F. Watson 1886.
    PG 2214*   Panel, 57.4 x 43.9 (22⅝ x 17¼), by unknown artist. Bequeathed by 13th
          Baron Elibank 1973.

MARCHMONT, Alexander Hume Campbell, 2nd Earl of, 1675–1740. *Statesman*
    PG 819*   Canvas, 75 x 62.6 (29½ x 24⅝), by unknown artist. Purchased 1913.

MARCHMONT, Hugh Hume, 3rd Earl of, 1708–94. *Statesman*
    PG 1184*   Canvas, 61 x 50.8 (24 x 20), by Pierre Falconet, 1769, signed. Purchased
          1932.

MARCHMONT, Sir Patrick Hume, 1st Earl of, 1641–1724. *Statesman*
    PGL 22*   Canvas, 77.2 x 64 (30⅜ x 25¼), by William Aikman. On loan from the
          National Museums of Scotland.

MARGARET, Queen, *c.* 1457–86. *Queen of James III*
    PG 1655   Water-colour, 13.8 x 7.7 (5⅜ x 3), by unknown artist after Hugo van der
          Goes. Bequeathed by W. F. Watson 1886.

MARIA FEODOROVNA, c. 1757–1828. *Empress of Paul I of Russia*
> PG 1883   Medallion (plaster replica), h. 5.9 (2⅜), after James Tassie. Provenance untraced.

MARISCHAL, George Keith, 10th Earl, 1694–1778. *Jacobite*
> PG 311*   Canvas, 124.5 x 99.1 (49 x 39), by Pierre Parrocel. Painted c. 1716. Bequeathed by W. F. Watson 1886.

MARISCHAL, William Keith, 7th Earl, 1614–61. *Leader of the Covenanters*
> PG 994*   Canvas, 67.3 x 56.5 (26½ x 22¼), by George Jamesone. Dated 1636. Purchased 1925.

MARSHALL, Henry, 1775–1851. *Physician and military hygienist*
> PG 552*   Canvas, 76.5 x 63.8 (30⅛ x 25⅛), by Sir Daniel Macnee. Given by W. E. Wingate 1896.

MARSHALL, Colonel William, 1780–1870. *Soldier*
> PG 2585   Water-colour on ivory, h. 7.6 (3), by unknown artist. Bequeathed by James Batley to the National Library of Scotland and transferred 1983.

MARSHALL, William Calder, 1813–94. *Sculptor*
> PG 1170   Plaster bust, h. 67 (24⁵⁄₁₆), self-portrait. Bequeathed by Mrs Annie Calder Orr 1932.

MARTIN, Lady; see FAUCIT

MARTIN, Very Rev. Alexander, 1857–1946. *Chaplain to the King in Scotland*
> PG 1794   Black chalk drawing, 46 x 29 (18⅛ x 11⅜), by David Foggie, 1934, signed. Given by Mrs M. Foggie 1955.

MARTIN, David, 1737–98. *Portrait painter*
> PG 194*   Canvas, 50.8 x 40.6 (20 x 16), self-portrait. Purchased 1887.

MARTIN, Rev. James, 1800–34. *Minister of St George's Church, Edinburgh*
> PG 1212   (With Rev. James Henderson.) Cut paper silhouette, h. 20.3 (8), by Augustin Edouart, signed. Purchased 1933.

MARTIN, Sir Theodore, 1816–1909. *Lawyer and writer*
> PG 694*   Canvas, 76.5 x 63.5 (39⅛ x 25⅛), by Thomas Duncan. Bequeathed by the sitter 1909.
> PG 955   Canvas, 54.6 x 49.5 (21½ x 19½), by Reginald Cholmondeley. Given by Miss Eliza H. Saville 1923.

MARTIN, William, fl. 1796.
> PG 1918   Medallion (plaster replica), h. 7.3 (2⅞), after James Tassie. Dated 1796. Provenance untraced.

Malcolm, Sir John
PG 1051

Malcolm, Sir John
PGL 321

Malcolm, Sir Pulteney
PG 2050

Mann, Harrington
PG 1391

Mann, Ludovic MacLellan
PG 2232

Mansfield, 1st Earl of
PG 598

Mansfield, 1st Earl of
PG 2589

Manson, George
PG 672

Mar, Countess of
PGL 238

Mar, 6th Earl of, with.
Lord Erskine   PGL 237

Mar, 2nd Earl of
PG 1628

Mar, 2nd Earl of
PG 2211

Mar, Countess of
PG 2214

Marchmont, 2nd Earl of
PG 819

Marchmont, 3rd Earl of
PG 1184

Marchmont, 1st Earl of
PGL 22

MARY II, 1662–94. *Reigned jointly with William III, 1688–94*

PG 921   (Commemorates Mary's regency.) Copper medal, dia. 4.9 (1¹⁵⁄₁₆), by John Roettier. Cast 1690. Purchased 1920.

PG 1385*   Canvas, 125.5 x 102.6 (49⅜ x 40⅜), by unknown artist after Willem Wissing. Purchased 1939.

PG 1533   Canvas, 126.4 x 101.6 (49¾ x 40), by J. J. Bakker after Sir Godfrey Kneller, signed. Purchased 1949.

PG 2766   (Coronation of William III and Mary II 1689.) Copper medal, dia. 4 (1⁹⁄₁₆), by George Hautsch. Purchased 1989.

PG 2767   (Coronation of William III and Mary II 1689.) Silver medal, dia. 4 (1⁹⁄₁₆), by George Hautsch. Purchased 1989.

MARY OF GUISE, 1515–60. *Queen of James V*

PG 977   Canvas, 96.5 x 71.1 (38 x 28), by Hugh Monro after the portrait by an unknown artist at Hardwick. Commissioned 1924.

PG 1558*   Panel, 22 x 15.1 (8¹¹⁄₁₆ x 5¹⁵⁄₁₆), attributed to Corneille de Lyon. Given by E. P. Jones 1950.

PG 2076   Water-colour, 13.6 x 10.9 (5¼ x 4¼), copy by unknown artist. Transferred from the National Gallery of Scotland 1950.

MARY, Princess, 1631–60. *Eldest daughter of Charles I; Princess of Orange*

PG 96   (With Charles II and James, Duke of York.) Canvas, 121.9 x 139.7 (48 x 55), by Henry Stone or Simon Stone after Sir Anthony Van Dyck. Purchased 1886.

PG 1308*   Canvas, 80.5 x 66 (31¹¹⁄₁₆ x 26), by Adriaen Hanneman, 1659, signed. Purchased 1936.

MARY, Princess, 1631–60. *Eldest daughter of Charles I; Princess of Orange*

PG 2763*   (Marriage to William of Nassau, Prince of Orange 1641.) Silver medal, dia. 7.2 (2¹³⁄₁₆), by Johann Blum. Purchased 1989.

MARY, Queen of Scots, 1542–87. *Reigned 1542–67*

PG 130   Panel, 25.2 x 20 (9¹⁵⁄₁₆ x 7⅞), by unknown artist. Purchased 1885.

PG 151   Bust (electrotype replica of tomb effigy in Westminster Abbey), h. 64.6 (25⁷⁄₁₆), after Cornelius and William Cure. Purchased 1885.

PG 161   Medal (electrotype replica), dia. 6.5 (2⁹⁄₁₆), after Jacopo Primavera. Given by J. M. Gray 1886.

PG 186*   (In white mourning.) Panel, 32.9 x 27.4 (13 x 10¹³⁄₁₆), by unknown artist after François Clouet. Probably a nineteenth-century replica. Purchased 1887.

PG 256   Bust (plaster cast of tomb effigy in Westminster Abbey), h. 64 (25¼), after Cornelius and William Cure. Provenance untraced.

PG 733   (With François II. Commemorates the marriage of Mary and the Dauphin.) Silver medal, dia. 5.1 (2), by unknown artist. Dated 1558. Purchased 1910.

PG 752   a (With Lord Darnley. Commemorates the marriage of Mary and Lord Darnley.) Silver medal, dia. 4.4 (1¾), by unknown artist. Dated 1565. Purchased 1910.

Marischal, 10th Earl
PG 311

Marischal, 7th Earl
PG 994

Marshall, Henry
PG 552

Martin, David
PG 194

Martin, Sir Theodore
PG 694

Mary II
PG 1385

Mary of Guise
PG 1558

Mary, Princess
PG 1308

Mary, Queen of Scots
PG 186

Mary, Queen of Scots
PG 1073

Execution of Mary, Queen of Scots
PG 1217

Mary, Queen of Scots (Anamorphosis)
PG 1989

Mary, Queen of Scots
PG 2508

Massey, William Ferguson
PG 1135

MARY, Queen of Scots (*continued*)

b (With Lord Darnley. Commemorates the marriage of Mary and Lord Darnley.) Silver medal (electrotype replica), dia. 4.3 (1¹¹⁄₁₆), after unknown artist. Dated 1565.

PG 1039   Coins (electrotype replicas).

a. Silver testoon, dia. 2.8 (1⅛). Issued 1553.

b. Penny, dia. 1.4 (⁹⁄₁₆). Issued 1542.

c. Penny, dia. 1.4 (⁹⁄₁₆). Issued 1547.

d. Silver half-testoon, dia. 2.4 (¹⁵⁄₁₆). Issued 1562.

e. Gold thirty-shilling piece, dia. 2.2 (⅞). Issued 1555.

f. Silver half-testoon, dia. 2.3 (⅞). Issued 1553.

g. Gold three pound piece, dia. 2.6 (1¹⁄₁₆). Issued 1555.

h. Silver testoon, dia. 2.8 (1⅛). Issued 1561.

i. Queen's gold ducat, dia. 3 (1³⁄₁₆). Issued 1558–59.

j. Silver ryal, dia. 4.2 (1⅝). Issued 1565. Purchased 1927.

PG 1073*   Canvas, 201.5 x 95.7 (79⅜ x 37¾), by unknown artist. Dated 1578, but painted *c.* 1610/15. Purchased 1925.

PG 1086   (Plaster cast of tomb effigy in Westminster Abbey.) Length 175.8 (69¼), after Cornelius and William Cure. Purchased 1928.

PG 1217*   (The Execution of Mary.) Water-colour, 21.9 x 26.4 (8⅝ x 10⅜), by unknown Dutch artist. Painted *c.* 1608. Purchased 1934.

PG 1765   Chalk drawing, 38.8 x 28.5 (15¼ x 11¼), copy by unknown artist. Purchased 1945.

PG 1989*   (Anamorphosis. Called Mary Queen of Scots.) Panel, 33 x 24.8 (13 x 9¾), by unknown artist. Given by A. H. Mayor 1962.

PG 2111   Pencil and chalk drawing, 26.6 x 18.6 (10½ x 7¼), copy by unknown artist. Transferred from the National Gallery of Scotland 1950.

PG 2313   Panel, 12.1 x 9.4 (4¾ x 3¹¹⁄₁₆), copy by unknown artist. Bequeathed by W. F. Watson 1886.

PG 2461   c. Pencil and brown ink drawing, 23.2 x 13.4 (9⅛ x 5¼), copy by David Allan.

e. (On one sheet with a study of Philip Herbert, 4th Earl of Pembroke.) Pencil, grey ink and wash drawing, 18.7 x 29.6 (7⅜ x 11⅝), copy by David Allan. Purchased 1980.

PG 2508*   Bronze bust, h. 27 (10⅝), by Ponce Jacquio. Executed *c.* 1559/60. Purchased 1982.

MASSEY, William Ferguson, 1856–1925. *Prime Minister of New Zealand*

PG 1135*   Canvas, 102.5 x 79.4 (40⅜ x 31¼), by Sir James Guthrie; study for portrait in *Statesmen of the Great War* (National Portrait Gallery, London). Given by W. G. Gardiner and Sir Frederick C. Gardiner 1930.

MASSON, Professor David, 1822–1907. *Historian and author*

PG 678*   Canvas, 62.2 x 48.9 (24½ x 19¼), by Sir George Reid. Dated 1896. Given by the artist 1909.

MATHIESON, William Law, 1868–1938. *Historian*
PG 1407*   Canvas, 102.2 x 76.2 (40¼ x 30), by D. Gordon Shields, 1934, signed.
            Purchased 1941.

MATY, Paul Henry, 1746–87. *Librarian of the British Museum*
PG 384   Medallion (plaster replica), h. 6.8 (2¹¹⁄₁₆), after James Tassie. Cast from a
            medallion in possession of W. G. Patterson 1889.

MAULE, Harry; see PANMURE (PGL 242).

MAURICE of Orange-Nassau, Prince 1567–1625. *General and Stadholder of the
            Netherlands*
PG 1374   (Formerly called 1st Marquess of Huntly.) Canvas, 60.5 x 47.7 (23¾ x
            18¾), by unknown artist after Jan Anthonisz van Ravesteyn.

MAVOR, Osborne Henry (nom de plume, 'James Bridie'), 1888–1951. *Playwright*
PG 2398   Pencil drawing, 23.2 x 18.4 (9⅛ x 7¼), by Sir William Oliphant Hutchison.
            Given by the executors of Margery, Lady Hutchison 1977.
PG 2636*   Black crayon drawing, 27.5 x 22.7 (10⅞ x 9) (irregular), by Mervyn Peake,
            signed. Executed 1939. Given by Mrs Rona B. Mavor 1985.
PG 2703*   Terracotta head, h. 31.1 (12¼), by Benno Schotz, signed. Sculpted 1953.
            Purchased 1987.

MAXTON, James, 1885–1946. *Labour politician*
PG 1416*   Panel, 111.1 x 85.7 (43¾ x 33¾), by Sir John Lavery, signed. Painted
            c. 1933 and apparently re-touched before 1939. Bequeathed by the artist
            1941.

MAXWELL, Sir Herbert Eustace, 1845–1937. *Historian, biographer and naturalist*
PG 1451*   Pastel drawing, 46.3 x 29.3 (18¼ x 11⁹⁄₁₆), by William Strang, 1917, signed.
            Given by Sir John Stirling Maxwell 1944.
PG 1713   Pencil drawing, 37.5 x 33.7 (14¾ x 13¼), by W. Graham Boss. Given by
            the artist.

MAXWELL, John, 1905–62. *Artist*
PG 2500   Ball-point, chalk, and water-colour drawing, 38.5 x 26.8 (15⅛ x 10⁹⁄₁₆), by
            Emilio Coia, signed. Purchased 1981.

MEADOWBANK, Alexander Maconochie-Welwood, 2nd Lord, 1777–1861. *Judge*
PG 1424*   Canvas, 76.2 x 63.5 (30 x 25), by Sir Martin Archer Shee. Purchased 1941.

MEADOWBANK, Allan Maconochie, 1st Lord, 1748–1816. *Judge*
PG 164   Paste medallion, h. 7.4 (2⅞), by James Tassie. Dated 1791. Given by the
            descendants of Rev. Alexander Bryce 1887.
PG 2188*   Canvas, 76.4 x 63.6 (30⅛ x 25), by Sir Henry Raeburn. Purchased 1970.

MEDINA, Sir John Baptiste de, 1659–1710. *Portrait painter*
  PG 1555* Canvas, 77.2 x 63.5 (30⅜ x 25), self-portrait. Purchased 1950.

MEDWYN, John Hay Forbes, Lord, 1776–1854. *Judge*
  PG 2528* Water-colour on ivory, 10.5 x 7.9 (4³⁄₁₆ x 3⅛) (sight), by Andrew
            Robertson. Transferred from the National Gallery of Scotland 1982.
  PG 2529   Water-colour on card, 12.5 x 10 (4¹⁵⁄₁₆ x 3¹⁵⁄₁₆) (irregular), copy by or after
            Andrew Robertson. Transferred from the National Gallery of Scotland 1982.

MELFORT, John Drummond, 1st Earl of, 1649–1714. *Secretary of State for Scotland and*
            Jacobite
  PG 1083* Canvas, 243.7 x 147.2 (96 x 58), by Sir Godfrey Kneller, 1688, signed.
            Purchased 1928.

MELVILLE, Elizabeth Rennie, Viscountess. *Wife of 1st Viscount Melville*
  PG 2746* Canvas, 127.6 x 101.3 (50¼ x 39⅞), by David Martin. Purchased with
            assistance from the National Heritage Memorial Fund and the National
            Art-Collections Fund 1988.

MELVILLE, George Melville, 1st Earl of, 1636–1707. *Statesman*
  PG 1532* Canvas, 127 x 101.8 (50 x 40⅛), by Sir John Baptiste de Medina, signed (on
            reverse). Purchased 1949.

MELVILLE, Henry Dundas, 1st Viscount, 1742–1811. *Statesman*
  PG 363   Wedgwood medallion, h. 8.9 (3½), after James Tassie. Given by Messrs.
            J. Wedgwood and Sons 1889.
  PG 1267   Paste medallion, h. 9.4 (3¾), by James Tassie. Purchased 1935.
  PG 2745* Canvas, 127.6 x 101.6 (50¼ x 40), by David Martin. painted 1770.
            Purchased with assistance from the National Heritage Memorial Fund and
            the National Art-Collections Fund 1988.
  PGL 123* Canvas, 127 x 101.9 (50 x 40⅛), by John Rising, signed. On loan from the
            Duke of Buccleuch and Queensberry.

MELVILLE of Bennochy and Strathkinness, John Whyte, 1797–1883/5. *Soldier*
  PGL 337* (*A Meet of the Fife Hounds.*) See GROUPS.

MELVILLE, General Robert, 1723–1809. *Soldier and antiquary*
  PG 497   Medallion (plaster replica), h. 7.3 (2⅞), after James Tassie. Dated 1791.
            Cast from a medallion in possession of R. W. Cochran Patrick 1894.
  PG 1852* Canvas, 72.4 x 62.2 (28½ x 24½), by Sir Henry Raeburn. Purchased 1958.

MELVILLE, Robert Saunders Dundas, 2nd Viscount, 1771–1851. *First Lord of the*
            Admiralty
  PG 252*   Canvas, 127 x 101.6 (50 x 40), by Colvin Smith. Given by
            Lieutenant-Colonel W. Hope to the National Gallery of Scotland and
            transferred 1889.

Masson, Professor David
PG 678

Mathieson, William Law
PG 1407

Mavor, Osborne Henry
PG 2636

Mavor, Osborne Henry
PG 2703

Maxton, James
PG 1416

Maxwell, Sir Herbert
Eustace   PG 1451

Meadowbank, 2nd Lord
PG 1424

Meadowbank, 1st Lord
PG 2188

Medina, Sir John de
PG 1555

Medwyn, Lord
PG 2528

Melfort, 1st Earl of
PG 1083

Melville, Viscountess
PG 2746

Melville, 1st Earl of
PG 1532

Melville, 1st Viscount
PG 2745

Melville, 1st Viscount
PGL 123

Melville, Robert
PG 1852

MENDIP, Welbore Ellis, 1st Baron, 1713–1802. *Statesman*
    PG 479   Medallion (plaster replica), h. 9 (3⁹⁄₁₆), after James Tassie. Dated 1780. Cast from a medallion in possession of Jeffery Whitehead 1894.

MENZIES, Colonel, fl. 1899. *Of Northwoodside Curling Club*
    PG 1856*   (*Curling at Carsebreck*.) See GROUPS.

MENZIES of Menzies, Lieutenant-Colonel Sir Robert, 7th Baronet, 1817–1903. *Of Weem Curling Club*
    PG 1856*   (*Curling at Carsebreck*.) See GROUPS.

MERCER, Sir Walter, 1890–1971. *Surgeon*
    PG 2399   Pencil drawing, 23.2 x 18.4 (9⅛ x 7¼), by Sir William Oliphant Hutchison. Given by the executors of Margery, Lady Hutchison 1977.

MEREDITH, George, 1828–1909. *Novelist and poet*
    PG 1018   Pencil drawing, 20.3 x 14.6 (8 x 5¾), by Violet, Duchess of Rutland, signed. Given by Sir Humphrey Rolleston 1926.

MERTOUN
    PG 1023   (Mertoun and the valley of the Tweed.) See SCOTT, Sir Walter

METHVEN, David Smythe, Lord, 1746–1806. *Judge*
    PG 1254   Paste medallion, h. 7.9 (3¹⁄₁₆), by James Tassie. Dated 1794. Purchased 1935.

MICHIE, David Alan Redpath, b. 1928. *Artist*
    PGL 328*   (*Gathering at 7 London Street*.) See GROUPS.

MILLAR, Dr James, 1762–1827. *Physician and author*
    PG 879*   Crayon drawing, 45.7 x 39.3 (18 x 15½), by John Henning. Bequeathed by the Misses C. and E. Gibson 1918.

MILLAR, Professor John, 1735–1801. *Professor of Law at Glasgow University*
    PG 158   Paste medallion, h. 7.6 (3), by James Tassie. Dated 1796. Purchased 1886.

MILLER, Hugh, 1802–56. *Geologist and author*
    PG 255*   Marble bust, h. 91.3 (36), by William Brodie, signed. Transferred from the National Gallery of Scotland 1889.

MILLER, Very Rev. John Harry, 1869–1940. *Principal of St Mary's College, St Andrews*
    PG 1790   Black chalk drawing, 45.5 x 28.6 (18 x 11¼), by David Foggie, 1933, signed. Given by Mrs M. Foggie 1955.

MILLER of Dalswinton, Patrick, 1731–1815. *Pioneer in steam navigation*
    PG 385   Medallion (plaster replica), h. 7.5 (2¹⁵⁄₁₆), after James Tassie. Dated 1789. Cast from a medallion in possession of W. G. Patterson 1889.

MILNE, George Francis Milne, 1st Baron, 1866–1948. *Field-Marshal*
  PG 1012*   (Study for portrait in *General Officers of World War I, 1914–18*, in the
                  National Portrait Gallery, London.) Canvas, 56 x 40.7 (22⅟16 x 16), by John
                  Singer Sargent. Purchased 1925.

MILNER, Sir Alfred Milner, 1st Viscount, 1845–1925. *Statesman*
  PG 1138*   Canvas, 76.5 x 102.3 (30⅛ x 40¼), by Sir James Guthrie; study for portrait
                  in *Statesmen of the Great War* (National Portrait Gallery, London). Given
                  by W. G. Gardiner and Sir Frederick C. Gardiner 1930.

MILTON, Andrew Fletcher, Lord, 1692–1766. *Lord Justice-Clerk*
  PG 1663   a. Water-colour, 16.2 x 11.3 (6⅜ x 4½), by Robert Scott after Allan
                  Ramsay, signed. Bequeathed by W. F. Watson 1886.
                  b. (View of the sitter's house.) Water-colour drawing, 6.6 x 8.2 (2⅝ x 3¼),
                  by unknown artist. Bequeathed by W. F. Watson 1886.
  PGL 263*   Canvas, 76 x 63.2 (29⅞ x 24⅞), by Allan Ramsay, 1748, signed. On loan
                  from J. T. T. Fletcher.

MILTON, John, 1608–74. *Poet and scholar*
  PG 1015*   Terracotta bust, h. 56.2 (22⅛), by Louis François Roubiliac. Probably
                  modelled in 1759. Purchased 1925.
  PG 1025   Bust (plaster replica), h. 29 (11⅜), after Edward Pierce. Purchased 1926.

MINTO, Gilbert Elliot, 1st Earl of, 1751–1814. *Statesman and Governor-General of India*
  PG 335   Ink and pencil drawing, 23.8 x 17.2 (9⅜ x 6¾), by James Atkinson. Given
                  by the Rev. Canon Atkinson 1892.
  PGL 301*   Canvas, 232.5 x 148.5 (91½ x 54¼), by George Chinnery. Painted
                  c. 1811–12. On loan from Roxburgh District Council.

MINTO, Gilbert Elliot, 2nd Earl of, 1782–1859. *Statesman*
  PG 931   Medallion (plaster replica), h. 7 (2¾), after unknown artist. Given by
                  Francis Scott 1922.

MITCHELL, Sir Arthur, 1826–1909. *Writer on insanity and antiquary*
  PG 769*   Pencil drawing, 32.8 x 24.2 (12¹⁵⁄16 x 9½), by John Henry Lorimer, 1891,
                  signed. Bequeathed by J. M. Gray 1894.
  PG 1464   Canvas, 127 x 101.6 (50 x 40), by Sir George Reid. Given by Sir George
                  A. Mitchell 1945.
  PG 1692   Pencil drawing, 37.5 x 33.7 (14¾ x 13¼), by W. Graham Boss. Given by
                  the artist.

MODENA, Mary of, 1658–1718. *Consort of James VII and II*
  PG 976*   Canvas, 125.1 x 101 (49¼ x 39¾), by Willem Wissing, 1687, signed.
                  Purchased 1924.
  PG 2116   Pencil drawing, 13.1 x 10.1 (5⅛ × 4), by Robert White. Transferred from
                  the National Gallery of Scotland 1950.

MOFFAT, Graham, 1866–1951. *Actor and playwright*
  PG 2307*   Canvas, 137.2 x 91.8 (54 x 36⅛), by Cowan Dobson, 1914, signed. Given by
             Dr R. L. Hutchison 1975.

MOFFAT, Margaret Liddel Lincks, Mrs Graham, d. 1943. *Actress*
  PG 2308   Canvas, 137.8 x 92.2 (54¼ x 36¼), by Cowan Dobson, 1914, signed. Given
             by Dr R. L. Hutchison 1975.

MOFFAT, Robert, 1795–1883. *Missionary*
  PG 2035*   (With John Mokoteri and Sarah Roby.) Canvas, 53.4 x 45.7 (21 x 18), by
             William Scott, 1842, signed. Purchased 1964.

MOIR, David Macbeth, 1798–1851. *Physician and author*
  PG 2179*   Water-colour, 23.5 x 18.4 (9¼ x 7¼), by John Faed, signed. Purchased 1970.
  PG 2512   Water-colour, 25.7 x 17.4 (10⅛ x 6⅞), by Daniel Maclise. Purchased 1982.
  PG 2752*   Canvas, 92 x 71.5 (36¼ x 28⅛), by Sir John Watson Gordon. Painted 1850.
             Purchased 1988.

MOIR, James, fl. *c.* 1830.
  PG 1359   Pencil drawing, 9.3 x 8.6 (3⅝ x 3⅜), attributed to George Meikle Kemp.
             Given by Thomas Ritchie 1938.

MONBODDO, James Burnett, Lord, 1714–99. *Judge and author*
  PG 362*   Pencil drawing, 55.5 x 43.5 (21⅞ x 17⅛), by John Brown. Purchased 1888.
  PG 946*   (*The Inauguration of Robert Burns as Poet Laureate of the Lodge
             Canongate, Kilwinning, 1787.*) See GROUPS.
  PG 1770*   (*Burns at an evening party of Lord Monboddo's 1786.*) See GROUPS.

MONCK, General George; see ALBEMARLE

MONCKTON, Lieutenant-General Robert, 1726–82. *Second in Command to Wolfe at
             Quebec and Governor of New York*
  PG 1256   Paste medallion, h. 8 (3½), by James Tassie. Purchased 1935.

MONCRIEFF, Colonel Sir Alexander, 1829–1906. *Engineer*
  PG 1076   Pencil drawing, 32.2 x 24.1 (12⅝ x 9½), by John Henry Lorimer, 1891,
             signed. Bequeathed by J. M. Gray 1894.

MONCRIEFF, Sir James Wellwood Moncrieff, Lord, 1776–1851. *Judge*
  PGL 51   Plaster bust, h. 72.4 (28½), by Samuel Joseph. Dated 1823. On loan from
             the Trustees of William Moncrieff.

MONMOUTH AND BUCCLEUCH, James Scott, Duke of, 1649–85. *Natural son of
             Charles II by Lucy Walter*
  PG 1459   Water-colour on ivory, 2.8 x 2.4 (1⅛ x 1), by Charles Boit. Bequeathed by
             Sir St Clair Thomson 1944.

Melville, 2nd Viscount
PG 252

Millar, Dr James
PG 879

Miller, Hugh
PG 255

Milne, 1st Baron
PG 1012

Milner, 1st Viscount
PG 1138

Milton, Lord
PGL 263

Milton, John
PG 1015

Minto, 1st Earl of
PGL 301

Mitchell, Sir Arthur
PG 769

Modena, Mary of
PG 976

Moffat, Graham
PG 2307

Moffat, Rev. Robert, with John
Mokoteri and Sarah Roby   PG 2035

Moir, David Macbeth
PG 2179

Moir, David Macbeth
PG 2752

Monboddo, Lord
PG 362

Montgomery, Sir James
William   PGL 87

MONMOUTH AND BUCCLEUCH, James Scott, Duke of (*continued*)

PG 2765   (Execution of the Duke of Monmouth and the 9th Earl of Argyll.) Silver medal, dia. 6.2 (2⁷⁄₁₆), by Regnier Arondeaux. Purchased 1989.

MONRO, Lady

PG 2568   Water-colour on ivory, 14.5 x 10.7 (5¾ x 4¼) (sight), by Robert Thorburn. Transferred from the National Gallery of Scotland 1982.

MONRO, Alexander, 'Secundus', 1733–1817. *Anatomist*

PG 232   Plaster bust, h. 74.5 (29⅜), by unknown artist. Purchased 1888.

MONRO, Alexander, 'Tertius', 1773–1859. *Anatomist*

PG 782   Cut paper silhouette, h. 21.6 (8½), by Augustin Edouart. Purchased 1912.

MONTGOMERY, Sir James, 1766–1839. *Lord Advocate*

PG 800   Cut paper silhouette, h. 16.2 (6⅜), by Augustin Edouart. Purchased 1912.

MONTGOMERY, Sir James William, 1721–1803. *Lord Advocate and Chief Baron of the Exchequer*

PGL 87*   Pencil drawing, 48.9 x 35.8 (19¼ x 14⅛), by John Brown. On loan from the National Museums of Scotland.

MONTGOMERY, Robert, 1774–1854. *Barrister*

PG 606*   Canvas, 73 x 61 (28¾ x 24), by Sir Henry Raeburn. Cut down from three-quarter length at an unknown date. Bequeathed by Dean Montgomery 1903.

MONTROSE, James Graham, 1st Marquess of, 1612–50. *Royalist*

PG 978   Canvas, 76.3 x 63.5 (30¹⁄₁₆ x 25), copy by William Hastie Geissler after Willem van Honthorst. Commissioned 1924.

PG 998*   Canvas, 128 x 105 (50⅜ x 41⅜), attributed to Willem van Honthorst. Purchased 1925.

PG 1773   Wash drawing, 26.3 x 19.8 (10⅜ x 7⅞), by unknown artist after William Dobson. Purchased 1948.

PG 2418*   Canvas, 75.6 x 58.4 (29¾ x 23), attributed to William Dobson. Bequeathed by Lady Malise Graham 1978.

MONTROSE, James Graham, 3rd Duke of, 1755–1836. *Lord Chamberlain*

PG 1040*   (*The entrance of George IV at Holyroodhouse.*) See GROUPS.

MOORE, James Carrick 1762/3–1834. *Surgeon and associate of Edward Jenner*

PG 2731*   Canvas, 76.2 x 63.5 (30 x 25), attributed to John Jackson. Purchased 1988.

MOORE, Dr John, 1729–1802. *Physician and author*

PG 571*   Canvas, 76.2 x 63.5 (30 x 25), by Sir Thomas Lawrence. Painted *c*. 1790. Given by Miss Carrick Moore 1898.

PG 1770*   (*Burns at an evening party of Lord Monboddo's 1786.*) See GROUPS.

MOORE, Lieutenant-General Sir John, 1761–1809. *Soldier*
  PG 1301*   (Fragment of the *Death of Abercromby*.) Canvas, 95.9 x 71.1 (37¾ x 28), by
                James Northcote. Purchased 1936.
  PG 2680*   (*The Battle of Alexandria, 21 March 1801*.) See GROUPS.

MOORE, Thomas, 1779–1851. *Poet*
  PG 825*   (*Sir Walter Scott and his friends at Abbotsford*.) See GROUPS.

MORAY, James Stewart, Earl of, *c.* 1531–70. *Regent of Scotland*
  PG 1002   Canvas, 38 x 28 (15 x 11), copy by Hugh Monro after unknown artist.
                Commissioned 1925.

MORE, Charles, fl. 1787. *Of the Royal Bank of Scotland*
  PG 946*   (As Depute-Master, in *The Inauguration of Robert Burns as Poet Laureate
                of the Lodge Canongate, Kilwinning, 1787*.) See GROUPS.

MORE, Hannah, 1745–1833. *Religious writer*
  PG 2280   Cut paper silhouette, h. 17.5 (6⅞), by Augustin Edouart, 1831, signed.
                Provenance untraced.

MORE, John Shank, *c.* 1784–1861. *Professor of Scots Law at Edinburgh University*
  PG 2159   Cut paper silhouette, h. 16.6 (6⁹⁄₁₆), by Augustin Edouart, 1830, signed.
                Given by Mrs J. H. G. Ross 1969.
  PG 2306   (Crombie Sketchbook, fo. 6r. Study for *Modern Athenians*, Pl. 25.) Pencil
                drawing, 15.6 x 20 (6⅛ x 7⅞), by Benjamin William Crombie. Purchased 1938.

MOREAU, General Jean-Victor, 1763–1813. *Soldier*
  PG 2682   e. (Study related to *The Battle of Alexandria* and *The Landing of British
                Troops at Aboukir*.) Water-colour, 12.7 x 8.9 (5 x 3½), by unknown artist
                after Charles François Levachez. Purchased 1986.

MORGAN, Edwin, b. 1920. *Poet*
  PG 2597*   (*Poets' Pub*.) See GROUPS.

MORISON, Sir Alexander, 1779–1866. *Alienist*
  PG 2623*   Canvas, 51.1 x 61.3 (20⅛ x 24⅛), by Richard Dadd, signed. Dated 1852.
                Purchased with assistance from the National Heritage Memorial Fund 1984.

MORRIS, Edward Patrick Morris, 1st Baron, 1858–1935. *Prime Minister of Newfoundland*
  PG 1141*   Canvas, 100.4 x 77.8 (39½ x 30⅝), by Sir James Guthrie; study for portrait
                in *Statesmen of the Great War* (National Portrait Gallery, London). Given
                by W. G. Gardiner and Sir Frederick Gardiner 1930.

MORRISON, Robert, 1782–1834. *Missionary in China*
  PG 1237*   Pencil and water-colour drawing, 22.5 x 18 (8⅞ x 7⅛)), by William
                Nicholson. Purchased 1934.

MORTON, 13th Earl of, Family of; see GROUPS (PG 2233).

MORTON, Agatha Halyburton, Countess of, d. 1748. *Wife of 13th Earl of Morton*
    PG 2233* See GROUPS.

MORTON, George Douglas, 15th Earl of, 1761–1827. *Lord High Commissioner to the Church of Scotland and Lord-Lieutenant of Fifeshire*
    PG 1040* (*The Entrance of George IV at Holyroodhouse.*) See GROUPS.

MORTON, James Douglas, 4th Earl of, d. 1581. *Regent of Scotland*
    PG 839   Canvas, 55.1 x 45.9 (21^{11}⁄$_{16}$ x 18^{1}⁄$_{16}$), by unknown artist. Dated 1577. Purchased 1914.
    PG 1857* Panel, 106.3 x 82.1 (41^{7}⁄$_{8}$ x 32^{5}⁄$_{16}$), attributed to Arnold Bronckorst. Painted *c.* 1580. Purchased 1959.
    PG 2461   d. Pencil, grey ink and wash drawing, 18.4 x 14.7 (7^{1}⁄$_{4}$ x 5^{3}⁄$_{4}$), copy by David Allan. Purchased 1980.

MORTON, James Douglas, 13th Earl of. *c.* 1702–1768. *Keeper of the Records of Scotland and President of the Royal Society*
    PG 2233* See GROUPS.

MORTON, Sholto Charles Douglas, 14th Earl of Morton, 1732–74.
    PG 2233* (As Lord Aberdour.) See GROUPS.

MORTON, William Douglas, 8th Earl of, 1582–1648. *Lord High Treasurer of Scotland*
    PG 1858   Canvas, 76.5 x 63.5 (30^{1}⁄$_{8}$ x 25), by unknown artist. Purchased 1959.

MOTHERWELL, William, 1797–1835. *Poet*
    PG 235   Wax medallion, h. 9.8 (3^{7}⁄$_{8}$), by John Fillans. Dated 1835. Purchased 1888.
    PG 236   Plaster bust, h. 58.4 (23), by James Fillans. Given by Sir Joseph Noël Paton 1888.
    PG 313   Canvas, 30.5 x 26 (12 x 10^{1}⁄$_{4}$), by Andrew Henderson. Bequeathed by W. F. Watson 1886.
    PG 790   Cut paper silhouette, h. 19.2 (7^{9}⁄$_{16}$), by Augustin Edouart. Purchased 1912.

MOUBRAY, John James, 1857–1928. *Of Naemoor Curling Club*
    PG 1856* (*Curling at Carsebreck.*) See GROUPS.

MOUNCEY, William, 1852–1901. *Landscape painter*
    PG 1386   Millboard, 25.3 x 35.5 (10 x 14), by William Stewart MacGeorge, signed. Purchased 1939.

MOUNT EDGECUMBE, Caroline Augusta Feilding, Countess of (d. 1881).
    PG 2571   Water-colour on ivory, 31 x 19 (12 x 11^{1}⁄$_{2}$), (irregular), by Robert Thorburn. Transferred from the National Gallery of Scotland 1982.

MOUNTSTUART, John Stuart, Viscount; see UNIDENTIFIED (PG 2243).

Montgomery, Robert
PG 606

Montrose, 1st Marquess of
PG 998

Montrose, 1st Marquess of
PG 2418

Moore, James Carrick
PG 2731

Moore, Dr John
PG 571

Moore, Sir John
PG 1301

Morison, Sir Alexander
PG 2623

Morris, 1st Baron
PG 1141

Morrison, Robert
PG 1237

Morton, 4th Earl of
PG 1857

Muir, Thomas
PG 1668

Muir, Willa
PG 2186

Munro, Neil
PG 928

Munro, Neil
PG 1161

Murdoch, William Garden Blaikie
PG 2430

MUIR, Thomas, 1765–98. *Parliamentary reformer*
PG 1668*   Chalk drawing, 29.8 x 18.6 (11¾ x 7⁵⁄₁₆), by David Martin, signed.
Bequeathed by W. F. Watson 1886.

MUIR, Thomas Scott, 1896–1928. *Geographical writer*
PG 2649   Bronze medal, dia. 5 (2), by Charles d'Orville Pilkington Jackson, signed on
the obverse. Dated 1930. Given by the trustees of the artist 1985.

MUIR, Willa Anderson, Mrs Edwin, d. 1970. *Writer and translator*
PG 2186*   Plywood, 59.9 x 53.3 (23⁹⁄₁₆ x 21), by Nigel McIsaac, 1944, signed. Given by
the artist 1970.

MUIRHEAD, David, 1867–1930. *Artist*
PG 1434   Pencil drawing, 23 x 17.4 (9 x 6⅞), by Dugald Sutherland MacColl, signed.
Dated *c.* 1898. Given by A. E. Borthwick 1943.

MULGRAVE, Edmund Sheffield, 1st Earl of, *c.* 1564–1646. *Vice-Admiral of Yorkshire*
PG 2092   Wash drawing, 14.5 x 8.8 (5⅝ x 3¾), attributed to George Perfect Harding
after engraving by Renold Elstrack. Transferred from the National Gallery
of Scotland 1950.

MUNRO, General Sir Hector, 1726–1805. *Soldier*
PG 468   Medallion (plaster replica), h. 8.3 (3¼), after James Tassie. Dated 1796.
Cast from a medallion in possession of R. W. Cochran Patrick 1893.

MUNRO of Lindertis, Sir Hugh Thomas, 4th Baronet, 1856–1919. *Writer on mountaineering*
PG 2630   (Called Sir Hugh Thomas Munro.) Chalk drawing, 57 x 42.3 (22½ x 16⅝),
by unknown artist. Provenance untraced.

MUNRO, Neil, 1864–1930. *Author*
PG 928*   Pastel drawing, 41.9 x 26.9 (16½ x 10⁹⁄₁₆), by William Strang, 1903, signed.
Purchased 1921.
PG 1161*   Canvas, 68.5 x 53.4 (25 x 21), by Stansmore Dean (Mrs Robert Macaulay
Stevenson), signed. Purchased 1931.

MUNRO, Robert, 1835–1920. *Anthropologist and archaeologist*
PG 1706   Pencil drawing, 37.5 x 33.6 (14¾ x 13¼), by W. Graham Boss. Given by
the artist.

MURCHISON, Sir Roderick Impey, 1792–1871. *Geologist*
PG 747   Plaster bust, h. 71.2 (28¹⁄₁₆), by Sir Richard Westmacott. Dated 1848. Given
by Miss A. F. Yule 1910.

MURDOCH, William Garden Blaikie, 1880–1934. *Art critic and writer*
PG 2430*   Canvas, 51.4 x 41.3 (20¼ x 16¼), by Horace Brodzky, 1917, signed.
Purchased 1978.

MURDOCK, William, 1754–1839. *Engineer; inventor of gas lighting*
  PG 808   Bust (plaster replica), h. 73.3 (24⅞), after Sir Francis Legatt Chantrey.
              Purchased 1912.

MURRAY, Alexander, 1712–78. *Jacobite*
  PGL 26*   Canvas, 76.5 x 63.5 (30⅛ x 25), by Allan Ramsay, 1742, signed. On loan
              from the National Museums of Scotland.

MURRAY, Professor Alexander, 1775–1813. *Linguist*
  PG 196*   Pencil drawing, 24.6 x 17.4 (9¹¹⁄₁₆ x 6⅞), by Andrew Geddes, 1812, signed.
              Purchased 1887.

MURRAY, Charles David Murray, Lord, 1866–1936. *Lord Advocate*
  PG 1797   Black chalk drawing, 44.9 x 28 (17⅝ x 11), by David Foggie, 1933, signed.
              Given by Mrs M. Foggie 1955.

MURRAY, Sir David, 1849–1933. *Artist*
  PG 1149   Millboard, 19.4 x 14.6 (7⅝ x 5¾), by James Archer. Given by the Royal
              Scottish Academy 1931.
  PG 1233*   Canvas, 42.3 x 35.5 (16⅝ x 14), by John Pettie, signed. Purchased 1934.
  PG 1234   Canvas, 61 x 51.1 (24 x 20⅛), by Reginald George Jennings, 1914, signed.
              Purchased 1934.

MURRAY of Elibank, Alexander Murray, 1st Baron, 1870–1920. *Parliamentarian*
  PG 1573   Water-colour over half-tone reproduction on synthetic ivory base, 12.7 x 10
              (5 x 3¹⁵⁄₁₆), by unknown artist. Given by Lord Elibank 1951.

MURRAY of Gorthy, Sir David, 1567–1629. *Poet*
  PGL 20*   Canvas, 54.1 x 43.8 (21⁵⁄₁₆ x 17¼), by unknown artist. Dated 1603. On loan
              from the National Museums of Scotland.

MURRAY, Lord George, c. 1700–60. *Jacobite general*
  PG 2635*   (*The Battle of Glenshiel 1719.*) See GROUPS.
  PG 2754*   Chinese ink drawing, 9 x 7.3 (3⅝ x 2⅞) (oval), by Sir Robert Strange,
              signed. Purchased 1988.

MURRAY, General Sir George, 1772–1846. *Soldier and statesman*
  PG 639*   Canvas, 63.8 x 38.7 (25⅛ x 15¼), by Henry William Pickersgill. Purchased
              1905.
  PG 889   Chalk drawing, 52.7 x 38.4 (20¾ x 15⅛), by John Linnell, 1836, signed.
              Purchased 1918.

MURRAY, Hugh, 1779–1846. *Geographer*
  PG 2674   Pencil drawing with chalk highlights, 29.4 x 24.5 (11⁹⁄₁₆ x 9⅝) (irregular),
              by Andrew Geddes, signed with initials. Dated indistinctly 181[3].
              Purchased 1985.

MURRAY, General James, 1719–94. *Governor of Quebec and Minorca*
   PG 2215*   Canvas, 76.1 x 63.5 (29¹⁵⁄₁₆ x 25), by Allan Ramsay, 1742, signed.
              Bequeathed by 13th Baron Elibank 1973.

MURRAY, John, 1745–93. *Publisher*
   PG 464   Medallion (plaster replica), h. 7.6 (3), after James Tassie. Dated 1790. Cast
             from a medallion in possession of Jeffery Whitehead 1893.

MURRAY, Sir John, c. 1768–1827. *Soldier*
   PG 2513*   (With Sir James Murray-Pulteney.) Canvas, 76.9 x 91.8 (30¼ x 36⅛),
              attributed to John Thomas Seton. Painted c. 1788/94. Purchased 1982.

MURRAY, Sir John Archibald Murray, Lord, 1779–1859. *Judge*
   PG 1066*   Canvas, 127 x 101.6 (50 x 40), by Sir John Watson Gordon, 1856, signed.
              Bequeathed by Lady Murray to the National Gallery of Scotland in 1861
              and transferred.

MURRAY, Sir Mungo, 1668–1700. *Son of 2nd Earl of Atholl*
   PG 997*   (Formerly known as Highland Chieftain.) Canvas, 224.8 x 154.3 (88½ x
              60¾), by John Michael Wright. Painted c. 1683. Purchased 1925.

MURRAY, R. G., fl. 1899. *Of Biggar Curling Club*
   PG 1856*   (*Curling at Carsebreck.*) See GROUPS.

MURRAY, William, 1737–78. *Soldier*
   PG 2710*   Wax medallion, h. 16.5 (6½), by Samuel Percy. Given by Mrs Iseude M.
              Smythe 1986.

MURRAY, William Henry, 1790–1852. *Actor and manager of Theatre Royal, Edinburgh*
   PG 190*   Panel, 18.6 x 14.3 (7⅜ x 5⅝), by Sir William Allan, 1848, signed.
              Purchased 1887.
   PG 904*   Canvas, 82 x 63.9 (32¼ x 25⅛), by Sir William Allan, 1843, signed.
              Bequeathed by Mrs Harriet Smythe 1919.
   PG 2306   (As Paul Pry; Crombie Sketchbook, fo. 4.) Pencil drawing, 15.6 x 20
              (6⅛ x 7⅞), by Benjamin William Crombie. Purchased 1938.

MURRAY of Ochtertyre, Sir William Keith, 9th Baronet, 1872–1956. *Of Ochtertyre
              Curling Club*
   PG 1856*   (*Curling at Carsebreck.*) See GROUPS.

MURRAY-PULTENEY, Sir James, c. 1751–1811. *Soldier and politician*
   PG 638   Canvas, 44.4 x 36.8 (17½ x 14½), by unknown artist. Purchased 1905.
   PG 2513*   (With Sir John Murray.) Canvas, 76.9 x 91.8 (30¼ x 36⅛), attributed to
              John Thomas Seton. Painted c. 1788/94. Purchased 1982.

Murray, Alexander
PG L 26

Murray, Professor Alexander
PG 196

Murray, Sir David
PG 1233

Murray of Gorthy, Sir David
PG L 20

Murray, Lord George
PG 2754

Murray, Sir George
PG 639

Murray, James
PG 2215

Murray, Sir John, with Sir James
Murray-Pulteney   PG 2513

Murray, Lord
PG 1066

Murray, Sir Mungo
PG 997

Murray, William
PG 2710

Murray, William Henry
PG 190

Murray, William Henry
PG 904

Mylne, John
PG 1536

MUSICIANS, two unidentified, fl. 1845
    PG 2293   Pencil drawing, 26.4 x 20.9 (10⅜ x 8¼), by J. E. Jones, 1845, signed.
                Provenance untraced.

MYLNE, John, 1611–67. *Master mason*
    PG 105   Pencil drawing, 24.4 x 17.3 (9⅝ x 6¾), by unknown artist. Bequeathed by
                W. F. Watson 1886.
    PG 1536*   Copper, 90.2 x 71.2 (35½ x 28⅛), by unknown artist. Probably painted
                c. 1650/60. Purchased 1949.

NAIRNE, Carolina Oliphant, Baroness, 1766–1845. *Songwriter*
PG 610*   (With her son William Murray Nairne.) Canvas, 90.9 x 70.2 (35¾ x 27⅝),
          by Sir John Watson Gordon. Bequeathed by K. Oliphant 1903.
PG 1125   Canvas, 76.2 x 63.4 (30 x 25), by Sir John Watson Gordon. Given by
          Dr R. F. Barbour 1930.

NAIRNE, William Murray Nairne, 6th Lord, 1808–37. *Son of Baroness Nairne*
PG 610*   (With Baroness Nairne.) Canvas, 90.9 x 70.2 (35¾ x 27⅝), by Sir John
          Watson Gordon. Bequeathed by K. Oliphant 1903.

NAPIER, Sir Archibald Napier, 1st Lord, 1576–1645. *Extraordinary Lord of Session*
PG 1833* Canvas (conjoined with 1st Earl of Airth PG 1834), 106.7 x 128.3 (42 x
          50½), by George Jamesone. Dated 1637. Purchased 1956.

NAPIER, Sir Charles, 1786–1860. *Admiral*
PG 7*   Canvas, 121.9 x 101.6 (48 x 40), by John Simpson. Purchased 1884.
PG 539   Medallion (plaster replica), h. 6.4 (2⅝), after John Henning. Dated 1811.
          Given by Miss Brown 1894.
PG 1680* a. Water-colour, 12.8 x 9.5 (5 1/16 x 3¾), by Benjamin William Crombie,
          1844, signed.
          b. (View of Napier's birthplace at Falkirk.) Water-colour, 6.4 x 10.8
          (2½ x 4¼), by unknown artist. Bequeathed by W. F. Watson 1886.

NAPIER, General Sir Charles James, 1782–1853. *Conqueror of Sind*
PG 586   Bronze bust, h. 37.5 (14¾), by George Gamon Adams. Dated 1853.
          Purchased 1899.
PG 1679   Ink drawing, 34.3 x 26 (13½ x 10¼), by John Faed after a bust by Patric
          Park. Dated 1854. Bequeathed by W. F. Watson 1886.

NAPIER, David, 1790–1869. *Marine engineer*
PG 587   Plaster bust, h. 90.7 (35¾), by Matthew Noble, 1870, signed. Given by
          C. B. Trollope 1900.

NAPIER of Merchiston, Francis Napier, 7th Lord, 1758–1823. *Soldier; Representative*
          Peer of Scotland and Lord-Lieutenant of the county of Selkirk
PG 946*   (*The Inauguration of Robert Burns as Poet Laureate of the Lodge*
          Canongate, Kilwinning, 1787.) See GROUPS.

NAPIER, Francis Napier, 10th Baron, and 1st Baron Ettrick, 1819–98. *Diplomat and*
          Governor of Madras
PG 811*   Panel, 61.6 x 51.4 (24¼ x 20¼), by George Frederic Watts, 1866, signed.
          Purchased 1912.

NAPIER of Merchiston, John, 1550–1617. *Discoverer of logarithms*
PG 987   Canvas, 63.5 x 76.7 (25 x 30¼), by Archibald McGlashan after unknown
          artist. Commissioned 1925.

NAPIER of Merchiston, John (*continued*)

PG 2228   Canvas, 110.7 x 99.5 (43⁹⁄₁₆ x 39³⁄₁₆), copy by unknown artist. Dated 1616.
            Purchased with assistance from the National Art-Collections Fund and
            the Pilgrim Trust 1974.

NAPIER, Professor Macvey, 1776–1847. *Editor of the* Edinburgh Review

PG 1689   Ink and wash drawing, 15.9 x 11 (6¼ x 4⅜), by P. Slater, signed.
            Bequeathed by W. F. Watson 1886.

NAPIER, Margaret Graham, Lady, d. *c.* 1626. *Sister of 1st Marquess of Montrose and
            wife of 1st Lord Napier*

PG 2608*   Canvas, 109.3 x 81 (43 x 32), attributed to Adam de Colone. Painted 1626.
            Purchased 1984.

NAPIER, Mark, 1798–1879. *Historical biographer*

PG 1388*   Canvas, 104.1 x 81.3 (41 x 32), by Colvin Smith. Painted 1867. Purchased
            1939.

NAPIER, Robert, 1791–1876. *Marine engineer*

PG 791*   Cut paper silhouette, h. 15.9 (6¼), by Augustin Edouart. Cut 1832.
            Purchased 1912.

NAPIER of Magdala, Robert Cornelis Napier, 1st Baron, 1810–90. *Field-marshal*

PG 566*   Canvas, 53.3 x 36.2 (21 x 14¼), by Michael Angelo Pittatore. Painted 1869.
            Purchased 1897.
PG 1977   Chalk drawing, 35.5 x 27 (14 x 10⅝), by T. Blake Wirgman, signed. Dated
            1886. Given by Aberdeen University 1961.

NAPIER, General Sir William Francis Patrick, 1785–1860. *Military historian*

PG 585   Bust (plaster replica), h. 68.5 (27), after George Gamon Adams. Dated 1855.
            Purchased 1899.

NAPOLEON BONAPARTE, 1769–1821. *Emperor of France*

PG 243   Plaster bust, h. 81.9 (32¼), by George Garrard. Dated 1802. Given by
            W. Calder Marshall 1889.
PG 1919   Medallion (plaster replica), h. 7.5 (2¹⁵⁄₁₆), after James Tassie. Provenance
            untraced.
PG 2324   Ivory, 7.9 x 6.2 (3⅛ x 2⁷⁄₁₆), attributed to J. R. Galland, 1817, signed.
            Bequeathed by W. F. Watson 1886.

NASMYTH, Alexander, Family of; see GROUPS (PG 2729a).

NASMYTH, Alexander, 1758–1840. *Artist*

PG 1381   (With Robert Burns at Roslin Castle.) Pencil drawing, 15.9 x 21 (6¼ x 8¼),
            by Alexander Nasmyth, 1786, signed. Transferred from the National
            Gallery of Scotland 1939.

Nairne, Baroness, with
William Murray Nairne
PG 610

Napier, Sir Charles
PG 7

Napier, Sir Charles
PG 1680a

Napier, 10th Baron, and
1st Baron Ettrick   PG 811

Napier, Lady
PG 2608

Napier, Mark
PG 1388

Napier, Robert
PG 791

Napier of Magdala, 1st Baron
PG 566

Nasmyth, Alexander, with
Barbara Nasmyth   PG 2729b

Nasmyth, Charlotte
PG 2039

Nasmyth, James
PG 1547

Neill, Alexander Sutherland
PG 2204

Neill, Alexander Sutherland
PG 2638

Nelson, Viscount
PG 965

Nelson, William
PG 1435

NASMYTH, Alexander (*continued*)

PG 2729*   (verso) b. (With his wife, Barbara Foulis.) Ink and wash drawing, 15.3 x 20 (6 x 7⅞), by David Octavius Hill, 1829. Purchased 1987.

NASMYTH, Charlotte, 1804–84. *Artist*

PG 2039*   Canvas, 76.5 x 63.8 (30⅛ x 25⅛), by William Nicholson. Transferred from the National Gallery of Scotland 1964.

PG 2729a.*   (The Nasmyth family.) See GROUPS.

NASMYTH, James, 1808–90. *Inventor of the steam hammer*

PG 1547*   Pastel drawing, 24.6 x 17.2 (9¹¹⁄₁₆ x 6¾), self-portrait. Dated 1881. Purchased 1950.

PG 2729a.*   (The Nasmyth family.) See GROUPS.

NEILL, Alexander Sutherland, 1883–1973. *Educationalist*

PG 2204*   Bronze head, h. 29.8 (11¾), by Alan Thornhill. Modelled 1971. Cast 1972. Purchased 1972.

PG 2638*   Canvas, 76.2 x 61 (30 x 24), by Ishbel McWhirter, signed. Dated 1964. Purchased 1985.

NELSON, Horatio Nelson, Viscount, 1758–1805. *Admiral; victor of Trafalgar*

PG 489   Medallion (plaster replica), h. 9 (3⁹⁄₁₆), after William Tassie. Dated 1805. Cast from a medallion in possession of Jeffery Whitehead 1894.

PG 863   Pastel drawing, 48.3 x 37.8 (19 x 14⅞), by unknown artist. Purchased 1917.

PG 965*   Canvas, 76.2 x 64 (30 x 25¼), by Lemuel Francis Abbott. Given by Andrew T. Reid 1924.

PG 1357   Medallion (plaster replica), 9.1 (3⁹⁄₁₆), after William Tassie. Dated 1805. Purchased 1938.

NELSON, William, 1816–87. *Publisher and philanthropist*

PG 1435*   Marble bust, h. 75.3 (29¹¹⁄₁₆), by William Brodie, 1880, signed. Given by Mrs W. I. Mitchell-Innes 1942.

NEWARK, David Leslie, 1st Lord, d. 1682. *Royalist general*

PG 1638   Pencil and chalk drawing, 34 x 27.8 (13⅜ x 10⅞), by the 11th Earl of Buchan, 1795, signed, after unknown artist. Bequeathed by W. F. Watson 1886.

PGL 267   Canvas, 68.9 x 54.7 (27⅛ x 21½), by or after George Jamesone. On loan from J. T. T. Fletcher.

NEWHALL, Sir Walter Pringle, Lord, *c.* 1664–1736. *Scottish judge*

PG 2174   Canvas, 74.3 x 61.2 (29¼ x 24¼), attributed to Andrew Allan. Purchased 1970.

NEWTON, Sir Charles Hay, Lord, *c.* 1740–1811. *Judge*

PG 668*   Ink drawing, 22.3 x 16.9 (9¾ x 6⅝), by John Clerk. Purchased from the Gray Bequest Fund 1908.

PGL 302*   Canvas, 76.4 x 63.1 (30¹⁄₁₆ x 24⅞), by Sir Henry Raeburn. Painted *c.* 1807.
           On loan from the National Gallery of Scotland.

NEWTON, Sir Isaac, 1642–1727. *Natural philosopher*
PG 1920   Medallion (plaster replica), h. 3.2 (1¼), after James Tassie. Provenance
           untraced.

NICHOLSON, Mabel Pryde, Mrs William, d. 1918. *Sister of James Pryde and wife of*
           (Sir) William Nicholson
PG 2653   (With her husband William Nicholson.) Water-colour, 16.4 x 11.6
           (6⁵⁄₁₆ x 4⁹⁄₁₆), by unknown artist. Given by Dr Camilla Uytman 1981.

NICHOLSON, William, 1781–1844. *Artist*
PG 1202*   Canvas, 68 x 58.4 (26¾ x 23), self-portrait. Purchased 1933.

NICHOLSON, Sir William, 1872–1949. *Artist*
PG 2653   (With his wife Mabel Pryde.) Water-colour, 16.4 x 11.6 (6⁵⁄₁₆ x 4⁹⁄₁₆),
           by unknown artist. Given by Dr Camilla Uytman 1981.

NICOL, Erskine, 1825–1904. *Artist*
PG 1103   Plaster bust, h. 65.5 (25¹³⁄₁₆), by George Clark Stanton, signed. Given by
           J. A. Geoghegan 1929.
PG 1145   Wash drawing, 23.5 x 18.1 (9¼ x 7⅛), by Thomas Faed. Purchased 1930.
PG 1160*   Charcoal drawing (oval) 35 x 32 (13¾ x 11⅞), self-portrait. Given by James
           Hannaford 1931.
PG 1723   Pencil drawing, 30 x 23.4 (11⅝ x 9¼), self-portrait, 1892, signed. Given by
           J. Kent Richardson 1943.

NIGHTINGALE, Florence, 1820–1910. *Nursing reformer*
PG 222   (Probably the artist's plaster.) Plaster bust, h. 50.5 (19⅞), by or after Sir
           John Steell. Purchased 1888.

NISBET of Dirleton, Sir John, *c.* 1609–87. *Lord Advocate and judge*
PG 1761   Ink drawing, 27.4 x 17.5 (10¾ x 6⅞), by John Brand, 1791, signed, after an
           engraving by Robert White. Given by Sir Hew Dalrymple 1944.
PGL 25   Water-colour on ivory, 5.7 x 4.5 (2¼ x 1¾), by unknown artist. On loan
           from the National Museums of Scotland.

NITHSDALE, Winifred Herbert, Countess of, d. 1749. *Jacobite and wife of the 5th Earl*
           of Nithsdale
PG 2415*   (*The Marriage of Prince James Francis Edward Stewart and Princess Maria*
           Clementina Sobieska.) See GROUPS.

NOBLE, James Campbell, 1846–1913. *Artist*
PG 1496*   Canvas, 82 x 64.5 (32¼ x 25⅜), by John Pettie, 1889, signed. Given by
           D. Campbell Noble 1947.

NOBLE, Robert, 1857–1917. *Artist*
    PG 2460*   (*Friendly Critics.*) See GROUPS.

NORFOLK, Charlotte Sophia, Duchess of, d. 1870.
    PG 1166   (Study for *The Landing of Queen Victoria at Dumbarton in 1847*, in the collection of Dumbarton District Council.) Pencil and water-colour drawing, 60.1 x 41 (23¾ x 16⅛), by Hope James Stewart. Painted 1849. Purchased 1931.

NORFOLK, Henry Charles Howard, 13th Duke of, 1791–1856.
    PG 1167   (Study for *The Landing of Queen Victoria at Dumbarton in 1847*, in the collection of Dumbarton District Council.) Pencil and water-colour drawing, 65.8 x 41 (25⅞ x 16⅛), by Hope James Stewart. Painted 1849. Purchased 1931.

NORIE, James, 1684–1757. *Artist*
    PGL 228*   Canvas, 77.2 x 64.3 (30⅜ x 25⁵⁄₁₆), self-portrait. On loan from the Royal Scottish Academy.

NORTH, Frederick North, 8th Lord (later 2nd Earl of Guilford), 1732–92. *Statesman*
    PG 506   Medallion (plaster replica), h. 8.2 (3³⁄₁₆), after James Tassie. Cast from a medallion in possession of Mrs Shadford Walker 1894.

NORTHUMBERLAND, Hugh Percy, 1st Duke of, 1715–86. *Statesman*
    PG 441   Medallion (plaster replica), h. 8.6 (3⅜), after James Tassie. Dated 1780. Given by the South Kensington Museum 1893.

NORTON, Caroline Sheridan, the Hon. Mrs George (afterwards Lady Stirling-Maxwell), 1808–77. *Poet*
    PG 332*   Water-colour, 18.1 x 13 (7¼ x 5⅛), attributed to Mrs Emma Ferguson of Raith. Dated 1860. Given by G. Waterson 1891.

NORTON, Christopher, d. 1799. *Engraver and business partner of James Byres of Tonley*
    PG 2601*   (*The Byres family.*) See GROUPS.

Newton, Lord
PG 668

Newton, Lord
PGL 302

Nicholson, William
PG 1202

Nicol, Erskine
PG 1160

Noble, James Campbell
PG 1496

Norie, James
PGL 228

Norton, Caroline
PG 332

OAKES, Brigadier-General Sir Hildebrand, 1754–1822. *Soldier*
  PG 2680*   (*The Battle of Alexandria, 21 March 1801.*) See GROUPS.

OCHTERLONY, Major-General Sir David, 1758–1825. *Soldier*
  PG 2651   Canvas, 76.2 x 63.5 (30 x 25), by Arthur William Devis. Painted *c*. 1816.
             Given by Ean W. Ramsay 1983.

OGILVIE, Sir Frederick Wolff, 1893–1949. *Economist*
  PG 1800*   Black chalk drawing, 45.1 x 28 (17¾ x 11), by David Foggie, 1932, signed.
             Given by Mrs M. Foggie 1955.

OGILVIE, William Henry, 1869–1963. *Author and journalist*
  PG 1507   Pencil drawing, 36.2 x 26.4 (14¼ x 10⅜), by Stuart Carnegie Alexander,
             signed. Given by the sitter 1947.

OLIPHANT, Margaret, 1828–97. *Novelist*
  PG 1788*   Pencil and black chalk drawing, 30.2 x 24.8 (11⅞ x 9¾), by Janet Mary
             Oliphant, 1895, signed. Given by Miss M. O. Valentine 1955.

OPIE, John, 1761–1807. *Artist*
  PGL 89*   Canvas, 35 x 28.3 (13¾ x 11⅛), self-portrait. On loan from the National
             Museums of Scotland.

ORCHARDSON, Sir William Quiller, 1832–1910. *Artist*
  PG 726   Millboard, 19.4 x 14.8 (7⅝ x 5⅞), by James Archer. Given by the Royal
             Scottish Academy 1910.
  PG 771   Pencil drawing, 35.5 x 25.4 (14 x 10), by John Henry Lorimer, 1892, signed.
             Bequeathed by J. M. Gray 1894.
  PG 828*   Canvas, 121.9 x 66.1 (48 x 26), by John Pettie. Purchased 1913.
  PG 875*   Canvas, 40.6 x 35.5 (16 x 14), by John Pettie. Bequeathed by Lady
             Orchardson 1917.
  PG 915   Bronze bust, h. 56.8 (22⅜), by Edward Onslow Ford. Dated 189[ ].
             Purchased 1920.
  PG 1092*   Bronze bust, h. 61 (24), by Edward Onslow Ford. Dated 1895. Given by the
             family of Lady Orchardson 1928.
  PG 1093   Plaster bust, h. 62.4 (24⅝), by John Hutchison. Given by the family of Lady
             Orchardson 1928.

ORKNEY, George Hamilton, 1st Earl of, 1666–1737. *Soldier*
  PG 1017   Canvas, 214 x 144.8 (84¼ x 57), by unknown artist. Given by C. J. C.
             Douglas 1926.

ORLEANS, Henrietta Anne, Duchess of, 1644–70. *Fifth daughter of Charles I*
  PG 899*   Canvas, 217.5 x 129.8 (85⅝ x 51⅛), by Pierre Mignard. Purchased 1919.

ORMISTON, Adam Cockburn, Lord, 1656–1735. *Lord Justice-Clerk*
  PG 1868*   Canvas, 127 x 101.5 (50 x 40), attributed to William Aikman. Purchased 1959.

Ogilvie, Sir Frederick
Wolff PG 1800

Oliphant, Margaret
PG 1788

Opie, John
PGL 89

Orchardson, Sir
William Quiller PG 828

Orchardson, Sir William Quiller
PG 875

Orchardson, Sir
William Quiller PG1092

Orleans, Duchess of
PG 899

Ormiston, Lord
PG 1868

Orpen, Sir William
PG 1447

Outram, Sir James
PG 1480

Owen, Robert
PG 1606

Oxford and Asquith, 1st Earl of
PG 1128

ORPEN, Sir William, 1878–1931. *Artist*
    PG 1447*   Ink drawing, 27.6 x 20.1 (10⅞ x 7⅞), self-portrait, signed. Bequeathed by
                Kenneth Sanderson 1944.

ORR, Professor John, 1885–1966. *French scholar*
    PG 2007   Black chalk drawing, 46.4 x 28.6 (18¼ x 11¼), by David Foggie, 1939,
                signed. Given by Mrs M. Foggie 1962.

OUGHTON, Sir James Adolphus, 1720–80. *Commander-in-Chief in Scotland*
    PG 1846   Canvas, 99 x 83.9 (39 x 33), attributed to John Downman. Given by Captain
                L. T. Ross 1957.

OUTRAM, Sir James, 1803–63. *General ('The Bayard of India')*
    PG 1480*   Paper mounted on canvas, 61 x 50.8 (24 x 20), attributed to Alfred Buxton,
                signed in monogram. Painted *c.* 1863. Purchased 1946.

OVERBURY, Sir Thomas, 1581–1613. *Poet*
    PG 2095   Ink drawing. 30.5 x 22.1 (12 x 8¾), copy by unknown artist. Transferred
                from the National Gallery of Scotland 1950.

OWEN, Robert, 1771–1858. *Pioneer socialist*
    PG 1606*   Water-colour. 28.1 x 21.3 (11 x 8⅜), by Mary Ann Knight. Given by Mrs
                James Watt 1953.

OXFORD, Henry de Vere, 18th Earl of, 1593–1625. *Hereditary Lord Great Chamberlain*
                    of England
    PG 314   Canvas, 44.5 x 35.5 (17½ x 14), by unknown artist. Bequeathed by W. F.
                Watson 1886.

OXFORD AND ASQUITH, Henry Herbert Asquith, 1st Earl of, 1852–1928. *Statesman*
    PG 1128*   Canvas, 111.8 x 86.3 (44 x 34), by Sir James Guthrie. Given by W. G.
                Gardiner and Sir Frederick C. Gardiner 1930.

PAIRMAN, John, 1788–1843. *Artist*
    PG 1461   Panel, 43 x 34.4 (16⅞ x 13⁹⁄₁₆), self-portrait. Given by W. R. Pairman 1944.

PAISLEY, Margaret Seton, Lady, d. 1616. *Wife of Claud Hamilton, Lord Paisley*
    PG 1020   (As a girl, with her father, 5th Lord Seton, and her brothers.) See
                 GROUPS.
    PGL 312*   (As a girl, with her father, 5th Lord Seton and her brothers.) See
                 GROUPS.

PANMURE, Harry Maule, Titular Earl of, d. 1734. *Jacobite and antiquarian*
    PGL 242*   Canvas, 75.2 x 62.2 (29⅝ x 24½), attributed to John Scougall. On loan from
                 the Earl of Mar and Kellie.

PANMURE, James Maule, 4th Earl of, c. 1659–1723. *Jacobite*
    PGL 233*   Canvas, 75.6 x 62.2 (29¾ x 24½), attributed to John Scougall. On loan from
                 the Earl of Mar and Kellie.

PANMURE, William Ramsay Maule, Lord, 1771–1852. *Parliamentarian*
    PG 2177*   Canvas, 92 x 71.4 (36¼ x 28⅛), by Colvin Smith. Purchased 1970.

PARK, James, 1857 x 1946. *Geologist*
    PG 1398   Canvas, 112.4 x 87 (44¼ x 34¼), by Annie Elizabeth Kelly. Given by the
                 sitter 1939.

PARK, Patric, 1811–55. *Sculptor*
    PG 654*   Water-colour, 37.6 x 30.4 (14⅞ x 12), by Kenneth Macleay, 1859, signed.
                 Probably based on a photograph. Given by Patric Park junior 1906.

PARKER, Charles Stuart, 1829–1910. *Politician*
    PG 913   Plaster medallion. dia. 18.4 (7⁵⁄₁₆), by unknown artist. Dated 1893. Given
                 by Dr George Neilson 1921.

PATERSON, Hamish Constable, 1890–1955. *Artist*
    PG 2491*   Canvas, 46.3 x 60.8 (18¼ x 24), self-portrait, signed. Purchased 1981.

PATERSON, Sir Hugh, 1686–1777. *Jacobite*
    PG 634*   Canvas, 76.2 x 64.2 (30 x 25¼), by John Thomas Seton, 1776, signed
                 (on reverse). Bequeathed by H. J. Rollo 1890.

PATERSON, James, 1854–1932. *Artist*
    PG 1180*   Chalk drawing, 40.6 x 28 (16 x 11), self-portrait, 1916, signed. Purchased 1932.

PATON, George, 1721–1807. *Antiquary*
    PG 200   Pencil drawing, 10.5 x 8.2 (4⅛ x 3¼), by John Brown. Purchased 1887.
    PGL 66*   Pencil drawing, 50.8 x 36.2 (20 x 14¼), by John Brown. On loan from the
                 National Museums of Scotland.

PATON, Sir Joseph Noël, 1821–1901. *Artist*
 PG 605* Pencil drawing, 48.9 x 27.3 (19¼ x 10¾), by Ranald Noël Paton, 1890, signed. Bequeathed by J. M. Gray 1894.
 PG 619* Marble bust, h. 88.3 (34¹³⁄₁₆), by Amelia Robertson Hill, 1872, signed. Given by the artist 1904.
 PG 1453 (In his studio). Canvas, 86.3 x 111.7 (34 x 44), by John Ballantyne, 1867, signed. Purchased 1944.
 PG 1701 Pencil drawing, 37.5 x 33.6 (14¾ x 13¼), by W. Graham Boss. Given by the artist.
 PG 2068 Plaster medallion, h. 10.3 (4¹⁄₁₆), by Amelia Robertson Hill. Executed *c.* 1851. Given by A. R. Cross 1967.
 PG 2181* Wax medallion, h. 10.5 (4⅛), by Amelia Robertson Hill. Executed *c.* 1851. Purchased 1970.

PATON, Waller Hugh, 1828–95. *Artist*
 PG 1235* Canvas, 49.3 x 34.3 (19⁷⁄₁₆ x 13½), by George Paul Chalmers, 1867, signed. Purchased 1934.

PAUL I, 1754–1801. *Emperor of Russia*
 PG 1921 Medallion (plaster replica), h. 4 (1⁹⁄₁₆), after James Tassie. Provenance untraced.

PAUL, Rev. Hamilton, 1773–1854. *Poet and humorist*
 PG 2185 Black ink silhouette, h. 6.5 (2⁹⁄₁₆), by unknown artist. Given by Miss Newbigging 1970.

PAUL, Sir James Balfour, 1846–1931. *Lyon King of Arms*
 PG 1157 Canvas, 152.7 x 76.7 (60⅛ x 30³⁄₁₆), by Percy Sturdee, 1901, signed. Bequeathed by the sitter 1931.

PAUL, Rev. John, 1795–1873. *Minister of St Cuthbert's, Edinburgh*
 PG 1178 Cut paper silhouette, h. 20.2 (7¹⁵⁄₁₆), by Augustin Edouart. Dated 1830. Purchased 1932.

PAUL, Robert, 1788–1866. *Manager of the Commercial Bank*
 PG 2160 Cut paper silhouette, h. 20.5 (8¹⁄₁₆), by Augustin Edouart, 1830, signed. Given by Mrs J. H. G. Ross 1969.

PEARSON, John, fl. 1899. *Of Sheffield Curling Club*
 PG 1856* (*Curling at Carsebreck.*) See GROUPS.

PEEL, Sir Robert, 1788–1850. *Statesman*
 PG 223 Plaster bust, h. 59 (23¼), by Sir John Steell. Probably executed 1850 and based on a bust by Sir Francis Chantrey. Purchased 1888.
 PG 975 (Commemorates Peel's visit to Glasgow as Lord Rector of the University 1837.) Copper medal, dia. 4.5 (1¾), by John Ottley. Dated 1837. Given by Sir J. R. Findlay 1925.

Panmure, Titular Earl of
PGL 242

Panmure, 4th Earl of
PGL 233

Panmure, Lord
PG 2177

Park, Patric
PG 654

Paterson, Hamish
PG 2491

Paterson, Sir Hugh
PG 634

Paterson, James
PG 1180

Paton, George
PGL 66

Paton, Sir Joseph Noël
PG 605

Paton, Sir Joseph Noël
PG 619

Paton, Sir Joseph Noël
PG 2181

Paton, Waller Hugh
PG 1235

Pencaitland, Lord
PG 1838

Peploe, Samuel John
PG 1831

Perth, 1st Titular Duke of
PG 1850

Perth, 1st Titular Duke of
PGL 223

PENCAITLAND, James Hamilton, Lord, 1659–1729. *Judge*
    PG 1838*   Canvas, 78.9 x 63.9 (31⅟16 x 25¼), by Juriaen Pool, signed. Given by
              J. Millar 1957.

PENNANT, Thomas, 1726–98. *Traveller and naturalist*
    PG 512   Medallion (plaster replica), h. 6.5 (2⁹⁄16), after Wedgwood. Cast from a
              medallion in possession of Mrs Shadford Walker 1894.

PEPLOE, Samuel John, 1871–1935. *Artist*
    PG 1831*   Canvas, 50.8 x 40.6 (20 x 16), self-portrait. Given to the National Gallery of
              Scotland by John Thorburn in 1947 and transferred 1956.

PERIGAL, Arthur, 1816–84. *Landscape painter*
    PG 1360   Canvas, 76.2 x 63.5 (30 x 25), by Sir Daniel Macnee, 1881, signed. Given by
              Dr A. F. Perigal 1938.

PERTH, Duchess of, fl. *c.* 1720. *1st wife of the 5th titular Duke of Perth*
    PG 1661   a. (Probable identification.) Wash drawing, oval 8.9 x 6.7 (3½ x 2⅝),
              by James Ferguson. Bequeathed by W. F. Watson 1886.

PERTH, James Drummond, 1st titular Duke of, 1648–1716. *Lord Chancellor of Scotland*
    PG 1850*   Canvas, oval 75.7 x 64.9 (29¹³⁄16 x 25½), by John Riley. Purchased 1958.
    PGL 223* Canvas, 77.2 x 59.4 (30⅜ x 23⅜), attributed to Alexis Simon Belle. On loan
              from A. Robertson.

PERTH, James Drummond, 2nd titular Duke of, 1673–1720. *Jacobite*
    PG 1531*   Canvas, 126.8 x 102.6 (49⅞ x 40⅜), by Sir John Baptiste de Medina.
              Painted *c.* 1700. Purchased 1949.

PERTH, James Drummond, 3rd titular Duke of, 1713–46. *Jacobite*
    PG 1662   (With Lord Seaforth.) Ink drawing, 37.2 x 24.4 (14⅝ x 9⅝), copy by John
              Sobieski Stuart, signed. Bequeathed by W. F. Watson 1886.

PERTH, John Drummond, 4th titular Duke of, 1714–47. *Jacobite*
    PG 1597*   Canvas, 61.5 x 46.6 (24¼ x 18⅜), by Domenico Dupra, 1739, signed
              (on reverse). Purchased 1953.

PERTH, John Drummond, 5th titular Duke of, 1679–1757.
    PG 1660   (Probable identification.) Wash drawing, oval 8.9 x 6.7 (3½ x 2⅝), by James
              Ferguson. Bequeathed by W. F. Watson 1886.

PERTH, Mary Stuart, Duchess of, 1702–73. *2nd wife of the 5th titular Duke of Perth*
    PG 1661   b. (Probable identification.) Wash drawing, oval 8.6 x 6.7 (3⅜ x 2⅝),
              by James Ferguson. Bequeathed by W. F. Watson 1886.

PETER I (the Great), 1672–1725. *Emperor of Russia*
  PG 1922   Medallion (plaster replica), h. 9.7 (3¹³⁄₁₆), after James Tassie. Provenance
             untraced.

PETTIE, John, 1839–93. *Artist*
  PG 720   Millboard, 19.4 x 14.7 (7⅝ x 5¾), by James Archer. Given by the Royal
             Scottish Academy 1910.
  PG 1091   Bronze bust, h. 51.4 (20¼), by George Anderson Lawson. Given by the
             family of Lady Orchardson 1928.
  PG 1423*   Millboard, 25.4 x 18.7 (10 x 7⅜), by George Paul Chalmers, signed.
             Purchased 1941.

PHILIP, HRH The Prince; see EDINBURGH.

PHILIPHAUGH, Sir James Murray, Lord, 1655–1708. *Lord Clerk Register of Scotland*
  PG 948   Canvas, 76.8 x 64.1 (30¼ x 25¼), by unknown artist. Purchased 1923.

PHILIPSON, Sir Robin, b. 1916. *Artist*
  PGL 328*   (*Gathering at 7 London Street.*) See GROUPS.

PHILLIP, John, 1817–67. *Artist*
  PG 626*   (In his studio.) Canvas, 71.1 x 92.1 (28 x 36¼), by John Ballantyne, signed.
             Painted *c.* 1864. Purchased 1903.
  PG 679   Plaster bust, h. 62 (25⅜), by John Hutchison. Given by Mrs Currie 1909.
  PG 1473*   Millboard, 48.2 x 40.5 (19 x 16), self-portrait. Given by Dr George Cathcart
             1945.

PILLANS, Professor James, 1778–1864. *Educational reformer*
  PG 2268   Ink and pencil drawing, 16.8 x 20.9 (6⅝ x 8¼), by unknown artist.
             Provenance untraced.

PINKERTON, John, 1758–1826. *Antiquary and historian*
  PG 2237*   Paste medallion, h. 7.5 (3), by James Tassie. Dated 1798. Purchased 1974.

PIRIE, Sir George, 1863–1946. *President of the Royal Scottish Academy*
  PG 1792   Pencil drawing, 47.3 x 29.2 (18⅝ x 11½), by David Foggie, 1933, signed.
             Given by Mrs M. Foggie 1955.

PIRRIE, Sandy, fl. 1847. *Golfer*
  PG 2021*   Oil on paper, 50.8 x 31.7 (20 x 12½), by Charles Lees, signed. Provenance
             untraced.

PITCAIRN, Robert, 1793–1855. *Lawyer and antiquary*
  PG 1242   Water-colour on ivory, 11 x 8.3 (4⅜ x 3¼), by unknown artist. Bequeathed
             by Miss Hester H. H. Pitcairn 1930.

PITT, William, 1759–1806. *Statesman*
> PG 203   Statuette (plaster replica), h. 96.6 (38⅞), after Sir Francis Legatt Chantrey. Given by W. Calder Marshall 1887.
> PG 204   Statuette (plaster replica), h. 49.5 (19⁹⁄₁₆), after John Flaxman. Given by W. Calder Marshall 1887.
> PG 447   Medallion (plaster replica), h. 2.3 (⅝), after James Tassie. Given by the South Kensington Museum 1893.
> PG 490   Medallion (plaster replica), h. 7.6 (3), after James Tassie. Modelled by John Flaxman. Cast from a medallion in possession of Jeffery Whitehead 1894.
> PG 607   Bust (plaster replica), h. 72.4 (28½), after Joseph Nollekens. Given by A. W. Inglis 1903.
> PG 1316   Statuette (bronze replica), h. 48.5 (19⅛), after John Flaxman. Purchased 1937.
> PG 1405* Marble bust, h. 71.8 (28⁵⁄₁₆), by Joseph Nollekens, 1807, signed. Given by H. D. Molesworth 1941.

PLAYFAIR, Professor John, 1748–1819. *Mathematician*
> PG 244   Plaster bust, h. 68.1 (26⅞), by Sir Francis Legatt Chantrey. Purchased 1889.
> PG 1688   Pencil drawing, 26.8 x 22.5 (10½ x 8⅞), by William Nicholson. Purchased 1887.
> PGL 44*   Pencil and water-colour drawing, 25.4 x 20.7 (10 x 8¼), by William Nicholson. On loan from the National Museums of Scotland.

PLUMMER, Andrew, 1747–99. *Antiquary*
> PG 472   Medallion (plaster replica), h. 8 (3⅛), after James Tassie. Dated 1796. Cast from a medallion in possession of R. W. Cochran Patrick 1893.

POELLNITZ, Lady Anne de, b. 1746. *Wife of Friedrich, Baron de Poellnitz*
> PG 1957   Paste medallion, h. 9.6 (3¹³⁄₁₆), by James Tassie. Transferred from the National Gallery of Scotland 1960.

POELLNITZ, Charles Louis, Baron de, c. 1691–1775. *Master of Ceremonies to Frederick the Great*
> PG 1923   Medallion (plaster replica), h. 2.7 (1¹⁄₁₆), after James Tassie. Provenance untraced.

POETS' PUB; see GROUPS (PG 2597).

POLE, Sir Charles Morice, 1757–1830. *Admiral*
> PG 2242   Black and white chalk drawing, 33 x 26.1 (13 x 10¼), attributed to Mather Brown. Provenance untraced.

POLLOCK, Sir John Donald, 1868–1962. *Physician and industrialist*
> PGL 257* Canvas, 92.1 x 71.4 (36¼ x 28⅛), by Ernest Stephen Lumsden, 1926, signed. On loan from the trustees of the Pollock Trust.

Perth, 2nd Titular Duke of
PG 1531

Perth, 4th Titular Duke of
PG 1597

Pettie, John
PG 1423

Phillip, John
PG 626

Phillip, John
PG 1473

Pinkerton, John
PG 2237

Pirrie, Sandy
PG 2021

Pitt, William
PG 1405

Playfair, Professor John
PGL 44

Pollock, Sir John Donald
PGL 257

Pollok, Robert
PG 293

Ponton, Mungo
PG 2725

Prestongrange, Lord
PG 1509

Pryde, James
PGL 325

Purdie, Thomas
PG 2463

POLLOK, Robert, 1798–1827. *Poet*
 PG 293* Chalk drawing, 27 x 21 (10⅝ x 8⁵⁄₁₆), by Sir Daniel Macnee. Given by
   Professor A. Crum Brown 1890.
 PG 1231 Painted silhouette, 11.4 x 7.7 (4½ x 3), by unknown artist. Given by Dr
   James Curle 1934.

PONTON, Mungo, 1802–80. *Advocate and pioneer photographer*
 PG 2725* Canvas, 76.5 x 63.7 (30⅛ x 25⅛), by Samuel Mackenzie. Painted *c.* 1837.
   Given by Edinburgh Photographic Society 1987.

PORTER, Anna Maria, 1780–1832. *Novelist*
 PG 824* (Probably Anna Maria Porter with the Porter family.) See GROUPS.

PORTER, Annette Frances, fl. 1829. *Probably the daughter of Sir Robert Ker Porter*
 PG 824* (The Porter family.) See GROUPS.

PORTER, Jane, 1776–1850. *Novelist*
 PG 824* (The Porter family.) See GROUPS.

PORTER, Sir Robert Ker, 1777–1842. *Artist and traveller*
 PG 824* (The Porter family.) See GROUPS.

PORTOBELLO
 PG 2458* (George IV at a military review on Portobello Sands 23 August 1822.) See
   GEORGE IV.
 PGL 326 (George IV at a review of cavalry on Portobello Sands 1822.) See GEORGE
   IV.

PRATTS, George, d. 1784. *Edinburgh Town Crier*
 PG 1670 Pen and water-colour drawing, 8.8 x 7.4 (3½ x 2⅞), by unknown artist.
   Bequeathed by W. F. Watson 1886.

PRESTONGRANGE, William Grant, Lord, *c.* 1701–64. *Judge*
 PG 1509* Canvas, 76.3 x 63.8 (30¹⁄₁₆ x 25⅛), by Allan Ramsay, 1751, signed.
   Purchased 1948.

PRIMROSE, Bouverie Francis, 1813–98. *Secretary to the Board of Trustees for
   Manufactures and Fisheries*
 PG 2655 Canvas, 127.5 x 102.2 (50³⁄₁₆ x 40¼), by Robert Herdman, signed in
   monogram. Dated 1883. Given by the sitter to the National Gallery of
   Scotland 1884 and transferred 1985.

PROUT, Samuel, 1783–1852. *Topographical artist*
 PG 1724 Pencil drawing, 15 x 12 (5⅞ x 4¾), self-portrait, signed. Purchased 1932.

PRYDE, James Ferrier, 1866–1941. *Artist*
>   PG 1525   Charcoal drawing on canvas, 91.4 x 71.1 (36 x 28), by Sir William Oliphant
>   Hutchison. Given by the artist 1949.
>   PGL 325* Canvas, 204.1 x 153 (80⅜ x 60¼), by Sir Herbert James Gunn, signed.
>   Painted *c.* 1931. On loan from Chloë Gunn.

PURDIE, Thomas ('Tam'), 1767–1829. *Personal attendant to Sir Walter Scott*
>   PG 2463* Canvas, 45.7 x 37.8 (18 x 15), by unknown artist (perhaps John Morrison).
>   Painted *c.* 1822. Given by Mrs M. B. Fairbairn 1980.

PURVES of Woodhouselee, Sir William, d. 1685. *Solicitor-General for Scotland*
>   PGL 21   Panel, 61.8 x 50.9 (24⅜ x 20), attributed to Sir Peter Lely. On loan from the
>   National Museums of Scotland.

Queensberry, 3rd Duke of   Queensberry, 2nd Duke of
PG 2166   PG 2045

QUEENSBERRY, Charles Douglas, 3rd Duke of, 1698–1778. *Keeper of the Great Seal of
>   Scotland*
>   PG 2166* Canvas, 126.7 x 101.2 (49⅞ x 39⅞), attributed to Thomas Hudson.
>   Purchased with assistance from the National Art-Collections Fund
>   (London-Scot Bequest) 1969.

QUEENSBERRY, James Douglas, 2nd Duke of, 1662–1711. *Statesman*
>   PG 1171   Canvas, 125.7 x 102.9 (49½ x 40½), by unknown artist. Given by Sir Hew
>   Dalrymple 1932.
>   PG 2045* Canvas on panel, 74 x 58.1 (29⅛ x 22⅞), attributed to Sir John Baptiste de
>   Medina. Given anonymously 1964.

RAE, John, 1813–93. *Arctic explorer*
  PG 1488* Millboard, 40 x 33.7 (15¾ x 13¼), by Stephen Pearce. Replica of a portrait painted *c.* 1853. Given by Dr J. H. Tallent 1947.

RAEBURN, Sir Henry, 1756–1823. *Portrait painter*
  PG 601* Camera lucida drawing in pencil, 29.3 x 21.4 (11⅝ x 8½), by Sir Francis Legatt Chantrey. Dated 1818. Given by F. Murray 1902.
  PG 936* Paste medallion, h. 7.6 (3), by James Tassie. Modelled by Sir Henry Raeburn. Dated 1792. Purchased 1922.
  PG 1037* Marble bust, h. 64.4 (25⅜), by Thomas Campbell, 1822, signed. Purchased 1926.
  PG 1968 Paste medallion, h. 7.6 (3), by James Tassie. Modelled by Sir Henry Raeburn. Dated 1792. Transferred from the National Gallery of Scotland 1960.

RAINY, Rev. Robert, 1826–1906. *Principal of New College, Edinburgh*
  PG 984 Canvas, 80 x 61 (31½ x 24), by John Bowie, signed. Commissioned and purchased 1925.
  PG 1485* Canvas, 72 x 56.6 (28⅜ x 22¼), by Sir George Reid, signed. Given by Mrs Margaret Marwood 1947.

RAMSAY, Allan, 1686–1758. *Poet*
  PG 3 Chalk drawing, oval 19.1 x 15.9 (7½ x 6¼), by unknown artist after William Aikman, 1745. Given by W. Bell Scott 1884.
  PG 316 Canvas, 34.4 x 34.4 (13½ x 13½), by unknown artist. Bequeathed by W. F. Watson 1886.
  PG 355 Wash drawing, 16.2 x 9.7 (6⅜ x 3¹³⁄₁₆), by Alexander Carse after John Smibert. Purchased 1889.
  PG 973* Canvas, 75.7 x 64 (29¹³⁄₁₆ x 25³⁄₁₆), by William Aikman. Painted 1722. Purchased 1924.
  PG 1470 Canvas, 77.5 x 65.5 (30½ x 25¾), by unknown artist after John Smibert. Given by Sir Hew Dalrymple 1946.
  PG 2023* Chalk drawing, 41.9 x 30.5 (16½ x 12), by Allan Ramsay. Dated 1729. Purchased 1962.

RAMSAY, Allan, 1713–84. *Artist*
  PG 189 Canvas, 38.2 x 31.7 (15 x 12½), by Alexander Nasmyth after Ramsay's self-portrait of 1739. Dated 1781. Purchased 1887.
  PG 641* Marble bust, h. 59.9 (24), by Michael Foye, 177[ ], signed. Purchased 1905.
  PG 727* Pastel drawing, 40.6 x 28.2 (16 x 11⅛), self-portrait. Given by the Royal Scottish Academy 1910.
  PGL 10* Chalk drawing, 40 x 26.7 (15¾ x 10½), self-portrait. On loan from the trustees of Lockhart Thomson.

RAMSAY, Anne Bayne, Mrs Allan Ramsay, d. 1743. *Wife of the artist Allan Ramsay*
  PG 2603* Canvas, 68.3 x 54.7 (26⅞ x 21½), by Allan Ramsay. Painted *c.* 1739/43. Purchased 1983.

Rae, John
PG 1488

Raeburn, Sir Henry
PG 601

Raeburn, Sir Henry
PG 936

Raeburn, Sir Henry
PG 1037

Rainy, Rev. Robert
PG 1485

Ramsay, Allan (senior)
PG 973

Ramsay, Allan (senior)
PG 2023

Ramsay, Allan
PG 641

Ramsay, Allan
PGL 10

Ramsay, Allan
PG 727

Ramsay, Anne
PG 2603

Ramsay, Very Rev.
Edward Bannerman   PG 950

Ramsay, John
PG 1478

•Ramsay, Margaret
PG 1104

Rankin, Walter
PG 2719

Raspe, Rudolf Erich
PG 258

RAMSAY, Charles Maule, 1859–1936. *Of Brechin Castle Curling Club*
  PG 1856* (*Curling at Carsebreck.*) See GROUPS.

RAMSAY, Very Rev. Edward Bannerman, 1793–1872. *Dean of Edinburgh*
  PG 176   (Artist's plaster.) Plaster bust, h. 71.4 (28⅛), by Sir John Steell, signed.
            Sculpted posthumously. Purchased 1887.
  PG 783   Cut paper silhouette, h. 21.8 (8⁹/₁₆), by Augustin Edouart. Purchased 1912.
  PG 950*   Millboard, 44.4 x 26.8 (17½ x 10⁹/₁₆), by Sir John Watson Gordon.
            Purchased 1923.

RAMSAY, John, 1768–1845. *Soldier; son of Allan Ramsay the artist*
  PG 1478* Water-colour on ivory, 8 x 6.6 (3⅛ x 2½), by François Ferrière, 1794,
            signed. Purchased 1946.

RAMSAY, Margaret Lindsay, Mrs Allan, c. 1726–82. *Wife of the artist*
  PG 1104* Chalk drawing, 40 x 26.7 (15¾ x 10½), by Allan Ramsay. Given by
            A. W. Inglis 1929.

RAMSAY, Professor William, 1806–65. *Classical scholar*
  PG 792   Cut paper silhouette, h. 20.6 (8⅛), by Augustin Edouart. Purchased 1912.

RAMSAY of Barnton, William, 1809–50. *Sportsman*
  PG 801   Cut paper silhouette, h. 22.2 (8¾), by Augustin Edouart. Purchased 1912.

RANKIN, Walter, fl. 1940. *Local Defence Volunteer*
  PG 2719* (*Home Guard.*) Canvas, 76 x 55.6 (29¹⁵/₁₆ x 21⅞), by Sir William Oliphant
            Hutchison, 1940, signed. Purchased 1987.

RANKINE, Andrew, fl. 1899. *Of New Monkland Curling Club*
  PG 1856* (*Curling at Carsebreck.*) See GROUPS.

RASPE, Rudolf Erich, 1737–94. *Author, antiquary and mineralogist*
  PG 258*   Paste medallion, h. 7 (2¾), by James Tassie. Dated 1784. Transferred from
            the National Gallery of Scotland 1889.

REDPATH, Anne, 1895–1965. *Artist*
  PG 2380* Chalk drawing, 49.2 x 38.9 (19⅜ x 15⁵/₁₆), self-portrait, signed. Purchased
            1977.
  PG 2486   Chalk drawing, 62.5 x 50.6 (24⅝ x 19⅞), by Suzanne Beadle, signed. Dated
            1963. Purchased 1981.
  PGL 328* (*Gathering at 7 London Street.*) See GROUPS.

REID, Sir George, 1841–1913. *Portrait painter*
  PG 854*   Bronze bust, h. 26 (10¼), by James Pittendrigh Macgillivray. Purchased
            1916.
  PG 2046* Canvas, 111.7 x 86.3 (44 x 34), by John Bowie, signed. Given by H. R. H.
            Woolford 1964.

REID, George Ogilvy, 1851–1928. *Portrait painter*
PG 1746   (In his studio.) Wash drawing, 54.9 x 38.9 (21⅝ x 15⅜), by
           J. R. Abercromby, signed. Drawn 1898. Purchased 1940.

REID, Janet, fl. 1795.
PG 2444 · Paste medallion, h. 7.9 (3⅛), by James Tassie. Dated 1795. Bequeathed by
           William Tassie to the National Gallery of Scotland 1860 and transferred
           1979.

REID, Robert, fl. 1887. *Dentist*
PG 1007   Bronze medallion, dia. 11.6 (4⁹⁄₁₆), by Charles Matthew. Dated 1887.
           Bequeathed by Mr and Mrs W. R. Macdonald 1925.

REID, Professor Thomas, 1710–96. *Philosopher*
PG 120   Wash drawing, 9.1 x 7.3 (3⅝ x 2⅞), by or after James Tassie, 1789, signed
           or inscribed. Bequeathed by W. F. Watson 1886.
PG 770   Medallion (plaster replica), h. 7.3 (2⅞), after James Tassie. Dated 1791.
           Provenance untraced.
PG 2144   Paste medallion, h. 7.5 (2¹⁵⁄₁₆), by James Tassie. Dated 1791. Purchased
           1968.

REITH of Stonehaven, John Reith, 1st Baron, 1889–1971. *Director-General of the*
           British Broadcasting Corporation
PG 2475*   Canvas, 127.5 x 102.3 (50¼ x 40¼) by Sir Oswald Birley, signed. Dated
           1933. Purchased 1981.

RENNIE, John, 1761–1821. *Engineer*
PG 544   Plaster bust, h. 78.1 (30¾), by Sir Francis Legatt Chantrey, 1818, signed.
           Purchased 1895.
PG 1840*   Canvas, 76.2 x 63.5 (30 x 25), by Sir Henry Raeburn. Painted *c*. 1810.
           Purchased with assistance from the National Art-Collections Fund (London
           Scot Bequest) 1957.
PG 2447*   Canvas, 127 x 101.6 (50 x 40), by Sir Martin Archer Shee. Painted *c*. 1794.
           Purchased 1979.

REYNIERE, Monsieur de la, fl. 1784. French postal administrator
PG 1924   Medallion (plaster replica), h. 6.8 (2¹¹⁄₁₆), after James Tassie. Dated 1784.
           Provenance untraced.

REYNOLDS, Sir Joshua, 1723–92. *Portrait painter*
PG 2323   Water-colour on ivory, oval 11.2 x 8.4 (4⅜ x 3⁵⁄₁₆), by unknown artist after
           Sir Joshua Reynolds. Bequeathed by W. F. Watson 1886.

RICHARDSON, Adam Black, d. 1909. *Antiquary and numismatist*
PG 1703   Pencil drawing, 37.5 x 33.7 (14¾ x 13¼), by W. Graham Boss. Given by
           the artist.

RICHMOND, 1st Duke of; see LENNOX (PG 1420).

RICHMOND AND LENNOX, , Frances Teresa Stewart, Duchess of, 1648–1702. *Mistress of Charles II*
   PG 707   Copper medal, dia. 7 (2¾), by John Roettier. Purchased 1910.

RIDDELL of Walton Health, George Allardice, 1st Baron, 1865–1934. *Newspaper proprietor and diarist*
   PG 1283   Canvas, 127.6 x 102.2 (50¼ x 40¼), by Sir William Orpen, 1919, signed. Bequeathed by the sitter 1935.

RIDDELL, James, fl. 1899. *Of Paisley Boreas Curling Club*
   PG 1856*   *(Curling at Carsebreck.)* See GROUPS.

RIDDELL, Dr John, fl. 1796. *Physician*
   PG 2643   Paste medallion, h. 7.7 (3), by James Tassie. Dated 1795. Purchased 1985.

RIDDING, Ellen
   PG 2560   Water-colour on ivory, h. 4 (1⅝) (sight), by James Scouler. Transferred from the National Gallery of Scotland 1982.

RIDDING, William
   PG 2559   Water-colour on ivory, h. 4.2 (1¹¹⁄₁₆) (sight), by James Scouler. Transferred from the National Gallery of Scotland 1982.

RITCHIE, William; see BROWN, Major Alexander.

ROBERT I (known as Robert the Bruce), 1274–1329. *Earl of Carrick and Lord of Annandale. Reigned 1306–29*
   PG 914   a. Plaster cast of skull with conjoined base, h. 41.5 (16¼), by William Scoular, signed. Taken 1819. Given by George Carfrae 1921.
              b. Bronze cast of skull, h. 22.8 (9), after William Scoular. Presumably cast from PG 914a. at an unknown date. Provenance untraced.

ROBERTON, Sir Hugh Stevenson, 1874–1952. *Founder of Glasgow Orpheus Choir*
   PG 2063*   Ink drawing, 38.1 x 28.9 (15 x 11⅜), by William Niven, signed. Given by M. Donnelly 1966.

ROBERTS, Alexander Fowler, 1844–1929. *Provost of Selkirk*
   PG 1856*   *(Curling at Carsebreck.)* See GROUPS.

ROBERTS, David, 1796–1864. *Artist*
   PG 599   (Laudatory medal commissioned by the Art Union of London.) Bronze medal, dia. 5.4 (2⅛), by George T. Morgan. Dated 1875. Purchased 1902.
   PG 2466*   (In Arab dress.) Canvas, 133 x 101.3, by Robert Scott Lauder. Painted 1840. Purchased 1980.

Redpath, Anne
PG 2380

Reid, Sir George
PG 854

Reid, Sir George
PG 2046

Reith, 1st Baron
PG 2475

Rennie, John
PG 1840

Rennie, John
PG 2447

Roberton, Sir Hugh
Stevenson   PG 2063

Roberts, David
PG 2466

Robertson, Alexander
PG 438

Robertson, Allan
PG 2020

Robertson, Andrew
PG 2741

Robertson, Sir Charles Grant
PG 1572

Robertson, Eben William
PG 1027

Robertson, Roger
PG L 65

Robertson, Rev. William
PG 1393

Roche, Alexander Ignatius
PG 1185

ROBERTSON of Struan, Alexander, *c.* 1670–1749. *Jacobite, poet and clan chieftain*
  PG 438*   Canvas, oval 79 x 61.9 (31⅛ x 24⅜), by unknown artist. Bequeathed by
            Mrs Robertson of Struan 1893.

ROBERTSON, Allan, fl. 1847. *Golf ball maker*
  PG 2020*   Oil on paper, 50.5 x 31.7 (19⅞ x 12½), by Charles Lees, signed. Provenance
            untraced.

ROBERTSON, Andrew, 1777–1845. *Miniature painter*
  PG 2741*   Water-colour on ivory, h. 3.2 (1¼), self-portrait. Painted 1811. Purchased
            1988.

ROBERTSON, Sir Charles Grant, 1869–1948. *Historian*
  PG 1572*   Canvas, 121.3 x 109.7 (47¾ x 43³⁄₁₆), by Meredith Frampton, 1941, signed.
            Given by Mrs Isobel Nevill 1951.

ROBERTSON, Eben William, 1815–1874. *Historian*
  PG 1027*   Water-colour on ivory, 24.2 x 17.6 (9½ x 7), by Sir William Charles Ross.
            Bequeathed by Mrs M. Robertson 1927.

ROBERTSON, Professor George Matthew, 1864–1932. *Psychiatrist*
  PG 2235   Canvas board, 38 x 24.6 (14⅞ x 9¹¹⁄₁₆), by Sir James Gunn. Painted 1930.
            Purchased 1974.

ROBERTSON, Professor James, 1714–95. *Orientalist*
  PG 388   Medallion (plaster replica), h. 7.3 (2⅞), after James Tassie. Cast from a
            medallion in possession of W. G. Patterson 1889.

ROBERTSON, Rev. Dr John, 1797–1843. *Minister at Cambuslang*
  PG 1752   Water-colour, 22.2 x 17.2 (8¾ x 6¾), attributed to James Howe. Given by
            the legatees of J. A. Gardiner.

ROBERTSON, Mary, fl. 1801. *Sister of Andrew Robertson*
  PG 2526   Water-colour on ivory, 11 x 8 (4⁵⁄₁₆ x 3³⁄₁₆) (irregular), by Andrew
            Robertson. Painted 1801. Transferred from the National Gallery of Scotland
            1982.

ROBERTSON, Patrick Robertson, Lord, 1794–1855. *Judge*
  PG 2306   (Crombie Sketchbook, fo. 9. Study for *Modern Athenians* Pl. 18.) Pencil
            drawing, 15.6 x 20 (6⅛ x 7⅞), by Benjamin William Crombie. Purchased
            1938.

ROBERTSON of Ladykirk, Roger, fl. 1780. *Antiquary*
  PGL 65*   Pencil drawing, 50.2 x 34.6 (19¾ x 13⅝), by John Brown. On loan from the
            National Museums of Scotland.

ROBERTSON, Rev. William, 1721–93. *Historian. Principal of Edinburgh University*
PG 185   Paste medallion, h. 7.2 (2¹³⁄₁₆), by James Tassie. Dated 1791. Purchased 1887.
PG 402   Medallion (plaster replica), h. 7.3 (2⅞), after James Tassie. Dated 1791.
            Cast from a medallion in possession of J. R. Findlay 1889.
PG 1393*   Canvas, 127.5 x 102.1 (50¼ x 40¼), by Sir Joshua Reynolds. Painted 1772.
            Purchased 1939.

ROBERTSON, William Robertson, Lord, 1753–1835. *Senator of the College of Justice*
PG 1277   Paste medallion, h. 6.5 (2⁹⁄₁₆), by John Henning, 1810. Purchased 1935.

ROBINSON, Mary Darby, Mrs, 1758–1800. *Actress*
PG 2326   Water-colour on ivory, 10.6 x 8.3 (4³⁄₁₆ x 3¼), by unknown artist after Sir
            Joshua Reynolds. Bequeathed by W. F. Watson 1886.

ROBISON, Professor John, 1739–1805. *Scientist*
PG 389   Medallion (plaster replica), h. 8.1 (3³⁄₁₆), after James Tassie. Dated 1791.
            Cast from a medallion in possession of W. G. Patterson 1889.

ROCHE, Alexander Ignatius, 1861–1921. *Artist*
PG 1185*   Canvas, 42.6 x 33 (16¾ x 13), self portrait. Purchased 1932.

ROCKINGHAM, Charles Watson-Wentworth, 2nd Marquess of, 1730–82. *Statesman*
PG 301   Paste medallion, h. 8.8 (3½), by James Tassie. Purchased 1891.
PG 1926   Medallion (plaster replica), h. 8.9 (3½), after James Tassie. Provenance
            untraced.

ROCKINGHAM, Mary, Marchioness of, d. 1804. *Wife of the 2nd Marquess*
PG 1927   Medallion (plaster replica), h. 8.9 (3½), after James Tassie. Cast from a
            medallion in possession of W. G. Patterson 1889.

ROGERS, James S., fl. 1899. *Of Strathmartine Curling Club*
PG 1856*   (*Curling at Carsebreck.*) See GROUPS.

ROGERSON, Dr John, 1740–1828. *Physician and adviser to Catherine the Great*
PG 2507*   Canvas, 76.4 x 63 (30 x 24⅞), by Johann Baptist Lampi. Purchased 1982.

ROKEBY, Richard Robinson, 1st Baron, 1709–94. *Archbishop of Armagh*
PG 473   Medallion (plaster replica), h. 9 (3½), after James Tassie. Cast from a
            medallion in possession of Jeffery Whitehead 1894.

ROLLAND of Gask, Adam, 1734–1819. *Advocate*
PG 2270   Paste medallion, h. 7.6 (3), by James Tassie. Dated 1794. Purchased 1975.

ROLLOCK, Rev. Robert, *c.* 1555–99. *First Principal of Edinburgh University*
PG 635*   Canvas, 76.1 x 63.1 (30 x 24¹³⁄₁₆), by unknown artist. Dated 1599.
            Bequeathed by H. J. Rollo 1890.

ROSEBERY, Archibald Philip Primrose, 5th Earl of. 1847–1929. *Politician*
    PG 1120*   Ink drawing, 17.6 x 11.3 (6⅞ x 4½), by unknown artist. Purchased 1929.

ROSEBERY, Sir Archibald Primrose, 1st Earl of, 1664–1723. *Privy Councillor*
    PGL 264   Canvas, 79.1 x 66.3 (31⅛ x 26⅛), by Sir John Baptiste de Medina. On loan from J. T. T. Fletcher.

ROSS, Admiral Sir John, 1777–1856. *Arctic explorer*
    PG 8*   Canvas, 94 x 72.4 (37 x 28½), by Benjamin Rawlinson Faulkner. Purchased 1884.

ROSS, Sir John Lockhart, 1721–90. *Vice-Admiral*
    PG 1287*   Water-colour on ivory, 3.2 x 2.8 (1¼ x 1⅛), by Samuel Cotes, 1758, signed. Purchased 1935.

ROSS, Thomas, d. 1930. *Architect and antiquarian*
    PG 1146*   Water-colour, 30.8 x 25.4 (12⅛ x 10), by Henry Wright Kerr, 1893, signed. Bequeathed by J. M. Gray 1894.
    PG 1147   Pencil drawing, 40 x 28.9 (15¾ x 11⅜), by James Paterson, 1920, signed. Purchased 1931.

ROSSLYN, Alexander Wedderburn, 1st Earl of, 1733–1805. *Lord Chancellor*
    PG 861*   (As Lord Loughborough.) Canvas, 127 x 101.9 (50 x 40⅛), by Mather Brown. Painted in or before 1791. Purchased 1917.

ROTHES, Anne Erskine, Countess of, d. 1640. *Wife of the 6th Earl of Rothes*
    PG 2456*   (With her daughters, Lady Margaret Leslie and Lady Mary Leslie.) Canvas, 219.4 x 135.5 (86⅜ x 53¼), by George Jamesone, signed. Dated 1626. Purchased 1980.

ROTHES, Lady Jean Hay, Countess of, d. 1731. *Wife of the 8th Earl*
    PG 897*   Panel, oval 29.7 x 24.7 (11¹¹⁄₁₆ x 9¹¹⁄₁₆), by unknown artist. Purchased 1919.

ROTHES, John Leslie, 7th Earl and 1st Duke of, 1630–81. *Lord Chancellor*
    PG 860*   Canvas, 126 x 102 (49⅝ x 40⅛), by L. Schuneman, 1667, signed. Purchased 1916.

ROTHES, John Leslie, 8th Earl of, 1697–1722. *Vice-Admiral of Scotland*
    PG 896*   Panel, oval 29.9 x 24.8 (11¾ x 9¾), by unknown artist. Purchased 1919.

ROXBURGHE, John Ker, 5th Earl and 1st Duke of, *c.* 1680–1741. *Statesman*
    PG 1021   Canvas, 127 x 102.2 (50 x 40¼), by unknown artist. Purchased 1926.

ROXBURGHE, John Ker, 3rd Duke of, 1740–1804. *Bibliophile*
    PG 288   Canvas, 76.2 x 63.5 (30 x 25), by unknown artist. Purchased 1889.

Rogerson, Dr John
PG 2507

Rollock, Rev. Robert
PG 635

Rosebery, 5th Earl of
PG 1120

Ross, Sir John
PG 8

Ross, Sir John Lockhart
PG 1287

Ross, Thomas
PG 1146

Rosslyn, 1st Earl of
PG 861

Rothes, Countess of, with
Lady Margaret Leslie and
Lady Mary Leslie   PG 2456

Rothes, Countess of
PG 897

Rothes, 1st Duke of
PG 860

Rothes, 8th Earl of
PG 896

Ruddiman, Anne
PG 2012

Ruddiman, Thomas
PG 2013

Runciman, Alexander
PGL 88

RUDDIMAN, Anne Smith, Mrs Thomas, fl. 1729–69. *Third wife of Thomas Ruddiman*
  PG 2012*   Canvas, 76.2 x 63.7 (30 x 25¹⁄₁₆), by William Denune, 1749, signed. Given
        by Miss S. Steuart 1962.

RUDDIMAN, Thomas, 1674–1757. *Philologist and publisher*
  PG 108   Water-colour, 40.3 x 29.5 (15⁷⁄₈ x 11⁵⁄₈), by the 11th Earl of Buchan, after
        unknown artist. Bequeathed by W. F. Watson 1886.
  PG 2013*   Canvas, 74 x 63.8 (29⅛ x 25⅛), by William Denune, 1749, signed. Given
        by Miss S. Steuart 1962.

RUMFORD, Benjamin Thompson, Count von, 1753–1814. *Soldier and scientist*
  PG 390   Medallion (plaster replica), h. 7.8 (3¹⁄₁₆), after James Tassie. Dated 1796.
        Cast from a medallion in possession of W. G. Patterson 1889.

RUNCIMAN, Alexander, 1736–85. *Artist*
  PG 2433   Pencil and chalk drawing, 23.4 x 17.2 (9³⁄₁₆ x 6¾), by unknown artist.
        Purchased 1979.
  PGL 31*   (With John Brown.) Canvas 63.6 x 76.5 (25 x 30⅛), self-portrait, 1784,
        signed. On loan from the National Museums of Scotland.
  PGL 88*   Pencil drawing, 7.3 x 9.5 (2⁷⁄₈ x 3¾), by John Brown, 1785, signed. On loan
        from the National Museums of Scotland.

RUNCIMAN, John, 1744–68. *Artist*
  PGL 32*   Canvas, 68.7 x 55.6 (27¹⁄₁₆ x 21⁷⁄₈), self-portrait, 1767, signed (on reverse).
        On loan from the National Museums of Scotland.

RUSHFORTH, Dr Winifred, 1885–1983. *Psycho-analyst*
  PG 2519*   Hardboard, 56 x 76.3 (22 x 30), by Victoria Crowe. Dated 1981/2.
        Purchased 1982.

RUSSEL, Alexander, 1814–76. *Editor of* The Scotsman
  PG 557*   Marble bust, h. 67.4 (26⁹⁄₁₆), by William Brodie. Given by the proprietors of
        The Scotsman 1896.

RUSSELL, James, d. 1773. *Professor of natural philosophy at Edinburgh University*
  PG 2014*   (With his son James.) Canvas, 101.6 x 127.7 (40 x 50¼), by David Martin,
        1769, signed. Purchased 1962.

RUSSELL, James, 1754–1836. *President of the Royal College of Surgeons of Edinburgh;
        Professor of clinical surgery at Edinburgh University*
  PG 2014*   (As a boy, with his father Professor James Russell.) Canvas, 101.6 x 127.7
        (40 x 50¼), by David Martin, 1769, signed. Purchased 1962.

RUSSELL, John Scott, 1808–82. *Naval architect*
  PG 876*   Canvas, 101.6 x 88.9 (40 x 35), by Henry Wyndham Phillips. Purchased
        1917.

Runciman, John
PGL 32

Rushforth, Dr Winifred
PG 2519

Russel, Alexander
PG 557

Russell, Professor James, with
James Russell   PG 2014

Russell, John Scott
PG 876

Rutherfurd, Lord
PG 710

Rutherfurd, Lord
PGL 40

RUTHERFURD, Andrew Rutherfurd, Lord, 1791–1854. *Judge*

PG 710*   Canvas, 238.4 x 148.5 (89⅞ x 58), by Sir John Watson Gordon. Given by
             the Royal Scottish Academy 1910.

PG 1497*   (With the Marquess of Breadalbane, the Marquess of Dalhousie and Lord
             Cockburn.) See GROUPS.

PG 1727   Chalk drawing, 24.9 x 17.6 (9¾ x 7), by Sir John Watson Gordon.
             Provenance untraced.

PGL 40*   Water-colour drawing, 26 x 20.8 (10¼ x 8³⁄₁₆), by Benjamin William
             Crombie. On loan from J. T. Brown.

SACKVILLE, George Sackville Germain, 1st Viscount, 1716–85. *Soldier and politician*
   PG 1258   Paste medallion, h. 8.9 (3½), by James Tassie. Purchased 1935.

SAGE, John, 1652–1711. *Non-juring Scottish bishop*
   PG 1848*   Chalk drawing, 33 x 27.3 (13 x 10¾), by unknown artist. Purchased 1958.

ST VINCENT, Sir John Jervis, Earl of, 1735–1823. *Admiral; victor of Cape St Vincent*
   PG 1951   Wedgwood medallion, h. 7.5 (3), after unknown artist. Provenance
           untraced.

SAKEOUSE, John, 1797–1819. *Eskimo whaler and draughtsman*
   PG 2488*   Panel, 29.9 x 22 (11¾ x 8¹¹⁄₁₆), by Alexander Nasmyth. Painted *c*. 1816.
           Purchased 1981.

SALVESEN, Edward Theodore Salvesen, Lord, 1857–1942. *Judge*
   PG 1799   Black chalk drawing, 46.5 x 28.8 (18¼ x 11⅜), by David Foggie, 1934,
           signed. Given by Mrs M. Foggie 1955.

SANDERSON, Kenneth, 1868–1943. *Connoisseur and collector; trustee of the National
           Galleries of Scotland*
   PG 1448   Black chalk drawing, 46.3 x 28.9 (18¼ x 11⅜), by David Foggie, 1933,
           signed. Bequeathed by the sitter 1944.

SANDFORD, Sir Daniel Keyte, 1798–1838. *Professor of Greek at Glasgow University*
   PG 793   Cut paper silhouette, h. 20.6 (8⅛), by Augustin Edouart. Purchased 1912.

SANDHURST, William Mansfield, 1st Baron, 1819–76. *Soldier*
   PG 1976   (With 1st Baron Clyde.) Chalk drawing, 25.7 x 34 (10⅛ x 13⅜), by T. Blake
           Wirgman after a photograph by Felice Beato taken 1857. Given by
           Aberdeen University 1961.

SANDILANDS, Isabella Byres of Tonley, Mrs Robert, b. 1737. *Sister of James Byres of
           Tonley*
   PG 2601*   (The Byres family.) See GROUPS.

SAUNDERS, Robert Crombie, b. 1914. *Poet*
   PG 2702*   (recto) a. Pencil drawing, 42.3 x 26.3 (16⅝ x 10⅜), by Hamish Lawrie,
           signed.
           (verso) b. Pencil drawing, 42.3 x 26.3 (16⅝ x 10⅜), by Hamish Lawrie.
           Given by the artist 1986.

SCHAFER, Sir Edward Sharpey, 1850–1935. *Physiologist*
   PG 1826   Bronze medal, dia. 2 (5), by C.d'O. Pilkington Jackson. Dated 1922. Given
           by the artist 1956.
   PG 1827   Bronze medal, dia. 2 (5), by C.d'O. Pilkington Jackson. Dated 1922. Given
           by the artist 1956.

SCHETKY, Johann Georg Christoph, d. 1824. *Composer and cellist*
  PG 946*   (Probably J. G. C. Schetky, in *The Inauguration of Robert Burns as Poet
             Laureate of the Lodge Canongate, Kilwinning, 1787.*) See GROUPS.

SCHETKY, Miss Mary, c. 1786–1877. *Sister of John Christian Schetky, the marine
                                    painter*
  PG 1173   Cut paper silhouette, h. 20 (7⅞), by Augustin Edouart. Cut 1830.
             Purchased 1932.

SCHILSKY, Eric, 1898–1974. *Sculptor*
  PGL 328*   (*Gathering at 7 London Street.*) See GROUPS.

SCHLAPP, Otto, 1859–1939. *Professor of German at Edinburgh University*
  PG 1816   Black chalk drawing, 45.1 x 28.6 (17¾ x 11¼), by David Foggie, 1932,
             signed. Given by Mrs M. Foggie 1955.

SCHOTZ, Benno, 1891–1984. *Sculptor*
  PG 2707*   Bronze bust, h. 48.5 (19⅛), by Vincent Butler, 1978, signed. Purchased
             1987.

SCOTLAND, THE HONOURS OF. *The discovery of the Scottish Regalia*
  PG 2069*   Pencil and water-colour, 13.7 x 18.7 (5⅜ x 7⅜), by Sir David Wilkie, 1822,
             signed. Purchased 1967.

SCOTT, Anne, 1803–33. *Daughter of Sir Walter Scott*
  PG 1303*   (*The Abbotsford Family.*) See GROUPS.

SCOTT, Anne Rutherford, Mrs Walter, d. 1819. *Mother of Sir Walter Scott*
  PG 656*   Canvas, 76.2 x 63.5 (30 x 25), by George Watson. Purchased 1907.

SCOTT, Charles, 1805–41. *Son of Sir Walter Scott*
  PG 1303*   (As a child in *The Abbotsford Family.*) See GROUPS.

SCOTT, David, 1806–49. *Artist*
  PG 1312   Plaster bust. h. 68.9 (27³⁄₁₆), by Sir John Steell. Bequeathed by Miss I. S.
             Brown 1937.
  PG 1450*   Canvas, 73.8 x 58.6 (29 x 23¹⁄₁₆), self-portrait, 1832, signed. Given by Mrs
             H. Sample 1944.
  PG 1608*   Canvas, 68.6 x 52.1 (27 x 20½), by Robert Scott Lauder, 1839, signed.
             Purchased 1954.

SCOTT, Francis George, 1880–1958. *Composer*
  PG 2592*   Bronze head, h. 34.4 (13½), by Benno Schotz, signed. Purchased 1983.
  PG 2639*   Canvas, 61.4 x 51.4 (24³⁄₁₆ x 20¼), by William Johnstone, signed on the
             reverse. Dated indistinctly 19[3]3. Purchased 1985.
  PGL 320*   Canvas, 96.5 x 71.1 (38 x 28), by William Johnstone, signed. On loan from
             George N. Scott.

SCOTT, George, fl. 1899. *Of Bothwell Curling Club*
   PG 1856*   (*Curling at Carsebreck.*) See GROUPS.

SCOTT, James Bruce, fl. 1893
   PG 2663   Cut paper silhouette, 59.5 x 45.6 (23$\frac{9}{16}$ x 17$\frac{15}{16}$), by unknown artist. Dated 1893. Provenance untraced.

SCOTT, John, 1783–1821. *Editor of* The Champion *and the* London Magazine
   PG 1969   Pencil drawing, 18.1 x 14.4 (7$\frac{1}{4}$ x 5$\frac{3}{4}$), by Seymour Kirkup, 1819, signed. Transferred from the National Gallery of Scotland 1960.

SCOTT, John, 1816–64. *Art dealer*
   PG 1864*   Chalk drawing, 56 x 44.4 (22 x 17$\frac{1}{2}$), by Johann Horrak, 1861, signed. Transferred from the National Gallery of Scotland 1959.

SCOTT, Marguerite Charlotte Charpentier, Lady, 1770–1826. *Wife of Sir Walter Scott*
   PG 140   a. (With Sir Walter Scott.) Pencil drawing, 12.3 x 9.8 (4$\frac{13}{16}$ x 3$\frac{7}{8}$), by Sir Edwin Landseer, signed. Provenance untraced.
   PG 1190   (Possible Lady Scott's dog.) Pencil and watercolour, 15.2 x 15.2 (6 x 6), by William Nicholson. Purchased 1932.
   PG 1303*   (*The Abbotsford Family.*) See GROUPS.

SCOTT, Michael, 1789–1835. *Author of* Tom Cringle's Log
   PG 794   Cut paper silhouette, h. 22.1 (8$\frac{11}{16}$), by Augustin Edouart. Purchased 1912.

SCOTT, Mrs Peggy, fl. 1831. *Nurse*
   PG 1769   Cut paper silhouette, h. 17.5 (6$\frac{7}{8}$), by Augustin Edouart, 1831, signed. Given by the Royal Scottish Museum 1947.

SCOTT, Robert, fl. 1830. *Druggist and Director of the Commercial Bank*
   PG 2155   Cut paper silhouette, h. 20.8 (8$\frac{3}{16}$), by Augustin Edouart, 1830, signed. Given by Mrs J. H. G. Ross 1969.

SCOTT, Robert Lyons, 1871–1939. *Shipbuilder and collector of armour*
   PG 2031*   Canvas, 72.5 x 50.7 (28$\frac{1}{2}$ x 20), by Thomas Cantrell Dugdale, signed. Painted *c.* 1936. Purchased 1963.

SCOTT, Thomas, fl. 1817. *Shepherd to Sir Walter Scott*
   PG 1303*   (*The Abbotsford Family.*) See GROUPS.

SCOTT, Thomas, 1854–1927. *Artist*
   PG 1730   Pencil drawing, 30.5 x 26.7 (12 x 10$\frac{1}{2}$), by George Rowland Halkett, signed. Dated 1887. Bequeated by J. M. Gray 1894.
   PG 2065*   Canvas, 69.2 x 56.2 (27$\frac{1}{4}$ x 22$\frac{1}{8}$), by William Johnstone after a portrait by George Fiddes Watt painted 1918. Bequeathed by Miss J. G. D. Miller 1967.

Sage, John
PG 1848

Sakeouse, John
PG 2488

Saunders, Robert
Crombie   PG 2702a

Schotz, Benno
PG 2707

Scotland, The Honours of
PG 2069

Scott, Anne Rutherford
PG 656

Scott, David
PG 1450

Scott, David
PG 1608

Scott, Francis George
PG 2592

Scott, Francis George
PG 2639

Scott, Francis George
PGL 320

Scott, John
PG 1864

Scott, Robert Lyons
PG 2031

Scott, Thomas
PG 2065

SCOTT, Sir Walter, 1771–1832. *Novelist and poet*

PG 95* (Study based on PG 572.) Pencil and chalk drawing, 22.2 x 16.9 (8¾ x 6¾), by Andrew Geddes, 1823, signed. Purchased 1885.

PG 103* Canvas, 76.2 x 64 (30 x 25⅛), by Sir Francis Grant. Painted 1831. Bequeathed by Lady Ruthven 1885.

PG 123* Water-colour drawing, 17.9 x 11.7 (7⅛ x 4⅝), by Benjamin William Crombie, signed. Executed 1831. Bequeathed by W. F. Watson 1886.

PG 140 a. (With Lady Scott.) Pencil drawing, 12.3 x 9.8 (4¹³⁄₁₆ x 3⅞), by Sir Edwin Landseer, signed. Provenance untraced.
b. Pencil drawing, 13 x 10.7 (5⅛ x 4¼), by Sir Edwin Landseer. Provenance untraced.
c. Pencil drawing, 22.5 x 17.3 (8⅞ x 6¾), by Peter Eduard Ströhling. Given by Sir H. H. Campbell 1886.

PG 180 Death mask (plaster replica), h. 33.2 (13⅛), after Sir Francis Legatt Chantrey. Given by W. Calder Marshall 1887.

PG 352 Bust (plaster replica), h. 76.2 (30), after Sir Francis Legatt Chantrey. Dated 1820. Purchased 1887.

PG 420 Medallion (plaster replica), h. 6 (2⅜), after John Henning. Original dated 1808. Cast from a medallion in possession of J. Kermack 1892.

PG 572* (Probably a study for *The Discovery of the Regalia*.) Panel, 55.7 x 41.9 (21¹⁵⁄₁₆ x 16½), by Andrew Geddes. Given by J. Rankin 1898.

PG 575 Canvas, 76.2 x 63.5 (30 x 25), by Sir John Watson Gordon. Painted 1830. Transferred from the National Gallery of Scotland 1898.

PG 628* Canvas, 127 x 101 (50 x 39¾), by James Saxon. Painted 1805. Purchased 1904.

PG 662* Marble bust, h. 74.2 (29¼), by Sir Francis Legatt Chantrey. Executed 1828. Given by an anonymous donor 1907.

PG 700 (Death of Scott 1832.) Copper medal, dia. 4.9 (1¹⁵⁄₁₆), by W. Bain and B. R. Faulkner. Purchased 1910.

PG 784 Cut paper silhouette, h. 14.9 (5⅞), by Augustin Edouart. Purchased 1912.

PG 825* (*Sir Walter Scott and his friends at Abbotsford*.) See GROUPS.

PG 937 Canvas, 238.7 x 147.3 (90 x 57¹⁵⁄₁₆), by James Hall, 1838, signed. Given by Brigadier-General Archibald Stirling.

PG 960 Chalk drawing, 23.5 x 18.8 (9⁵⁄₁₆ x 7½), by Gilbert Stuart Newton, signed. Given by M. H. Spielmann through the National Art-Collections Fund 1923.

PG 1023 (Mertoun and the Valley of the Tweed.) Pencil and water-colour, 25.4 x 50.2 (10 x 19¾), by James Ward, signed. Purchased 1926.

PG 1031* Canvas, 76.2 x 63.5 (30 x 25), by Colvin Smith. Purchased 1926.

PG 1074* Cut paper silhouette, h. 14.7 (5¾), by Augustin Edouart, 1831, signed. Provenance untraced.

PG 1097 Chalk drawing, 47.5 x 35 (18¾ x 13¾), by Joseph Slater. Drawn *c*. 1821. Purchased 1928.

PG 1099 Water-colour, 27.3 x 22.4 (10¾ x 8⅞), by William Nicholson. Painted 1815. Purchased 1928.

Scott, Sir Walter
PG 95

Scott, Sir Walter
PG 103

Scott, Sir Walter
PG 123

Scott, Sir Walter
PG 572

Scott, Sir Walter
PG 628

Scott, Sir Walter
PG 662

Scott, Sir Walter
PG 1031

Scott, Sir Walter
PG 1074

Scott, Sir Walter
PG 1188

Scott, Sir Walter (Gala Day at Abbotsford)
PG 1193

Scott, Sir Walter
PG 1286

Scott, Sir Walter
PG 1366

Scott, Sir Walter
PGL 41

Funeral of Sir Walter Scott
PGL 268

SCOTT, Sir Walter (*continued*)

PG 1105   a. Pencil and water-colour drawing, 12.7 x 9.6 (5 x 3¾), by Michelangelo
           Gaetani. Drawn 1832.
           b. Ink drawing, 12.1 x 9.9 (4¾ x 3⅞), by Michelangelo Gaetani. 1832,
           signed.
           c. Pencil drawing, 10.9 x 13.6 (4¾ x 5⅜), by Michelangelo Gaetani. Dated
           1832. Given by Baron C. A. de Cosson 1929.

PG 1172   Electrotype medallion, dia. 9.6 (3¾), after Thomas Crawford. Given by Sir
           Hew Dalrymple 1932.

PG 1188*   Pencil and water-colour, 31.7 x 27 (12½ x 10⅝), by William Nicholson.
           Executed 1815. Purchased 1932.

PG 1189   (Scott's dog Maida.) Pencil and water-colour, 18.6 x 17.4 (7⅜ x 6⅞), by
           William Nicholson. Purchased 1932.

PG 1192   Wash drawing (shadowgraph), 33.5 x 24.5 (13⅛ x 9⅝), by William Simson.
           Purchased 1932.

PG 1193*   (*Gala Day at Abbotsford.*) Panel, 27.9 x 40.6 (11 x 16), by Sir William
           Allan. Purchased 1932.

PG 1204   Pencil drawing, 11.3 x 18 (4½ x 7), by Michelangelo Gaetani, 1832, signed.
           Purchased 1933.

PG 1241   Pencil drawing, 11.4 x 7.1 (4½ x 2¾), by Gilbert Stuart Newton, signed.
           Purchased 1934.

PG 1249   Canvas, 99.3 x 75.1 (39¹⁄₁₆ x 29⁹⁄₁₆), by Sir John Watson Gordon. Purchased
           1935.

PG 1286*   Canvas, 76.2 x 63.5 (30 x 25), by Sir Henry Raeburn. Painted 1822.
           Purchased with assistance from the National Art-Collections Fund 1935.

PG 1302   Porcelain statuette, h. 33.2 (13⅛), after Sir John Steell. Dated 1850.
           Purchased 1936.

PG 1303*   (*The Abbotsford Family.*) See GROUPS.

PG 1362   Wax relief, h. 10.2 (4), by unknown artist. Purchased 1938.

PG 1365   Canvas, 105.4 x 75.9 (41½ x 29⅞), by James Howe. Given by Sir John
           Stirling Maxwell 1938.

PG 1366*   Canvas, 93.1 x 73.3 (36⅝ x 28⅞), by Sir William Allan, signed. Given by
           the National Art-Collections Fund (London Scot Bequest) 1938.

PG 1367   Canvas, 91.1 x 71.1 (35⅞ x 28), by Henry M. Baird after Robert G. Baird.
           Given by A. N. G. Aitken 1938.

PG 1379   Water-colour on ivory, 9.3 x 7 (3⅝ x 2¾), by Jessica Landseer after Sir
           Edwin Landseer. Painted 1845. Purchased 1939.

PG 1387   Millboard, 33 x 28 (13 x 11), by or after Sir John Watson Gordon. Purchased
           1939.

PG 1452   (Death of Scott 1832.) Silver medal, dia. 4.9 (1¹⁵⁄₁₆), by W. Bain. Given by
           General Sir J. A. Haldane 1944.

PG 1483   Millboard, 13.1 x 11.2 (5⅛ x 4⅜), by Gilbert Stuart Newton. Purchased 1946.

PG 1499   Pencil drawing, 26.2 x 18.1 (7⅛ x 10¼), by James Eckford Lauder. Given by
           Dr Lauder Thomson 1947.

PG 1522   Bust (plaster replica), h. 76.5 (30⅛), after Sir Francis Legatt Chantrey.
           Dated 1820. Bequeathed by A. N. G. Aitken 1949.

PG 1523   Plaster statuette, h. 66.1 (26¹⁄₁₆), by Sir John Steell, 1865, signed.
           Bequeathed by A. N. G. Aitken 1949.

PG 1524   Plaster statuette, h. 57.6 (22¾), by John Greenshields. Bequeathed by
           A. N. G. Aitken 1949.

PG 1569   Marble bust, h. 64.1 (25¼), by Sir Francis Legatt Chantrey. Bequeathed by
           Professor R. W. Seton-Watson 1953.

PG 1678   a. Pencil and water-colour, 16 x 12.9 (6⅜ x 5⅛), by the Rev. John
           Thomson. Dated 1829.
           b. (Scott's pocket-knife.) Water-colour, 7.1 x 17.8 (2¹³⁄₁₆ x 7), by unknown
           artist. Bequeathed by W. F. Watson 1886.

PG 1731   (Scott's death at Abbotsford, 21st September 1832.) Water-colour, 22.2 x
           29.2 (8¾ x 11½), by Sir William Allan, 1832, signed. Provenance untraced.

PG 1810   Wash drawing, 11.6 x 10.7 (4½ x 4¼), by Sir Edwin Landseer. Purchased
           1955.

PG 1860   Electrotype medallion, dia. 9.6 (3¾), by Thomas Crawford. Given by Lady
           Foster 1959.

PG 1986   Pencil drawing with chalk highlights, 29.6 x 21.2 (11⅝ x 8⅜), by Gilbert
           Stuart Newton. Dated 1834 but probably drawn in 1824. Given by Giles H.
           Robertson in memory of Professor D. S. Robertson 1962.

PG 2132   (With Lady Scott.) Panel, 35.4 x 30.6 (13¹⁵⁄₁₆ x 12¹⁄₁₆), by Sir William Allan.
           Bequeathed by Miss E. H. Ross 1968.

PG 2217   Panel, 21 x 17.9 (8¼ x 7¹⁄₁₆), by Sir John Watson Gordon, signed or
           inscribed. Bequeathed by Sir William Younger 1973.

PG 2230   Pencil and chalk drawing, 17.9 x 13 (7¹⁄₁₆ x 5⅛), by Sir William Allan.
           Purchased 1974.

PG 2295   a. (Birthplace of Scott in College Wynd, Edinburgh.) Wash drawing,
           28.3 x 20.6 (11⅛ x 8⅛), by Henry G. Duguid, signed (on reverse).
           b. Ink and water-colour drawing, oval 3.8 x 3 (1½ x 1³⁄₁₆), copy by unknown
           artist. Bequeathed by W. F. Watson to the National Gallery of Scotland
           1886 and transferred 1975.

PG 2656   (Study for PG 937.) Millboard, 45.4 x 35.5 (17⅞ x 14)
           by James Hall, 1837/8. Given anonymously c. 1932.

PG 2657   (Study for PG 937.) Pencil drawing on millboard, 45.4 x 35.5 (17⅞ x 14),
           by James Hall or Captain Basil Hall. Given anonymously c. 1932.

PG 2658   a. (Study for PG 937.) Camera lucida sketch in pencil on tracing paper,
           21 x 10.1 (8⁵⁄₁₆ x 4) (irregular), by Captain Basil Hall, 1830.
           b. (Study for PG 937.) Camera lucida sketch in pencil on tracing paper,
           21.4 x 20.9 (8⁷⁄₁₆ x 8¼) (irregular), by Captain Basil Hall, 1830.
           c. (Study for PG 937.) Camera lucida sketch in pencil on tracing paper,
           19.8 x 20.9 (7¹³⁄₁₆ x 8¼) (irregular), by Captain Basil Hall, 1830. Given
           anonymously c. 1932.

PG 2659   (Drawing of hand and, verso, drawing of head, studies for PG 937.) Pencil
           drawing, 32.4 x 19.6 (12¾ x 7¹¹⁄₁₆), by James Hall, 1838. Given
           anonymously c. 1932.

PG 2660   (Plan of the hall pavement at Abbotsford.) Pencil drawing, 66 x 101.6 (26 x
           40), by James Hall, 1843. Given anonymously c. 1932.

SCOTT, Sir Walter (*continued*)

PG 2661   Pencil drawing on millboard, 35.7 x 30 (14 x 11¹³⁄₁₆) (irregular), by James
          Hall or Captain Basil Hall after Sir John Watson Gordon, 1830. Given
          anonymously *c.* 1932.

PG 2662   Pencil drawing on millboard, 35.7 x 28 (14 x 11), by James Hall or Captain
          Basil Hall after Sir John Watson Gordon 1830. Given anonymously *c.* 1932.

PG 2776   (Commemorative medal issued by the Royal High School, Edinburgh.)
          Silver medal, dia. 5 (2), by C. d'O. Pilkington Jackson, 1932, signed.
          Probably given by the artist 1956.

PGL 41*   Water-colour on ivory, 4.4 x 3.5 (1¾ x 1⅜), by unknown artist. On loan
          from the National Museums of Scotland.

PGL 268* (The Funeral of Sir Walter Scott.) Water-colour, 40 x 53.3 (15¾ x 21),
          by Captain James Edward Alexander. On loan from A. A. Alexander.

SCOTT, Lieutenant-Colonel Sir Walter, 2nd Baronet, 1801–47. *Soldier; son of Sir Walter*
          Scott

PG 1303* (*The Abbotsford Family.*) See GROUPS.

SCOTT, William Bell, 1811–90. *Poet and artist*

PG 1849* Canvas, 53.1 x 35 (20⅞ x 14), self-portrait, 1867, signed. Given by Sir
          James Fergusson 1958.

PGL 314* Canvas, 76.5 x 64.1 (30⅛ x 25¼), by David Scott, signed. Painted 1832. On
          loan from the National Gallery of Scotland.

SCOTT-MONCRIEFF, Charles Kenneth, 1889–1930. *Translator of Proust*

PG 2199* Canvas, 111.7 x 86.3 (44 x 34), by Edward Stanley Mercer. Purchased 1972.

SCOTT-MONCRIEFF, George, 1910–74. *Author*

PG 2008* Black chalk drawing, 47 x 29.5 (18½ x 11⅝), by David Foggie, 1934, signed.
          Given by Mrs M. Foggie 1962.

SCOTTISH ARTS CLUB, THE SMOKING ROOM; see GROUPS (PG 2737).

SCOTTISH NATIONAL PORTRAIT GALLERY; *designs for a window*

PG 2278   a. (Royal Arms of Great Britain.) Pencil drawing, 45.9 x 39 (18¹⁄₃₂ x 15⅜),
          by W. Graham Boss.
          b. (Arms of the Society of Antiquaries of Scotland.) Pencil drawing, 45.9 x
          39 (18¹⁄₁₆ x 15⅜); by W. Graham Boss.
          c. ('The 13th day of August 1891.') Pencil drawing, 46.4 x 39.2 (18¼ x
          15⁷⁄₁₆), by W. Graham Boss. Given by the artist.

SCOTTISH NATIONAL PORTRAIT GALLERY; *interior and exterior views*

PG 1760* a. Ink drawing, 15.3 x 13.5 (6 x 5⅜), by Thomas Crawford Hamilton,
          signed. Drawn 1890.
      *   b. Ink drawing, 17.9 x 25 (7 x 9¾), by Thomas Crawford Hamilton, 1890,
          signed. Given by J. Kent Richardson 1944.

Scott, William Bell
PG 1849

Scott, William Bell
PGL 314

Scott-Moncrieff, Charles
Kenneth   PG 2199

Scott-Moncrieff, George
PG 2008

Scottish National Portrait Gallery
PG 1760a

Scottish National Portrait Gallery
PG 1760b

Scottish National Portrait Gallery
(Cartoons for Frieze)   PG 2631a

Seafield, 1st Earl of
PG 1064

Selkirk, 6th Earl of
PG 1557

Seton Palace
PG 2696

Seton, 5th Lord
PGL 309

Shanks, William Somerville
PG 2405

Sharp, James
PG 1529

Sharp, William
PG 1214

SCOTTISH NATIONAL PORTRAIT GALLERY; *cartoons for processional frieze*

PG 2631*   a. (From Septimius Severus to figures representing the Stone Age.) Sepia wash over pencil drawing, 35.5 x 76.8 (14 x 30¼), by William Hole, signed. Drawn *c.* 1898.

b. (From Thomas Carlyle to Thomas Campbell.) Sepia wash over pencil drawing, 35.5 x 83.5 (14 x 32⅞), by William Hole. Drawn *c.* 1898.

c. (From Robert II to Margaret, Queen of Scots.) Sepia wash over pencil drawing, 35.4 x 66 (13¹⁵⁄₁₆ x 26), by William Hole. Drawn *c.* 1898.

d. (From Thomas the Rhymer to Duncan I.) Sepia wash over pencil drawing, 35.4 x 65.9 (13⅞ x 25¹⁵⁄₁₆), by William Hole. Drawn *c.* 1898.

e. (From the Vikings to Septimius Severus.) Sepia wash over pencil drawing, 35.5 x 65.6 (14 x 25¹³⁄₁₆), by William Hole. Drawn *c.* 1898.

f. (From James VI and I to Mary of Guise.) Sepia wash over pencil drawing, 33.7 x 64.8 (13¹³⁄₁₆ x 25½), by William Hole. Drawn *c.* 1898.

g. (From Cardinal David Beaton, Archbishop of St Andrews, to Robert Boyd, Lord Boyd.) Sepia wash over pencil drawing, 35.3 x 66 (13⅞ x 26), by William Hole. Drawn *c.* 1898.

h. (From William Crichton, Lord Crichton, to Edward Balliol.) Sepia wash over pencil drawing, 35.4 x 66 (13¹⁵⁄₁₆ x 26), by William Hole. Drawn *c.* 1898.

i. (From Mungo Park to James Bruce.) Sepia wash over pencil drawing, 35.5 x 66.2 (14 x 26¹⁄₁₆), by William Hole. Drawn *c.* 1898.

j. (From James Boswell to James Thomson.) Sepia wash over pencil drawing, 35.5 x 66.2 (14 x 26¹⁄₁₆), by William Hole. Drawn *c.* 1898.

k. (From John Erskine, 6th Earl of Mar, to William Kerr, 1st Earl of Lothian.) Sepia wash over pencil drawing, 34.9 x 66 (13¾ x 26), by William Hole. Drawn *c.* 1898. Purchased 1984.

SEAFIELD, James Ogilvy, 1st Earl of, 1664–1730. *Lord Chancellor of Scotland*

PG 1064*   Canvas, 125.7 x 103.1 (49½ x 40⅝), by Sir John Baptiste de Medina, 1695, signed. Bequeathed by Lady Ogilvie Dalgleish to the National Gallery of Scotland and transferred.

SEAFORTH, Francis Humberston Mackenzie, Lord, 1754–1815. *Soldier and Governor of Barbados*

PG 1662   (With the 3rd titular Duke of Perth.) Ink drawing, 37.1 x 24.4 (14⅝ x 9⅝), by John Sobieski Stuart, signed, after unknown artist. Bequeathed by W. F. Watson 1886.

SEAFORTH, Kenneth Mackenzie, 1st Earl of, 1744–81. *Collector*

PG 2610*   (As Viscount Fortrose, at home in Naples: fencing scene.) See GROUPS.
PG 2611*   (As Viscount Fortrose, at home in Naples: concert party.) See GROUPS.

SELKIRK, James Dunbar Douglas, 6th Earl of, 1809–85. *Representative Peer for Scotland*

PG 1557*   Water-colour, 30.7 x 18 (12⅛ x 7⅛), by Leslie Ward ('Spy'), signed. Purchased 1950.

SEMPILL, Hugh Sempill, 14th Lord, 1758–1830. *Soldier*
PG 1671   Water-colour, 18.6 x 11.6 (7⅜ x 4⁹⁄₁₆), by J. Jenkins, 1800, signed.
            Bequeathed by W. F. Watson 1886.

SETON, 5th Lord; Family of; See GROUPS (PG 1020, PGL 312).

SETON PALACE AND THE FORTH ESTUARY
PG 2696*   Panel, 45.6 x 68.5 (17¹⁵⁄₁₆ x 27), by Alexander Keirincx, signed in
            monogram. Painted *c*. 1635–40. Purchased 1986.

SETON, George Seton, Lord, 1613–48. *Royalist*
PGL 336*   (With his father, the 3rd Earl of Winton, and his brother, 1st Viscount
            Kingston.) Canvas, 113 x 83.8 (44½ x 33), by Adam de Colone, 1625.
            On loan from the Kintore Trust.

SETON, George, 1822–1908. *Advocate*
PG 1815   Pencil drawing, 35.5 x 24.8 (14 x 9¾), by Thomas Crawford Hamilton,
            1890, signed. Bequeathed by J. M. Gray 1894.

SETON, George Seton, 5th Lord, 1531–85. *Supporter of Mary Queen of Scots*
PG 1020   (With his family.) See GROUPS.
PGL 309*   Panel, 120 x 105.7 (47½ x 41⅝), by unknown artist. Dated 157[–]. On loan
            from the National Gallery of Scotland.
PGL 312*   (With his family.) See GROUPS.

SETON, Sir William, *c*. 1562–1635. *Sheriff of Edinburgh and Postmaster-General of
            Scotland*
PG 1020   (Probably Sir William Seton. As a boy, with his father, 5th Lord Seton,
            his brothers and sister.) See GROUPS.
PGL 312*   (Probably Sir William Seton. As a boy, with his father, 5th Lord Seton,
            his brothers and sister.) See GROUPS.

SEYMOUR, Lord John Webb. 1777–1819. *Son of the 10th Duke of Somerset*
PG 1540   Porcelain medallion, h. 5.8 (2⁵⁄₁₆), by John Henning. Dated 1807. Purchased
            1949.

SHANKS, William Somerville, 1864–1951. *Artist*
PG 2405*   Canvas, 77.5 x 64.2 (30½ x 25¼), self-portrait, signed. Given by the Fine
            Art Society Ltd 1977.

SHARP, Granville, 1735–1813. *Pioneer for the abolition of slavery*
PG 455   Medallion (plaster replica), h. 5.4 (2⅛), after Catherine Andras. Given by
            J. M. Gray 1893.

SHARP, James, 1613–79. *Archbishop of St Andrews*
PG 1529*   Canvas, 76.8 x 64.1 (30¼ x 25¼), by unknown artist after Sir Peter Lely.
            Purchased 1949.

SHARP, William, 1749–1824; see UNIDENTIFIED (PG 2258).

SHARP, William (nom de plume, 'Fiona Macleod'), 1855–1905. *Author and poet*
   PG 1214*   Canvas, 125.4 x 73.7 (49⅜ x 29), by Daniel Albert Wehrschmidt, 1898,
               signed. Purchased 1934.

SHARPE, Charles Kirkpatrick, *c.* 1781–1851. *Antiquary*
   PG 193   Panel, 25.4 x 21.1 (10 x 8⁵⁄₁₆), by John Irvine. Purchased 1887.
   PG 1677   Wash drawing, 18.3 x 14.3 (7¼ x 5⅝), by the sitter after Thomas Fraser.
              Bequeathed by W. F. Watson 1886.
   PGL 35*   Canvas, 76.2 x 63.5 (30 x 25), by Thomas Fraser. Painted 1829. On loan
              from the National Museums of Scotland.

SHAW, Peter, fl. 1899. *Of Merchiston Curling Club*
   PG 1856*   (*Curling at Carsebreck.*) See GROUPS.

SHAW, Sax Roland, b. 1916. *Artist*
   PGL 328*   (*Gathering at 7 London Street.*) See GROUPS.

SHEIL, Richard Lalor, 1791–1851. *Dramatist and politician*
   PG 1719   Chalk drawing, 52 x 37.5 (20½ x 14¾), by William Bewick. Dated 1824.
              Purchased 1927.

SHEPHERD, Sir Samuel, 1760–1840. *Lord Chief Baron of the Scottish Exchequer*
   PG 1279   Wax medallion, h. 9.5 (3¾), by unknown artist. Purchased 1935.

SHERIFF, John, 1816–44. *Artist*
   PG 1681   Pencil drawing, 11.8 x 7.9 (4⅝ x 3⅛), by Sir Daniel Macnee, signed.
              Bequeathed by W. F. Watson 1886.

SHERWILL SILHOUETTE ALBUM
   PGL 250   130 silhouettes, some cut and some printed, by Lucy Maria Lind, Mrs
              Sherwill. On loan from the National Museums of Scotland.

SHORT, James, 1710–68. *Mathematician and optician*
   PG 1644   Pencil and chalk drawing, 36 x 25.5 (14¼ x 10), by the 11th Earl of Buchan.
              Bequeathed by W. F. Watson 1886.

SHREWSBURY, Sir John Talbot, 1st Earl of, 1390–1453. *Lord High Steward of Ireland*
   PG 2078   Water-colour, 16 x 11 (6¼ x 4¼), copy by unknown artist. Transferred
              from the National Gallery of Scotland 1950.

SIBBALD, James, 1745–1803. *Author and bookseller*
   PG 322*   Canvas, oval 25.9 x 19.7 (10³⁄₁₆ x 7¾), by unknown artist. Bequeathed by
              W. F. Watson 1886.

SIDDONS, Harriet Murray, Mrs Henry, 1783–1844. *Actress and theatrical manager*
    PG 214   Canvas, 64.5 x 54.3 (25⅜ x 21⅜), by John Wood. Purchased 1888.

SIDDONS, Henry, 1774–1815. *Actor; eldest son of Sarah Siddons*
    PG 1487   (As a child, study for a double portrait with his mother.) Canvas, 68.3 x
                52.9 (26⅞ x 20¾), by William Hamilton. Given by Mrs F. T. Saintsbury
                1947.

SIDDONS, Henry, b. 1814. *Theatre manager*
    PG 2209   Pencil and water-colour drawing, 27.7 x 22 (10⅞ x 8¹¹⁄₁₆), by unknown
                artist. Purchased 1973.

SIDDONS, Sarah Kemble, Mrs William, 1755–1831. *Actress*
    PG 537   Medallion (plaster replica), h. 4.1 (1⅝), after John Henning. Dated 1807.
                Given by Miss Brown 1894.
    PG 2542   (Probably Sarah Siddons.) Water-colour on card, h. 9 (3½), by J. Brown,
                signed. Transferred from the National Gallery of Scotland 1982.

SILHOUETTE ALBUM *c.* 1782–*c.* 1818
    PG 2584   See GROUPS.

SILLERY, Charles Doyne, 1807–1837. *Poet*
    PG 1174   Cut paper silhouette, h. 20 (7⅞), by Augustin Edouart. Cut 1830.
                Purchased 1932.

SIMPSON, Sir James Young, 1811–70. *Discoverer of chloroform*
    PG 426*   Marble bust, h. 79.5 (31¾), by John Stevenson Rhind, signed, after Patric
                Park. Given by Sir W. G. Simpson 1889.

SIMPSON, Joseph, 1879–1939. *Artist*
    PG 1383*   Millboard, 34.9 x 25.7 (13¾ x 10⅛), by George Fiddes Watt, 1897, signed.
                Given by J. Kent Richardson 1939.

SIMSON, Harriet Elizabeth, 1826/7–32.
    PG 2556   Water-colour on ivory, dia. 4.8 (1¾), by Sir William Charles Ross.
                Transferred from the National Gallery of Scotland 1982.

SIMSON, William, 1800–47. *Artist*
    PG 179   Plaster bust, h. 68.7 (27¹⁄₁₆), by David Simson. Given by G. W. Simson
                1886.

SINCLAIR, Sir John, 1754–1835. *Politician, statistician and agriculturist*
    PG 459   Medallion (plaster replica), h. 8.4 (3⁵⁄₁₆), after James Tassie. Dated 1797.
                Cast from a medallion in possession of Jeffery Whitehead 1893.

SIVELL, Robert, 1888–1958. *Artist*

PG 1997* Black chalk drawing, 42.6 x 27.6 (16¾ x 10⅞), by David Foggie, 1938, signed. Given by Mrs M. Foggie 1962.

PG 2401 Pencil drawing, 36.5 x 25.2 (14⅜ x 9¹⁵⁄₁₆), by Sir William Oliphant Hutchison. Drawn from memory. Given by the executors of Margery, Lady Hutchison 1977.

PG 2490* Canvas, 73.9 x 56.9 (29⅛ x 22⅜), by Hamish Paterson. Dated indistinctly 193[3]. Purchased 1981.

SKELTON, Sir John, 1831–97. *Author*

PG 570 Wax medallion, dia. 14.6 (5¾), by Charles Matthew, 1890, signed. Bequeathed by J. M. Gray 1894.

SKENE, Andrew, 1784–1835. *Solicitor General for Scotland*

PG 1508 Canvas, 127 x 101.6 (50 x 40), by Colvin Smith. Given by Brigadier A. H. R. Dodd 1948.

PG 2306 (Crombie Sketchbook, fo. 9.) Pencil drawing, 15.6 x 20 (6⅛ x 7), by Benjamin William Crombie. Purchased 1938.

SKENE, James, 1775–1864. *Antiquarian, artist, and friend of Scott*

PG 2051 Wash drawing, 17.8 x 16.2 (7 x 6⅜), by unknown artist. Transferred from the National Gallery of Scotland 1965.

SKENE, William Forbes. 1809–92. *Historian and Celtic scholar*

PG 428* Canvas, 75.2 x 53.2 (29⅝ x 20¹⁵⁄₁₆), by Sir George Reid, signed. Painted 1888. Given by anonymous subscribers 1892.

PG 802 Cut paper silhouette, h. 22.1 (8¹¹⁄₁₆), by Augustin Edouart. Purchased 1912.

SKINNER, James Scott, 1843–1927. *Violinist and composer*

PG 2024* Canvas, 73.7 x 55.8 (29 x 22), by David Waterson, signed. Dated 1912 (on the reverse). Purchased 1962.

SKINNER, Rev. John, 1721–1807. *Minister and songwriter*

PG 1770* (*Burns at an evening party of Lord Monboddo's 1786.*) See GROUPS.

SKIRVING, Adam, 1719–1803. *Song writer: author of* Hey, Johnnie Cope

PG 596* Canvas, 76.2 x 72.9 (30 x 24), by Archibald Skirving. Bequeathed by D. Ainslie 1901.

SKIRVING, Archibald, 1749–1819. *Artist*

PG 595* Chalk drawing, 71.4 x 54.9 (28⅛ x 21⅝), self-portrait. Bequeathed by D. Ainslie 1901.

PG 713* Canvas, 90.3 x 69.4 (35½ x 27¼), by George Watson. Given by the Royal Scottish Academy 1910.

PGL 313* Canvas, 72.7 x 60 (28⅝ x 23⅝), by Andrew Geddes. On loan from the National Gallery of Scotland.

Sharpe, Charles Kirkpatrick
PGL 35

Sibbald, James
PG 322

Simpson, Sir James Young
PG 426

Simpson, Joseph
PG 1383

Sivell, Robert
PG 1997

Sivell, Robert
PG 2490

Skene, William Forbes
PG 428

Skinner, James Scott
PG 2024

Skirving, Adam
PG 596

Skirving, Archibald
PG 595

Skirving, Archibald
PG 713

Skirving, Archibald
PGL 313

Smellie, William
PGL 29

Smellie, William
PGL 52

Smellie, William
PGL 64

Smiles, Samuel
PG 631

SKIRVING of Croys, Captain Robert, 1757–1843. *Of the East India Company; brother of Archibald Skirving*
PG 2473   Panel, 66 x 45 (26 x 17½), by Andrew Geddes. Painted 1813. Given by Mrs Leila Hoskins 1981.

SMALL, James, fl. 1899. *Of Strathardle Curling Club*
PG 1856*   (*Curling at Carsebreck.*) See GROUPS.

SMALL, Major-General John, 1726–96. *Soldier*
PG 671   Chalk drawing, 47.2 x 40 (18⅝ x 15¾), copy by unknown artist. Purchased 1908.

SMART, John, 1741–1811. *Miniature painter*
PG 2254   Black and white chalk drawing, 35.3 x 28.4 (13⅞ x 11³⁄₁₆), by Mather Brown. Drawn *c.* 1784/5. Provenance untraced.

SMART, John, 1838–99. *Landscape painter*
PG 1747   (In his studio.) Wash drawing, 41.4 x 38.1 (16¼ x 15), by J. R. Abercromby, signed. Executed 1898. Purchased 1940.

SMELLIE, William, 1740–95. *Printer, naturalist and antiquary*
PG 1770*   (*Burns at an evening party of Lord Monboddo's 1786.*) See GROUPS.
PGL 29*   Canvas, 127 x 101.6 (50 x 40), by George Watson. On loan from the National Museums of Scotland.
PGL 52*   Plaster bust, h. 65.5 (25¹³⁄₁₆), by Robert Cummins, signed. On loan from the National Museums of Scotland.
PGL 64*   Pencil drawing, 49.8 x 34 (19⅝ x 13⅜), by John Brown. On loan from the National Museums of Scotland.

SMILES, Samuel, 1812–1904. *Author and reformer*
PG 631*   Canvas, 34.3 x 24.8 (13½ x 9¾), by Sir George Reid, 1891, signed. Bequeathed by J. M. Gray 1894.
PG 1243*   Canvas, 32.1 x 31.9 (12⅝ x 12⁹⁄₁₆), by Sir George Reid, 1879, signed. Given by Mrs Lucy Smiles 1934.

SMITH, Mr, fl. *c.* 1840. *Bookseller*
PG 2018   (With James Smith of Deanstone.) Pencil drawing, 10 x 12.1 (3⅞ x 4¾), attributed to William Home Lizars. Given by E. Kersley 1962.

SMITH SKETCHBOOK
PG 2309   Portrait and other sketches by Charles Smith. Dated 1810. Provenance untraced.

SMITH, A. Davidson, fl. 1899. *Secretary of the Royal Caledonian Curling Club*
PG 1856*   (*Curling at Carsebreck.*) See GROUPS.

SMITH, Adam, 1723–90. *Political economist*
  PG 157   Paste medallion, h. 7.5 (2¹⁵⁄₁₆), by James Tassie. Dated 1787. Purchased 1886.
  PG 403   Medallion (plaster replica), h. 7.3 (2⅞), after James Tassie. Dated 1787.
             Cast from a medallion in possession of J. R. Findlay 1889.
  PG 1472   Canvas, 77.9 x 64.5 (30⅝ x 25⅜), by unknown artist. Given by J. H.
             Romanes 1945.
  PG 1949*   Paste medallion, h. 7.3 (2¹⁵⁄₁₆), by James Tassie. Dated 1787. Transferred
             from the National Gallery of Scotland 1960.

SMITH, Alexander, 1830–67. *Poet and writer*
  PG 883*   Plaster medallion, dia. 36.5 (14⅜), by William Brodie. Given by Miss
             Maclennan 1918.
  PG 2453*   Canvas, 61 x 50.8 (24 x 20), by James Archer. Painted *c.* 1856. Given by
             Mrs Marion St Johnston 1980.

SMITH, Iain Crichton, b. 1928. *Poet*
  PG 2597*   (*Poets' Pub.*) See GROUPS.

SMITH, James, of Deanstone, 1789–1850. *Agriculturist*
  PG 2018   (With Smith, bookseller.) Pencil drawing, 10 x 12.1 (3⅞ x 4¾), attributed
             to William Home Lizars. Given by E. Kersley 1962.

SMITH of Dalry, John, 1846–1930. *Geologist, antiquary and botanist*
  PG 1201   Bronze medallion, dia. 14 (5½), by Robert Bryden. Dated 1930. Purchased
             1933.

SMITH, Dr John, 1825–1910. *Dental surgeon and founder of Edinburgh Dental Hospital*
  PG 2625   Chalk drawing, 36.7 x 27 (14⁷⁄₁₆ x 10⅝), by James Paterson, signed. Dated
             1908. Provenance untraced.

SMITH, John Guthrie Spence, 1880–1951. *Artist*
  PG 2737*   (*The Smoking Room, the Scottish Arts Club.*) See GROUPS.

SMITH, Norman Kemp, 1872–1958. *Philosopher*
  PG 1803   Black chalk drawing, 44.9 x 28 (17⅝ x 11), by David Foggie, 1932, signed.
             Given by Mrs M. Foggie 1955.

SMITH, Rev. Sydney, 1771–1845. *Wit and author*
  PG 528   Porcelain medallion, h. 5.2 (2¹⁄₁₆), by John Henning. Dated 1803. Given by
             Miss Brown 1894.
  PG 1948   Medallion (plaster replica), h. 5.1 (2), after John Henning. Provenance untraced.

SMITH, Professor Sir Sydney Alfred, 1884–1969. *Professor of Forensic Medicine at
             Edinburgh University*
  PG 2402   Charcoal drawing, 41 x 25.9 (16⅛ x 10³⁄₁₆), by Sir William Oliphant
             Hutchison. Given by the executors of Margery, Lady Hutchison 1977.

SMITH, Sydney Goodsir, 1915–75. *Poet*
>PG 2368* (Landscape sketch on the reverse.) Canvas, 76.2 x 63.5 (30 x 25), by Denis Peploe, signed. Given by Mrs Hazel Goodsir Smith 1976.
>PG 2597* (*Poets' Pub.*) See GROUPS.

SMITH, Rev. Walter Chalmers, 1824–1908. *Free Church minister and poet*
>PG 2207* Canvas, 64.8 x 55.8 (25½ x 22), by Sir George Reid, signed. Painted *c.* 1894. Bequeathed by Miss M. M. Carlyle 1972.

SMITH, William, 1703–73. *Principal Clerk of Chancery*
>PG 1762 Wash drawing, 17.1 x 13.6 (6¾ x 5⅜), copy by unknown artist. Purchased 1945.

SMITH, Sir William Alexander, 1854–1914. *Founder of the Boys' Brigade*
>PG 1404* (Cut down from three-quarter length.) Canvas, 76.2 x 62.9 (30 x 24¾), by Alexander Roche. Given by G. S. Smith and D. P. Smith 1940.

SMITH, Professor William Robertson, 1846–94. *Theologist and Semitic scholar*
>PG 680* Canvas, 34.5 x 29.8 (13⁹⁄₁₆ x 11¾), by Sir George Reid, signed. Purchased 1909.

SMITH, Sir (William) Sidney, 1764–1840. *Admiral*
>PG 2680* (*The Battle of Alexandria, 21 March 1801.*) See GROUPS.
>PG 2681* (*The Landing of British Troops at Aboukir, 8 March 1801.*) See GROUPS.
>PG 2682 *c.* (Study for *The Landing of British Troops at Aboukir.*) Water-colour and pencil drawing, 18.5 x 14.7 (7⁵⁄₁₆ x 5¹³⁄₁₆) (irregular), attributed to Philip James de Loutherbourg. Purchased 1986.

SMOLLET of Bonhill, Alexander, 1801–81. *Member of Parliament for Dunbartonshire*
>PG 1165 (Study for *The Landing of Queen Victoria at Dumbarton in 1847,* in the collection of Dumbarton District Council.) Pencil and water-colour, 68.6 x 50.8 (27 x 20) by Hope James Stewart. Drawn 1849. Purchased 1931.

SMOLLET, Miss Cecilia, fl. 1849. *Sister of Alexander Smollet*
>PG 1980 (Study for *The Landing of Queen Victoria at Dumbarton in 1847,* in the collection of Dumbarton District Council.) Water-colour, 58.4 x 41 (23 x 16⅛), by Hope James Stewart. Painted 1849. Purchased 1931.

SMOLLET, Miss Helen, fl. 1849. *Sister of Alexander Smollet*
>PG 1979 (Study for *The Landing of Queen Victoria at Dumbarton in 1847,* in the collection of Dumbarton District Council.) Water-colour, 59.5 x 41 (23½ x 16⅛), by Hope James Stewart. Painted 1849. Purchased 1931.

SOBIESKA, Princess Maria Clementina, 1702–35. *Wife of Prince James Francis Edward Stewart*
>PG 704 (With Prince James Francis Edward Stewart. Commemorates the marriage of Prince James and Princess Clementina.) Silver medal, dia. 4.1 (1⅝), by Otto Hamerani. Dated 1719. Purchased 1910.

Smiles, Samuel
PG 1243

Smith, Adam
PG 1949

Smith, Alexander
PG 883

Smith, Alexander
PG 2453

Smith, Sydney Goodsir
PG 2368

Smith, Rev. Walter Chalmers
PG 2207

Smith, Sir William Alexander
PG 1404

Smith, Professor William
Robertson   PG 680

Sobieska, Princess Maria
Clementina   PG 886

Sobieska, Princess Maria
Clementina   PG 1837

Somerville, Mary
PG 1115

Southesk, 5th Earl of
PG 2452

Spark, Muriel
PG 2617

SOBIESKA, Princess Maria Clementina (*continued*)

PG 735 (Commemorates the escape of Princess Clementina from Innsbruck.) Silver medal, dia. 4.7 (1⅞), by Otto Hamerani. Dated 1719. Purchased 1910.

PG 886* Canvas, 98 x 73 (38⁹⁄₁₆ x 28¾), by unknown artist. Purchased 1918.

PG 1330 (Commemorates the escape of Princess Clementina from Innsbruck.) Copper medal, dia. 4.8 (1⅞), by Otto Hamerani. Dated 1719. Purchased 1937.

PG 1331 (With Prince James Francis Edward Stewart. Commemorates the marriage of Prince James and Princess Clementina.) Copper medal, dia. 4.1 (1⅝), by Otto Hamerani. Dated 1719. Purchased 1937.

PG 1332 (With Prince James Francis Edward Stewart. Commemorates the birth of Prince Charles Edward.) Copper medal, dia. 4.1 (1⅝), by Otto Hamerani. Dated 1720. Purchased 1937.

PG 1457 Enamel, 4.8 x 3.9 (1⅞ x 1½), by unknown artist. Bequeathed by Sir St Clair Thomson 1944.

PG 1837* Canvas, 76.5 x 63.7 (30⅛ x 25⅛), by unknown artist after Louis Gabriel Blanchet. Bequeathed by Miss B. S. Parr 1956.

PG 2415* (*The Marriage of Prince James Francis Edward Stewart and Princess Maria Clementina Sobieska.*) See GROUPS.

PGL 201 (Commemorates the marriage of Prince James and Princess Clementina.) Silver medal, dia. 4.8 (1⅞), by Otto Hamerani. Struck 1719. Obverse: Prince James Francis Edward Stewart. On loan from the National Museums of Scotland.

PGL 202 (With Prince James Francis Edward Stewart. Commemorates the marriage of Prince James and Princess Clementina.) Silver medal, dia 4.1 (1⅝), by Otto Hamerani. Dated 1719. On loan from the National Museums of Scotland.

SOLDIER, STUDY OF A

PG 2264 Black and white chalk drawing, 35.2 x 29.4 (13⅞ x 11⁹⁄₁₆), attributed to Mather Brown. Provenance untraced.

SOMERVILLE, Mary Fairfax, Mrs William, 1780–1872. *Writer on science*

PG 279 Medallion (plaster replica), h. 4.2 (1⅝), after Lawrence Macdonald. Given by Sir W. Ramsay-Fairfax 1889.

PG 354 Medallion (plaster replica), h. 10.8 (4¼), after Robert Macpherson. Cast from an electrotype medallion in possession of Sir J. D. Hope 1889.

PG 1115* Canvas, 76.2 x 63.5 (30 x 25), by Thomas Phillips. Painted *c.* 1834. Purchased 1929.

SOMERVILLE, Robert, fl. 1899. *Of St Boswells Curling Club*

PG 1856* (*Curling at Carsebreck.*) See GROUPS.

SOUTHESK, James Carnegie, 5th Earl of, 1692–1730. *Jacobite*

PG 2452* Ink drawing, 31.7 x 22.2 (12½ x 8¾) (irregular), by Pier Leone Ghezzi. Purchased 1979.

SPARK, Muriel Sarah Camberg, Mrs S., b. 1919. *Writer*
    PG 2617*   Canvas, 183 x 91.4 (72 x 36), by Alexander Moffat, signed on the reverse.
             Dated 1984. Purchased by commission 1984.

SPENCE, David, d. *c.* 1860. *Dentist, and friend of William Tassie*
    PG 1929   Medallion (plaster replica), h. 7.2 (2¹³⁄₁₆), after William Tassie. Provenance
             untraced.

SPENCE, Lewis, 1874–1954. *Poet and scholar*
    PG 1817   Black chalk drawing, 46.4 x 29.2 (18¼ x 11½), by David Foggie, 1933,
             signed. Given by Mrs M. Foggie 1955.

SPENCER, Sir Brent, 1760–1828. *Soldier*
    PG 2680*   (*The Battle of Alexandria, 21 March 1801.*) See GROUPS.

SPENCER, Herbert, 1820–1903. *Philosopher*
    PG 618*   Canvas, 143.5 x 112.4 (56½ x 44¼), by Sir Hubert von Herkomer, 1898,
             signed. Given by the Herbert Spencer Portrait Committee 1904.

SPOTTISWOOD, Sir Robert, 1596–1646. *Lord President of the Court of Session*
    PG 1288   Canvas, 71.1 x 60.4 (28 x 23¾), by unknown artist. Dated 1636. Purchased
             1935.

SPREULL, James, d. 1769. *Merchant in Glasgow and benefactor of the Society for the
             Propagation of the Gospel in the Highlands and Islands*
    PG 2477*   Canvas, 127 x 101 (50 x 39¾), by unknown artist. Purchased 1981.

STAIR, John Dalrymple, 2nd Earl of, 1673–1747. *General and diplomat*
    PG 324   Canvas, 20.2 x 17.5 (7¹⁵⁄₁₆ x 6⅞), by unknown artist. Bequeathed by
             W. F. Watson 1886.
    PG 2195   Water-colour on ivory, oval 7 x 5.4 (2¾ x 2⅛), by unknown artist.
             Purchased 1971.

STARK, William fl. *c.* 1810–20 *Architect*
    PG 2386   (Possibly William Stark 1770–1813.) Water-colour, 15 x 11.6 (5¹⁵⁄₁₆ x 4⁹⁄₁₆),
             by unknown artist. Given by Mrs Gore Browne Henderson to the National
             Gallery of Scotland 1976 and transferred 1977.

STATESMEN, Some Statesmen of the Great War; See GROUPS (PG 1466).

STEDMAN (or STEEDMAN) John, d. 1791. *Physician*
    PG 2269   Paste medallion, h. 7.4 (2⅞), by James Tassie, after a portrait by John
             Thomas Seton. Dated 1791. Purchased 1975.

STEELL, Sir John, 1804–91. *Sculptor*
    PG 611   (Probably the artist's plaster.) Plaster bust, h. 85.4 (33⅜), by David Watson
             Stevenson. Purchased 1903.

STEELL, Sir John (*continued*)
    PG 2042*   Canvas, oval 21.1 x 17.3 (8⁵⁄₁₆ x 6¹³⁄₁₆), by Robert Scott Lauder. Painted 1832. Given by Miss Steell to the National Gallery of Scotland 1893 and transferred 1964.

STEPHENS, Henry, 1795–1874. *Agricultural writer*
    PG 2753*   Canvas, 91.5 x 71.3 (36 x 28⅛), by Sir John Watson Gordon. Purchased 1988.

STEUART, George, *c.* 1735–1806. *Artist and architect*
    PG 1399*   Copper, 43.1 x 31.7 (17 x 12½), by Sir William Beechey. Dated 1775. Given by Mrs B. G. Steuart 1940.

STEUART, George Drummond, 1798–1847. *Of Braco Castle*
    PG 1575   Millboard, 27.6 x 22.5 (10⅞ x 8⅞), by John Maclaren Barclay. Purchased 1951.

STEUART of Goodtrees, Sir James, 1635–1713. *Lord Advocate*
    PG 776*   Canvas, 76.2 x 63.5 (30 x 25), attributed to Sir John Baptiste de Medina. Purchased 1912.

STEUART, John, d. 1865. *Grandson of the 4th Baronet of Grandtully*
    PG 1574   Millboard, 27.6 x 22.6 (10⅞ x 8⅞), by John Maclaren Barclay, 1844, signed. Purchased 1951.

STEUART of Allanbank, Sir John James, 1779–1849. *Etcher and draughtsman*
    PG 1855   Water-colour, oval 14.2 x 11.1 (5½ x 4⅜), by 'PMᶜ[ ]', 1803, signed (with monogram). Given by Miss F. Egerton 1959.
    PG 1987   Canvas, 127.4 x 102.3 (50⅛ x 40¼), by Andrew Geddes, signed. Given by Lady Mitchison 1962.

STEUART, Robert, b. 1789. *Grandson of the 4th Baronet of Grandtully*
    PG 1576   Millboard, 27.6 x 22.7 (10⅞ x 8⅞), by John Maclaren Barclay, 1844, signed (on reverse). Purchased 1951.

STEUART of Grandtully, Thomas, 1802–46. *The Abbé Chevalier Steuart*
    PG 1755   Millboard, 27.7 x 22.5 (10⅞ x 8⅞), by John Maclaren Barclay after unknown artist. Purchased 1951.

STEVENSON, Flora Clift, 1840–1905. *Educationist and philanthropist*
    PG 643*   Canvas, 127 x 106.7 (50 x 42), by Alexander Roche, signed. Presented to the sitter by public subscription 1904 and bequeathed 1905.

STEVENSON, Joseph, 1806–95. *Historian and archivist*
    PG 550   Wax medallion, dia. 14.3 (5⅝), by Charles Matthew, 1889, signed. Bequeathed by J. M. Gray 1894.
    PG 1008   Bronze medallion, dia. 14 (5½), by Charles Matthew. Dated 1889. Bequeathed by Mr and Mrs W. R. Macdonald 1925.

Spencer, Herbert
PG 618

Spreull, James
PG 2477

Steell, Sir John
PG 2042

Stephens, Henry
PG 2753

Steuart, George
PG 1399

Steuart, Sir James
PG 776

Stevenson, Flora Clift
PG 643

Stevenson, Robert
PG 657

Stevenson, Robert Louis
PG 548

Stevenson, Robert Louis
PG 847

Stevenson, Robert Macaulay,
with Margaret Gauld and
Stansmore Dean Stevenson
PG 2704

Stevenson, Ronald
PG 2599

Stevenson, Thomas
PG 568

STEVENSON, Robert, 1772–1850. *Lighthouse engineer*

PG 272 Bust (plaster replica), h. 56.8 (22⅜), after Samuel Joseph. Given by Sir R. Murdoch Smith 1889.

PG 657* (Cut down from three-quarter length.) Canvas, 85.1 x 74.9 (33½ x 29½), by John Syme. Painted *c.* 1833. Purchased 1907.

STEVENSON, Robert Louis, 1850–94. *Essayist, poet and novelist*

PG 548* Marble bust, h. 77.1 (30⅜), by David Watson Stevenson, 1894/5, signed. Given by R. Cox 1895.

PG 847* Canvas, 61 x 35.5 (24 x 14), by Count Girolamo Nerli, signed. Painted 1892. Bequeathed by Mrs Turnbull 1915.

PG 1361 Pastel, 29.2 x 21 (11½ x 8¼), by Count Girolamo Nerli, 1892, signed. Purchased 1938.

STEVENSON, Robert Macaulay, 1854–1952. *Artist and critic*

PG 2403 Writing ink drawing, 20.3 x 12.6 (8 x 5), by Sir William Oliphant Hutchison. Given by the executors of Margery, Lady Hutchison 1977.

PG 2704* (In *Broadway*, with his wife (probably Stansmore Dean) and Margaret Paterson, Mrs David Gauld.) Water-colour and pencil drawing, 35.3 x 25.2 (13⅞ x 9⅞), by David Gauld, signed. Bequeathed by Mrs Isabel M. Traill 1986.

STEVENSON, Roger, fl. 1784.

PG 1273 Paste medallion, h. 7.6 (3), by James Tassie. Modelled 1784. Purchased 1935.

STEVENSON, Ronald, b. 1928. *Composer and pianist*

PG 2599* Hardboard, 71.2 x 91.4 (28 x 36), by Victoria Crowe, signed. Dated 1983. Purchased 1983.

STEVENSON, Stansmore Richmond Dean, Mrs Robert Macaulay, 1866–1944. *Artist*

PG 2704* (Probably Stansmore Dean, in *Broadway*, with Robert Macaulay Stevenson and Mrs David Gauld.) Water-colour and pencil drawing, 35.3 x 25.2 (13⅞ x 9⅞), by David Gauld, signed. Bequeathed by Mrs Isabel M. Traill 1986.

STEVENSON, Thomas, 1818–87. *Lighthouse and harbour engineer*

PG 568* Canvas, 86.3 x 63.5 (34 x 25), by Sir George Reid, signed. Bequeathed by Mrs Thomas Stevenson 1897.

STEVENSON, Professor William Barron, 1869–1954. *Professor of Hebrew and Semitic Languages at Glasgow University*

PG 2404 Charcoal and white chalk drawing, 62.3 x 48 (24½ x 18⅞), by Sir William Oliphant Hutchison. Given by the executors of Margery, Lady Hutchison 1977.

STEVENSON, William Grant, 1849–1919. *Painter and sculptor*
> PG 2455*   Canvas, 76.2 x 63.5 (30 x 25), by Charles Martin Hardie, signed. Dated
> 1893. Purchased 1980.

STEWART Family-Tree. *Genealogy of the Royal House of Stewart*
> PG 749   Panel, 70.8 x 66.8 (27⅞ x 26⁵⁄₁₆), by unknown artist. Purchased 1910.

STEWART, Anthony, 1773–1846. *Miniature painter*
> PG 430*   Canvas, 61.4 x 46.4 (24⅛ x 18¼), by Andrew Geddes. Dated 1812.
> Purchased 1892.

STEWART, Mrs Anthony, fl. 1795–1804.
> PG 1959   Paste medallion, h. 7.4 (2¹⁵⁄₁₆), by James Tassie. Dated 1795. Transferred
> from the National Gallery of Scotland 1960.

STEWART, Prince Charles Edward, 1720–88. *Eldest son of Prince James Francis Edward*
> *Stewart*
> PG 594*   Bust (plaster replica), h. 48.3 (19), after Jean-Baptiste Lemoyne. Dated
> 1746. Purchased 1900.
> PG 622*   Canvas, 25.7 x 22 (10⅛ x 8⅝), by Hugh Douglas Hamilton. Painted 1775.
> Purchased 1903.
> PG 736   Silver medal, dia. 4.1 (1⅝), by Otto Hamerani. Executed 1729. Reverse:
> Prince Henry Benedict Stewart. Purchased 1910.
> PG 737   (Expected arrival in Britain 1745.) Silver medal, dia. 4.1 (1⅝), by Thomas
> Pingo. Dated 1745. Purchased 1911.
> PG 887*   Canvas, 73.4 x 60.3 (28⅞ x 23¾), by Antonio David, 1732, signed.
> Purchased 1918.
> PG 929   Water-colour and ink, 2.6 x 2.1 (1 x ⅞), by unknown artist. Given by
> C. Stewart 1922.
> PG 930   (The 'Oak Medal'.) Copper medal, dia. 3.4 (1⁵⁄₁₆), by Thomas Pingo. Dated
> 1750. Given by C. Stewart 1922.
> PG 1024   Bronze bust, h. 48.1 (19), after Jean-Baptiste Lemoyne. Dated 1746. Cast
> from PG 594, 1926.
> PG 1272   Paste medallion, h. 8.9 (3½), by James Tassie. Purchased 1935.
> PG 1278   Paste medallion, h. 7.6 (2¹⁵⁄₁₆), by James Tassie. Modelled by Giovanni
> Battista Weder. Purchased 1935.
> PG 1333*   Copper medal, dia. 4.1 (1⅝), by Otto Hamerani. Struck 1729. Reverse:
> Prince Henry Benedict Stewart. Purchased 1937.
> PG 1346   (The 'Oak Medal'.) Copper medal, dia. 3.4 (1⁵⁄₁₆), by Thomas Pingo. Dated
> 1750. Purchased 1937.
> PG 1510   Canvas, 76.2 x 63.8 (30 x 25⅛), by unknown artist. Bequeathed by
> Miss F. D. Robertson 1948.
> PG 1519*   Canvas, 63.5 x 48.5 (25 x 19⅛), by unknown artist after Louis Gabriel
> Blanchet. Purchased 1949.
> PG 1535*   Canvas, 68.9 x 54.5 (27⅛ x 21⁷⁄₁₆), by unknown artist after Maurice
> Quentin de la Tour. Purchased 1949.

STEWART, Prince Charles Edward (*continued*)

PG 1613   Canvas, 76.2 x 63.5 (30 x 25), by unknown artist. Given by
           A. Miller-Stirling 1954.

PG 1690   Ink drawing, 35.5 x 25.4 (14 x 10), by Charles Elphinstone Dalrymple after
           unknown artist. Given by the artist 1887.

PG 2060*   (As a child.) Copper, 12.1 x 8.9 (4¾ x 3½), by unknown artist. Purchased
           1966.

PG 2318   Water-colour on ivory, 8.2 x 6.2 (3³⁄₁₆ x 2⁵⁄₁₆), copy by unknown artist.
           Bequeathed by W. F. Watson 1886.

PG 2320   Gouache, dia. 2.7 (1¹⁄₁₆), copy by unknown artist. Bequeathed by
           W. F. Watson 1886.

PG 2330   Water-colour on synthetic ivory, oval 7 x 5.3 (2¾ x 2⅛), by unknown artist
           after Louis Tocqué. Bequeathed by W. F. Watson 1886.

PG 2333   Water-colour on card, oval 3.9 x 3.5 (1⁹⁄₁₆ x 1⁷⁄₁₆), copy by unknown artist.
           Bequeathed by W. F. Watson 1886.

PG 2511*   (*The Baptism of Prince Charles Edward Stewart.*) See GROUPS.

PG 2522   (With Prince Henry Benedict Stewart.) Watercolour on ivory, 5.3 x 7.3
           (2¹⁄₁₆ x 2⅞), attributed to Giacomo Galletti. Given by Mrs C. Elizabeth
           Lockett and Sir Donald Bannerman 1982.

PG 2738   (Marriage to Princess Louisa of Stolberg.) Copper medal dia. 3.2 (1¼), by
           unknown artist. Struck 1772. Purchased 1988.

PGL 191   Water-colour on card, 6 x 5 (2⅜ x 2), by unknown artist. On loan from the
           National Museums of Scotland.

PGL 192   Water-colour on ivory, 4.4 x 3.7 (1¾ x 1½), by unknown artist. On loan
           from the National Museums of Scotland.

PGL 203   Silver medal, dia. 4.1 (1⅝), by Otto Hamerani. Executed 1729. Reverse:
           Prince Henry Benedict Stewart. On loan from the National Museums of
           Scotland.

PGL 204   (Expected arrival in Britain 1745.) Copper medal, dia. 4.1 (1⅝), by Thomas
           Pingo. Dated 1745. On loan from the National Museums of Scotland.

PGL 205   (Expected arrival in Britain 1745.) Silver medal, dia. 4.1 (1⅝), by Thomas
           Pingo. Dated 1745. On loan from the National Museums of Scotland.

PGL 294   Electrotype death mask, h. 25.4 (10), after unknown artist. On loan from
           the Duddingston Preservation Society.

PGL 340   Bronze medal, dia. 4.5 (1¾), by Otto Hamerani, 1729. Reverse: Prince
           Henry Benedict Stewart. On loan from the National Museums of Scotland.

STEWART, Princess Clementina; see SOBIESKA

STEWART, Sir Donald Martin, 1824–1900. *Commander-in-Chief in India*

PG 1560*   Water-colour, 30.8 x 18.2 (12⅛ x 7⅛), by Carlo Pellegrini ('Ape'), signed.
           Purchased 1950.

STEWART, Professor Dugald, 1753–1828. *Philosopher*

PG 209   Bronze bust, h. 38.7 (15¼), by Samuel Joseph. Given by J. Maxtone
           Grahame 1887.

Stevenson, William Grant
PG 2455

Stewart, Anthony
PG 430

Stewart, Prince Charles
Edward   PG 594

Stewart, Prince Charles Edward
PG 622

Stewart, Prince Charles Edward
PG 887

Stewart, Prince Charles Edward
PG 1333

Stewart, Prince Charles Edward
PG 1519

Stewart, Prince Charles Edward
PG 1535

Stewart, Prince Charles Edward
PG 2060

Stewart, Sir Donald
Martin   PG 1560

Stewart, Professor Dugald
PG 821

Stewart, Professor Dugald
PG 1985

Stewart, Professor Dugald
PGL 36

STEWART, Professor Dugald (*continued*)

PG 266   Paste medallion, h. 7.7 (3¹⁄₁₆), by James Tassie. Dated 1797. Transferred from the National Gallery of Scotland 1889.

PG 416   Medallion (plaster replica), h. 5.3 (2⅛), after John Henning. Original cast 1811. Cast from a medallion in the Museum of Science and Art, Edinburgh 1892.

PG 821*   Canvas, 76.2 x 62.2 (30 x 24½), by Sir Henry Raeburn. Painted *c*. 1810. Purchased 1913.

PG 1542   Porcelain medallion, h. 5.5 (2⅛), by John Henning. Dated 1811. Purchased 1949.

PG 1985* Chalk drawing, 50.8 x 41.9 (20 x 16½), by Sir David Wilkie, 1824, signed. Purchased 1962.

PG 1770* (*Burns at an evening party of Lord Monboddo's 1786.*) See GROUPS.

PG 2497   Ink silhouette, 41 x 33.2 (16⅛ x 13⅛), by Louisa Emma Fox-Strangways, Marchioness of Lansdowne. Drawn 1819. Given by Mrs Christina Edgeworth Colvin 1981.

PGL 36*   Chalk drawing, 49.5 x 41.9 (19½ x 16½), attributed to John Henning. On loan from R. K. Miller.

STEWART, Helen D'Arcy Cranstoun, Mrs Dugald, 1765–1838. *Song writer*

PG 417   Medallion (plaster replica), h. 5.6 (2³⁄₁₆), after John Henning. Cast from a medallion in the Museum of Science and Art, Edinburgh 1892.

PG 2503   Pencil and water-colour drawing, 14.4 x 13.3 (5⅝ x 5³⁄₁₆), by Thomas Heaphy. Executed 1802. Given by Lieutenant-Colonel James Bannatyne 1981.

STEWART, Prince Henry Benedict Clement, 1725–1807. *Cardinal York; younger brother of Prince Charles Edward Stewart*

PG 579   Water-colour on ivory, 10.9 x 8.5 (4¼ x 3⅜), attributed to Veronica Stern. Transferred from the National Gallery of Scotland 1898.

PG 624   Canvas, 68.6 x 53.4 (27 x 21), by unknown artist after Domenico Corvi. Purchased 1903.

PG 736   Silver medal, dia. 4.1 (1⅝), by Otto Hamerani. Executed 1729. Obverse: Prince Charles Edward Stewart. Purchased 1910.

PG 738   (Death of Prince Charles Edward Stewart.) Silver medal, dia. 5.2 (2¹⁄₁₆), by Gioacchino Hamerani. Dated 1788. Obverse: Cardinal York as Henry IX. Purchased 1910.

PG 888*   Canvas, 73.4 x 60.6 (28⅞ x 23⅞), by Antonio David, 1732, signed. Purchased 1918.

PG 1333* Copper medal, dia. 4.1 (1⅝), by Otto Hamerani. Struck 1729. Obverse: Prince Charles Edward Stewart. Purchased 1937.

PG 1518* Canvas, 63.5 x 47.3 (25 x 18⅝), by unknown artist after Louis Gabriel Blanchet. Purchased 1949.

PG 2360   Pen and water-colour drawing, 18.6 x 11.4 (7⁵⁄₁₆ x 4½), by unknown artist. Provenance untraced.

PG 2522   (With Prince Charles Edward Stewart.) Water-colour on ivory, 5.3 x 7.3
           (2¹⁄₁₆ x 2⅞), attributed to Giacomo Galletti. Given by Mrs C. Elizabeth
           Lockett and Sir Donald Bannerman 1982.

PGL 190   Water-colour on card, 5.4 x 7.3 (2⅛ x 2⅞), by unknown artist. On loan
           from the National Museums of Scotland.

PGL 203   Silver medal, dia. 4.1 (1⅝), by Otto Hamerani. Executed 1729. Obverse:
           Prince Charles Edward Stewart. On loan from the National Museums of
           Scotland.

PGL 206   (Death of Prince Charles Edward Stewart.) Copper medal, dia. 5.2 (2¹⁄₁₆), by
           Gioacchino Hamerani. Dated 1788. Obverse: Cardinal York as Henry IX.
           On loan from the National Museums of Scotland.

PGL 298*   Water-colour on ivory, oval 6.7 x 5.1 (2⅝ x 2), by unknown artist after
           Louis Gabriel Blanchet. On loan from the National Museums of Scotland.

PGL 300   Wash drawing, oval 6.1 x 4.7 (2⅜ x 1¹¹⁄₁₆), attributed to Sir Robert Strange.
           On loan from the National Museums of Scotland.

PGL 340   Bronze medal, dia. 4.5 (1¾), by Otto Hamerani, 1729. Obverse: Prince
           Charles Edward Stewart. On loan from the National Museums of Scotland.

STEWART, J. W., fl. 1899. *Of East Kilpatrick Curling Club*
    PG 1856*   (*Curling at Carsebreck.*) See GROUPS.

STEWART, Prince James Francis Edward, 1688–1766. *Son of James VII and II*
    PG 159*   Canvas, 96.8 x 73.8 (38⅛ x 29), by unknown artist. Purchased 1886.
    PG 305   Canvas, 76.2 x 62.9 (30 x 24⅜), by unknown artist. Bequeathed by
               W. F. Watson 1886.
    PG 703   (Succession of Prince James.) Silver medal, dia. 2.6 (1), by Norbert Roettier.
               Dated 1699. Purchased 1910.
    PG 704   (With Princess Clementina Sobieska. Commemorates the marriage of
               Prince James and Princess Clementina Sobieska.) Silver medal, dia. 4.1
               (1⅝), by Otto Hamerani. Dated 1719. Purchased 1910.
    PG 739   Silver pattern crown piece, dia. 4.1 (1⅝), by Norbert Roettier. Dated 1716.
               Purchased 1910.
    PG 744   Silver gilt medal, dia. 3.6 (1⁷⁄₁₆), by Norbert Roettier. Dated 1699. Obverse:
               James VII and II. Purchased 1910.
    PG 764   (Appeal against the House of Hanover.) Copper medal, dia. 4.9 (1¹⁵⁄₁₆),
               by Otto Hamerani. Dated 1721. Purchased 1911.
    PG 909*   Canvas, 76.8 x 64.2 (30⅛ x 25¼), by François de Troy, 1701, signed
               (on reverse). Given by C. E. Price 1920.
    PG 922   (Birth of Prince James.) Pewter medal, dia. 6 (2⅜), by Jan Smeltzing. Dated
               1688. Purchased 1920.
    PG 923   (Commemorates the birth of Prince James.) Pewter medal, dia. 5.9 (2⁵⁄₁₆),
               by Jan Smeltzing. Dated 1688. Purchased 1920.
    PG 1043   Copper, 12.1 x 9 (4¾ x 3½), by unknown artist. Given by Miss
               M. E. Wilson 1927.
    PG 1210*   Water-colour on card, 6 x 4.8 (2⅜ x 1⅞), by Marie Anne Chéron, 1704,
               signed (on reverse). Purchased 1933.

STEWART, Prince James Francis Edward (*continued*)

PG 1215 Canvas, oval 75.3 x 62.9 (29⅝ x 24¾), by a follower of Nicolas de Largillièrre. Purchased 1934.

PG 1311* Water-colour on card, 7.4 x 5.9 (2⅞ x 2⅜), by Lawrence Crosse, signed. Purchased 1936.

PG 1322 Copper medal, dia. 2.4 (¹⁵⁄₁₆), by Norbert Roettier. Dated 1697. Purchased 1937.

PG 1323 Copper medal, dia. 2.4 (¹⁵⁄₁₆), by Norbert Roettier. Dated 1697. Purchased 1937.

PG 1324 Copper medal, dia. 2.5 (1), by Norbert Roettier. Dated 1697. Purchased 1937.

PG 1325 Silver medal, dia. 2.4 (¹⁵⁄₁₆), by Norbert Roettier. Dated 1697. Purchased 1937.

PG 1326 Copper medal, dia. 2.4 (¹⁵⁄₁₆), by Norbert Roettier. Dated 1697. Purchased 1937.

PG 1327 Silver medal, dia. 2.8 (1⅛), by Norbert Roettier. Dated 1704. Purchased 1937.

PG 1328 (Restoration of the kingdom.) Copper medal, dia. 3.7 (1⁷⁄₁₆), by Norbert Roettier. Struck 1708. Purchased 1937.

PG 1329 (Restoration of the kingdom.) Copper medal, dia. 2.9 (1⅛), by Norbert Roettier. Struck 1708. Purchased 1937.

PG 1331 (With Princess Clementina Sobieska. Commemorates the marriage of Prince James and Princess Clementina.) Copper medal, dia. 4.1 (1⅝), by Otto Hamerani. Dated 1719. Purchased 1937.

PG 1332 (With Princess Clementina Sobieska. Commemorates the birth of Prince Charles Edward.) Copper medal, dia. 4.1 (1⅝), by Otto Hamerani. Dated 1720. Purchased 1937.

PG 1527 Copper, oval 17.5 x 14.7 (6⅞ x 5¾), attributed to Veronica Stern. Bequeathed by Miss F. D. Robertson 1949.

PG 1836* Canvas, 76.4 x 63.5 (30¹⁄₁₆ x 25), by unknown artist. Bequeathed by Miss B. S. Parr 1956.

PG 2191* Canvas, 101.2 x 81.3 (39⅞ x 32), by Nicolas de Largillière, 1691, signed. Purchased 1971.

PG 2415* (*The Marriage of Prince James Francis Edward Stewart and Princess Maria Clementina Sobieska.*) See GROUPS.

PG 2511* (*The Baptism of Prince Charles Edward Stewart.*) See GROUPS.

PG 2769* (Memorial to Princess Louisa Stewart. Portrait bust on obverse.) Silver medal, dia. 5.2 (2¹⁄₁₆), by Norbert Roettier. Struck 1712. Purchased 1989.

PGL 194 Copper medal, dia. 2.4 (¹⁵⁄₁₆), by Norbert Roettier. Dated 1697. On loan from the National Museums of Scotland.

PGL 195 Copper medal, dia. 2.5 (1), by Norbert Roettier. Dated 1697. On loan from the National Museums of Scotland.

PGL 196 Copper medal, dia. 2.4 (¹⁵⁄₁₆), by Norbert Roettier. Dated 1697. On loan from the National Museums of Scotland.

PGL 197 (Succession of Prince James.) Silver medal, dia. 2.6 (1), by Norbert Roettier. Dated 1699. On loan from the National Museums of Scotland.

Stewart, Prince Henry Benedict
PG 888

Stewart, Prince Henry Benedict
PG 1333

Stewart, Prince Henry Benedict
PG 1518

Stewart, Prince Henry Benedict
PGL 298

Stewart, Prince James Francis
Edward   PG 159

Stewart, Prince James Francis
Edward   PG 909

Stewart, Prince James Francis Edward
PG 1210

Stewart, Prince James Francis Edward
PG 1311

Stewart, Prince James Francis Edward
PG 1836

Stewart, Prince James Francis Edward
PG 2191

Stewart, Prince James Francis Edward
PG 2769

Stewart, Prince James Francis Edward
PGL 297

STEWART, Prince James Francis Edward (*continued*)

PGL 198   Silver medal, dia. 2.7 ($^{11}\!/_{16}$), by Norbert Roettier. Dated 1699. On loan from the National Museums of Scotland.

PGL 199   (Restoration of the kingdom.) Silver medal, dia. 3.7 ($1^7\!/_{16}$), by Norbert Roettier. Struck 1708. On loan from the National Museums of Scotland.

PGL 200   (Appeal against the House of Hanover.) Copper medal, dia. 4.9 ($1^{15}\!/_{16}$), by Otto Hamerani. Dated 1721. On loan from the National Museums of Scotland.

PGL 201   (Commemorates the marriage of Prince James and Princess Clementina.) Silver medal, dia. 4.8 ($1^7\!/_8$), by Otto Hamerani. Struck 1719. Reverse: Princess Clementina Sobieska. On loan from the National Museums of Scotland.

PGL 202   (With Princess Clementina Sobieska. Commemorates the marriage of Prince James and Princess Clementina.) Silver medal, dia. 4.1 ($1^5\!/_8$), by Otto Hamerani. Dated 1719. On loan from the National Museums of Scotland.

PGL 297*   Water-colour drawing, oval 5.9 x 4.6 ($2^5\!/_{16}$ x $1^{13}\!/_{16}$), by Jacques Antoine Arlaud, 1702, signed (on reverse). On loan from the National Museums of Scotland.

STEWART, Princess Louisa Maria Teresa, 1692–1712. *Daughter of James VII and II*

PG 1216*   Canvas, oval 73 x 59 ($28^3\!/_4$ x $23^1\!/_4$), by a follower of Nicolas de Largillièrre. Painted *c.* 1700. Purchased 1934.

PG 2769*   (Memorial to Princess Louisa.) Silver medal, dia. 5.2 ($2^1\!/_{16}$), by Norbert Roettier. Struck 1712. Purchased 1989.

STEWART, Margaret Ferooza McNeill, Mrs Duncan, 1834–71. *Daughter of Sir John McNeill*

PG 2646   Water-colour on ivory, h. 3.7 ($1^1\!/_2$), by unknown artist. Given by John R. Ingram 1985.

STEWART, Colonel Matthew, d. 1851. *Soldier; son of Professor Dugald Stewart*

PG 2504*   Pencil and water-colour drawing, 25.5 x 20.3 (10 x 8), by Thomas Heaphy, 1805, signed. Given by Lieutenant-Colonel James Bannatyne 1981.

STEWART, Peter, fl. 1800. *Of Glasgow*

PG 1932   Medallion (plaster replica), h. 7.3 ($2^7\!/_8$), after William Tassie. Dated 1800. Provenance untraced.

STIRLING, William Alexander, Earl of, *c.* 1567–1640. *Poet and statesman*

PGL 141*   Canvas, 73 x 55.2 ($28^3\!/_4$ x $21^3\!/_4$), by unknown artist. On loan from A. Alexander.

STIRLING-MAXWELL, Sir William, 1818–78. *Spanish scholar, and historian*

PG 558*   Bronze bust, h. 76.7 ($30^1\!/_4$), by Francis John Williamson. Dated 1873. Given by Sir J. Stirling-Maxwell and A. Stirling 1896.

STOLBERG, Princess Louisa of, 1753–1824. *Wife of Prince Charles Edward Stewart*
PG 1520   Canvas, 56.4 x 43.3 (22¼ x 17), by unknown artist. Purchased 1949.
PG 2738   (Marriage to Prince Charles Edward Stewart.) Copper medal, dia. 3.2 (1¼),
           by unknown artist. Struck 1772. Purchased 1988.
PGL 299*   Water-colour on ivory, oval 4.2 x 3.3 (1¹¹/₁₆ x 1⁵/₁₆), by unknown artist.
           On loan from the National Museums of Scotland.

STORMONT, Sir David Murray, 1st Viscount, d. 1631.
PG 1111*   (Previously called 1st Viscount Stormont.) See DERRY, Tom.

STRACHEY, Jane Maria Grant, Lady, c. 1840–1928. *Writer*
PG 2169*   Canvas, 76.2 x 61 (30 x 24), by Dora Carrington. Painted 1920. Given by
           Mrs James Strachey 1969.

STRANG, William, 1859–1921. *Artist*
PG 966*   Canvas, 53.3 x 38.1 (21 x 15), self-portrait. Purchased 1924.
PG 2198*   Canvas, 107 x 92.1 (42⅛ x 36¼), self-portrait, signed. Purchased 1972.

STRANGE, Mary Bruce, 1748–84. *Eldest daughter of Sir Robert Strange*
PG 1961   Paste medallion, h. 7.2 (2⅞), by James Tassie. Transferred from the
           National Gallery of Scotland 1960.

STRANGE, Sir Robert, 1721–92. *Engraver*
PG 1847   Copper plate, 15.2 x 15.2 (6 x 6), engraved by Sir Robert Strange after Jean
           Baptiste Greuze. Engraved 1791. Given by Miss F. M. McNeill 1957.
PG 1992*   Canvas, 75.5 x 62.9 (29¾ x 24¾), by Joseph Samuel Webster, 1750, signed.
           Given by Mrs G. Beck 1962.
PGL 296*   Wash drawing, dia. 10.6 (4³/₁₆), by Jean Baptiste Greuze. Drawn c. 1760.
           On loan from the National Museums of Scotland.

STRANGE, Sir Thomas, 1756–1841. *Chief Justice in Madras*
PG 1991*   Canvas, 91.4 x 71.1 (36 x 28), by Benjamin West, 1799, signed. Given by
           Mrs G. Beck 1962.
PGL 295   Water-colour on ivory, oval 3.5 x 2.8 (1⅜ x 1⅛), by unknown artist.
           On loan from the National Museums of Scotland.

STRATHALLAN, William Drummond, 1st Viscount, c. 1617–88. *Royalist general*
PG 1433*   Canvas, 125.4 x 102 (49¾ x 40⅛), attributed to L. Schuneman. Purchased 1942.

STRATHMORE, Patrick Lyon, 1st Earl of, 1643–95. *Privy Councillor*
PG 1609   Canvas, 124.9 x 100.7 (49³/₁₆ x 39⅝), attributed to L. Schuneman.
           Purchased 1954.

STRATHNAIRN, Hugh Henry Rose, Baron, 1801–85. *Commander-in-Chief in India*
PG 1736   Water-colour and pencil (caricature), 16.6 x 20.4 (6½ x 8), by unknown
           artist. Purchased 1936.

STRUTHERS, Rev. James., c. 1770–1807. *Moderator of the Relief Church Synod of 1799*
  PG 1934   Medallion (plaster replica), h. 8.1 (3³⁄₁₆), after William Tassie. Dated 1807.
             Provenance untraced.

STRUTHERS, Sir John, 1857–1925. *Educationist*
  PG 1019   Canvas, 113.7 x 95.2 (44¾ x 37½), by Maurice Greiffenhagen, 1922,
             signed. Given by a group of subscribers 1926.

STUART, Lady Arabella, c. 1577–1615. *Only daughter of the 6th Earl of Lennox*
  PG 9*   Panel, oval 90.2 x 70.4 (35½ x 27¾), attributed to Robert Peake. Dated
             1605. Purchased 1884.

STUART, Sir Charles, 1753–1801. *General*
  PG 458   Medallion (plaster replica), h. 8.9 (3½), after James Tassie. Given by
             J. M. Gray 1893.

STUART, James, 1713–88. *Painter and architect*
  PG 364   Wedgwood medallion, h. 7.6 (3). Given by Messrs J. Wedgwood and Sons
             1889.

STUART, Major-General James, c. 1735–93. *Commander-in-Chief in Madras*
  PG 1832*   Canvas, 151.1 x 118.7 (59½ x 46¾), by George Romney. Painted 1786/8.
             Purchased with assistance from the National Art-Collections Fund 1956.

STUART of Dunearn, James, 1775–1849. *Duellist and pamphleteer*
  PG 1143*   (Cut down from a half-length.) Canvas, 62.9 x 51.4 (24¾ x 20¼), by Sir
             Daniel Macnee. Given by M. V. Erskine Stuart 1930.

STUART, Sir John, 1759–1815. *General*
  PG 2680*   (*The Battle of Alexandria, 21 March 1801.*) See GROUPS.

STURROCK, Alick Riddell, 1885–1953. *Artist*
  PG 2737*   (*The Smoking Room, the Scottish Arts Club.*) See GROUPS.
  PGL 328*   (*Gathering at 7 London Street.*) See GROUPS.

STURROCK, Mary Newbery, 1892–1985. *Artist*
  PGL 328*   (*Gathering at 7 London Street.*) See GROUPS.

SUTHERLAND, Dorothy Johnstone, Mrs David Macbeth, 1892–1980. *Artist*
  PG 2397   Pencil drawing, 56.2 x 38.4 (22⅛ x 15⅛), by Sir William Oliphant
             Hutchison. Given by the executors of Margery, Lady Hutchison 1977.

SUTHERLAND, Sir Thomas, 1834–1922. *Chairman of P. and O. Steamship Company*
  PG 2055   Canvas, 127 x 101.6 (50 x 40), by John Henry Lorimer, 1882, signed. Given
             by Miss H. Sutherland 1966.

Stewart, Princess Louisa
PG 1216

Stewart, Princess Louisa
PG 2769

Stewart, Colonel Matthew
PG 2504

Stirling, Earl of
PGL 141

Stirling-Maxwell, Sir William
PG 558

Stolberg, Princess Louisa of
PGL 299

Strachey, Lady
PG 2169

Strang, William
PG 966

Strang, William
PG 2198

Strange, Sir Robert
PG 1992

Strange, Sir Robert
PGL 296

Strange, Sir Thomas
PG 1991

Strathallan, 1st Viscount
PG 1433

SUTTON, Sir Charles, 1775–1828. *Soldier*
    PG 2684   b. (Possibly Sir Charles Sutton. Study related to *The Battle of Alexandria* and *The Landing of British Troops at Aboukir*.) Water-colour, 10.2 x 8.1 (4 x 3³⁄₁₆), attributed to Philip James de Loutherbourg. Purchased 1986.

SUVOROV, Prince Alexander Vasilievich Italysky, Count, 1729–1800. *Russian field-marshal*
    PG 2338   Pencil and wax crayons, oval 18.8 x 13.8 (7³⁄₈ x 5⁷⁄₁₆), attributed to Adam Buck, signed. Bequeathed by W. F. Watson 1886.

SWAN of Longniddry, 'Cooper', fl. *c.* 1850.
    PG 1779   Pencil drawing, 28.7 x 22 (11¼ x 8⅝), by J. D. Finlayson, signed. Given by William Finlayson 1951.

SYM, Robert, 1752–1845. *Writer to the Signet; 'Timothy Tickler' of* Noctes Ambrosianae
    PG 2645   Wax profile medallion, h. 6.3 (2½) (sight), by Michael Wilson. Given by John R. Ingram 1985.

SYME, James, 1799–1870. *Surgeon*
    PG 616*   Chalk drawing, 60 x 46 (23⅝ x 18), by George Richmond, 1857, signed. Bequeathed by Mrs Syme 1903.
    PG 768*   Canvas, 127 x 101.6 (50 x 40), by George Richmond. Purchased 1911.

SYME, John, 1795–1861. *Artist*
    PG 1544*   Canvas, 76.2 x 63.5 (30 x 25) self-portrait. Given by Miss E. S. Boswell 1950.
    PG 1545   Canvas, 46 x 35.9 (18⅛ x 14⅛), self-portrait. Given by Miss E. S. Boswell 1950.

Stuart, Lady Arabella
PG 9

Stuart, Major-General James
PG 1832

Stuart, James
PG 1143

Syme, James
PG 616

Syme, James
PG 768

Syme, John
PG 1544

TAIT, Professor Peter Guthrie, 1831–1901. *Physicist*
  PG 600*   Canvas, 94.6 x 66.7 (37¼ x 26¼), by Sir George Reid, signed. Given by the
             artist 1902.

TASSIE, James, 1735–99. *Sculptor and gem engraver*
  PG 259   Paste medallion, h. 7.6 (3), by William Tassie. Transferred from the
             National Gallery of Scotland 1889.
  PG 260*   Paste medallion, h. 8.2 (3¼), by William Tassie. Transferred from the
             National Gallery of Scotland 1889.
  PG 576*   Canvas, 76.6 x 64.9 (30⅛ x 25½), by David Allan. Painted *c.* 1781.
             Bequeathed by William Tassie to the National Gallery of Scotland and
             transferred 1898.
  PG 1225   Ink silhouette, 18.9 x 11.5 (7⅝ x 4½), by unknown artist. Dated 1776.
             Purchased 1934.
  PGL 33   Canvas, 76.2 x 63.5 (30 x 25), by John Paxton. On loan from the National
             Museums of Scotland.

TASSIE, John, b. 1740. *Younger brother of James Tassie*
  PG 1842   Medallion (plaster replica), h. 7.2 (2¹³⁄₁₆), after James Tassie. Dated 1791.
             Bequeathed by Miss M. E. Laidlaw 1957.

TASSIE, Mrs Margaret, fl. 1796. *Wife of John Tassie*
  PG 1843*   Paste medallion, h. 7.6 (3), by James Tassie. Dated 1796. Bequeathed by
             Miss M. E. Laidlaw 1957.

TAYLOR, Alfred Edward, 1869–1945. *Professor of Moral Philosophy at Edinburgh University*
  PG 1795   Black chalk drawing, 46.7 x 29.2 (18⅜ x 11½), by David Foggie, 1934,
             signed. Given by Mrs M. Foggie 1955.

TAYLOR, James, 1753–1825. *Engineer*
  PG 1259   Paste medallion, h. 8 (3⅛), by William Tassie. Dated 1801. Purchased 1935.

TAYLOR, Rev. James, 1813–92. *Minister and author*
  PG 690*   Canvas, 128.9 x 102.9 (50½ x 40½), by Sir Daniel Macnee, 1873, signed.
             Given by J. Pringle Taylor 1910.

TAYLOR, Jessie Marion King, Mrs Ernest Archibald, 1875–1949. *Decorative artist and
             illustrator*
  PG 2406*   Ink and crayon drawing, 50 x 39.3 (19⅞ x 15½), by Helen Paxton Brown,
             signed. Purchased 1977.
  PG 2756   Cut paper silhouette, h. 20.2 (7⁹⁄₁₀), by James Gunyeon Jeffs. Cut 1932.
             Purchased 1989.

TAYMOUTH CASTLE
  PG 2359*   (View of Taymouth Castle from the south.) Canvas, 66 x 133 (26 x 52⅜), by
             James Norie and Jan Griffier. Begun 1733 and repainted 1739. Purchased 1976.

TEBBS, Sir Benjamin, fl. 1793. *Sheriff of London*
    PG 2248   Black and white chalk drawing, 32.8 x 26 (12⅞ x 10¼), by Mather Brown.
                 Provenance untraced.

TELFORD, James, fl. 1899. *Of Newcastle-upon-Tyne Curling Club*
    PG 1856*   (*Curling at Carsebreck.*) See GROUPS.

TENNANT, William, 1784–1848. *Poet and linguist*
    PG 124   Pencil and water-colour, 12.3 x 10.9 (4⅞ x 4¼), by unknown artist.
               Bequeathed by W. F. Watson 1886.
    PG 1156   Canvas, 76.2 x 63.5 (30 x 25), by unknown artist. Bequeathed by Miss
               A. T. F. Whyte 1931.

TERRY, Daniel, c. 1780–1829. *Actor and dramatist*
    PG 1082*   Water-colour, 26.8 x 21.7 (10⁹⁄₁₆ x 8⁹⁄₁₆), by William Nicholson.
               Bequeathed by Mrs M. L. Turnbull 1928.
    PG 2594*   Canvas, 76.2 x 63.5 (30 x 25), by Henry William Pickersgill. Painted
               c. 1813. Purchased 1983.

THACKERAY, William Makepeace, 1811–63. *Novelist*
    PG 143   Pencil and water-colour, 17.1 x 13.2 (6¾ x 5¼), by Richard Doyle. Dated
               1848. Bequeathed by W. F. Watson 1886.

THATCHER, Margaret Hilda Roberts, Mrs Denis, b. 1925. *Prime Minister*
    PG 2706*   Canvas, 101 x 91.5 (39¾ x 36), by David Donaldson, signed. Given by Sir
               Norman Macfarlane 1986.

THOMAS, Mrs Mary, fl. 1798.
    PG 2445   Paste medallion, h. 8 (3⅛), by James Tassie. Dated 1798. Bequeathed by
               William Tassie to the National Gallery of Scotland 1860 and transferred
               1979.

THOMSON, Sir Adam, b. 1926. *Founder and chairman of British Caledonian Airways*
    PG 2697*   Oil on board, 243.9 x 243.9 (96 x 96), by John Wonnacott, 1986, signed.
               Purchased by commission 1986.
    PG 2739   a. (In hangar 3 at Gatwick airport.) Pencil drawing, 54 x 52.7 (21¼ x 20¾),
               by John Wonnacott.
               b. (In hangar 3 at Gatwick airport.) Pencil drawing, 47.4 x 57.8 (18⅝ x 22¾)
               (irregular), by John Wonnacott.
               c. (Interior of hangar with details of aircraft.) Pencil drawing, 43.3 x 41.8
               (17¹⁄₁₆ x 16⁷⁄₁₆), by John Wonnacott.
               d. (Fuselage of aircraft.) Pencil drawing, 14.7 x 20.3 (5¾ x 8), by John
               Wonnacott.
               e. (Aircraft mechanic with machinery in hangar.) Pencil drawing,
               22.3 x 18.8 (8¾ x 7⅜), by John Wonnacott.
               f. (Aircraft in hangar with detail of engine.) Pencil drawing, 21 x 29.5
               (8¼ x 11⅝), by John Wonnacott.

THOMSON, Sir Adam (*continued*)

g. (Interior of hangar.) Pencil drawing, 29.5 x 21 (11⅝ x 8¼), by John Wonnacott.

h. (View from hangar showing aircraft grounded and others landing.) Pencil drawing, 21 x 29.5 (8¼ x 11⅝), by John Wonnacott. Purchased 1988.

PG 2740   a. Pencil drawing, 55.5 x 38.1 (21⅞ x 15) (irregular), by John Wonnacott.

b. Pencil drawing, 29.5 x 21 (11⅝ x 8¼), by John Wonnacott. Purchased 1988.

THOMSON, David Cleghorn, b. 1900. *Poet*

PG 2001*   Black chalk drawing, 45.4 x 28 (17⅞ x 11), by David Foggie, 1932, signed. Given by Mrs M. Foggie 1962.

THOMSON, George, 1757–1851. *Collector of Scottish songs*

PG 273*   Canvas, 125.4 x 101.3 (49⅜ x 39⅞), by William Smellie Watson. Purchased 1889.

PG 961   Millboard, 20 x 14.2 (7⅞ x 5⅝), by unknown artist after Sir Henry Raeburn. Purchased 1923.

PG 1061*   Water-colour, 28.5 x 22.5 (11¼ x 8⅞), by William Nicholson. Painted *c*. 1817. Given by Mrs A. Fisher and Miss M. Thomson to the National Gallery of Scotland 1879 and transferred 1913.

PG 1770*   (*Burns at an evening party of Lord Monboddo's 1786.*) See GROUPS.

THOMSON, James, 1700–48. *Poet*

PG 331*   Canvas, oval 56.1 x 43.9 (22⅛ x 17⁵⁄₁₆), by William Aikman, 1720, signed (on reverse). Purchased 1891.

PG 642*   Canvas, 76.8 x 64.1 (30¼ x 25¼), by John Vanderbank, 1726, signed. Purchased 1905.

PG 1026   Canvas, 52.8 x 41.3 (20¹³⁄₁₆ x 16¼), by unknown artist after an engraving by James Basire. Purchased 1926.

THOMSON, John, 1856–1926. *Paediatrician*

PG 2352   Bronze medal, dia. 5.1 (2), by C. d'O. Pilkington Jackson. Dated 1929. Given by the artist 1956.

THOMSON of Duddingston, Rev. John, 1778–1840. *Landscape painter*

PG 1049   Chalk drawing, 52 x 36.5 (20½ x 14⅜), by William Bewick. Dated 1824. Purchased 1927.

PG 1069*   Canvas, 83.8 x 66 (33 x 26), by William Wallace. Bequeathed by Professor James Pillans to the National Gallery of Scotland in 1863 and transferred 1913.

PG 1285*   Pencil drawing, 27.5 x 21.8 (10¾ x 8½), by Sir Thomas Dick Lauder. Dated 1831. Given by Captain D. M. Anderson 1935.

PGL 14   Canvas, 96.5 x 66 (38 x 26), by William Wallace. On loan from the trustees of Lockhart Thomson.

THOMSON, Sir Mitchell Mitchell-, 1st Baronet, 1846–1918. *Lord Provost of Edinburgh*

PG 1856*   (*Curling at Carsebreck.*) See GROUPS.

Tait, Professor Peter Guthrie
PG 600

Tassie, James
PG 260

Tassie, James
PG 576

Tassie, Margaret
PG 1843

Taylor, Rev. James
PG 690

Taylor, Jessie Marion
PG 2406

Taymouth Castle
PG 2359

Terry, Daniel
PG 1082

Terry, Daniel
PG 2594

Thatcher, Margaret
PG 2706

Thomson, Sir Adam
PG 2697

Thomson, David
Cleghorn   PG 2001

Thomson, George
PG 273

Thomson, George
PG 1061

THOMSON, T. D., fl. 1899. *Of Dirleton Curling Club*
    PG 1856*   (*Curling at Carsebreck.*) See GROUPS.
    PG 2011   Canvas, 40.7 x 30.5 (16 x 12), by Charles Martin Hardie, 1899, signed.
                Given by H. R. H. Woolford 1962.

THOMSON, Thomas, 1768–1852. *Lawyer and legal antiquary*
    PG 211*   Canvas, 76.2 x 63.5 (30 x 25), by Robert Scott Lauder. Given by G. Seton
                1888.
    PG 224   (Probably the artist's plaster.) Plaster bust, h. 55.5 (21⅞), by Sir John
                Steell. Purchased 1888.
    PG 825*   (*Sir Walter Scott and his friends at Abbotsford.*) See GROUPS.
    PG 1050   Chalk drawing, 51.8 x 38.4 (21⅜ x 15⅛), by William Bewick. Purchased
                1927.

THOMSON, Thomas, 1773–1852. *Chemist*
    PG 1148   Canvas, 58.4 x 48.2 (23 x 19), by unknown artist. Bequeathed by Miss
                A. Thomson 1931.

THOMSON, William
    PG 2389   (As a child, possibly a son of the artist. A pair to PG 2390 Unidentified girl.)
                Pencil drawing, 24.7 x 17.8 (9¾ x 7), by Peter Thomson. Given by Mrs
                Gore Browne Henderson to the National Gallery of Scotland 1976 and
                transferred 1977.

THURLOW, Edward Thurlow, 1st Baron, 1731–1806. *Lord Chancellor*
    PG 498   Medallion (plaster replica), h. 6.3 (2½), after Catherine Andras. Cast from a
                medallion in possession of R. W. Cochran Patrick 1894.

THURSO, Archibald Henry Macdonald Sinclair, 1st Baronet of Ulbster and 1st Viscount,
                1890–1970. *Liberal statesman, Secretary of State for Scotland and*
                Secretary of State for Air
    PG 2009*   Black chalk drawing, 46.1 x 28.7 (18⅛ x 11⁵⁄₁₆), by David Foggie, 1939,
                signed. Given by Mrs M. Foggie 1962.
    PG 2634*   Canvas, 101.6 x 75.7 (40 x 29⅞), by Augustus John, signed. Painted
                c. 1920/4. Purchased 1984.

TILLOCH, Alexander, 1759–1825. *Printer*
    PG 336   Pencil drawing, 17.2 x 13 (6¾ x 5⅛), attributed to John Henning. Dated
                1815. Purchased 1892.

TINWALD, Charles Erskine, Lord, 1680–1763. *Lord Justice-Clerk*
    PG 1515*   Canvas, 76.6 x 64.1 (30⅛ x 25¼), by Allan Ramsay, 1750, signed.
                Purchased 1948.

TONGE, John A. *Critic*
    PG 2597*   (*Poets' Pub.*) See GROUPS.

TOOKE, John Horne, 1736–1812. *Politician and philologist*
PG 460   Medallion (plaster replica), h. 7.7 (3), after James Tassie. Dated 1793. Cast
from a medallion in possession of Jeffery Whitehead 1893.

TORPHICHEN, James Sandilands, 9th Baron, 1759–1815. *Soldier and Representative*
Peer of Scotland
PG 946*   (*The Inauguration of Robert Burns as Poet Laureate of the Lodge*
Canongate, Kilwinning, 1787.) See GROUPS.

TRAIL, Rev. James, 1681–1723. *Covenanting minister of Montrose*
PG 1418   c. Canvas, 20.3 x 15.2 (8 x 6), copy by unknown artist. Given by
T. Gascoigne 1941.

TRAIL, Rev. Robert, 1603–78. *Covenanting minister of Edinburgh*
PG 1418   b. Millboard, 20.3 x 15.2 (8 x 6), copy by unknown artist. Given by
T. Gascoigne 1941.
PG 1641   Pencil and chalk drawing, 27.7 x 21.3 (10⅞ x 8⅜), by the 11th Earl of
Buchan after unknown artist. Bequeathed by W. F. Watson 1886.

TRAILL, Isabel Davidson, Mrs David, d. 1986. *Benefactress of the National Galleries of*
Scotland; wife of Dr David Traill
PG 2705*   Canvas, 32 x 27¼ (81.3 x 69.2), by David Donaldson, signed. Purchased
1986.

TRAILL, Thomas Stewart, 1781–1862. *Professor of medical jurisprudence at Edinburgh*
University
PG 1851*   Canvas, 50.2 x 41.3 (19¾ x 16¼), by Alexander Mosses. Purchased 1958.

TRAQUAIR, Phoebe Anna, 1852–1936. *Artist*
PG 1463*   Marble bust, h. 68.1 (26⅞), by James Pittendrigh Macgillivray, signed.
Sculpted *c.* 1895. Transferred from the Scottish Modern Arts Association
1944.
PG 1594*   Panel, 29.9 x 34.1 (11¾ x 13⁷⁄₁₆), self-portrait, 1911, signed. Bequeathed by
Professor Ramsay Traquair 1952.

TRAQUAIR, Ramsay Heatley, 1840–1912. *Zoologist and palaeontologist*
PG 1071   Bronze medallion, dia. 13.9 (5½), by Charles Matthew. Bequeathed by
J. M. Gray 1894.

TULLOCH of Tannachie, Francis, fl. 1797.
PG 1958   Paste medallion, h. 8.3 (3⁵⁄₁₆), by James Tassie. Dated 1797. Transferred
from the National Gallery of Scotland 1960.

TULLOCH, Rev. John, 1823–86. *Theologian and Principal of St Andrews University*
PG 219*   Canvas, 137.8 x 111.7 (54¼ x 44), by Robert Herdman, 1880, signed. Given
by Mrs Robert Herdman 1888.

TURNER, Joseph Mallord William, 1775–1851. *Artist*
    PG 1786   Ink drawing, 26.6 x 17.9 (10½ x 7), by Sir William Allan. Transferred from
    the National Gallery of Scotland 1952.

TURNER, Sir William, 1832–1916. *Principal of Edinburgh University*
    PG 1709   Pencil drawing, 37.5 x 33 (14¾ x 13), by W. Graham Boss. Given by the
    artist.

TWEEDDALE, George Hay, 8th Marquess of, 1787–1876. *Agriculturist*
    PG 1571*   Canvas, 238 x 147.5 (93^{11}⁄₁₆ x 58¹⁄₁₆), by Sir Francis Grant. Given by the
    Marquess of Tweeddale 1951.
    PG 2457*   Canvas, 302.9 x 206.6 (119¼ x 81⅜), by Sir Henry Raeburn and Colvin
    Smith. Begun *c.* 1823 and completed *c.* 1843. Purchased 1980.

TWEEDDALE, John Hay, 1st Marquess of, 1626–97. *Lord High Chancellor of Scotland*
    PG 2225*   Canvas, 126.3 x 103.5 (49¾ x 40¾), by Sir Peter Lely. Purchased with
    assistance from the National Art-Collections Fund and the Pilgrim Trust
    1974.

TWEEDDALE, John Hay, 2nd Marquess of, 1645–1713. *Parliamentarian*
    PG 2224*   Canvas, oval 75.5 x 62.6 (29¾ x 24⅝), attributed to Jacob Ferdinand Voet.
    Purchased with assistance from the National Art-Collections Fund and the
    Pilgrim Trust 1973.

TWEEDDALE, John Hay, 4th Marquess of, *c.* 1695–1762. *Lord Justice-General for
    Scotland*
    PG 2226*   Canvas, 128.2 x 102.2 (50½ x 40¼), by William Aikman. Painted *c.* 1728.
    Purchased with assistance from The National Art-Collections Fund and the
    Pilgrim Trust 1974.

TWEEDDALE, William Montagu Hay, 10th Marquess of, 1826–1911.
    PG 1856*   (*Curling at Carsebreck.*) See GROUPS.

TWEEDSMUIR, Sir John Buchan, 1st Baron, 1875–1940. *Author; Governor General of
    Canada*
    PG 1400*   Bronze head, h. 35 (13¾), by Thomas John Clapperton. Modelled 1935.
    Cast 1940. Purchased 1940.

TYTLER, Patrick Fraser, 1791–1849. *Historian*
    PG 187   Panel, 20.6 x 16.4 (8⅛ x 6½), by Sir John Watson Gordon. Purchased 1887.
    PG 666*   Canvas, 76.2 x 63.5 (30 x 25), by Sir John Watson Gordon. Purchased 1909.

TYTLER of Woodhouselee, William, 1711–92. *Historian*
    PG 1770*   (*Burns at an evening party of Lord Monboddo's 1786.*) See GROUPS.

Thomson, James
PG 331

Thomson, James
PG 642

Thomson, Rev. John
PG 1069

Thomson, Rev. John
PG 1285

Thomson, Thomas
PG 211

Thurso, 1st Viscount
PG 2009

Thurso, 1st Viscount
PG 2634

Tinwald, Lord
PG 1515

Traill, Isabel
PG 2705

Traill, Professor Thomas
Stewart   PG 1851

Traquair, Phoebe
PG 1463

Traquair, Phoebe
PG 1594

Tulloch, Rev. John
PG 219

Tweeddale,
8th Marquess of
PG 1571

Tweeddale,
8th Marquess of
PG 2457

URE, George, fl. 1899. *Of Bonnybridge Curling Club*
   PG 1856*   (*Curling at Carsebreck.*) See GROUPS.

VALLANCE, William Fleming, 1827–1904. *Artist*
   PG 1748   (In his studio.) Wash drawing, 48.9 x 39 (19¼ x 15⅜), by J. R.
            Abercromby, signed. Executed 1898. Purchased 1940.

VEITCH, William, 1794–1885. *Classical scholar*
   PG 150*   Canvas, 127.6 x 101.6 (50¼ x 40), by James Irvine. Bequeathed by the sitter
            1885.

VERNON, Sir Edward, 1723–94. *Admiral*
   PG 480   Medallion (plaster replica), h. 9.5 (3¾), after James Tassie. Dated 1785.
            Cast from a medallion in possession of Jeffery Whitehead 1893.

VICTORIA, Queen, 1819–1901. *Reigned 1837–1901*
   PG 168*   (Artist's plaster.) Plaster bust, h. 56.2 (22⅛), by Sir John Steell, 1838,
            signed. Purchased 1886.
   PG 1000* Water-colour, 44.5 x 31 (17½ x 12³⁄₁₆), by Alfred Edward Chalon, 1838,
            signed. Purchased 1925.
   PG 1068   Marble bust, h. 67.7 (26¹¹⁄₁₆), by Alexander and William Brodie, 1865,
            signed by William Brodie. Transferred from the National Gallery of Scotland.
   PG 1117* Canvas, 92.1 x 71.1 (36¼ x 28), by Franz Xaver Winterhalter. Purchased 1929.
   PG 1124   Canvas, 178.4 x 121.7 (70¼ x 47⅞), by Sir James Jebusa Shannon.
            Purchased 1930.
   PG 1169   (With Prince Albert, the Prince of Wales and the Princess Royal.) See
            GROUPS.
   PG 1306* (*The Baptism of Prince Maurice of Battenberg.*) See GROUPS.
   PG 1559   (Diamond Jubilee.) Copper medal, dia. 5.5 (2³⁄₁₆), by G. W. de Saulles after
            T. Brock and W. Wyon. Struck 1897. Given by A. Cope 1950.
   PG 1715   Pencil drawing, 42 x 42 (16½ x 16½), by W. Graham Boss. Given by the
            artist.
   PG 1780   (Key to the painting *The Landing of Queen Victoria at Dumbarton in 1847*,
            in the collection of Dumbarton District Council.) Ink drawing, 25.1 x 31.2
            (9⅞ x 12¼), by Hope James Stewart. Purchased 1931.
   PG 1822   (Department of Science and Art prize medal.) Copper medal, dia. 5.4 (2⅛),
            by William Wyon. Dated 1856. Given by T. I. Hunter 1955.
   PG 2417* (*The Visit of Queen Victoria and Prince Albert to Hawthornden.*) See
            GROUPS.

VICTORIA, Princess; Victoria Adelaide Mary Louise, Princess Royal, 1840–1901.
            Eldest child of Queen Victoria; Empress of Germany
   PG 1169   (As a child, with Queen Victoria, Prince Albert and the Prince of Wales.)
            See GROUPS.

Tweeddale, 1st Marquess of
PG 2225

Tweeddale, 2nd Marquess of
PG 2224

Tweeddale, 4th Marquess of
PG 2226

Tweedsmuir, 1st Baron
PG 1400

Tytler, Patrick Fraser
PG 666

Veitch, William
PG 150

Victoria, Queen
PG 168

Victoria, Queen
PG 1000

Victoria, Queen
PG 1117

WADE, Field-Marshal George, 1673–1748. *Commander-in-chief in Scotland*
- PG 353* Pencil and chalk drawing, 32.4 x 42.8 (12¾ x 16⅞), by Alexander van Haecken after Jan van der Banck. Given by W. G. Patterson 1889.
- PG 2416* Canvas, 75 x 63.2 (29½ x 24⅞), attributed to Johan van Diest. Purchased 1977.
- PGL 28* Canvas, 119.6 x 65.4 (47⅛ x 25¾), by unknown artist. On loan from the National Museums of Scotland.

WAITT, Richard, d. 1732. *Portrait painter*
- PG 2142* Canvas, 60.7 x 127 (42 x 50), self-portrait, 1728, signed. Purchased 1968.

WALES, Augusta of Saxe-Gotha, Princess of, 1719–72. *Mother of George III*
- PGL 273 Chalk drawing, 39 x 24.4 (15⅜ x 9⅝), by Allan Ramsay. On loan from the National Gallery of Scotland.

WALES, Frederick Lewis, Prince of, 1707–51. *Eldest son of George II; father of George III.*
- PG 964 Panel, 28.8 x 24.9 (11⅜ x 9¹³⁄₁₆), by unknown artist. Purchased 1923.

WALES, Henry, Prince of, 1594–1612. *Eldest son of James VI and I*
- PG 846 Panel, 54.6 x 41 (21½ x 16⅛), by unknown artist. Dated 1612. Purchased 1915.
- PGL 240* Canvas, 134 x 101 (52¾ x 39¾), attributed to Robert Peake. On loan from the Earl of Mar and Kellie.

WALKER, Adam, c. 1731–1821. *Astronomer and inventor*
- PG 392 Medallion (plaster replica), h. 8.1 (3³⁄₁₆), after James Tassie. Dated 1795. Cast from a medallion in possession of W. G. Patterson 1889.

WALKER, Archibald Stodart, 1869–1934. *Author*
- PG 1229 Pencil drawing, 35.5 x 25.3 (14 x 9⅞), by James Paterson, 1904, signed. Bequeathed by the sitter 1934.

WALKER, Thomas, 1749–1817. *Political reformer*
- PG 651 Paste medallion, h. 7.9 (3⅛), by James Tassie. Dated 1798. Purchased 1905.

WALKINSHAW, Clementina, c. 1726–1802. *Mistress of Prince Charles Edward Stewart*
- PG 1102* Canvas, 76.2 x 62.5 (30 x 24⅝), by unknown artist. Purchased 1928.

WALKINSHAW of Barrowfield and Camlachie, Katherine Paterson, Mrs John (called Lady Barrowfield), c. 1683–1780. *Mother of Clementina Walkinshaw*
- PGL 311* Canvas, 77.8 x 65.1 (30⅝ x 25⅝), by John Thomas Seton, 1776, signed. On loan from the National Gallery of Scotland.

WALLACE, Robert, fl. 1795. *Surgeon*
- PG 2641 Paste medallion, h. 7.5 (2⅞), by James Tassie. Dated 1795. Purchased 1985.

Wade, George
PG 353

Wade, George
PG 2416

Wade, George
PGL 28

Waitt, Richard
PG 2142

Wales, Prince of
PGL 240

Walkinshaw, Clementina
PG 1102

Walkinshaw, Katherine
PGL 311

Wallace, Sir William
PG 1616

Walpole, Sir Hugh Seymour
PG 1489

Walton, Edward Arthur, with
Helen Law   PG 2467

Walton, Edward Arthur
PG 2482

Warriston, Lord
PG 2721

Watson, George
PG 714

Watson, Robert
PGL 38

WALLACE, Sir William, *c.* 1272–1305. *Scottish patriot*
    PG 1616*   Chalk and pencil drawing, 43.5 x 32.7 (17⅛ x 12¾), by the 11th Earl of
            Buchan after unknown artist. Bequeathed by W. F. Watson 1886.

WALLACE, Professor William 1768–1843. *Mathematician*
    PG 195   Pencil and chalk drawing, 24.2 x 17.9 (9½ x 7⁷⁄₁₆), by Andrew Geddes,
            signed. Purchased 1887.

WALPOLE, Sir Hugh Seymour, 1884–1941. *Novelist*
    PG 1489*   Bronze head, h. 28.9 (11⅜), by Benno Schotz. Sculpted 1924. Given by Sir
            Alexander Walker 1947.

WALTON, Edward Arthur, 1860–1922. *Artist*
    PG 2467*   (With his fiancée Helen Law, as *Hokusai and the Butterfly*.) Canvas, 61.1 x
            45.7 (24 x 18), by Sir John Lavery, signed. Dated 1889. Purchased 1980.
    PG 2482*   Pencil drawing, 24.8 x 20.2 (9¾ x 7¹⁵⁄₁₆), by Helen Walton, signed. Dated
            1913. Given by Dr Camilla Uytman 1981.
    PG 2484   (With Joseph Crawhall and Sir James Guthrie.) Ink drawing (caricature),
            9 x 11.3 (3½ x 4⁷⁄₁₆), by Sir James Guthrie. Given by Dr Camilla Uytman to
            the National Gallery of Scotland and transferred 1981.
    PG 2485   Ink drawing (caricature), 17.9 x 11.1 (7 x 4⅜), by Sir James Guthrie. Given
            by Dr Camilla Uytman to the National Gallery of Scotland and transferred
            1981.

WALTON, Helen Law or Henderson, Mrs Edward Arthur, 1859–1945.
    PG 2467*   (With her fiancé E. A. Walton as *Hokusai and the Butterfly*.) Canvas, 61.1
            x 45.7 (24 x 18), by Sir John Lavery, signed. Dated 1889. Purchased 1980.

WALTON, Professor John, 1895–1971. *Professor of Botany at Glasgow University*
    PG 2481   (As a child.) Pencil drawing on cardboard, 14.5 x 11.2 (6¹¹⁄₁₆ x 4⅜), by
            Edward Arthur Walton. Dated 1901. Given by Dr Camilla Uytman 1981.

WARDLAW, Agnes, fl. 1791. *Daughter of Sir William Wardlaw*
    PG 2277   (With Margaret Wardlaw.) Paste medallion, h. 3.1 (1¼), by James Tassie.
            Dated 1791. Purchased 1975.

WARDLAW, Margaret, d. 1847. *Eldest daughter of Sir William Wardlaw*
    PG 2277   (With Agnes Wardlaw.) Paste medallion, h. 3.5 (1⅜), by James Tassie.
            Dated 1791. Purchased 1975.

WARDLAW, Rev Ralph, 1779–1853. *Congregationalist and Professor of Systematic*
            Theology
    PG 2420   (Perhaps Rev. Ralph Wardlaw. Seated study for a portrait.) Ink and wash
            drawing, 17.8 x 11.2 (7 x 4⅜), by Sir Daniel Macnee. Given by Dr Ruth
            Waddell 1978.

WARDLAW, Susan, d. 1815. *Youngest daughter of Sir William Wardlaw*
    PG 1966   Paste medallion, h. 7.5 (2^{15}⁄$_{16}$), by James Tassie. Dated 1791. Transferred
                from the National Gallery of Scotland 1960.

WARDLAW, Sir William, b. 1794. 12th baronet of Pitreavie
    PG 2203   Paste medallion, h. 7.4 (2^{15}⁄$_{16}$), by James Tassie. Dated 1791. Purchased
                1972.

WARDROP, James, 1782–1869. *Surgeon*
    PG 1113   Canvas, 68.6 x 57.1 (27 x 22½), by Thomas Musgrove Joy. Given by J. C.
                Wardrop 1929.

WARRISTON, Archibald Johnston, Lord, c. 1610–63. *Statesman*
    PG 2721*   Canvas, 47 x 46 (18½ x 16), by George Jamesone. Purchased 1987.

WATERFORD, Louisa Stuart, Marchioness of, 1818–91. *Artist*
    PG 1530*   (With her sister Charlotte Stuart, Countess Canning.) Water-colour on
                ivory, 50.5 x 34 (19⅞ x 13⅜), by Robert Thorburn. Purchased 1949.

WATSON, George, 1767–1837. *Artist and first President of the Royal Scottish Academy*
    PG 714*   Canvas, 92 x 71.8, (36¼ x 28¼), self-portrait. Given by the Royal Scottish
                Academy 1910.

WATSON, Robert, 1746–1838. *Adventurer*
    PGL 38*   Panel, 30.1 x 23.8 (11⅞ x 9⅜), by Carl Christian Vogel von Vogelstein.
                Painted 1817. On loan from the National Museums of Scotland.

WATSON, Walter, 1780–1854. *Poet*
    PG 2715   Chalk drawing 37.1 x 29.7 (14⅝ x 11⅝), by Alexander Duff Robertson,
                1849, inscribed. Purchased 1987.

WATT, George Fiddes, 1873–1960. *Artist*
    PG 2521*   Canvas, 101.6 x 75.9 (40 x 30), by Hugh Adam Crawford, signed. Purchased
                1982.

WATT, James, 1736–1819. *Engineer, inventor of the steam engine*
    PG 126   Pencil and wash-drawing, 23.5 x 14.8 (9¼ x 5⅞), by George Dawe after Sir
                Francis Legatt Chantrey. Purchased 1885.
    PG 294*   Chalk drawing, 53 x 43.8 (20⅞ x 17¼), by John Henning, 1809, signed.
                Given by Miss M. Campbell 1891.
    PG 347   Plaster bust, h. 67.5 (26⅝), by Sir Francis Legatt Chantrey, 1818, signed.
                Purchased 1887.
    PG 419   Porcelain medallion, h. 7 (2¾), by John Henning. Dated 1809. Provenance
                untraced.
    PG 636   Panel, 27.3 x 21.3 (10¾ x 8⅜), by unknown artist after Sir William
                Beechey. Bequeathed by W. F. Watson 1886.

WATT, James (*continued*)

PG 766   (Memorial.) Copper medal, dia. 4.7 (1⅞), by Joseph Shepherd Wyon. Probably struck *c*. 1858. Purchased 1911.

PG 1186*   Marble bust, h. 52.3 (20⅝), by Sir Francis Legatt Chantrey. Purchased 1932.

PG 1763   Pencil drawing, 25.5 x 17.1 (10 x 6¾), by unknown artist after Sir Francis Legatt Chantrey. Purchased 1945.

PG 1953   (Laudatory medal.) Bronze medal, dia. 6.2 (2⁷⁄₁₆), by Alfred Joseph Stothard after Sir Francis Legatt Chantrey. Dated 1826. Given by General Sir H. C. Jackson 1960.

PG 2612*   Canvas, 76.8 x 64.2 (30¼ x 25¼), by John Partridge after Sir William Beechey. Purchased 1984.

WAUCHOPE, James, 1767–97.

PG 2550   Water-colour on ivory, h. 6.6 (2⅝), by François Ferrière after Sir Henry Raeburn, signed. Dated indistinctly 180[   ]. Transferred from the National Gallery of Scotland 1982.

WAUCHOPE, Sir John, d. 1682. *Covenanter*

PG 1789   Canvas, 125 x 103.2 (49¼ x 40⅝), by unknown artist. Purchased 1955.

WAUGH, Rev. Alexander, 1754–1827. *Minister of the Secession Church*

PG 516   Medallion (plaster replica), h. 7.9 (3⅛), after James Tassie. Dated 1794. Cast from a medallion in possession of J. M. Gray 1894.

PG 523   Medallion (plaster replica), h. 8.1 (3³⁄₁₆), after James Tassie. Dated 1794. Cast from a medallion in possession of J. M. Gray 1894.

PG 1107   Paste medallion, h. 2.6 (1), by William Tassie. Purchased 1929.

PG 1307   Paste medallion, h. 2.7 (1¹⁄₁₆), by James Tassie. Dated 1791. Purchased 1936.

PG 2356   Paste medallion, h. 8 (3⅛), by James Tassie. Dated 1794. Purchased 1976.

WEBSTER, Rev. Alexander, 1707–84. *Moderator of the General Assembly*

PG 812   Canvas, 38.2 x 28.1 (15¹⁄₁₆ x 11¹⁄₁₆), by David Martin. Purchased 1913.

WEBSTER, David, d. *c*. 1829. *Bookseller and printer*

PG 2712   Cut paper silhouette, h. 7.7 (3), by unknown artist, 1825. Purchased 1986.

WELLINGTON, Arthur Wellesley, 1st Duke of, 1769–1852. *Soldier and statesman*

PG 538   Medallion (plaster replica), h. 5.1 (2), after John Henning. Given by Miss Brown 1894.

PG 866*   Pencil and water-colour, 45.3 x 30.5 (17⅞ x 12), by Sir David Wilkie, 1833, signed. Purchased 1916.

PG 905   a. Chalk drawing, 52.6 x 37.6 (20⅝ x 14¾), by James Hall. Dated 1836.
          b. Chalk drawing, 46.4 x 35 (18¼ x 13¾), by James Hall. Dated 1836. Given by General Archibald Stirling of Keir 1919.

PG 967   Marble bust, h. 77.2 (30⁷⁄₁₆), by Sir John Steell, 1845, signed. Transferred from the National Gallery of Scotland 1924.

Watt, George Fiddes
PG 2521

Watt, James
PG 294

Watt, James
PG 1186

Watt, James
PG 2612

Wellington, 1st Duke of
PG 866

Wellwood, Rev. Sir Henry
Moncrieff   PG L 151

Wemyss, 10th Earl of
PG 1403

Whitelaw, Alexander
PG 2376

Whittaker, Charles
Richard   PG 2000

Whyte, Rev. Alexander
PG 2194

Whyte, Ian
PG 1998

Wilkie, Sir David
PG 573

Wilkie, Sir David
PG 719

Wilkie, Sir David
PG 1220

Wilkie, Sir David
PG 1443

William III
PG 1122

WELLINGTON, Arthur Wellesley, 1st Duke of (*continued*)
 PG 991   Canvas, 91.1 x 70.8 (35⅞ x 27⅞), by Henry Perronet Briggs. Painted
          c. 1837. Bequeathed by A. Abercromby Trotter 1925.
 PG 1505 Panel, 27.9 x 22.5 (11 x 8⅞), by James Miller, 1853, signed (on reverse).
          Purchased 1948.

WELLINGTON, Hubert, 1879–1967. *Principal of Edinburgh College of Art*
 PG 2004 Black chalk drawing. 46.1 x 28.9 (18³⁄₁₆ x 11⅜), by David Foggie, 1934,
          signed. Given by Mrs M. Foggie 1962.

WELLWOOD, Rev. Sir Henry Moncrieff, 1750–1827. *Chaplain to George III*
 PG 527   Porcelain medallion, h. 6 (2½), by John Henning. Dated 1809. Given by
          Miss Brown 1894.
 PGL 48   Plaster bust, h. 75.2 (29⅝), by Samuel Joseph. Dated 1822. On loan from
          the Trustees of William Moncrieff.
 PGL 151* Marble bust, h. 74.9 (29½), by Samuel Joseph, 1825, signed. On loan from
          Sir H. R. Wellwood Moncrieff.

WELSH, Jane Baillie; see CARLYLE.

WEMYSS, Francis Wemyss-Charteris-Douglas, 10th Earl of, 1818–1914. *Politician*
 PG 778   Cut paper silhouette, h. 17.3 (6¹³⁄₁₆), by Augustin Edouart. Purchased 1912.
 PG 963   Pastel drawing, 33 x 25.4 (13 x 10), by unknown artist. Purchased 1923.
 PG 1403* Panel, 100.3 x 74.9 (39½ x 29½), by Philip Alexius de Laszlo, 1908, signed.
          Purchased 1941.

WEMYSS of Wemyss and Torrie, James Erskine, 1789–1854. *Admiral*
 PGL 337* (*A Meet of the Fife Hounds.*) See GROUPS.

WESLEY, Rev. John, 1703–91. *Founder of Methodism*
 PG 2113 Pencil and chalk drawing, 23.1 x 18.5 (9⅛ x 7¼), by Henry Bone.
          Transferred from the National Gallery of Scotland 1950.

WHITE, Adam, fl. 1830. *Provost of Leith*
 PG 2161 Cut paper silhouette, h. 20.2 (8), by Augustin Edouart, 1830, signed. Given
          by Mrs J. H. G. Ross 1969.

WHITEFOORD, Caleb, 1734–1810. *Diplomat and wit*
 PG 946* (*The Inauguration of Burns as Poet Laureate of the Lodge Canongate,
          Kilwinning, 1787.*) See GROUPS.
 PG 1770* (*Burns at an evening party of Lord Monboddo's 1786.*) See GROUPS.

WHITEFOORD of Whitefoord and Ballochmyle, Sir John, d. 1803. *Patron of Burns*
 PG 946* (*The Inauguration of Robert Burns as Poet Laureate of the Lodge
          Canongate, Kilwinning, 1787.*) See GROUPS.

WHITELAW, Alexander, 1823–79. *Industrialist and philanthropist*
PG 2376* Canvas, 127 x 101.6 (50 x 40), attributed to Sir Daniel Macnee. Given by William Whitelaw 1977.

WHITTAKER, Dr Charles Richard, 1879–1967. *Surgeon*
PG 2000* Black chalk drawing, 45.1 x 28 (17¾ x 11), by David Foggie, 1932, signed. Given by Mrs M. Foggie 1962.
PG 2737* (*The Smoking Room, the Scottish Arts Club.*) See GROUPS.

WHYTE, Rev. Alexander, 1836–1921. *Principal of New College, Edinburgh*
PG 855   Bronze medallion, dia. 51 (20¹⁄₁₆), by Paul Wissaert. Dated 1915. Given by a body of subscribers 1916.
PG 2194* Canvas, 91.5 x 71.3 (36 x 28¹⁄₁₆), by Sir James Guthrie, signed. Given by A. H. Whyte and Mrs A. Thoms 1971.

WHYTE, Ian, 1901–60. *Musician and composer*
PG 1998* Black chalk drawing, 43.8 x 28 (17¼ x 11), by David Foggie, 1932, signed. Given by Mrs M. Foggie 1962.

WHYTE, James Huntington, fl. 1933. *Editor of* The Modern Scot
PG 2310   Black chalk drawing, 46.5 x 28.6 (17¹⁵⁄₁₆ x 11¼), by David Foggie, 1933, signed. Given by J. Tonge 1975.

WIGHTMAN, General Joseph, d. 1722. *Hanoverian general*
PG 2635* (*The Battle of Glenshiel 1719.*) See GROUPS.

WILKIE, Sir David, 1785–1841. *Artist*
PG 181   Plaster head (life mask), h. 30.8 (12⅛), by 'Smith, a Phrenologist'. Given by W. Calder Marshall 1887.
PG 251   Canvas, 92.7 x 71.4 (36½ x 28⅛), by Sir William Beechey. Transferred from the National Gallery of Scotland 1889.
PG 573* Canvas, 76.5 x 63.5 (30⅛ x 25), self-portrait. Painted *c.* 1804/5. Given by J. Rankin 1898.
PG 584   Canvas, 36 x 31.5 (14⅛ x 12⅜), self-portrait. Given by the Archbishop of York 1899.
PG 719* Canvas, 99.7 x 76.8 (39¼ x 30¼), by Thomas Phillips. Given by the Royal Scottish Academy 1910.
PG 825* (*Sir Walter Scott and his friends at Abbotsford.*) See GROUPS.
PG 1220* Marble bust, h. 68.2 (26⅞), by Samuel Joseph, 1842, signed. Transferred from the National Gallery of Scotland 1934.
PG 1443* Panel, 66 x 48.2 (26 x 19), by Andrew Geddes, 1816, signed. Bequeathed by Kenneth Sanderson 1944.
PG 2197   Panel, 14.1 x 9.6 (5⁹⁄₁₆ x 3¾), self-portrait. Purchased by the National Gallery of Scotland 1971 and transferred 1972.

WILKIE, Sir David Dalbreck, 1882–1938. *Professor of Surgery at Edinburgh University*
    PG 1808   Black chalk drawing, 47 x 29.9 (18½ x 11¾), by David Foggie, 1933, signed. Given by Mrs M. Foggie 1955.

WILLIAM III, 1650–1702. *Reigned 1688–1702*
    PG 807   Canvas, 76.2 x 63.5 (30 x 25), by unknown artist after Sir Godfrey Kneller. Purchased 1912.
    PG 1122*   Polychrome wax bust, h. 29.7 (11¾), by Anna Maria Braunin, signed. Purchased 1929.
    PG 1471   Chalk drawing, 46.4 x 38.9 (18¼ x 15⁵⁄₁₆), by Sir Godfrey Kneller. Purchased 1945.
    PG 2766   (Coronation of William III and Mary II 1689.) Copper medal, dia. 4 (1⁹⁄₁₆), by George Hautsch. Purchased 1989.
    PG 2767   (Coronation of William III and Mary II 1689.) Silver medal, dia. 4 (1⁹⁄₁₆), by George Hautsch. Purchased 1989.

WILLIAM IV, 1765–1837. *Reigned 1830–1837*
    PG 534   Medal (plaster replica), dia. 6.4 (2½), after John Henning. Dated 1827. Given by Miss Brown 1894.
    PG 806*   Canvas, 76.2 x 63.5 (30 x 25), by Sir David Wilkie, 1837, signed. Purchased 1912.
    PG 850   Bronze bust, h. 14.3 (5⅝), copy by unknown artist. Dated 1831. Given by J. R. Findlay 1916.

WILLIAM of Nassau, 1626–50. *Prince of Orange; father of William III*
    PG 2763*   (Marriage to Princess Mary 1641.) Silver medal, dia. 7.2 (2¹³⁄₁₆), by Johann Blum. Purchased 1989.

WILLIAMS, David, (nom de guerre, 'Dave Willis'), 1895–1973. *Comedian*
    PG 2465*   Canvas, 61 x 50.6 (24 x 20), by Henry Raeburn Dobson, signed. Painted *c.* 1940. Purchased 1980.

WILLIAMS, Hugh William, 1773–1829. *Artist*
    PG 716*   Canvas, 76.2 x 63.5 (30 x 25), by William Nicholson. Given by the Royal Scottish Academy 1910.

WILLIAMSON, David, fl. 1899. *Of the Canadian branch of the Royal Caledonian Curling Club*
    PG 1856*   (*Curling at Carsebreck.*) See GROUPS.

WILLISON, George, 1741–97. *Portrait painter*
    PG 2134*   Paste medallion, h. 6.6 (2⅝), by James Tassie. Modelled by Guilliobe. Purchased 1968.

WILSFORD, Sir James 1515–50. *English commander at the siege of Haddington, 1547*
    PG 427*   Panel, 90.8 x 74.6 (35¾ x 29⅜), by unknown artist. Dated 1547. Given by the Marquess of Tweeddale 1892.

William IV
PG 806

William of Nassau with
Princess Mary   PG 2763

Williams, David
PG 2465

Williams, Hugh William
PG 716

Willison, George
PG 2134

Wilsford, Sir James
PG 427

Wilson, Sir Daniel
PG 429

Wilson, James
PG 968

Wilson, John
PG 755

Wilson, Professor John
PG 604

Wilson, Professor John
PG 708

Wilson, Professor John
PG 1369

Wilson, Professor John
PG 2751

Wilson, Margaret
PG 2613

WILSON, Alexander, 1714–86. *Astronomer and type-founder*
PG 750   Oil on card, 27.5 x 20.4 (10⅞ x 8), by unknown artist. Given by J. Parker Smith 1912.

WILSON, Alexander, 1766–1813. *Ornithologist*
PG 282   Cut paper silhouette, h. 7.3 (2⅞), by unknown artist. Given by the representatives of the late Robert Gray 1890.

WILSON, Andrew, fl. *c.* 1889. *Dentist and naturalist*
PG 1728   Pencil drawing, 20.6 x 14.7 (8 x 5¾), by Charles Matthew. Dated *c.* 1889. Bequeathed by J. M. Gray 1894.

WILSON, Christina Lawrie, Mrs Alexander, 1766–1803. *Friend of Burns*
PG 508   Medallion (plaster replica), h. 7.7 (3), after James Tassie. Dated 1791. Cast from a medallion in possession of Mrs Shadford Walker 1894.
PG 509   Medallion (plaster replica), h. 7.7 (3), after William Tassie. Dated 1800. Cast from a medallion in possession of Mrs Shadford Walker 1894.
PG 1268   Paste medallion, h. 7.7 (3), by James Tassie. Modelled 1791. Purchased 1935.

WILSON, Sir Daniel, 1816–92. *Antiquary*
PG 429*   Canvas, 40 x 66.7 (15¾ x 26¼), by Sir George Reid, 1891, signed. Given by the artist 1893.

WILSON, George, 1818–59. *Chemist and religious writer*
PG 2628   Sepia drawing, 19.5 x 16.6 (7¾ x 6⁹⁄₁₆), by —— Fox. Executed 1839/40. Provenance untraced.

WILSON, James, 1742–98. *Possibly American jurist and politician*
PG 1940   Medallion (plaster replica), h. 8 (3⅛), after James Tassie. Dated 1798. Provenance untraced.

WILSON, James, 1805–60. *Politician and founder of* The Economist
PG 968*   Marble bust, h. 73.8 (29⅛), by Sir John Steell, 1859, signed. Transferred from the National Gallery of Scotland 1924.

WILSON, 'Daft Jamie', d. 1828. *Murdered by Burke and Hare*
PG 1973   Panel, 17.4 x 12.2 (6⅞ x 4¾), attributed to James Howe. Given anonymously 1961.

WILSON, John, 1800–49. *Singer and composer of songs*
PG 755*   Millboard, 18 x 14 (7 x 5½), by Sir Daniel Macnee. Given by Alexander Inglis 1911.

WILSON, Professor John (nom de plume, 'Christopher North'), 1785–1854. *Author and moral philosopher*
    PG 604*   Bust (plaster replica), h. 86.2 (34), after James Fillans. Dated 1845. Given by Sir James Caw 1902.
    PG 646   Canvas, 91.4 x 70.5 (36 x 27¾), by Sir John Watson Gordon, 1829, signed. Purchased 1906.
    PG 708*   Canvas, 236 x 149.3 (86¾ x 58¾), by Sir Henry Raeburn. Given by the Royal Scottish Academy 1910.
    PG 825*   (*Sir Walter Scott and his friends at Abbotsford.*) See GROUPS.
    PG 1369*   Millboard, 60.6 x 42.5 (23⅞ x 16¾), by Thomas Duncan, signed. Given by the National Art-Collections Fund (London Scot Bequest) 1938.
    PG 1475   Porcelain bust (Worcester), h. 29.4 (11½), copy by unknown artist. Given by Lieutenant-Colonel N. V. C. Dalrymple Hamilton 1946.
    PG 2306   (Crombie Sketchbook, fo. 6v. Study for *Modern Athenians* Pl. 12.) Pencil and water-colour drawing, 16.5 x 20 (6⅛ x 7⅞), by Benjamin William Crombie. Purchased 1938.
    PG 2751*   Canvas, 127 x 101.9 (50 x 40), by Sir John Watson Gordon, signed. Dated 1852. Purchased 1988.

WILSON, John Mackay, 1804–35. *Author of* Tales of the Borders
    PG 1300   Millboard, 29.9 x 25.7 (11¾ x 10⅛), by James Sinclair. Painted 1831. Purchased 1936.

WILSON, Margaret Sym, Mrs John, 1753–1824. *Mother of Professor John Wilson*
    PG 2613*   Pastel, 68.5 x 56 (27 x 22), by Archibald Skirving. Executed between 1797 and 1807. Given by Miss Marjorie A. Wilson 1984.

WILSON, Patrick, 1743–1811. *Astronomer*
    PG 2236*   Paste medallion, h. 7.4 (2¹⁵⁄₁₆), by James Tassie. Dated 1796. Purchased 1974.

WILSON, Scottie, 1889–1972. *Artist*
    PG 2492*   Pencil drawing, 35.5 x 25.4 (14 x 10), by Marie Levy, signed. Dated 1962. Purchased 1981.

WILSON, William, 1905–72. *Etcher*
    PG 2431*   (In his Edinburgh studio.) Pencil and chalk drawing, 28.6 x 39.4 (11¼ x 15½) (irregular), by Edgar Holloway, 1937, signed. Purchased 1978.
    PGL 328*   (*Gathering at 7 London Street.*) See GROUPS.

WINGATE, Sir James Lawton, 1846–1924. *Artist*
    PG 2140   Water-colour, 51.5 x 39 (20¼ x 15⅜), by Henry Wright Kerr, 1917, signed. Given by Sir William MacTaggart 1968.

WINTON, Lady Anne Hay, Countess of, *c.* 1592–1625/8. *Wife of the 3rd Earl of Winton*
    PG 2173*   Canvas, 109.5 x 83.7 (43⅛ x 33), by Adam de Colone. Dated 1625. Bequeathed by Sir Theophilus Biddulph 1969.

WINTON, George Seton, 8th Lord Seton and 3rd Earl of, 1584–1650. *Royalist*
  PGL 336* (With his sons, 1st Viscount Kingston and Lord Seton.) Canvas, 113 x 83.8
            (44½ x 33), by Adam de Colone, 1625. On loan from the Kintore Trust.

WINTON, Robert Seton, 6th Lord Seton and 1st Earl of, 1550–1603.
  PG 1020   (With his father, 5th Lord Seton, and his brother and sister.) See
            GROUPS.
  PGL 312* (With his father, 5th Lord Seton, and his brothers and sister.)
            See GROUPS.

WISHART, George, c. 1513–46. *Reformer and martyr*
  PG 580*   Panel, 60.3 x 45.7 (23¾ x 18), by unknown artist. Dated 1543. Bequeathed
            by Mrs May 1898.

WITHERSPOON, Rev. John, 1723–94. *Principal of Princeton College, New Jersey*
  PG 481   Medallion (plaster replica), h. 6.9 (2¹¹⁄₁₆), after James Tassie. Dated 1784.
            Cast from a medallion in possession of Jeffery Whitehead 1894.

WOLFE, General James, 1729–59. *Victor at Quebec*
  PG 1716   Pencil and chalk drawing, 32.4 x 29.2 (12¾ x 11½), by James Anthony
            Minasi, signed, after Benjamin West. Purchased 1906.

WOOD, Alexander, 1725–1807. *Surgeon*
  PG 1368   Canvas, 76.2 x 63.5 (30 x 25), by D. Alison. Given by Kenneth Sanderson
            1938.

WOOD, Wendy, 1892–1981. *Scottish Nationalist*
  PG 2006* Black chalk drawing, 44.8 x 29.2 (17⅝ x 11½), by David Foggie, 1932,
            signed. Given by Mrs M. Foggie 1962.
  PG 2673   Canvas, 91.4 x 71.2 (36 x 28), by Florence St John Cadell, signed. Dated
            1959. Purchased 1985.

WOOLRICH, Philip, fl. c. 1675.
  PG 2082   Wash drawing, 12.3 x 8.6 (4⅞ x 3⅜), attributed to George Perfect Harding
            after an engraving by Francis Place. Transferred from the National Gallery
            of Scotland 1950.

WORDSWORTH, William, 1770–1850. *Poet*
  PG 825*   (*Sir Walter Scott and his friends at Abbotsford.*) See GROUPS.

WRAY, Robert Bateman, 1715–79. *Gem engraver*
  PG 396   Medallion (plaster replica), h. 6.4 (2½), after James Tassie. Cast from a
            medallion in possession of W. G. Patterson 1889.

WRIGHT, James, fl. 1800.
  PG 1941   Medallion (plaster replica), h. 7.6 (3), after William Tassie. Dated 1800.
            Provenance untraced.

Wilson, Patrick
PG 2236

Wilson, Scottie
PG 2492

Wilson, William
PG 2431

Winton, Countess of
PG 2173

Winton, 3rd Earl of, with
1st Viscount Kingston and
Lord Seton   PGL 336

Wishart, George
PG 580

Wood, Wendy
PG 2006

WRIGHT, Peter, fl. 1791–1818. *Physician, and friend of David Allan*
  PG 1942   Medallion (plaster replica), h. 7.6 (3), after James Tassie. Dated 1791.
             Provenance untraced.

WYLD, James, fl. 1830. *Director of the Commercial Bank*
  PG 2162   Cut paper silhouette, h. 21.5 (8⁷⁄16), by Augustin Edouart, 1830, signed.
             Given by Mrs J. H. G. Ross 1969.

WYNDHAM, Robert Henry, 1814–1894. *Actor and theatrical manager*
  PG 849   Canvas, 76.2 x 63.3 (30 x 24¹⁵⁄16), by Hugh Collins, 1872, signed. Purchased
            1915.

YELLOWLEES, William, 1796–*c*. 1859. *Artist*
PG 1247* Panel, 24.1 x 19.7 (9½ x 7¾), self-portrait, 1814, signed. Bequeathed by G. Yellowlees 1934.
PG 1859 Ivory medallion, h. 4.1 (1⅝), by William Ewing, 1818, signed. Given by A. G. Yellowlees 1959.

YESTER HOUSE
PG 2366* (View of the policies, including the canal and cascades.) Canvas, 111.2 x 87.6 (43¾ x 35¼), by unknown artist. Painted *c*. 1700. Purchased 1976.

YORK, Anne Hyde, Duchess of, 1637–71. *First wife of James VII and II*
PG 1179* Canvas, 182.2 x 143.8 (71¾ x 56⅝), by Sir Peter Lely. Purchased 1932.
PGL 125 Canvas, 64.5 x 52.1 (25⅜ x 20½), by unknown artist after Jacob Huysmans. On loan from the Duke of Buccleuch.

YORK AND ALBANY, H. R. H. Frederick Augustus, Duke of, 1763–1827. *Second son of George III*
PG 237 Canvas, 28.6 x 22.8 (11¼ x 9), by William Yellowlees after Sir William Beechey. Purchased 1888.
PG 446 Medallion (plaster replica), h. 3.8 (1½), after John Wilson. Given by the Trustees of the British Museum 1893.
PG 510 Medallion (plaster replica), h. 3.1 (1³⁄₁₆), after John Wilson. Purchased 1894.

YOUNG, Douglas, 1913–73. *Poet*
PG 2586* (With George Blake and Neil Gunn.) Ink, chalk and pencil drawing, 35 x 41.4 (13¾ x 16⁵⁄₁₆) (irregular), by Emilio Coia, signed. Executed 1957. Given by Christopher Blake 1983.

YOUNG, John Brown, fl. 1886. *Civil engineer*
PG 1005 Bronze medallion, dia. 14.4 (5¹¹⁄₁₆), by Charles Matthew. Dated 1886. Bequeathed by Mr and Mrs W. R. Macdonald 1925.

YOUNG, Sir Peter, 1544–1628. *Tutor to James VI and I and Charles I*
PG 627* Canvas, 108.2 x 93.1 (42⁹⁄₁₆ x 36⅝), by unknown artist. Dated 1622. Purchased 1904.

YOUNG, Captain Walter, d. 1781. *Sailor*
PG 1943 Medallion (plaster replica), h. 9.5 (3¾), after James Tassie. Provenance untraced.

YULE, Sir Henry, 1820–89. *Geographer*
PG 1988 Ink drawing, 25.7 x 23 (10⅛ x 9), by T. Blake Wirgman, signed. Bequeathed by Mrs L. K. Haldane 1962.

Yellowlees, William
PG 1247

Yester House
PG 2366

York, Duchess of
PG 1179

Young, Sir Peter
PG 627

GROUPS

SIR ROBERT KER PORTER AND MEMBERS OF HIS FAMILY

PG 824*   A set of four cut paper silhouettes by Augustin Edouart, 1829: Sir Robert
Ker Porter (1777–1842), h. 20.5 (8⅛); Jane Porter (1776–1850), h. 19.2
(7⁹⁄₁₆); (probably) Anna Maria Porter (1780–1832), h. 21.5 (8⁷⁄₁₆); Annette
Frances Porter (fl. 1829), h. 13.8 (5⁷⁄₁₆). Purchased 1913.

SIR WALTER SCOTT AND HIS FRIENDS AT ABBOTSFORD

PG 825*   Canvas, 118.2 x 163.2 (46½ x 64¼), by Thomas Faed. Painted 1849.
Imaginary group including Sir Walter Scott (1771–1832), James Hogg
(1770–1835), Henry Mackenzie (1745–1831), Professor John Wilson
(1785–1854), Rev. George Crabbe (1754–1832), John Gibson Lockhart
(1794–1854), William Wordsworth (1770–1850), Francis Jeffrey, Lord
Jeffrey (1773–1850), Sir Adam Ferguson (1771–1855), Thomas Moore
(1779–1852), Thomas Campbell (1777–1844), Sir William Allan
(1782–1850), Sir David Wilkie (1785–1841), Archibald Constable
(1774–1827), James Ballantyne (1772–1833), Sir Humphry Davy
(1778–1829) and Thomas Thomson (1768–1852). Purchased 1913.

THE INAUGURATION OF ROBERT BURNS AS POET LAUREATE OF THE LODGE CANONGATE, KILWINNING, 1787

PG 946*   Canvas, 83.8 x 132.1 (33 x 52), by William Stewart Watson. Imaginary
group of forty-four figures including Robert Burns (1759–96), Alexander
Ferguson of Craigdarroch (d. 1796), (probably) Francis Charteris, Lord
Elcho (1749–1808), James Sandilands, 9th Baron Torphichen (1759–1815),
Archibald Montgomerie, 11th Earl of Eglinton (1726–96), Charles More (fl.
1787), James Dalrymple of Orangefield (fl. 1787), Sir John Whitefoord of
Whitefoord and Ballochmyle (d. 1803), Sir William Forbes of Pitsligo
(1739–1806), James Burnett, Lord Monboddo (1714–99), William Dunbar
(fl. 1787), (probably) Johann Schetky (d. 1824), James Boswell (1740–95),
(probably) Sir James Hunter Blair (1741–87), Captain Francis Grose
(c. 1731–91), Caleb Whitefoord (1734–1810), and Francis Napier, 7th Lord
Napier (1758–1823). Purchased 1923.

GEORGE, 5TH LORD SETON AND HIS FAMILY

PG 1020   Canvas, 111.7 x 84.5 (44 x 33¼), by unknown artist after Frans Pourbus.
Original painted 1572 (see GROUPS, PGL 312.) Group including George
Seton, 5th Lord Seton (1531–85), Robert Seton, 1st Earl of Winton
(1550–1603), Sir John Seton, later Lord Barnes (d. 1594), Alexander Seton,
1st Earl of Dunfermline (1555–1622), (probably) Sir William Seton
(c. 1562–1635) and Margaret Seton, later Lady Paisley (d. 1616). Purchased
1925.

by A. EDOUART.

SIR ROBERT KER PORTER, B.1777.– D. 1842.
Painter & Traveller.

MISS JANE PORTER, B 1776.–D. 1850.
Author of "The Scottish Chiefs".

MISS A.F. PORTER.

MISS PORTER.

Porter Family   PG 824

Scott and his Friends   PG 825

Inauguration of Burns   PG 946

Entrance of George IV   PG 1040

Cockburn Family   PG 1175

Boswell Family   PG 1250

THE ENTRANCE OF GEORGE IV AT HOLYROODHOUSE

PG 1040*   Panel, 55.6 x 91.4 (21⅞ x 36), by Sir David Wilkie, 1828, signed. Group
including George IV (1762–1830), Alexander Douglas-Hamilton, 10th Duke
of Hamilton (1767–1852), James Graham, 3rd Duke of Montrose
(1755–1836), George Campbell, 6th Duke of Argyll (1768–1839), Sir
Alexander Keith (d. 1832), Lord Francis Leveson-Gower (later Earl of
Ellesmere) (1800–57), George Douglas, 15th Earl of Morton (1761–1827)
and John Hope, 4th Earl of Hopetoun (1765–1823). Purchased 1927.

QUEEN VICTORIA, PRINCE ALBERT AND THEIR CHILDREN

PG 1169   (Study for *The Landing of Queen Victoria at Dumbarton in 1847*, in the
collection of Dumbarton District Council.) Pencil and water-colour drawing,
66.7 x 50.1 (26 x 19¾), by Hope James Stewart. Drawn 1849. Four figures
including Queen Victoria (1819–1901), Prince Albert (1819–61), Albert
Edward, Prince of Wales (later Edward VII) (1841–1910) and Victoria,
Princess Royal (1840–1901). Purchased 1931.

HENRY COCKBURN, LORD COCKBURN AND HIS FAMILY

PG 1175*   A set of eleven cut paper silhouettes by Augustin Edouart, 1830: Henry
Cockburn, Lord Cockburn (1779–1854), h. 19.4 (7⅝); Elizabeth Macdowall,
Lady Cockburn (fl. 1830), h. 17.5 (7); Miss Jane Cockburn (d. 1878), h. 19.7
(7¾); James Macdowall Cockburn (fl. 1830), h. 19.9 (7⅞); Archibald
William Cockburn (1814–62), h. 19.4 (7⅝); Miss Graham Cockburn
(1817–97), h. 17.9 (7⅛); George Cockburn (1818–66), h. 16.3 (6½); Henry
Cockburn (1820–67), h. 16.3 (6½); Laurence Cockburn (1822–71), h. 16.6
(6⅝); Francis Jeffrey Cockburn (1825–93), h. 17.5 (7); Elizabeth Cockburn,
later Mrs Thomas Cleghorn (fl. 1830), h. 11 (4⅜). Purchased 1932.

JAMES BOSWELL AND HIS FAMILY

PG 1250*   Canvas, 104.1 x 125.1 (41 x 49¼), by Henry Singleton. Group including
James Boswell (1740–95), Margaret Montgomerie, Mrs James Boswell
(d. 1789) and three of their children, probably Veronica (b. 1773), James
(1778–1822) and Elizabeth (b. 1780). Purchased 1935.

THE ABBOTSFORD FAMILY

PG 1303*   Panel, 28 x 37.6 (11 x 14¹³⁄₁₆), by Sir David Wilkie, 1817, signed. Group
including Sir Walter Scott (1771–1832), Marguerite Charpentier, Lady
Scott (1770–1826), Charlotte Sophia Scott, Mrs John Gibson Lockhart
(1799–1837), Anne Scott (1803–33), Sir Adam Ferguson (1771–1855),
Walter Scott, 2nd Baronet (1801–47), Charles Scott (1805–41) and Thomas
Scott (fl. 1817). Transferred from the National Gallery of Scotland 1936.

THE BAPTISM OF PRINCE MAURICE OF BATTENBERG

PG 1306*   (Exhibited as *The First Baptism for 300 years of a Royal Prince in Scotland,
Balmoral Castle, October 31, 1891*. Study for the finished picture in the
Royal Collection.) Canvas, 23.8 x 35.7 (9⅜ x 14¹⁄₁₆), by George Ogilvy

Abbotsford Family   PG 1303

Battenberg Baptism   PG 1306

Statesmen of the Great War   PG 1466

Breadalbane, Cockburn, Dalhousie and Rutherfurd   PG 1497

Burns at Lord Monboddo's   PG 1770

Curling at Carsebreck   PG 1856

THE BAPTISM OF PRINCE MAURICE OF BATTENBERG (*continued*)

Reid, 1891, signed. Group including Queen Victoria (1819–1901), Prince Maurice of Battenberg (1891–1914), Princess Beatrice (1857–1944) and Prince Henry of Battenberg (d. 1896). Purchased 1936.

SOME STATESMEN OF THE GREAT WAR

PG 1466*   (Sketch for the finished picture in the National Portrait Gallery, London.) Canvas, 55.8 x 81.9 (22 x 32¼), by Sir James Guthrie. Group of sixteen figures including recognisable likenesses of Arthur James Balfour, 1st Earl of Balfour (1848–1930), David Lloyd George, 1st Earl Lloyd-George (1863–1945) and Horatio Herbert Kitchener, 1st Earl Kitchener (1850–1916). Purchased 1945.

THE MARQUESS OF BREADALBANE WITH LORD COCKBURN, THE MARQUESS OF DALHOUSIE AND LORD RUTHERFURD

PG 1497*   (Study for *Quitting the Manse*.) Millboard, 57.1 x 46.3 (22½ x 18¼), by Sir George Harvey. Group including John Campbell, 2nd Marquess of Breadalbane (1796–1862), Henry Cockburn, Lord Cockburn (1779–1854), James Ramsay, 1st Marquess of Dalhousie (1812–60) and Andrew Rutherfurd, Lord Rutherfurd (1791–1854). Given by Mrs E. M. Pearse 1947.

ROBERT BURNS AT AN EVENING PARTY OF LORD MONBODDO'S 1786

PG 1770*   Wash drawing, 38.1 x 54.3 (15 x 21⅜), by James Edgar. Drawn *c*. 1854. Imaginary group including Robert Burns (1759–96), Eliza Burnett (1767–90), Jane Maxwell, Duchess of Gordon (*c*. 1749–1812), James Cunningham, 13th Earl of Glencairn (1749–91), Rev. Dr Thomas Blacklock (1721–91), Dr John Moore (1729–1802), Hugh Blair (1718–1800), Rev. John Skinner (1721–1807), William Tytler (1711–92), Katherine Bruce of Clackmannan (d. 1791), Frances Dunlop (1730–1815), William Smellie (1740–1795), George Thomson (1757–1851), Robert Dundas (1713–87), James Burnett, Lord Monboddo (1714–99), Captain Francis Grose (*c*. 1731–91), Professor Dugald Stewart (1753–1828), Professor Adam Ferguson (1723–1816) and Caleb Whitefoord (1734–1810). Given by E. H. Gordon 1947.

CURLING AT CARSEBRECK

PG 1856*   (The Diamond Jubilee of the Royal Caledonian Curling Club.) Canvas, 75.6 x 121.9 (29¾ x 48), by Charles Martin Hardie, 1899, signed. Sixty-one identified figures include Colonel Thomas Stokes Robertson-Aikman (1860–1948), W. Ainslie (fl. 1899), R. S. Anderson (fl. 1899), Arthur James Balfour, 1st Earl of Balfour (1848–1930), Alexander Bruce, 6th Lord Balfour of Burleigh (1849–1921), James Bowie (fl. 1899), Gavin Campbell, 1st Marquess of Breadalbane (1851–1922), William Montagu Douglas Scott, 6th Duke of Buccleuch (1831–1914), R. Cathcart (fl. 1899), W. W. Chapman (fl. 1899), Charles Christie (fl. 1899), Sir James Gibson Craig (1841–1908), John Craig (fl. 1899), Laurence Cunningham (fl. 1899),

J. Scott Davidson (fl. 1899), Arthur Johnstone-Douglas (1846–1923),
Lieutenant-Colonel Henry Home Drummond (1846–1911), Alexander Dun
(fl. 1899), Janetta Maxwell Durham (fl. 1899), Victor Bruce, 9th Earl of
Elgin (1849–1917), Alexander Fairley (fl. 1899), W. S. Fergusson (fl. 1899),
Very Rev. Dr John Gillespie (1836–1912), Lady Henrietta Gilmour
(fl. 1899), Hugh Gilmour (fl. 1899), R. Gordon (fl. 1899), Sir Richard
Waldie-Griffith (1850–1933), William J. I'Anson (fl. 1899), Rev. John Kerr
(1852–1920), Algernon Keith-Falconer, 9th Earl of Kintore (1852–1930),
R. Knox (fl. 1899), James Law (fl. 1899), John Hope, 1st Marquess of
Linlithgow (1860–1908), Charles Lodder (fl. 1899), William Logan
(fl. 1899), W. McClymont (fl. 1899), Sir Allan Russell Mackenzie (1850–
1916), William Murray, 4th Earl of Mansfield (1806–93), Colonel Menzies
(fl. 1899), Lieutenant-Colonel Sir Robert Menzies (1817–1903), John James
Moubray (1857–1928), R. G. Murray (fl. 1899), Sir William Keith Murray
(1872–1956), John Pearson (fl. 1899), Charles Maule Ramsay (1859–1936),
Andrew Rankine (fl. 1899), James Riddell (fl. 1899), Alexander F. Roberts
(1844–1929), James S. Rogers (fl. 1899), George Scott (fl. 1899), Peter Shaw
(fl. 1899), James Small (fl. 1899), A. Davidson Smith (fl. 1899), Robert
Somerville (fl. 1899), J. W. Stewart (fl. 1899), James Telford (fl. 1899), Sir
Mitchell Mitchell-Thomson (1846–1918), T. D. Thomson (fl. 1899),
William Hay, 10th Marquess of Tweeddale (1826–1911), George Ure
(fl. 1899) and David Williamson (fl. 1899). Purchased 1959.

DUNMORE CHILDREN

PG 1889   Medallion (plaster replica), h. 5.4 (2³⁄₁₆), after James Tassie. Dated 1791.
Group of the four sons of Robert Dunmore of Kelvinside, including Thomas
(1777–1855), John (1779–1821), William (1782–1810) and George (fl.
1791). Provenance untraced.

AN INCIDENT DURING THE VISIT OF GEORGE IV TO EDINBURGH 1822

PG 2218*   Pencil and water-colour drawing, 19.5 x 23.6 (7¹¹⁄₁₆ x 9⁵⁄₁₆), by Sir David
Wilkie, 1822, signed. Group of six unidentified figures including two in
Highland dress and one in the uniform of the Royal Company of Archers.
Purchased 1973.

JAMES DOUGLAS, 13TH EARL OF MORTON AND HIS FAMILY

PG 2233*   Canvas, 241.3 x 284.7 (95 x 112⅛), by Jeremiah Davison, 1740, signed.
Group including James Douglas, 13th Earl of Morton (c. 1702–68), Agatha
Halyburton, Countess of Morton (d. 1748), Sholto Charles Douglas, 14th
Earl of Morton (1732–74), Lord James Douglas (1734–46), Lady Frances
Douglas (d. 1739), Lady Mary Douglas (d. 1816) and Lord George Douglas
(b. 1738). Purchased 1974.

LADY HONYMAN AND HER FAMILY

PG 2303*   Canvas, 111.2 x 151.2 (43¾ x 59½), by Alexander Nasmyth. Painted
c. 1790. Group including Mary McQueen, Lady Honyman (d. 1846), Robert

Incident during George IV's Visit   PG 2218

Morton Family   PG 2233

Honyman Family   PG 2303

Stewart Marriage   PG 2415

LADY HONYMAN AND HER FAMILY (*continued*)

Honyman (*c.* 1782–1809), Sir Richard Bemptde Johnstone Honyman, 2nd Baronet (1787–1842), and an unidentified Honyman daughter. Bequeathed by Miss C. H. E. F. Wilson-MacQueen 1975.

THE SOLEMNIZATION OF THE MARRIAGE OF PRINCE JAMES FRANCIS EDWARD STEWART AND PRINCESS MARIA CLEMENTINA SOBIESKA AT MONTEFIASCONE 1 SEPTEMBER 1719

PG 2415*   Canvas, 243.5 x 342 (95⅞ x 134⅝) by Agostino Masucci. Painted *c.* 1735. Figures include Prince James Francis Edward Stewart (1688–1766), Princess Clementina Sobieska (1702–35), Winifred Herbert, Countess of Nithsdale (d. 1749) and Sebastiano Pompilio Bonaventura, Bishop of Montefiascone. Purchased with assistance from the National Art-Collections Fund, the Pilgrim Trust, and private donors 1977.

THE VISIT OF QUEEN VICTORIA AND PRINCE ALBERT TO HAWTHORNDEN, 14 SEPTEMBER 1842

PG 2417*   Canvas, 162.5 x 123.8 (64 x 48¾), by Sir William Allan, 1844, signed. Figures include Queen Victoria (1819–1901), Prince Albert (1819–61) and Charlotte Anne Thynne, Duchess of Buccleuch (1811–95). Purchased 1977.

FRIENDLY CRITICS

PG 2460*   Canvas, 102.2 x 132.2 (40½ x 52), by Charles Martin Hardie, 1882/3, signed. Figures include Charles Martin Hardie (1858–1916), Alexander Anderson (1845–1909), Robert Noble (1857–1917), George Whitton Johnstone (1849–1901), John Simpson Fraser (fl. 1879–83) and Thomas Stuart Burnett (1853–88). Purchased 1980.

HISTORICAL COSTUME STUDIES BY DAVID ALLAN

PG 2461   f. Pencil, grey ink and water-colour, 14.5 x 24.3 (5¾ x 9⁹⁄₁₆), by David Allan. Seven figures on a single sheet, including Henry, Prince of Wales, Robert Devereux, 2nd Earl of Essex, Sir Thomas More, Dr John Caius and George Clifford, 3rd Earl of Cumberland.

PG 2461   g. Pencil, grey ink and wash drawing, 23.7 x 19.4 (9⁵⁄₁₆ x 7⅝), by David Allan. Five figures on a single sheet, including William Herbert, 3rd Earl of Pembroke, William Laud, Archbishop of Canterbury, Sir Thomas Bodley, Sir Kenelm Digby and John Selden. Purchased 1980.

THE BAPTISM OF PRINCE CHARLES EDWARD STEWART

PG 2511*   Canvas, 243.9 x 350.3 (96 x 138), by Pier Leone Ghezzi. Probably painted between 1722 and 1735. Figures include Prince James Francis Edward Stewart (1688–1766), Prince Charles Edward Stewart (1720–88) as an infant, and Sebastiano Pompilio Bonaventura, Bishop of Montefiascone. Purchased 1982.

Queen Victoria at Hawthornden   PG 2417

Friendly Critics   PG 2460

SILHOUETTE ALBUM *c.* 1782–*c.* 1818

PG 2584   Album of 319 silhouettes, mostly printed or painted and some cut, by an unknown artist. Executed *c.* 1782–*c.* 1818. Acquired *c.* 1951.

All named sitters are identified by contemporary or near-contemporary inscriptions. Sitters marked with a dagger [+] are also entered in the main text of the catalogue.

(1)   J. M. Clayhills 1800
(2)   G. D. Clayhills (as a child) 1800
(3)   George III copy after a silhouette cut by Princess Elizabeth
(4)   Mrs Dunbar
(5)   Adam Mure of Livingston
(6)   Miss Weir
(7)   Mrs Charles Dunbar
(8)   Jocelyn Atkinson
(9)   Miss Nugent
(10) Mrs Blair, wife of Colonel Blair
(11) Walter Lawrie
(12) Miss Thompson
(13) Lieutenant-Colonel Gordon of the 77th Regiment
(14) John Hely-Hutchinson, Baron Hutchinson, later 2nd Earl of Donoughmore (when Major Hutchinson of the 77th Regiment)+
(15) Major Morison of the 77th Regiment
(16) Lieutenant Mackay of the 77th Regiment
(17) Captain Clayhills of the 77th Regiment
(18) Captain Balnavis of the 77th Regiment
(19) Rev. Alexander Mackenzie of the 77th Regiment
(20) Captain Wood of the 77th Regiment
(21) Lieutenant Scott of the 77th Regiment
(22) Mrs Wright
(23) Dr Wright
(24) Miss Hodgson
(25) Mrs Wensley
(26) Mr Wensley
(27) Mrs Pye
(28) Mrs Burchall
(29) Dr Burchall
(30) Mrs Pringle
(31) Mrs Cummin, wife of Major Cummin
(32) Major Cummin of the Antient British Regiment (8th Fencible Cavalry Regiment)
(33) Miss Welch
(34) Major Blacker of the 65th Regiment
(35) Mrs Maddison, wife of Major Maddison
(36) Major Maddison of the 65th Regiment
(37) Mrs Blacker, wife of Major Blacker
(38) Lieutenant-Colonel William Duncan of the 1st Battalion of the 1st Royals+

(39)   Mrs Duncan, wife of Lieutenant-Colonel Duncan
(40)   John Readshaw
(41)   Mrs Dyer
(42)   Rev. Caleb Readshaw
(43)   Mrs Curry, wife of Leonard Curry
(44)   D. P. Okeden [? Oakden]
(45)   Miss Margaret Close
(46)   Captain Morley
(47)   Miss Carter
(48)   Henry Morley
(49)   Captain Charles Stewart
(50)   Anne Stewart, Countess of Airlie†
(51)   Captain John Stewart
(52)   Miss Stewart
(53)   Miss Ann Moir
(54)   Miss Margaret Stewart
(55)   Mr Moir of Newgrange
(56)   Mrs Moir of Newgrange
(57)   William Moir
(58)   Mrs Newsam
(59)   Mr Newsam
(60)   Miss Newsam
(61)   Mrs Hogg
(62)   Mr Hogg
(63)   Mrs Hogg, formerly Mrs Hamilton Brown
(64)   Miss Hogg
(65)   Thomas Charge
(66)   Miss Ann Hogg
(67)   Mrs Buck, wife of Stukely Buck
(68)   Captain Charles Murray of the 77th Regiment
(69)   Mrs Buck of Dadden, Devonshire
(70)   Miss Gladstone
(71)   George Renny, surgeon, of the 77th Regiment
(72)   Mrs Gladstone, wife of Colonel Gladstone
(73)   Lieutenant Patrick Mackenzie of the 77th Regiment
(74)   Mrs Southcote
(75)   Andrew Brown
(76)   Honble. Miss Barbara Gray
(77)   William Gray of Balledgarno
(78)   Miss Ann Gray
(79)   Mrs Hunter, senior, of Burnside
(80)   David Fyffe
(81)   Mrs Fyffe
(82)   Alexander Graham of Duntrune
(83)   Mrs Stirling of Craigbarnet
(84)   Mrs Gray of Carse

SILHOUETTE ALBUM (*continued*)

(85)	Mrs Read of Logie
(86)	Fletcher Read of Logie
(87)	Mrs Read, wife of Fletcher Read
(88)	Miss Lindsay 1796
(89)	Mr Lindsay 1796
(90)	Mrs Lindsay 1796
(91)	James Yeaman of Murie
(92)	Miss Yeaman
(93)	George Yeaman
(94)	Miss Lily Ramsay
(95)	George Yeaman
(96)	Mrs Jobson, wife of James Jobson 1796
(97)	James Jobson 1796
(98)	Miss Helen Jobson 1796
(99)	Miss Ann Douglas
(100)	Miss Ann Crawford
(101)	Lieutenant-Colonel Mackenzie of the 90th Regiment
(102)	Mrs Bower of Kincaldrum
(103)	Alexander Bower of Kincaldrum
(104)	Miss Mary Bower
(105)	Mrs Graham, senior, of Fintry
(106)	Robert Graham of Fintry
(107)	Mrs (Margaret Elizabeth) Graham of Fintry
(108)	Mrs Fletcher of Ballinshoe
(109)	Mrs Douglas of Brigton
(110)	Miss Graham of Fintry
(111)	Mrs Crawford of Monorgan
(112)	Henry Crawford of Monorgan
(113)	Miss Marion Crawford
(114)	John Crawford junior
(115)	John Crawford senior
(116)	Charles Crawford
(117)	Miss Ann Crawford
(118)	Mungo Murray of Lintrose
(119)	Mrs Murray of Lintrose
(120)	Mrs Richardson
(121)	Thomas Richardson
(122)	Miss Richardson
(123)	Miss Hunter
(124)	Rev. John Ella
(125)	Miss Hebden
(126)	Rev. John Richardson of Cleaves
(127)	Miss Eliza Richardson (as a child)
(128)	Mrs Richardson of Cleaves
(129)	Mrs Menzies of Invergowrie

(130)	Lieutenant Alexander Menzies RN
(131)	Miss Menzies
(132)	Miss Menzies senior
(133)	Miss Mary Menzies
(134)	Miss Betty Menzies
(135)	Sir Alexander Douglas
(136)	Lady Douglas
(137)	Unidentified young man
(138)	Mrs Butler
(139)	Major Butler
(140)	Miss Susan Mylne
(141)	Miss Laird
(142)	Emanuel Stephenson
(143)	Mrs Laird of Strathmartine
(144)	Miss Ogilvie
(145)	Miss Ann Kinloch
(146)	Sir Alexander Douglas
(147)	David Kinloch of Gourdie
(148)	Mrs Kinloch of Gourdie
(149)	Captain Charles Kinloch of the 52nd Regiment 1814
(150)	Miss Kinloch of Gourdie 1814
(151)	Miss Margaret Kinloch of Gourdie 1814
(152)	Miss Jemina G. Kinloch 1814
(153)	James Rattray of Arthurstone
(154)	Lieutenant D. Kinloch of the 52nd Regiment 1816
(155)	Captain James Menzies Clayhills of the Royal Regiment 1813
(156)	Lieutenant-Colonel Sandiaman [Sandeman ?] of the 9th Regiment
(157)	Thomas Mylne
(158)	Miss Lucy Mercer of Andover
(159)	Unidentified young woman
(160)	Miss Walker of Thirsk
(161)	Miss M. Metcalf
(162)	William Chalmers (identified by a later inscription as Rev. William Chalmers of the 52nd Regiment)
(163)	Miss Campbell
(164)	Unidentified woman
(165)	Major Bunbury
(166)	Mrs Bunbury
(167)	Miss Weir
(168)	Mrs Duff
(169)	Lieutenant-Colonel Skelly of the Scots Brigade
(170)	Mrs Skelly
(171)	Mr Mackenzie
(172)	Mrs Mackenzie
(173)	Captain James Stewart of the 10th Regiment
(174)	Miss Mylne of Mylnefield

SILHOUETTE ALBUM (*continued*)

- (175) Colonel Mylne of Mylnefield
- (176) Mrs Mylne, wife of Colonel Mylne
- (177) Miss Agnes Mylne of Mylnefield (later Mrs Charles Kinloch of Gourdie) 1818
- (178) John Mylne
- (179) Thomas Mylne of Mylnefield 1818
- (180) George Mylne
- (181) Mrs Mylne, wife of George Mylne
- (182) Elizabeth Jane Guthrie, Mrs Thomas Mylne of Mylnefield 1818
- (183) Mrs Scott, senior, of Criggie
- (184) Charles Scott of Criggie
- (185) Mrs Scott, wife of Charles Scott
- (186) James Small
- (187) Mr Smith of Rosebank
- (188) Mrs Scott, wife of Alexander Scott
- (189) Alexander Scott
- (190) Mrs Scott of Criggie
- (191) Miss Jane Becket
- (192) Mrs Becket
- (193) Miss Bridget Beckett
- (194) Miss Crawford of Newcastle
- (195) Thomas Becket
- (196) Miss Ann Crawford of Newcastle
- (197) Miss Mary Addison
- (198) John Raper
- (199) Miss Juliet Richardson
- (200) Miss Cross
- (201) Captain Cross
- (202) Miss Elizabeth Mair
- (203) Dr Usher
- (204) Miss Grantham
- (205) Mrs Cumby
- (206) Miss Mary Metcalf
- (207) Mrs Metcalf
- (208) Miss Margaret Metcalf
- (209) George Brown
- (210) George Cuit
- (211) Mr Langhorn
- (212) Mr Coatsworth
- (213) George Brown
- (214) Mr Priestman
- (215) John Robinson of Friary
- (216) Thomas Hutchinson
- (217) James Robinson
- (218) Jane Murray, Lady Mackenzie of Delvine†
- (219) Sir Alexander Muir Mackenzie, 1st Baronet, of Delvine†

(220)   Mrs Tobin
(221)   James Keay of Snaigo
(222)   Miss Hamilton Brown of Glaswell
(223)   Lieutenant-Colonel John Graham
(224)   Miss Ann Graham
(225)   Captain Mackay of Scotstown
(226)   Mrs Mackay of Scotstown
(227)   William Scott 1813
(228)   Mrs Scott 1813
(229)   Ensign John Bell of the 52nd Regiment
(230)   George Kinloch of Kinloch
(231)   Mrs Renny of Borrowfield
(232)   Mr Renny of Borrowfield
(233)   Charles Landall
(234)   Miss Michie
(235)   Miss Harriet Ramsay
(236)   Mrs Horsbrugh [? Horsburgh], wife of Major Horsbrugh of Lochmalony
(237)   Major Scott of Lochmalony
(238)   Mrs Warren 1812
(239)   Mrs Ker of Chatto
(240)   Miss Fyffe of Drumneith
(241)   Miss Weir
(242)   Rev. R. Aikman
(243)   Miss Palmer
(244)   Charles Clayhills (as a child) 1808
(245)   Miss Fraser
(246)   Patrick Scrymsour [? Scrymgeour] of Tealing 1814
(247)   Mrs Scrymsour [? Scrymgeour] of Tealing 1814
(248)   James Wedderburn 1813
(249)   Miss Guthrie of Craigie 1813
(250)   Mrs Guthrie of Craigie 1813
(251)   Miss Rose Guthrie 1813
(252)   Lieutenant McKay of the 77th Regiment
(253)   Captain Adamson
(254)   Mr Mant of the Royal Marines
(255)   Mr Green of Rathbone Place, London
(256)   Mrs Dick of Perth
(257)   Mr Dick of Perth
(258)   Thomas Monro Scott 1813
(259)   James O. Lockhart-Mure of Livingston 1815
(260)   Miss Inman
(261)   Mrs Lindsay 1812
(262)   William Lindsay 1812
(263)   Miss Jane Lindsay 1816
(264)   Miss Ann Lindsay 1816
(265)   Martin Lindsay 1816
(266)   Miss Mary Lindsay 1817

SILHOUETTE ALBUM (*continued*)

(267) Miss Katherine Lindsay 1818
(268) Miss Janet Lindsay 1817
(269) Miss Helen Lindsay 1818
(270) Sir W. Douglas 1800
(271) Charles Clayhills 1816
(272) G. D. Clayhills, Midshipman of HMS Indefatigable 1812
(273) Lieutenant-Colonel Bell
(274) Lieutenant Thomas Graham RN
(275) Mrs Hay of Newhall 1783
(276) William Hay (as a child) 1783
(277) Unidentified boy
(278) Ian Mylne (as a child)
(279) A. Mylne (as a child)
(280) Unidentified girl
(281) Unidentified child
(282) Unidentified child
(283) Unidentified child
(284) Unidentified girl
(285) Unidentified child
(286) Captain Morley
(287) Mrs Chaytor of [Spinni]thorn
(288) Unidentified man
(289) Mrs Mylne, wife of George Mylne
(290) James Clayhills of Invergowrie 1787
(291) Mrs Clayhills of Invergowrie 1800
(292) Thomas Becket (same sitter as no. 195)
(293) Miss Catriona Robinson
(294) James Menzies Clayhills (same sitter as no. 155) 1800
(295) Miss Mary Kirkcaldy 1817
(296) William Brown (as a child) 1817
(297) Miss Kirkcaldy 1817
(298) Captain Scott RN 1817
(299) Lawrence Brown (as a child) 1817
(300) Miss Hunter of Burnside 1818
(301) Miss Sarah Lawrenson 1818
(302) Miss Susan Loyd 1818
(303) Miss Anne Lawrenson 1818
(304) Miss Janet Maxwell 1783
(305) Miss Gladstanes 1782
(306) Miss Lillias Maxwell 1783
(307) Miss Ann Crawford 1783
(308) Unidentified woman
(309) Miss Mushet
(310) Miss Kitty Sandiaman [? Sandeman] 1783
(311) Miss Barbara Walker of St Fort 1783

(312)   Miss Mary Menzies
(313)   General Kerr (possibly John Manners Kerr) 1818
(314)   Mrs Kerr, wife of Herbert Kerr 1818
(315)   Herbert Kerr 1818
(316)   Miss Goodchild
(317)   Miss Beckett 1819
(318)   Lady Wiseman 1818
(319)   Miss Miller of Balumby 1819

POETS' PUB

PG 2597*   Canvas, 183 x 244 (72 x 96), by Alexander Moffat, 1980, signed on the reverse. Figures include Norman MacCaig (b. 1910), Sorley MacLean (b. 1911), Christopher Murray Grieve (1892–1978), Iain Crichton Smith (b. 1928), George Mackay Brown (b. 1921), Sydney Goodsir Smith (1915–75), Edwin Morgan (b. 1920), Robert Garioch (1909–81), Alan Bold (b. 1943) and John A. Tonge. Purchased 1983.

JAMES BYRES OF TONLEY AND MEMBERS OF HIS FAMILY

PG 2601*   Canvas, 63.2 x 75.8 (24⅞ x 29⅞), by Franciszek Smuglevicz. Painted c. 1775/8. Figures include James Byres of Tonley (1733–1817), Patrick Byres of Tonley (1713–78), Janet Moir, Mrs Patrick Byres (1711–87), Christopher Norton (d. 1799) and Isabella Byres, Mrs Robert Sandilands (b. 1737). Purchased with assistance from the National Art-Collections Fund 1983.

KENNETH MACKENZIE, 1ST EARL OF SEAFORTH AT HOME IN NAPLES: FENCING SCENE

PG 2610*   Canvas, 35.5 x 47.6 (14 x 18¾), by Pietro Fabris. Signed and dated 1771 on the reverse. Figures include Kenneth Mackenzie, 1st Earl of Seaforth (1744–81) (as Viscount Fortrose) and Nicolo Jomelli (1714–74). Purchased with assistance from the National Art-Collections Fund 1984.

KENNETH MACKENZIE, 1ST EARL OF SEAFORTH AT HOME IN NAPLES: CONCERT PARTY

PG 2611*   Canvas, 35.5 x 47.6 (14 x 18¾), by Pietro Fabris. Signed and dated 1771 on the reverse. Figures include Kenneth Mackenzie, 1st Earl of Seaforth (1744–81) (as Viscount Fortrose), Sir William Hamilton (1730–1803), Gaetano Pugnani (1731–98) and Pietro Fabris (fl. 1768–78). Purchased with assistance from the National Art-Collections Fund 1984.

THE BATTLE OF GLENSHIEL 1719

PG 2635*   Canvas, 118 x 164.5 (46½ x 64¾), by Peter Tillemans, signed. Figures probably include Lord George Murray (c. 1700–60), Rob Roy MacGregor (1671–1734) and General Joseph Wightman (d. 1722). Purchased with assistance from the National Heritage Memorial Fund and the National Art-Collections Fund 1984.

Stewart Baptism   PG 2511

Poets' Pub   PG 2597

Seaforth Fencing Scene   PG 2610

Seaforth Concert Party   PG 2611

Byres Family   PG 2601

Battle of Glenshiel   PG 2635

Battle of Alexandria   PG 2680

Landing at Aboukir   PG 2681

THE BATTLE OF ALEXANDRIA, 21 MARCH 1801

PG 2680*   Canvas, 106.6 x 152.6 (42 x 60$\frac{1}{16}$), by Philip James de Loutherbourg, 1802, signed. Figures include Sir Ralph Abercromby (1734–1801), Sir Thomas Dyer of Tottenham, (c. 1770–1838), Sir John Moore (1761–1809), Sir (William) Sidney Smith (1764–1840), Sir John Stuart (1759–1815), John Francis Cradock or Caradoc, 1st Baron Howden (1762–1839), Sir William Houston (1766–1842), Sir Brent Spencer (1760–1828), John Hely-Hutchinson, Baron Hutchinson of Alexandria and 2nd Earl of Donoughmore (1757–1832), John Hope, 4th Earl of Hopetoun (1765–1823), and Sir Hildebrand Oakes (1754–1822). Purchased 1986.

THE LANDING OF BRITISH TROOPS AT ABOUKIR, 8 MARCH 1801

PG 2681*   Canvas, 106.4 x 152.8 (41$\frac{7}{8}$ x 60$\frac{1}{8}$), by Philip James de Loutherbourg, 1802, signed. Figures include Sir (William) Sidney Smith (1764–1840), Lieutenant-Colonel J. Duncan (fl. 1801), Colonel Samuel Dalrymple (fl. 1801), George James Ludlow, 3rd and last Earl Ludlow (1758–1842) and Sir Eyre Coote (1762–1823). Purchased 1986.

ALEXANDER NASMYTH AND HIS FAMILY

PG 2729*   (recto) a. Ink and wash drawing, 15.3 x 20 (6 x 7$\frac{7}{8}$), by David Octavius Hill, 1829. Group at 47 York Place, Edinburgh, including Alexander Nasmyth (1758–1840), Barbara Foulis, (Mrs Alexander Nasmyth), James Nasmyth, (1808–90), Charlotte Nasmyth (1804–84), and an unidentified Nasmyth daughter. Purchased 1987.

THE SMOKING ROOM, THE SCOTTISH ARTS CLUB

PG 2737*   Canvas, 62.2 x 91.5 (24$\frac{1}{2}$ x 36), by Sir William Oliphant Hutchison, 1945, signed. Figures include William Miller Frazer (1864–1961), James W. Herries, Dr J. R. Peddie, Dr Charles Richard Whittaker (1879–1967), William Mumford, Adrian Moncrieff, Colin Swanson, Alexander Black, John Guthrie Spence Smith (1880–1951) and Alick Riddell Sturrock (1885–1953). Purchased 1988.

JOHN FRANCIS ERSKINE, 7TH EARL OF MAR AND HIS FAMILY

PGL 243*   (View of Alloa House in the background.) Canvas, 153.4 x 216.7 (60$\frac{3}{8}$ x 85$\frac{1}{4}$), by David Allan, 1783, signed (on reverse.) Group including John Francis Erskine, 7th Earl of Mar (1741–1825), Frances Floyer, Countess of Mar (d. 1798), James Floyer Erskine (c. 1773–98), Charlotte Frances Erskine (c. 1771–1837), Mary Anne Erskine (c. 1774–1844), Henry David Erskine (1776–1846), Charlotte Erskine (d. 1852), Jane Erskine (1782/3–1857) and Rachel Erskine (1719–1793). On loan from the Earl of Mar and Kellie.

GEORGE, 5TH LORD SETON AND HIS FAMILY

PGL 312*   Panel, 108.9 x 79.3, by Frans Pourbus the elder, 1572, signed. Group including George Seton, 5th Lord Seton (1531–85), Robert Seton, 1st Earl of Winton (1550–1603), Sir John Seton, later Lord Barnes (d. 1594),

Nasmyth Family   PG 2729a

Scottish Arts Club   PG 2737

Mar Family PGL 243

Seton Family PGL 312

Gathering at 7 London Street   PGL 328

Erskine Family   PGL 333

GEORGE, 5TH LORD SETON AND HIS FAMILY (*continued*)

Alexander Seton, 1st Earl of Dunfermline (1555–1622), (probably) Sir William Seton (*c.* 1562–1635) and Margaret Seton, later Lady Paisley (d. 1616). On loan from the National Gallery of Scotland.

GATHERING AT 7 LONDON STREET

PGL 328* (Anne Redpath's studio.) Canvas, 137.7 x 183.2 (54³/₁₆ x 72⅛), by Sir Robin Philipson. Painted *c.* 1952. Figures include Anne Redpath (1895–1965), David Michie (b. 1928), Eileen Michie, Brenda Mark (Philipson), Alastair Flattely (b. 1922), Hamish Reid, Joyce McClure, Maisie Shaw, Katie Horsman, David McClure (b. 1926), Victorine Foot (Schilsky) (b. 1920), Sax Shaw (b. 1916), Isobel Blyth, Mary Newbery Sturrock (1892–1985), Alick Riddell Sturrock (1885–1953), Eric Schilsky (1898–1974), Ellen Kemp, Robert Henderson Blyth (1919–70), William Wilson (1905–72), Sir William Gillies (1898–1973) and Sir Robin Philipson (b. 1916). On loan from Sir Robin Philipson.

SIR WILLIAM ERSKINE OF TORRIE AND HIS FAMILY

PGL 333* Canvas, 153.7 x 240 (60½ x 94½), by David Allan, 1788. Group including Sir William Erskine of Torrie, 1st Baronet, (1728–95), Lady Frances Erskine (d. 1793), William Erskine, 2nd Baronet (1770–1813), James Erskine, 3rd Baronet (1772–1825), and John Drummond Erskine, 4th and last Baronet (1776–1836), Frances, Henrietta, Elizabeth and Magdalene Erskine. On loan from the Trustees of the late Mrs Magdalene Sharpe Erskine.

A MEET OF THE FIFE HOUNDS 1833

PGL 337* Canvas, 91.5 x 122 (36 x 48), by Sir Francis Grant, 1834. Group including John Grant of Kilgraston (1798–1873), John Whyte Melville of Bennochy and Strathkinness (1797–1883/5), John Dalyell of Lingo and Ticknerin, (d. 1843), and James Erskine Wemyss of Wemyss and Torrie (1789–1854). On loan from the Kintore Trust.

Fife Hounds   PGL 337

UNIDENTIFIED SUBJECTS

16TH CENTURY

PG 2315   WOMAN. Water-colour on ivory, oval, 10.1 x 8.5 (4 x 3⅜), copy by unknown
           artist. Bequeathed by W. F. Watson 1886.
PG 2332   MAN. Copper, oval, 5.6 x 4.5 (2³⁄₁₆ x 1¾), copy by unknown artist. Bequeathed
           by W. F. Watson 1886.
PG 2461   h. MAN. (Scots Guard. Costume study.) Pencil, grey ink and wash drawing,
           15.7 x 24 (6¼ x 9⁷⁄₁₆), copy by David Allan. Purchased 1980.
PGL 157   WOMAN. Panel, 46.3 x 32.4 (18¼ x 12¾) (irregular), by unknown artist. On
           loan from the National Museums of Scotland.

17TH CENTURY

PG 1781*   (Formerly called Frederick, King of Bohemia, with Elizabeth, Queen of
           Bohemia. Probably a leaf from an album amicorum.) MAN AND WOMAN.
           Water-colour, 8.9 x 11.7 (3½ x 5⅝), by unknown artist. Executed c. 1620.
           Transferred from the National Gallery of Scotland 1952.
PG 2103   MAN. Wash and ink drawing, 12.6 x 12.2 (5 x 4⅞), copy by unknown artist.
           Transferred from the National Gallery of Scotland 1950.
PG 2104   MAN. Ink drawing, 11.6 x 10.6 (4½ x 4⅛), by unknown artist after Crispin de
           Passe. Transferred from the National Gallery of Scotland 1950.
PG 2105   MAN. Wash drawing, oval, 15.2 x 11.3 (6 x 4½), copy by unknown artist.
           Transferred from the National Gallery of Scotland 1950.
PG 2107   MAN. Red chalk drawing, 13.2 x 11.1 (5⅛ x 4⅜), by unknown artist.
           Transferred from the National Gallery of Scotland 1950.
PG 2110   MAN. Chalk drawing, 27.5 x 21 (10¾ x 8¼), by unknown artist. Transferred
           from the National Gallery of Scotland 1950.
PG 2112   MAN. Wash drawing, 20.1 x 16.4 (7⅞ x 6⅜), copy by unknown artist.
           Transferred from the National Gallery of Scotland 1950.
PG 2118   MAN. Pen, wash and white chalk drawing, 33.5 x 25.2 (13¼ x 9⅞), attributed
           to Edward Byng after Sir Godfrey Kneller. Transferred from the National
           Gallery of Scotland 1950.
PG 2121   WOMAN. Oil on paper, 34.5 x 24.3 (13½ x 9½), by unknown artist after Sir
           Godfrey Kneller. Transferred from the National Gallery of Scotland 1950.
PG 2316   MAN. Water-colour, oval, 5.4 x 4.3 (2⅛ x 1¹¹⁄₁₆), by unknown artist. Dated
           1661. Bequeathed by W. F. Watson 1886.
PG 2317   WOMAN. Water-colour, oval, 5.2 x 4.4 (2¹⁄₁₆ x 1¾), by unknown artist after
           Isaac Oliver. Bequeathed by W. F. Watson 1886.
PG 2334   MAN. Copper, oval, 6.5 x 5.3 (2⁹⁄₁₆ x 2¹⁄₁₆), copy by unknown artist.
           Bequeathed by W. F. Watson 1886.

PG 2336   WOMAN. Copper, oval, 9.5 x 7.7 (3¾ x 3), by unknown artist. Bequeathed by
           W. F. Watson 1886.

PG 2337   MAN. Copper, oval, 6.1 x 5.1 (2⁷⁄₁₆ x 2), by unknown artist. Bequeathed by
           W. F. Watson 1886.

PG 2339   MAN. Copper, oval, 10.6 x 8.1 (4⅛ x 3³⁄₁₆), by unknown artist. Bequeathed by
           W. F. Watson 1886.

PG 2351   MAN. Copper, 11.2 x 9.7 (4⁷⁄₁₆ x 3¹³⁄₁₆), by unknown artist. Provenance
           untraced.

PGL 158   MAN. Canvas, 86.3 x 67.3 (34 x 26½), by unknown artist. Inscribed with the
           date 1613. On loan from the National Museums of Scotland.

18TH CENTURY

PG 531   MAN. Plaster medallion, h. 8.9 (3½), attributed to Henry Webber, signed
           'H. W. Roma'. Given by Miss Brown 1894.

PG 1255   MAN. Paste medallion, h. 5.8 (2⁵⁄₁₆), by James Tassie. Purchased 1935.

PG 1260   WOMAN. Paste medallion, h. 8.8 (3½), by James Tassie. Purchased 1935.

PG 1373*   MAN. Canvas, 111 x 87.5 (43½ x 34⅜), by Andrea Soldi, signed. Given by the
           National Art-Collections Fund (London Scot Bequest) 1938.

PG 1967   MAN. Paste medallion, h. 7 (2¾), by James Tassie. Transferred from the
           National Gallery of Scotland 1960.

PG 2098*   MAN. Chalk drawing, 32.5 x 20 (12¾ x 7⅞), by Martin Ferdinand Quadal,
           1779, signed. Transferred from the National Gallery of Scotland 1950.

PG 2099   MAN. Pencil drawing, 19.4 x 15.2 (7⅝ x 6), copy by unknown artist.
           Transferred from the National Gallery of Scotland 1950.

PG 2100   MAN. See JOSEPH II.

PG 2101   MAN. Pencil drawing, 16.9 x 11.6 (6¾ x 4½), copy by unknown artist.
           Transferred from the National Gallery of Scotland 1950.

PG 2102   MAN. Chalk and wash drawing, 29.5 x 21.7 (11⅝ x 8½), by unknown artist.
           Transferred from the National Gallery of Scotland 1950.

PG 2117   MAN. Water-colour, 28.9 x 22.6 (11⅜ x 8⅞), by unknown artist. Transferred
           from the National Gallery of Scotland 1967.

PG 2119   MAN. Chalk drawing, 18 x 15 (7⅛ x 5⅝), by unknown artist. Transferred from
           the National Gallery of Scotland 1950.

PG 2123   WOMAN. Pencil and wash drawing, 17.3 x 12.5 (6⅞ x 4⅝), by unknown
           artist. Transferred from the National Gallery of Scotland 1950.

PG 2239   MAN. Black and white chalk drawing, 32.8 x 27.5 (12⅞ x 10¹³⁄₁₆), attributed to
           Mather Brown. Provenance untraced.

PG 2240   MAN. Black and white chalk drawing, 35 x 28 (13¹³⁄₁₆ x 11), attributed to
           Mather Brown. Provenance untraced.

PG 2241   MAN. Black and white chalk drawing, 35.5 x 28.6 (14 x 11¼), attributed to
           Mather Brown. Provenance untraced.

PG 2243   (Previously called Viscount Mountstuart.) MAN. Black and white chalk
           drawing, 36 x 28.6 (14³⁄₁₆ x 11¼), by Mather Brown. Provenance untraced.

PG 2244   MAN. Black and white chalk drawing, 31.3 x 26.2 (12¼ x 10⁵⁄₁₆), attributed to Mather Brown. Provenance untraced.

PG 2245   WOMAN. Black and white chalk drawing, 36 x 28.6 (14³⁄₁₆ x 11¼), attributed to Mather Brown. Provenance untraced.

PG 2246   (Previously called Duchess of Devonshire.) WOMAN. Black and white chalk drawing, 34.6 x 29.4 (13⅝ x 11⁹⁄₁₆), by Mather Brown. Drawn c. 1785/95. Provenance untraced.

PG 2247   WOMAN. Black, white and red chalk drawing, 35.8 x 28.7 (14⅛ x 11¼), by Mather Brown. Drawn c. 1785/95. Provenance untraced.

PG 2249   MAN. Black and white chalk drawing, 36.2 x 28.6 (14¼ x 11¼), by Mather Brown. Provenance untraced.

PG 2250   WOMAN. Black and white chalk, and ink drawing, 35.5 x 28.3 (14 x 11⅛), by Mather Brown. Drawn c. 1785/95. Provenance untraced.

PG 2251   MAN. Black and white chalk drawing, 36 x 28.5 (14⅛ x 11¼), attributed to Mather Brown. Provenance untraced.

PG 2252   MAN. Black and white chalk drawing, 35.5 x 28.9 (14 x 11⅜), by Mather Brown. Drawn c. 1792. Provenance untraced.

PG 2253   MAN. Black and white chalk drawing, 34.9 x 28.9 (13¾ x 11⅜), by Mather Brown. Provenance untraced.

PG 2255   MAN. Black and white chalk drawing, 36.2 x 29 (14¼ x 11⁷⁄₁₆), by Mather Brown. Drawn c. 1785/95. Provenance untraced.

PG 2257   WOMAN. Black and white chalk drawing, 35.8 x 28.7 (14⅛ x 11¼), by Mather Brown. Drawn c. 1785/95. Provenance untraced.

PG 2258   (Previously called William Sharp, 1749–1824.) MAN. Black and white chalk drawing, 35 x 28.3 (13¾ x 11⅛), attributed to Mather Brown. Provenance untraced.

PG 2259   MAN. Black and white chalk, and pencil drawing, 35.8 x 28.4 (14⅛ x 11³⁄₁₆), attributed to Mather Brown. Provenance untraced.

PG 2260   MAN. Black and white chalk drawing, 35.5 x 28.7 (14 x 11⁵⁄₁₆), attributed to Mather Brown. Provenance untraced.

PG 2261   MAN. Black and white chalk drawing, 31.2 x 26.6 (12¼ x 10½), attributed to Mather Brown. Provenance untraced.

PG 2262   YOUTH. Black and white chalk drawing, 35.8 x 28.7 (14¹⁄₁₆ x 11¼), attributed to Mather Brown. Provenance untraced.

PG 2263   MAN. Black, white and red chalk drawing, 35.6 x 28.7 (14 x 11⁵⁄₁₆), by Mather Brown. Drawn c. 1785/95. Provenance untraced.

PG 2273   MAN. Wash drawing, 16.4 x 13.2 (6⁷⁄₁₆ x 5³⁄₁₆), by unknown artist. Purchased 1950.

PG 2284   MAN. Water-colour, 7.4 x 5.5 (2¹⁵⁄₁₆ x 2³⁄₁₆), by unknown artist. Provenance untraced.

PG 2287   MAN. Water-colour, 23.5 x 16 (9¼ x 6⁵⁄₁₆), by unknown artist. Provenance untraced.

PG 2299   WOMAN. Pencil and pastel drawing, 26.6 x 18.1 (10½ x 7⅛), copy by unknown artist. Provenance untraced.

PG 2300   MAN. Pencil and pastel drawing, 27.5 x 18.4 (10¹³⁄₁₆ x 7¼), copy by unknown artist. Provenance untraced.

Unidentified
PG 1781

Unidentified
PG 1373

Unidentified
PG 2098

Unidentified
PGL 54

Unidentified
PGL 55

Unidentified
PGL 61

Unidentified
PGL 62

PG 2321   MAN. Copper, oval, 2.6 x 2.2 (1$\frac{1}{16}$ x $\frac{7}{8}$), copy by unknown artist. Bequeathed by W. F. Watson 1886.

PG 2327   MAN. Pen and wash drawing, oval, 4.2 x 3.4 (1$\frac{11}{16}$ x 1$\frac{5}{16}$), attributed to James Ferguson. Bequeathed by W. F. Watson 1886.

PG 2328   WOMAN. Copper, oval, 6 x 4.7 (2$\frac{3}{8}$ x 1$\frac{13}{16}$), by unknown artist. Bequeathed by W. F. Watson 1886.

PG 2329   MAN. Water-colour on ivory, oval, 3.7 x 3 (1$\frac{1}{2}$ x 1$\frac{3}{16}$), by unknown artist. Bequeathed by W. F. Watson 1886.

PG 2331   MAN. Water-colour on synthetic ivory, oval, 7.3 x 5.8 (2$\frac{7}{8}$ x 2$\frac{5}{16}$), copy by unknown artist. Bequeathed by W. F. Watson 1886.

PG 2342   MAN. Water-colour on ivory, oval, 9.9 x 7.3 (3$\frac{7}{8}$ x 2$\frac{7}{8}$), by unknown artist. Bequeathed by W. F. Watson 1886.

PG 2343   MAN. Water-colour on ivory, dia. 7.3 (2$\frac{7}{8}$), by 'I.B.', 1784, signed. Bequeathed by W. F. Watson 1886.

PG 2346   MAN. Water-colour on ivory, oval, 5.1 x 3.9 (2 x 1$\frac{9}{16}$), by unknown artist. Bequeathed by W. F. Watson 1886.

PG 2347   MAN. Water-colour on ivory, oval, 3.3 x 2.8 (1$\frac{5}{16}$ x 1$\frac{1}{8}$), by unknown artist. Bequeathed by W. F. Watson 1886.

PG 2348   MAN. Metal, oval, 4 x 3.4 (1$\frac{9}{16}$ x 1$\frac{3}{8}$), by unknown artist. Bequeathed by W. F. Watson 1886.

PG 2349   WOMAN. Water-colour on ivory, oval, 2 x 1.3 ($^{13}/_{16}$ x ½), by unknown artist. Bequeathed by W. F. Watson 1886.

PG 2350   MAN. Water-colour, oval, 1.7 x 1.4 ($^{11}/_{16}$ x $^{9}/_{16}$), by unknown artist. Bequeathed by W. F. Watson 1886.

PG 2413   GIRL. Pencil drawing, 46.2 x 35.4 (18$^{3}/_{16}$ x 13$^{15}/_{16}$), by John Brown. Provenance untraced.

PG 2534   MAN. Water-colour on ivory, h. 3.5 (1⅜), by John Bogle, signed. Dated 1784. Transferred from the National Gallery of Scotland 1982.

PG 2536   MAN. Water-colour on ivory, h. 3.5 (1⅜), by John Bogle, signed. Dated 1781. Transferred from the National Gallery of Scotland 1982.

PG 2537   MAN. Water-colour on ivory, h. 3.5 (1⅜) (sight), by John Bogle, signed. Dated 1775. Transferred from the National Gallery of Scotland 1982.

PG 2538   WOMAN. Water-colour on ivory, h. 3.3 (1$^{5}/_{16}$) (sight), by John Bogle. Transferred from the National Gallery of Scotland 1982.

PG 2539   MAN. Water-colour on ivory, h. 4.7 (1⅞) (sight), by John Bogle, signed. Dated 1788. Transferred from the National Gallery of Scotland 1982.

PG 2540   MAN. Water-colour on ivory, h. 4 (1⅝) (sight), by John Bogle, signed. Dated 1789. Transferred from the National Gallery of Scotland 1982.

PG 2544   MAN. Water-colour on ivory, h. 3.8 (1½), by Richard Crosse. Transferred from the National Gallery of Scotland 1982.

PG 2545   WOMAN. Water-colour on ivory, h. 4 (1⅝), by John Donaldson, signed. Dated 1787. Transferred from the National Gallery of Scotland 1982.

PG 2552   a. MAN. Water-colour on ivory, h. 4 (1⅝) (sight), by Alexander Gallaway. b. WOMAN. Water-colour on ivory, h. 4 (1⅝) (sight), by Alexander Gallaway. Transferred from the National Gallery of Scotland 1982.

PG 2596   MAN. Wash drawing, 9.9 x 7.8 (3⅞ x 3$^{1}/_{16}$) (irregular oval), by Allan Ramsay senior. Provenance untraced.

PGL 24   MAN. Canvas, 44.2 x 38.4 (17⅜ x 15⅛), by Adriaen de Lelie, 1786, signed. On loan from the National Museums of Scotland.

PGL 54*   WOMAN. Pencil drawing, 54.8 x 39.4 (21$^{9}/_{16}$ x 15½), by John Brown. On loan from the National Museums of Scotland.

PGL 55*   MAN. Pencil drawing, 57.5 x 41.3 (22⅝ x 16¼), by John Brown. On loan from the National Museums of Scotland.

PGL 56   MAN. Pencil drawing, 53.9 x 40.2 (21¼ x 15⅞), by John Brown. On loan from the National Museums of Scotland.

PGL 57   MAN. Pencil drawing, 61.4 x 41.8 (24⅛ x 16$^{7}/_{16}$), by John Brown. On loan from the National Museums of Scotland.

PGL 58   MAN. Pencil drawing, 49 x 35 (19$^{5}/_{16}$ x 13¾), by John Brown. On loan from the National Museums of Scotland.

PGL 61*   MAN. Pencil drawing, 40 x 28.9 (15¾ x 11⅜), by John Brown. On loan from the National Museums of Scotland.

PGL 62*   MAN. Pencil drawing, 51.9 x 34.5 (20$^{7}/_{16}$ x 13$^{9}/_{16}$), by John Brown. On loan from the National Museums of Scotland.

PGL 63   MAN. Pencil drawing, 49.6 x 33.5 (19½ x 13$^{3}/_{16}$), by John Brown. On loan from the National Museums of Scotland.

PGL 81   MAN. Pencil drawing, 50.8 x 36.5 (20 x 14⅜), by John Brown. On loan from the National Museums of Scotland.

Unidentified
PG 1280

Unidentified
PG 1717

Unidentified
PG 1718

Unidentified
PG 2388

Unidentified
PG 2524

Unidentified
PG 2566

19TH CENTURY

PG 1280*   MAN. Water-colour, 46.4 x 61.6 (18¼ x 24¼), by Daniel Maclise, signed.
Purchased 1934.

PG 1377   MAN. Canvas, 35.1 x 29.2 (13¹³⁄₁₆ x 11½), by Sir George Reid, 1898, signed.
Purchased 1938.

PG 1717*   MAN. Chalk drawing, 55.8 x 40.6 (22 x 16), by William Bewick. Purchased
1927.

PG 1718*   MAN. Pencil and chalk drawing, 53.4 x 39.2 (21 x 15⁷⁄₁₆), by William Bewick.
Purchased 1927.

PG 1767   MAN. Pencil and water-colour, 23.9 x 17 (9⁷⁄₁₆ x 6¾), by Richard Dighton,
signed. Purchased 1946.

PG 1774   MAN. Water-colour, 48.4 x 40 (19 x 15¾), by Hope James Stewart, 1848,
signed. Purchased 1949.

PG 2122   MAN. Pencil and water-colour, 23.6 x 17.6 (9¼ x 6⅞), attributed to William
Nicholson. Transferred from the National Gallery of Scotland 1950.

PG 2163   MAN. Cut paper silhouette, h. 21 (8¼), by Augustin Edouart, 1830, signed.
Given by Mrs J. H. G. Ross 1969.

PG 2164   MAN. Cut paper silhouette, h. 15.4 (6¹⁄₁₆), by Augustin Edouart, 1830, signed.
Given by Mrs J. H. G. Ross 1969.

PG 2266   MAN. Pencil and white gouache drawing, 24.8 x 17.7 (9¾ x 7), by unknown
           artist. Dated 1843. Provenance untraced.

PG 2267   MAN. Pencil, red and white chalk drawing, 51.3 x 40.4 (20³/₁₆ x 15⅞), copy by
           unknown artist. Provenance untraced.

PG 2272   WOMAN. Pencil and water-colour drawing, 20.3 x 14.5 (8 x 5¾), by unknown
           artist. Dated 1842. Provenance untraced.

PG 2283   a. MAN. Cut paper silhouette, h. 20.9 (8¼), by Augustin Edouart, 1831,
           signed. Provenance untraced.
           b. MAN. Cut paper silhouette, h. 21.5 (8½), by Augustin Edouart, 1831,
           signed. Provenance untraced.

PG 2285   WOMAN. Water-colour, 24.5 x 19.8 (9¹¹/₁₆ x 7¹³/₁₆), by William Greenlees,
           1844, signed. Provenance untraced.

PG 2286   MAN. Ink drawing, 16.5 x 23.2 (6½ x 9⅛), by P. Benson Maxwell, 1873,
           signed. Provenance untraced.

PG 2288   WOMAN. Pencil drawing, 27.4 x 21.9 (10¾ x 8⅝), copy by unknown artist.
           Given by the legatees of J. A. Gardiner.

PG 2289   WOMAN. Pencil drawing, 27.5 x 22 (10¹³/₁₆ x 8⅝), copy by unknown artist.
           Given by the legatees of J. A. Gardiner.

PG 2290   MAN. Pencil drawing, 13.9 x 11.4 (5½ x 4½), copy by J. A. Gardiner after
           unknown artist. Given by the legatees of J. A. Gardiner.

PG 2292   MAN. Pencil drawing, 15.6 x 13.4 (6⅛ x 5¼), by unknown artist. Provenance
           untraced.

PG 2296   MAN. Pencil and red chalk drawing, 18.7 x 15.3 (7⅜ x 6), by unknown artist.
           Provenance untraced.

PG 2319   MAN. Water-colour on ivory, oval, 5.6 x 4.5 (2³/₁₆ x 1¾), attributed to Charles
           Robertson. Bequeathed by W. F. Watson 1886.

PG 2345   MAN. Ivory, oval, 5.9 x 4.5 (2⅜ x 1¾), by unknown artist. Bequeathed by
           W. F. Watson 1886.

PG 2388*   MAN. Pencil drawing, 24.4 x 20.4 (9⅝ x 8), by William Scoular, 1823, signed.
           Given by Mrs Gore Browne Henderson to the National Gallery of Scotland 1976
           and transferred 1977.

PG 2390   GIRL. (Possibly a daughter of the artist. A pair to PG 2389 William Thomson.)
           Pencil drawing, 25.5 x 20 (10 x 7⅞), by Peter Thomson. Given by Mrs Gore
           Browne Henderson to the National Gallery of Scotland 1976 and transferred
           1977.

PG 2411   MAN. Pencil, ink and wask drawing, 16.3 x 11.2 (6⁷/₁₆ x 4⅜), by Sir John
           Watson Gordon. Given by Miss Helen W. Thornton 1977.

PG 2412   TWO GIRLS. (With a large dog.) Pencil, chalk and wash drawing, 14.2 x 12
           (5⁹/₁₆ x 4¹¹/₁₆), by Sir John Watson Gordon. Given by Miss Helen W. Thornton
           1977.

PG 2421   MAN. Pencil, ink and wash drawing, 18.2 x 11.5 (7⁵/₃₂ x 4½), by Sir Daniel
           Macnee. Given by Dr Ruth Waddell 1978.

PG 2422   MAN. Pencil and ink drawing, 17.8 x 11.5 (7 x 4½), by Sir Daniel Macnee.
           Given by Dr Ruth Waddell 1978.

PG 2423   WOMAN. Pencil, ink and wash drawing, 18.2 x 11.6 (7³/₁₆ x 4⁹/₁₆), by Sir
           Daniel Macnee. Given by Dr Ruth Waddell 1978.

PG 2424   MAN. (Recto: five head studies. Verso: three head studies.) Ink drawing, 11.2 x 17.8 (4⅜ x 7), by Sir Daniel Macnee. Given by Dr Ruth Waddell 1978.

PG 2425   BOY AND GIRL. Pencil and ink drawing, 11.5 x 17.6 (4½ x 6¹⁵⁄₁₆), by Sir Daniel Macnee. Given by Dr Ruth Waddell 1978.

PG 2426   GIRL. (Probably the same sitter as PG 2428.) Pencil and ink drawing, 11.5 x 15.4 (4½ x 6¹⁄₁₆), by Sir Daniel Macnee. Given by Dr Ruth Waddell 1978.

PG 2427   TWO GIRLS. Pencil and ink drawing, 11.5 x 18 (4½ x 7⅛), by Sir Daniel Macnee. Given by Dr Ruth Waddell 1978.

PG 2428   GIRL. (Probably the same sitter as PG 2426.) Pencil drawing, 13.5 x 10.2 (5⁵⁄₁₆ x 4¹⁄₃₂), by Sir Daniel Macnee. Given by Dr Ruth Waddell 1978.

PG 2524*   MAN. Water-colour on ivory, h. 7.3 (2⅞), by Andrew Robertson, signed in monogram. Dated 1814. Transferred from the National Gallery of Scotland 1982.

PG 2527   WOMAN. Water-colour on ivory, h. 7.5 (2¹⁵⁄₁₆), by Andrew Robertson, signed in monogram. Dated 1807. Transferred from the National Gallery of Scotland 1982.

PG 2531   MAN. Water-colour on ivory, h. 7 (2¾), by Peter Paillou, signed. Dated 1809. Transferred from the National Gallery of Scotland 1982.

PG 2532   a. MAN. Water-colour on ivory, h. 7.5 (2¹⁵⁄₁₆), by Peter Paillou, signed. Dated 1819.
           b. WOMAN. (Probably the wife of a.) Water-colour on ivory, h. 7 (2¾) (sight), attributed to Peter Paillou.
           c. GIRL. Water-colour on ivory, h. 6.2 (2⁷⁄₁₆) (sight), by unknown artist.
           d. GIRL. Water-colour on ivory, h. 6.3 (2½) (sight), by unknown artist.
           e. GIRL. Water-colour on ivory, h. 6.3 (2½) (sight), by unknown artist.
           Transferred from the National Gallery of Scotland 1982.

PG 2535   GIRL. Water-colour on ivory, h. 7 (2¾), by John Bogle, signed. Transferred from the National Gallery of Scotland 1982.

PG 2548   MAN. Water-colour on ivory, h. 7.5 (2¹⁵⁄₁₆), by William Douglas. Transferred from the National Gallery of Scotland 1982.

PG 2549   GIRL. Water-colour on ivory, h. 5 (2) (sight), by Miss Archibald Ramsay Douglas or Mrs Robert Stuart. Transferred from the National Gallery of Scotland 1982.

PG 2555   WOMAN. Water-colour on ivory, h. 10.4 (4⅛), by Sir William Charles Ross. Painted 1842. Transferred from the National Gallery of Scotland 1982.

PG 2558   WOMAN. Water-colour on ivory, 10.2 x 7.7 (4 x 3) (octagonal), by George Sanders. Transferred from the National Gallery of Scotland 1982.

PG 2566*   MAN. Water-colour on ivory, 10.7 x 8.3 (4¼ x 3¼), by William John Thomson. Painted 1816. Transferred from the National Gallery of Scotland 1982.

PG 2567   GIRL. Water-colour on ivory, 17.8 x 11.4 (7 x 4½) (sight), by Robert Thorburn. Transferred from the National Gallery of Scotland 1982.

PG 2569   WOMAN. Water-colour on ivory, 15.2 x 10.7 (6 x 4¼) (sight), by Robert Thorburn. Transferred from the National Gallery of Scotland 1982.

PG 2570   WOMAN. Water-colour on ivory, 15.8 x 24.4 (6¼ x 9⅝) (sight), by Robert Thorburn. Transferred from the National Gallery of Scotland 1982.

PG 2572   WOMAN. Water-colour on ivory, 10.1 x 7.6 (4 x 3), by unknown artist.
Transferred from the National Gallery of Scotland 1982.

PG 2577   MAN. Bronzed silhouette in ink on plaster, h. 8.2 (3¼), by or after John Miers.
Transferred from the National Gallery of Scotland 1982.

PG 2579   MAN. Silhouette in ink on plaster, h. 8.2 (3¼), by or after John Miers.
Transferred from the National Gallery of Scotland 1982.

PG 2580   WOMAN. Silhouette painted on glass, 10.6 x 8.2 (4³⁄₁₆ x 3¼), by unknown
artist. Transferred from the National Gallery of Scotland 1982.

PG 2652   MAN. Canvas, 35.6 x 28 (14 x 11), by Robert Innes, signed on the reverse.
Dated 1825. Provenance untraced.

PG 2682   a. INFANTRY OFFICER. (Study for *The Battle of Alexandria* or *The
Landing of British Troops at Aboukir.*) Water-colour and pencil drawing,
8.5 x 7.3 (3⅜ x 2⅞) (irregular), attributed to Philip James de Loutherbourg.
Purchased 1986.
b. ARMY OFFICER. (Study for *The Battle of Alexandria* or *The Landing of
British Troops at Aboukir.*) Water-colour, 10.6 x 9.1 (4³⁄₁₆ x 3⁹⁄₁₆) (irregular),
attributed to Philip James de Loutherbourg. Purchased 1986.
d. MIDSHIPMAN. (Study for *The Landing of British Troops at Aboukir.*)
Water-colour, 7.6 x 6.3 (3¹⁄₁₆ x 2½), attributed to Philip James de Loutherbourg.
Purchased 1986.

PG 2713   MINISTER. Millboard, 13 x 11.7 (5⅛ x 4⅝) (irregular), by David Octavius
Hill. Given by Miss Aileen Graham 1987.

PG 2714   MINISTER. Millboard, 18.4 x 14.9 (7¼ x 5⅞) (irregular), by David Octavius
Hill. Given by Miss Aileen Graham 1987.

NUMERICAL INDEX OF THE PERMANENT COLLECTION

PG 571	Moore, Dr John
PG 572	Scott, Sir Walter
PG 573	Wilkie, Sir David
PG 574	Cockburn of Ormiston, John
PG 575	Scott, Sir Walter
PG 576	Tassie, James
PG 577	Geddes, Andrew
PG 578	Hume, David
PG 579	Stewart, Prince Henry Benedict
PG 580	Wishart, George
PG 581	De Quincey, Thomas
PG 582	Mackay, Charles
PG 583	Argyll, 1st Marquess of
PG 584	Wilkie, Sir David
PG 585	Napier, Sir William
PG 586	Napier, Sir Charles James
PG 587	Napier, David
PG 588	Dundee, Viscount
PG 589	Anstruther, Sir John
PG 590	Findlay, John Ritchie
PG 591	Chalmers, Rev. Thomas
PG 592	Jamesone, George
PG 593	Lauder, Robert Scott
PG 594	Stewart, Prince Charles Edward
PG 595	Skirving, Archibald
PG 596	Skirving, Adam
PG 597	Clyde, 1st Baron
PG 598	Mansfield, 1st Earl
PG 599	Roberts, David
PG 600	Tait, Professor Peter Guthrie
PG 601	Raeburn, Sir Henry
PG 602	Chantrey, Sir Francis Legatt
PG 603	Dewar, Professor Sir James
PG 604	Wilson, Professor John
PG 605	Paton, Sir Joseph Noël
PG 606	Montgomery, Robert
PG 607	Pitt, William
PG 608	Jeffrey, Lord
PG 609	Constable, Archibald
PG 610	Nairne, Baroness, with William Murray Nairne
PG 611	Steell, Sir John
PG 612	Fowler, Sir John
PG 613	Arrol, Sir William
PG 614	Linlithgow, 1st Marquess of
PG 615	Hume, David
PG 616	Syme, James
PG 617	Cunningham, Rev. William
PG 618	Spencer, Hubert
PG 619	Paton, Sir Joseph Noël
PG 620	Hill, David Octavius
PG 621	Dalrymple, Sir Hew
PG 622	Stewart, Prince Charles Edward
PG 623	Albany, Duchess of
PG 624	Stewart, Prince Henry Benedict
PG 625	Eldin, Lord
PG 626	Philip, John
PG 627	Young, Sir Peter
PG 628	Scott, Sir Walter
PG 629	Chambers, Sir William
PG 630	Colville, Sir Charles
PG 631	Smiles, Samuel
PG 632	Hill, Amelia Robertson
PG 633	Macleod, Rev. Norman
PG 634	Paterson, Sir Hugh
PG 635	Rollock, Rev. Robert
PG 636	Watt, James
PG 637	Carlyle, Thomas
PG 638	Murray-Pulteney, Sir James
PG 639	Murray, Sir George
PG 640	Duff, Rev. Alexander
PG 641	Ramsay, Allan (junior)
PG 642	Thomson, James
PG 643	Stevenson, Flora Clift
PG 644	Baird, Sir David
PG 645	Campbell, Lady Charlotte
PG 646	Wilson, Professor John
PG 647	Macpherson, Sir John
PG 648	Anderson, James Robertson
PG 649	Faucit, Helen
PG 650	Leitch, William Leighton
PG 651	Walker, Thomas
PG 652	Henderson, John
PG 653	Mar, 1st Earl of
PG 654	Park, Patric
PG 655	Hope of Hopetoun, Sir James
PG 656	Scott, Anne Rutherford
PG 657	Stevenson, Robert
PG 658	Brown, Andrew Betts
PG 659	Cunningham, Allan
PG 660	Leslie, Professor Sir John
PG 661	Glencairn, 9th Earl of
PG 662	Scott, Sir Walter
PG 663	Dick, Professor William
PG 664	Edward VII
PG 665	Macdonald, George
PG 666	Tytler, Patrick Fraser
PG 667	Jeffrey, Lord
PG 668	Newton, Lord
PG 669	Jones, John Paul
PG 670	Gladstone, William Ewart
PG 671	Small, John
PG 672	Manson, George
PG 673	Bough, Samuel
PG 674	Faed, Thomas
PG 675	Lauder, James Eckford
PG 676	Blackie, Professor John Stuart
PG 677	Brougham and Vaux, 1st Baron
PG 678	Masson, Professor David
PG 679	Phillip, John
PG 680	Smith, Professor William Robertson
PG 681	Kelvin, Baron
PG 682	James I
PG 683	James II
PG 684	James III
PG 685	James IV
PG 686	James V
PG 687	Chalmers, Rev. Thomas
PG 688	Cunningham, Rev. William
PG 689	Clason, Rev. Dr Patrick
PG 690	Taylor, Rev. James
PG 691	Balfour, 1st Earl of

PG 812 Webster, Rev. Alexander
PG 813 Keith, James
PG 814 Hamilton, Duchess of
PG 815 Charles I
PG 816 Dunbar, Earl of
PG 817 Crawford, 17th Earl of
PG 818 Haddington, 1st Earl of
PG 819 Marchmont, 2nd Earl of
PG 820 Irving, Rev. Edward
PG 821 Stewart, Professor Dugald
PG 822 Kames, Lord
PG 823 McAdam, John Loudoun
PG 824 Porter, Sir Robert Ker, with his family
PG 825 Scott, Sir Walter, and his friends at Abbotsford
PG 826 Beaton, Mary
PG 827 Graham, Thomas
PG 828 Orchardson, Sir William Quiller
PG 829 Drummond, Sir George
PG 830 Ferrier, Susan
PG 831 Knox, Dr Robert
PG 832 Inglis, Rev. Dr John
PG 833 Mackenzie, William Forbes
PG 834 Mackenzie, Sir George
PG 835 Cathcart, 1st Earl of
PG 836 Chalmers, Rev. Thomas
PG 837 Gladstone, William Ewart
PG 838 Henley, William Ernest
PG 839 Morton, 4th Earl of
PG 840 Hamilton, 4th Duke of
PG 841 Burke, William
PG 842 Finlay, Justine. Transferred to the National Gallery of Scotland (NG 1192)
PG 843 Bell, Henry Glassford
PG 844 Livingstone, David
PG 845 Carlyle, Thomas
PG 846 Wales, Henry, Prince of
PG 847 Stevenson, Robert Louis
PG 848 Harvey, Sir George
PG 849 Wyndham, Robert Henry
PG 850 William IV
PG 851 Brougham and Vaux, 1st Baron
PG 852 Brown, Dr John
PG 853 Chalmers, Rev. Thomas
PG 854 Reid, Sir George
PG 855 Whyte, Rev. Alexander
PG 856 Chalmers, George Paul
PG 857 Argyll, 8th Duke of
PG 858 Charles I with James VII and II (as Duke of York)
PG 859 Hamilton, 2nd Duke of
PG 860 Rothes, 1st Duke of
PG 861 Rosslyn, 1st Earl of
PG 862 Henderson, Alexander
PG 863 Nelson, Viscount
PG 864 Lennox, 2nd Duke of
PG 865 Anderson, Joseph
PG 866 Wellington, 1st Duke of
PG 867 Donald, John Milne
PG 868 Irving, Rev. Edward
PG 869 Bothwell, 4th Earl of

PG 870 Bothwell, Countess of
PG 871 Elgin, 9th Earl of
PG 872 Balfour of Burleigh, 6th Lord
PG 873 Gillespie, Rev. John
PG 874 MacCunn, Hamish
PG 875 Orchardson, Sir William Quiller
PG 876 Russell, John Scott
PG 877 Haldane, 1st Viscount
PG 878 Bryce, 1st Viscount
PG 879 Millar, Dr James
PG 880 Gardner, Alexander
PG 881 Chalmers, George Paul
PG 882 Brougham and Vaux, 1st Baron
PG 883 Smith, Alexander
PG 884 Kelvin, Baron
PG 885 Graham, Robert Cunningham
PG 886 Sobieska, Princess Clementina
PG 887 Stewart, Prince Charles Edward
PG 888 Stewart, Prince Henry Benedict
PG 889 Murray, Sir George
PG 890 Fletcher of Saltoun, Andrew
PG 891 Grose, Francis
PG 892 Kay, John
PG 893 Carlyle, Thomas
PG 894 Bruce, Sir William
PG 895 Fergusson, Robert
PG 896 Rothes, 8th Earl of
PG 897 Rothes, Countess of
PG 898 Carlyle, Thomas (Carlyle's house at Craigenputtock)
PG 899 Orleans, Duchess of
PG 900 Albemarle, 1st Duke of
PG 901 James VII and II
PG 902 Huntly, 2nd Marquess of
PG 903 Drummond, Robert Hay
PG 904 Murray, William Henry
PG 905a,b Wellington, 1st Duke of
PG 906 Buccleuch, 5th Duke of
PG 907 Belhaven, 2nd Lord
PG 908 Argyll, 3rd Duke of
PG 909 Stewart, Prince James Francis Edward
PG 910 Cumberland, Duke of
PG 911 Bell, Henry
PG 912 Campbell, 1st Baron
PG 913 Parker, Charles Stuart
PG 914a,b Robert I (Robert the Bruce)
PG 915 Orchardson, Sir William Quiller
PG 916 Charles I
PG 917 Anne, Queen
PG 918 George I
PG 919 Forbes, Professor Edward
PG 920 Liston, Robert
PG 921 Mary II
PG 922 James VII and II
PG 923 Stewart, Prince James Francis Edward
PG 924 Balfour, 1st Earl of
PG 925 Atholl, 2nd Duke of
PG 926 Kelvin, Baron
PG 927 Gordon, Duchess of with Lady Wallace
PG 928 Munro, Neil
PG 929 Stewart, Prince Charles Edward

PG 1522   Scott, Sir Walter
PG 1523   Scott, Sir Walter
PG 1524   Scott, Sir Walter
PG 1525   Pryde, James
PG 1526   Hope, Sir Thomas
PG 1527   Stewart, Prince James Francis Edward
PG 1528   Leven, 3rd Earl of
PG 1529   Sharp, James
PG 1530   Waterford, Marchioness of,
           with Countess Canning
PG 1531   Perth, 2nd titular Duke of
PG 1532   Melville, 1st Earl of
PG 1533   Mary II
PG 1534   Blackadder, John
PG 1535   Stewart, Prince Charles Edward
PG 1536   Mylne, John
PG 1537   Horner, Francis
PG 1538   Lauderdale, 8th Earl of
PG 1539   Jeffrey, Lord
PG 1540   Seymour, Lord John Webb
PG 1541   Grahame, Rev. James
PG 1542   Stewart, Dugald
PG 1543   Bell, Charles
PG 1544   Syme, John
PG 1545   Syme, John
PG 1546   Macpherson of Cluny, Andrew
PG 1547   Nasmyth, James
PG 1548   Horne, Viscount
PG 1549   Abercromby, Sir Ralph
PG 1550   Forbes of Culloden, John
PG 1551   Balfour, Sir James
PG 1552   Lauder, Sir Harry
PG 1553   Belhaven, 2nd Baron
PG 1554   Kimmerghame, Lord
PG 1555   Medina, Sir John
PG 1556   Hyndford, 3rd Earl of
PG 1557   Selkirk, 6th Earl of
PG 1558   Mary of Guise
PG 1559   Victoria, Queen
PG 1560   Stewart, Sir Donald Martin
PG 1561   Byron, 6th Lord
PG 1562   Edward VII
PG 1563   Alexandra, Queen
PG 1564   Home, Rev. John
PG 1565   Hay of Edington, William
PG 1566   Keith, George Skene
PG 1567   Inglis, Charles
PG 1568   Gordon, Sir Alexander Hamilton
PG 1569   Scott, Sir Walter
PG 1570   Caw, Sir James Lewis
PG 1571   Tweeddale, 8th Marquess of
PG 1572   Robertson, Sir Charles Grant
PG 1573   Murray of Elibank, 1st Baron
PG 1574   Steuart, John
PG 1575   Steuart, George Drummond
PG 1576   Steuart, Robert
PG 1577   Steuart, Thomas
PG 1578   Cochrane, Sir Alexander
PG 1579   Gillespie, William
PG 1580   Hardie, James Keir
PG 1581   Kennedy, David

PG 1582   Erskine, Henry
PG 1583   Gosford, Lord
PG 1584   McArthur, John
PG 1585   Macaulay, 1st Baron
PG 1586   Lumisden, Andrew
PG 1587   Adam, Patrick William
PG 1588   Lockhart, John Gibson
PG 1589   Faed, Thomas, with John Ballantyne
           and Sir William Fettes Douglas
PG 1590   Faed, James
PG 1591   Faed, Thomas
PG 1592   Guthrie, Rev. Thomas
PG 1593   Carlyle, Thomas
PG 1594   Traquair, Phoebe Anna
PG 1595   Farquhar, Sir Arthur
PG 1596   Argyll, 4th Duke of
PG 1597   Perth, 4th titular Duke of
PG 1598   Irwin, Dr John
PG 1599   Bruce, Thomas
PG 1600   Henderson of Fordell, Sir John
PG 1601   Henderson of Fordell, Sir Robert
PG 1602   Henderson of Fordell, Sir James
PG 1603   Henderson of Fordell, Sir Francis
PG 1604   Arab Princess
PG 1605   Durham, Sir Philip Charles
PG 1606   Owen, Robert
PG 1607   Carrington, Lord
PG 1608   Scott, David
PG 1609   Strathmore, 1st Earl of
PG 1610   Haddington, 6th Earl of
PG 1611   Argyll, 9th Earl of
PG 1612   Constable, Thomas
PG 1613   Stewart, Prince Charles Edward
PG 1614   James VII and II. Transferred to PGL 230
           (loan since returned)
PG 1615   Braxfield, Lord
PG 1616   Wallace, Sir William
PG 1617   Buchan, Earl of
PG 1618   James II
PG 1619   Elphinstone, William
PG 1620   Knox, John, the younger
PG 1621   Maitland of Lethington, William
PG 1622   Buchanan, George
PG 1623   Crichton, James
PG 1624   Lennox, 1st Duke of
PG 1625   Erskine of Gogar, Sir Alexander
PG 1626   Leslie, John
PG 1627   Fraser, Sir Alexander
PG 1628   Mar, 2nd Earl of
PG 1629   Forbes, Bishop William
PG 1630   Johnston, Arthur
PG 1631   Mar, Countess of
PG 1632   Gordon of Straloch, Robert
PG 1633   Gordon of Straloch, Robert
PG 1634   Erskine, Alexander
PG 1635   Buchan, 6th Earl of
PG 1636   Cardross, 2nd Lord
PG 1637   Gregory, Professor James
PG 1638   Newark, 1st Lord
PG 1639   Belhaven, 2nd Baron
PG 1640   Gregory, Professor James

PG 1641	Trail, Rev. Robert		PG 1701	Paton, Sir Joseph Noël
PG 1642	Fletcher of Saltoun, Andrew		PG 1702	Findlay, John Ritchie
PG 1643	MacLaurin, Colin		PG 1703	Richardson, Adam Black
PG 1644	Short, James		PG 1704	Carfrae, Robert
PG 1645	Buchan, Countess of		PG 1705	Dickson, Thomas
PG 1646	James I		PG 1706	Munro, Robert
PG 1647	James V		PG 1707	Brodie, Sir Thomas Dawson
PG 1648	James VI and I		PG 1708	Cochran-Patrick, R. W.
PG 1649	Anne of Denmark		PG 1709	Turner, Professor Sir William
PG 1650	James I		PG 1710	Bute, 3rd Marquess of
PG 1651	James V		PG 1711	Goudie, Gilbert
PG 1652	James VI and I		PG 1712	Brown, John Taylor
PG 1653	Anne of Denmark		PG 1713	Maxwell, Sir Herbert Eustace
PG 1654	James III		PG 1714	Lothian, 9th Marquess of
PG 1655	Margaret, Queen		PG 1715	Victoria, Queen
PG 1656	Boncle, Sir Edward		PG 1716	Wolfe, James
PG 1657	James III		PG 1717	Unidentified
PG 1658	Knox, John		PG 1718	Unidentified
PG 1659	Charles I		PG 1719	Sheil, Richard Lalor
PG 1660	Perth, 5th titular Duke of		PG 1720	Anderson, Alexander
PG 1661	Perth, Duchess of		PG 1721	Same as PG 1120; number eliminated
PG 1662	Perth, 3rd titular Duke of, with Lord Seaforth		PG 1722	Maguire, William
			PG 1723	Nicol, Erskine
PG 1663	Milton, Lord		PG 1724	Prout, Samuel
PG 1664	Arniston, Lord		PG 1725	Bridgeman, John
PG 1665	Macdonald, Flora		PG 1726	Charlotte Augusta, Princess
PG 1666	Douglass, Robert		PG 1727	Rutherfurd, Lord
PG 1667	Bruce of Kinnaird, James		PG 1728	Wilson, Andrew
PG 1668	Muir, Thomas		PG 1729	Gray, John Miller
PG 1669	Hay, Katherine		PG 1730	Scott, Thomas
PG 1670	Pratts, George		PG 1731	Scott, Sir Walter
PG 1671	Sempill, 14th Lord		PG 1732	James III
PG 1672	Elliot, Jane or Jean		PG 1733	James II
PG 1673	Ballantyne, John		PG 1734	Grant, John
PG 1674	Lindsay, Lady Anne		PG 1735	Bruce, Alexander
PG 1675	Laing, Malcolm		PG 1736	Strathnairn, Baron
PG 1676	Ainslie, John		PG 1737	Huntly, 1st Marquess of, with Marchioness of Huntly
PG 1677	Sharpe, Charles Kirkpatrick			
PG 1678	Scott, Sir Walter		PG 1738	Louise, Princess (Duchess of Argyll)
PG 1679	Napier, Sir Charles James		PG 1739	Brown, William Beattie
PG 1680a,b	Napier, Sir Charles		PG 1740	Cameron, Hugh
PG 1681	Sheriff, John		PG 1741	Cameron, Mary
PG 1682	Johnstone, William Borthwick		PG 1742	Gibb, Robert
PG 1683	Jardine, Sir William		PG 1743	Macdonald, John Blake
PG 1684	Bridges, David		PG 1744	McKay, William Darling
PG 1685	Daer, Lord		PG 1745	Hardie, Charles Martin
PG 1686	Leyden, John		PG 1746	Reid, George Ogilvy
PG 1687	Bain, Sir James		PG 1747	Smart, John
PG 1688	Playfair, Professor John		PG 1748	Vallance, William Fleming
PG 1689	Napier, Professor Macvey		PG 1749	Clason, Rev. Dr Patrick
PG 1690	Stewart, Prince Charles Edward		PG 1750	Clason, Rev. Robert
PG 1691	Black, Adam		PG 1751	Lockhart, Rev. Dr John
PG 1692	Mitchell, Sir Arthur		PG 1752	Robertson, Rev. Dr John
PG 1693	Christison, David		PG 1753	Logan, Rev. George
PG 1694	Duns, Professor John		PG 1754	Hutchison, Rev. Alexander
PG 1695	Anderson, Joseph		PG 1755	Livingston, Rev. Archibald
PG 1696	Macdonald, James		PG 1756	Gordon, Mr
PG 1697	Macleod, Sir Reginald		PG 1757a,b	Hodgson, Rev. Dr John
PG 1698	Mackay, Aeneas James George		PG 1758	French, Rev. James
PG 1699	Anderson, Sir Robert Rowand		PG 1759	Tent Preaching at Bothwell
PG 1700	Douglas, Sir William Fettes		PG 1760a,b	Scottish National Portrait Gallery

PG 2466	Roberts, David	PG 2524	Unidentified
PG 2467	Walton, E. A., with Helen Law	PG 2525	Lieven, Princess
PG 2468	Fordyce, Rev. James	PG 2526	Robertson, Mary
PG 2469	Cowan, Charles	PG 2527	Unidentified
PG 2470	Cowan, Alexander	PG 2528	Medwyn, Lord
PG 2471	Darnley, Lord	PG 2529	Medwyn, Lord
PG 2472	Hamilton, Gavin	PG 2530	Crooks, Adam
PG 2473	Skirving of Croys, Robert	PG 2531	Unidentified
PG 2474	Grant of Laggan, Anne	PG 2532a	Unidentified
PG 2475	Reith, 1st Baron	b	Unidentified
PG 2476	Glenorchy, Viscountess	c	Unidentified
PG 2477	Spreull, James	d	Unidentified
PG 2478	Hutton, Lady	PG 2533	Kerr of Buchtrigg, Captain Charles Kerr
PG 2479	Hutton, Lady	PG 2534	Unidentified
PG 2480	Crawhall, Joseph	PG 2535	Unidentified
PG 2481	Walton, Professor John	PG 2536	Unidentified
PG 2482	Walton, E. A.	PG 2537	Unidentified
PG 2483	Carnegie, Andrew	PG 2538	Unidentified
PG 2484	Walton, E. A., with Joseph Crawhall	PG 2539	Unidentified
	and Sir James Guthrie	PG 2540	Unidentified
PG 2485	Walton, E. A.	PG 2541	Ferguson, James
PG 2486	Redpath, Anne	PG 2542	Siddons, Sarah
PG 2487	Colquhoun, Robert with Robert MacBryde	PG 2543	Crooks, Miss
PG 2488	Sakeouse, John	PG 2544	Unidentified
PG 2489	Douglas, George Norman	PG 2545	Unidentified
PG 2490	Sivell, Robert	PG 2546	Bulstrode, Richard
PG 2491	Paterson, Hamish	PG 2547	Jeffrey, Rev. Robert
PG 2492	Wilson, Scottie	PG 2548	Unidentified
PG 2493	Lamond, Frederic	PG 2549	Unidentified
PG 2494	Crozier, William	PG 2550	Wauchope, James
PG 2495	MacTaggart, Sir William	PG 2551	Dymock, Wilhelmina
PG 2496	MacTaggart, Sir William	PG 2552a	Unidentified
PG 2497	Stewart, Professor Dugald	b	Unidentified
PG 2498	Anderson, William	PG 2553	Cathcart, Mr
PG 2499	Charlotte Augusta, Princess	PG 2554	Cathcart, Mrs
PG 2500	Maxwell, John	PG 2555	Unidentified
PG 2501	McGlashan, Archibald	PG 2556	Simson, Harriet Elizabeth
PG 2502	Crawford, 28th Earl of	PG 2557	Hunter, Oswald
PG 2503	Stewart, Helen	PG 2558	Unidentified
PG 2504	Stewart, Colonel Matthew	PG 2559	Ridding, William
PG 2505	Mackenzie, Sir Compton	PG 2560	Ridding, Ellen
PG 2506	Hunter, Rev. Dr Henry	PG 2561	Dalrymple, Sir Hew Whitefoord
PG 2507	Rogerson, John	PG 2562	Dalrymple, Sir John Adolphus
PG 2508	Mary, Queen of Scots	PG 2563	Fanshawe, General Sir Edward
PG 2509	Dobson, Henry John	PG 2564	Fanshawe, Lady
PG 2510	Dempster of Dunnichen, George	PG 2565	Fanshawe, Sir Edward Gennys
PG 2511	Baptism of Prince Charles Edward Stewart	PG 2566	Unidentified
PG 2512	Moir, David Macbeth	PG 2567	Unidentified
PG 2513	Murray-Pulteney, Sir James	PG 2568	Monro, Lady
	with Sir John Murray	PG 2569	Unidentified
PG 2514	Dott, Aitken	PG 2570	Unidentified
PG 2515	Fergusson, John Duncan	PG 2571	Mount Edgecumbe, Countess of
PG 2516	Barnes, Sir Harry Jefferson	PG 2572	Unidentified
PG 2517	Barnes, Sir Harry Jefferson	PG 2573	Bagot, Lady [de-accessioned]
PG 2518	Barnes, Sir Harry Jefferson	PG 2574	Plimer, Joanna [de-accessioned]
PG 2519	Rushforth, Dr Winifred	PG 2575	Plimer, Charlotte, with Andrew, Louisa and
PG 2520	Crawford, Hugh Adam		Joanna Plimer [de-accessioned]
PG 2521	Watt, George Fiddes	PG 2576	Bute, 2nd Marquess of
PG 2522	Stewart, Prince Charles Edward, with Prince	PG 2577	Unidentified
	Henry Benedict Stewart	PG 2578	Aspinall, Mr
PG 2523	Johnstone, Commodore George	PG 2579	Unidentified

PG 2580 Unidentified
PG 2581 Dalyell, Sir John Graham
PG 2582 Innes, Gilbert
PG 2583 Adam, Patrick William
PG 2584 Silhouette Album c. 1782–c. 1818
PG 2585 Marshall, Colonel William
PG 2586 Blake, George with Neil Gunn and Douglas
         Young
PG 2587 Crozier, William
PG 2588 MacTaggart, Sir William
PG 2589 Mansfield, 1st Earl of
PG 2590 Adam, Robert
PG 2591 Black, Professor Joseph
PG 2592 Scott, Francis George
PG 2593 Macrae, Duncan
PG 2594 Terry, Daniel
PG 2595 Easton, Rev. Alexander
PG 2596 Unidentified
PG 2597 Poets' Pub
PG 2598 Elizabeth, the Queen Mother
PG 2599 Stevenson, Ronald
PG 2600 Allan, Shirley
PG 2601 Byres of Tonley, James, with his family
PG 2602 Dott, Peter McOmish
PG 2603 Ramsay, Anne
PG 2604 Grieve, Christopher Murray
PG 2605 Dott, Jean Morton
PG 2606 McGlashan, Archibald
PG 2607 Cameron, Sir David Young
PG 2608 Napier, Lady
PG 2609 Macdonald, Sir Alexander
PG 2610 Seaforth, 1st Earl of: fencing scene
PG 2611 Seaforth, 1st Earl of: concert party
PG 2612 Watt, James
PG 2613 Wilson, Margaret
PG 2614 Ewart, David
PG 2615 Grant of Laggan, Anne
PG 2616 Laing, Ronald David
PG 2617 Spark, Muriel
PG 2618 Grieve, Christopher Murray
PG 2619 Edinburgh from Canonmills
PG 2620 Graham of Gartmore, Robert Cunninghame
PG 2621 Fleming, Sir Sandford
PG 2622 Brown, Major Alexander
PG 2623 Morison, Sir Alexander
PG 2624 Leslie, Charles
PG 2625 Smith, Dr John
PG 2626 Douglas, Sir William Fettes
PG 2627 Alexander, Robert
PG 2628 Wilson, George
PG 2629 Form versus Fashion [ex-catalogue]
PG 2630 Munro, Sir Hugh Thomas
PG 2631a–k Scottish National Portrait Gallery
         (cartoons for processional frieze)
PG 2632 Davie, Alan, with John Bellany
PG 2633 Guthrie, Rev. Thomas
PG 2634 Thurso, 1st Viscount
PG 2635 Glenshiel, Battle of
PG 2636 Mavor, Osborne Henry
PG 2637 Grieve, Christopher Murray
PG 2638 Neill, Alexander Sutherland

PG 2639 Scott, Francis George
PG 2640 Duncan, 1st Viscount
PG 2641 Wallace, Robert
PG 2642 Erskine, Rev. Dr John
PG 2643 Riddell, John
PG 2644 Freer, Robert
PG 2645 Sym, Robert
PG 2646 Stewart, Margaret Ferooza
PG 2647 Hunter, William
PG 2648 Bruce, Sir John
PG 2649 Muir, Thomas Scott
PG 2650 Crawhall, Joseph
PG 2651 Ochterlony, Sir David
PG 2652 Unidentified
PG 2653 Nicholson, Sir William,
         with Mabel Nicholson
PG 2654 Grose, Francis
PG 2655 Primrose, Bouverie Francis
PG 2656 Scott, Sir Walter
PG 2657 Scott, Sir Walter
PG 2658 Scott, Sir Walter
PG 2659 Scott, Sir Walter
PG 2660 Scott, Sir Walter (plan of the hall pavement
         at Abbotsford)
PG 2661 Scott, Sir Walter
PG 2662 Scott, Sir Walter
PG 2663 Scott, James Bruce
PG 2664 Lee, R. A.
PG 2665 W. O. Hutchison Sketchbook 1952
PG 2666 W. O. Hutchison Sketchbook 1957
PG 2667 W. O. Hutchison Sketchbook 1966
PG 2668 Hutchison, Sir William Oliphant
PG 2669 Hutchison, Sir William Oliphant
PG 2670 Hutchison, Lady, with Henry Peter
         Hutchison and Robert Edward Hutchison
PG 2671a–e W. O. Hutchison landscape sketches
         [ex-catalogue]
PG 2672 Lockhart, John Gibson,
         with Charlotte Sophia Lockhart
PG 2673 Wood, Wendy
PG 2674 Murray, Hugh
PG 2675 MacGregor, John
PG 2676 Gibson, Sir Alexander
PG 2677 Blackie, Professor John Stuart
PG 2678 Buchanan, George
PG 2679 Manson, James Bolivar
PG 2680 Battle of Alexandria
PG 2681 Landing at Aboukir
PG 2682a Unidentified
      b Unidentified
      c Smith, Sir William Sydney
      d Unidentified
      e Moreau, General Jean-Victor
PG 2683a Doyle, Sir John
      b Finch, Edward
      c Baird, Sir David
      d Duncan, J.
PG 2684a Dyer, Sir Thomas
      b Sutton, Sir Charles
      c Ludlow, 3rd Earl
      d Cavan, 7th Earl of

LONG-TERM LOANS TO THE COLLECTION

PGL 1   Arran, 2nd Earl of [loan returned]
PGL 2   Arran, 3rd Earl of [loan returned]
PGL 3   Hamilton, Marchioness of [loan returned]
PGL 4   Hamilton, Marchioness of [loan returned]
PGL 5   Hamilton, 2nd Duke of, with 1st Duke of Lauderdale [loan returned]
PGL 6   Hamilton, 1st Duke of [acquired, PG 2722]
PGL 7   Sharp, James [loan returned]
PGL 8   Orkney, 1st Earl of [loan returned]
PGL 9   Hamilton, Count Anthony [loan returned]
PGL 10   Ramsay, Allan (junior) [loan returned]
PGL 11   Hamilton, 4th Duke of [loan returned]
PGL 12   Hamilton, 4th Duke of
PGL 13   Hamilton, 8th Duke of, with Dr John Moore and (Sir) John Moore [loan returned]
PGL 14   Thomson, Rev. John
PGL 15   Hogg, James
PGL 16   Wilkie, Sir David
         Wilkie, Isabella [loans returned]
PGL 17   James VI and I
PGL 18   Inglis or Kello, Esther
PGL 19   Anderson of Finzeauch, David
PGL 20   Murray of Gorthy, Sir David
PGL 21   Purves, Sir William
PGL 22   Marchmont, 1st Earl of
PGL 23   Lockhart, Sir George
PGL 24   Unidentified
PGL 25   Nisbet, Sir John
PGL 26   Murray, Alexander
PGL 27   Burnet, Gilbert
PGL 28   Wade, George
PGL 29   Smellie, William
PGL 30   Clerk of Eldin, John
PGL 31   Runciman, Alexander, with John Brown
PGL 32   Runciman, John
PGL 33   Tassie, James
PGL 34   Macfarlan, Walter
PGL 35   Sharpe, Charles Kirkpatrick
PGL 36   Stewart, Professor Dugald
PGL 37   Henry, Rev. Robert
PGL 38   Watson, Dr Robert
PGL 39   Hastings, 1st Marquess of
PGL 40   Rutherfurd, Lord
PGL 41   Scott, Sir Walter
PGL 42   Geddes, Andrew
PGL 43   Hamilton, Professor Sir William
PGL 44   Playfair, Professor John
PGL 45   Laing, David
PGL 46   Burns, Robert [acquired, PG 1085]
PGL 47   Halkett, Samuel
PGL 48   Wellwood, Rev. Sir Henry Moncrieff
PGL 49   Monro, Alexander ('Primus') [loan returned]
PGL 50   Meadowbank, Lord [loan returned]
PGL 51   Moncrieff, Lord

PGL 52   Smellie, William
PGL 53   Terry, Daniel, with Elizabeth Terry (Dull Readings) [loan returned]
PGL 54   Unidentified
PGL 55   Unidentified
PGL 56   Unidentified
PGL 57   Unidentified
PGL 58   Unidentified
PGL 59   Reid, Professor Thomas [loan returned]
PGL 60   Douglas, Sir Neil [acquired, PG 1866]
PGL 61   Unidentified
PGL 62   Unidentified
PGL 63   Unidentified
PGL 64   Smellie, William
PGL 65   Robertson, Roger
PGL 66   Paton, George
PGL 67   Anderson, William
PGL 68   Barclay, Rev. George
PGL 69   Baxter, John
PGL 70   Brown, Alexander
PGL 71   Brown, Dr John
PGL 72   Buchan, 11th Earl of
PGL 73   Cardonnel, Adam de
PGL 74   Dalrymple, Sir John
PGL 75   Deuchar, David
PGL 76   Drummond, Alexander
PGL 77   Duncan, Andrew
PGL 78   Erskine of Cambus, John
PGL 79   Gordon, Rev. Alexander
PGL 80   Henderson of Fordell, Sir John
PGL 81   Unidentified
PGL 82   Jeans, William
PGL 83   Dick, Sir Alexander
PGL 84   Caw, John
PGL 85   Little, William Charles
PGL 86   Cummyng, James
PGL 87   Montgomery, Sir James William
PGL 88   Runciman, Alexander
PGL 89   Opie, John
PGL 90   Macdonell, Sir James [acquired, PG 1465]
PGL 91   Pope, Alexander [loan returned]
PGL 92   Scott, Sir Walter [loan returned]
PGL 93   Wales, Henry, Prince of [loan returned]
PGL 94   Craighall, Lord
PGL 95   Hope, Lady
PGL 96   Ferguson, James [loan returned]
PGL 97   Napier, Sir Charles James [loan returned]
PGL 98   Campbell, Thomas [loan returned]
PGL 99   Lyell, Sir Charles [loan returned]
PGL 100 Middleton, 2nd Earl of [loan returned]
PGL 101 Brown, Robert [loan returned]
PGL 102 Sinclair, Sir John [acquired by the National Gallery of Scotland, NG 2301]
PGL 103 Nicol, Erskine [acquired, PG 1160]

PGL 104 Jones, John Paul
PGL 105 Owen, Robert [loan returned]
PGL 106 Bothwell, 4th Earl of '
PGL 107 Forbes of Pitsligo, Sir William [loan returned]
PGL 108 Macdonald, George
PGL 109 Bothwell, 4th Earl of (called) [loan returned]
PGL 110 Morton, 4th Earl of [acquired, PG 1857]
PGL 111 Morton, 8th Earl of [acquired, PG 1858]
PGL 112 Southesk, 1st Earl of [loan returned]
PGL 113 Montrose, 1st Marquess of [loan returned]
PGL 114 Lauderdale, 1st Duke of [loan returned]
PGL 115 Carrington, Lord [loan returned]
PGL 116 Sharp, Archbishop James [loan returned]
PGL 117 Hamilton, 2nd Duke of [loan returned]
PGL 118 Charles I [loan returned]
PGL 119 Lockhart, John Gibson [loan returned]
PGL 120 Monmouth and Buccleuch, Duke of [loan returned]
PGL 121 Beaton, Cardinal David [loan returned]
PGL 122 Elcho, Lord [loan returned]
PGL 123 Melville, 1st Viscount
PGL 124 Braganza, Catherine of
PGL 125 York, Duchess of
PGL 126 Prestongrange, Lord [acquired, PG 1509]
PGL 127 Queensberry, 2nd Duke of [acquired, PG 1171]
PGL 128 Argyll, Countess of [acquired, PG 1409]
PGL 129 Argyll, 1st Marquess of [acquired, PG 1408]
PGL 130 Ancram, 1st Earl of [loan returned]
PGL 131 Lothian, 1st Marquess of [acquired, PG 1414]
PGL 132 Lothian, Marchioness of [acquired, PG 1415]
PGL 133 Argyll, 9th Earl of [acquired, PG 1412]
PGL 134 Argyll, Marchioness of [acquired, PG 1413]
PGL 135 Lothian, 1st Marquess of [acquired, PG 1410]
PGL 136 Leven, 1st Earl of [acquired, PG 1411]
PGL 137 George IV [loan returned]
PGL 138 Cameron of Lochiel, Sir Ewen
PGL 139 Burns, Robert
PGL 140 Mary, Princess
PGL 141 Stirling, Earl of
PGL 142 Monmouth and Buccleuch, Duke of [loan returned]
PGL 143 Balfour, 1st Earl of [loan returned]
PGL 144 Balfour, 1st Earl of
PGL 145 Grey of Fallodon, Viscount
PGL 146 Hughes, William Morris
PGL 147 Napier of Merchiston, John [loan returned]
PGL 148 Buchanan, George [loan returned]
PGL 149 Harvie-Brown, John Alexander
PGL 150 Brown, Rev. John
PGL 151 Wellwood, Rev. Sir Henry Moncrieff
PGL 152 Fountainhall, Lord [loan returned]
PGL 153 James VI and I
PGL 154 Carlyle, Rev. Alexander
PGL 155 'Innes, Cardinal George'
PGL 156 Charles I

PGL 157 Unidentified
PGL 158 Unidentified
PGL 159 W. B. Blaikie collection of Jacobite portrait engravings [ex-catalogue]
PGL 160 Taylor, Peter [loan returned]
PGL 161 Steuart, George [acquired, PG 1399]
PGL 162 William III [acquired, PG 1471]
PGL 163 Dunmore, 4th Earl of
PGL 164 Burns, Robert [loan returned]
PGL 165 Hamilton, 2nd Duke of, with 1st Duke of Lauderdale [loan returned]
PGL 166 Hamilton, 3rd Duke of
PGL 167 Dundee, Viscount [loan returned]
PGL 168 Lothian, 1st Marquess of [acquired, PG 1414]
PGL 169 Lothian, Marchioness of [acquired, PG 1415]
PGL 170 Adam, Robert [loan returned]
PGL 171 Macdonald, Sir George
PGL 172 Belsches, Williamina
PGL 173 Agnew of Lochnaw, Sir Andrew
PGL 174 Charles I [acquired, PG 2212]
PGL 175 Mar, 2nd Earl of [acquired, PG 2211]
PGL 176 Mar, Countess of [acquired, PG 2214]
PGL 177 Lennox, 1st Duke of [acquired, PG 2213]
PGL 178 Dundee, Viscount [acquired, PG 2183]
PGL 179 Stewart, Prince Charles Edward [loan returned]
PGL 180 Stewart, Prince Henry Benedict [loan returned]
PGL 181 Stewart, Prince James Francis Edward [loan returned]
PGL 182 Sobieska, Princess Clementina [loan returned]
PGL 183 Stewart, Prince Charles Edward
PGL 184 Charles I with Henrietta Maria
PGL 185 Somerset, Earl of [loan returned]
PGL 186 Argyll and Greenwich, 2nd Duke of
PGL 187 Cromwell, Oliver
PGL 188 Cromwell, Oliver
PGL 189 Kinnoull, 1st Earl of
PGL 190 Stewart, Prince Henry Benedict
PGL 191 Stewart, Prince Charles Edward
PGL 192 Stewart, Prince Charles Edward
PGL 193 Charles I
PGL 194 Stewart, Prince James Francis Edward
PGL 195 Stewart, Prince James Francis Edward
PGL 196 Stewart, Prince James Francis Edward
PGL 197 Stewart, Prince James Francis Edward
PGL 198 Stewart, Prince James Francis Edward
PGL 199 Stewart, Prince James Francis Edward
PGL 200 Stewart, Prince James Francis Edward
PGL 201 Stewart, Prince James Francis Edward, with Princess Clementina Sobieska
PGL 202 Stewart, Prince James Francis Edward, with Princess Clementina Sobieska
PGL 203 Stewart, Prince Charles Edward, with Prince Henry Benedict Stewart
PGL 204 Stewart, Prince Charles Edward
PGL 205 Stewart, Prince Charles Edward
PGL 206 Stewart, Prince Henry Benedict

PGL 207 Shaw, George Bernard [loan returned]
PGL 208 Charles I, Execution of
PGL 209 Douglas, 1st Lord [loan returned]
PGL 210 Ancram, 1st Earl of
PGL 211 Lothian, 1st Marquess of
PGL 212 Scougal, Patrick [loan returned]
PGL 213 Monro, Alexander ('Tertius') [loan returned]
PGL 214 Woodhouselee, Lord [loan returned]
PGL 215 Granton, Lord
PGL 216 Grant, Abbé Peter [loan returned]
PGL 217 Moray of Abercairny, James [loan returned]
PGL 218 Moray of Abercairny, Christian [loan returned]
PGL 219 Graeme, Patrick [loan returned]
PGL 220 Kames, Lord [loan returned]
PGL 221 Murray, Sir John [loan returned]
PGL 222 Meadowbank, Lady [loan returned]
PGL 223 Perth, 1st titular Duke of
PGL 224 Dunmore, 1st Earl of
PGL 225 Murray, General James [acquired, PG 2215]
PGL 226 Low, William
PGL 227 Allan, David
PGL 228 Norie, James
PGL 229 Herdman, Robert
PGL 230 James VII and II [loan returned]
PGL 231 Tytler, William [loan returned]
PGL 232 Moir, David Macbeth [acquired, PG 2179]
PGL 233 Panmure, 4th Earl of
PGL 234 Buchan, 6th Earl of
PGL 235 Grange, Lady
PGL 236 Grange, Lord
PGL 237 Mar, 6th Earl of with Lord Erskine
PGL 238 Mar, Countess of
PGL 239 Charles I
PGL 240 Wales, Henry, Prince of
PGL 241 Kellie, 6th Earl of
PGL 242 Panmure, Titular Earl of
PGL 243 Mar, 7th Earl of, with his family
PGL 244 Scott-Moncrieff, Charles Kenneth [acquired, PG 2199]
PGL 245 Monboddo, Lord [loan returned]
PGL 246 Burnett, Elizabeth [loan returned]
PGL 247 Grieve, James [loan returned]
PGL 248 Elder, Thomas [loan returned]
PGL 249 Scott, Sir Walter [loan returned]
PGL 250 Sherwill Silhouette Album
PGL 251 George IV at St Giles [loan returned]
PGL 252 Burnet, Gilbert [loan returned]
PGL 253 Stewart, Prince Henry Benedict [loan returned]
PGL 254 Richmond and Lennox, 3rd Duke of [loan returned]
PGL 255 Macdonald, Sir Alexander [acquired, PG 2609]
PGL 256 Macdonald, Sir Alexander, with Sir James Macdonald [acquired, PG 2127]
PGL 257 Pollock, Sir John Donald
PGL 258 Duncan, Andrew
PGL 259 Black, Joseph
PGL 260 Cullen, William

PGL 261 Irvine, Sir James Colquhoun [loan returned]
PGL 262 Fletcher, Andrew
PGL 263 Milton, Lord
PGL 264 Rosebery, 1st Earl of
PGL 265 Fletcher, Henry
PGL 266 Fletcher-Campbell, John
PGL 267 Newark, 1st Lord
PGL 268 Scott, Funeral of Sir Walter
PGL 269 Haldane, Professor John Scott
PGL 270 Niven, William [loan returned]
PGL 271 Stewart, Prince James Francis Edward [acquired, PG 2191]
PGL 272 Waitt, Richard [acquired, PG 2142]
PGL 273 Wales, Augusta, Princess of
PGL 274 Charlotte, Queen
PGL 275 Lumsden, Sir James
PGL 276 Fraser of Castle Leathers, Major James
PGL 277 Hamilton, Captain Thomas [acquired, PG 2750]
PGL 278 Stuart, Andrew [loan returned]
PGL 279 Craig, Lord [loan returned]
PGL 280 Reith, 1st Baron [acquired, PG 2475]
PGL 281 Hamilton, 5th Duke of
PGL 282 Stephens, Henry [acquired, PG 2753]
PGL 283 Martin, Sir Theodore [loan returned]
PGL 284 Moir, David Macbeth [acquired, PG 2752]
PGL 285 Alison, Sir Archibald [loan returned]
PGL 286 Warren, Samuel [loan returned]
PGL 287 Drummore, Lord
PGL 288 Gillies, Sir William [acquired, PG 2448]
PGL 289 Hamilton, 14th Duke of, with Duchess of Hamilton [acquired, PG 2723]
PGL 290 Lockhart of Lee, Sir William
PGL 291 Lee, Lord
PGL 292 Lockhart, Sir George
PGL 293 Lockhart of Carnwath, George
PGL 294 Stewart, Prince Charles Edward
PGL 295 Strange, Sir Thomas
PGL 296 Strange, Sir Robert
PGL 297 Stewart, Prince James Francis Edward
PGL 298 Stewart, Prince Henry Benedict
PGL 299 Stolberg, Princess Louisa of
PGL 300 Stewart, Prince Henry Benedict
PGL 301 Minto, 1st Earl of
PGL 302 Newton, Lord
PGL 303 Bonnar, William
PGL 304 Elgin, Countess of [loan returned]
PGL 305 Ker, Mark
PGL 306 Leslie, Lady Helen
PGL 307 Wilkie, Rev. David, with Isabella Wilkie [loan returned]
PGL 308 McTaggart, William [loan returned]
PGL 309 Seton, 5th Lord
PGL 310 Morton, 12th Earl of [loan returned]
PGL 311 Barrowfield, Lady (Katherine Walkinshaw)
PGL 312 Seton, 5th Lord, with his family
PGL 313 Skirving, Archibald
PGL 314 Scott, William Bell
PGL 315 Brisbane, Sir Charles
PGL 316 Grant of Dalvey, Sir Alexander [loan returned]

PGL 317   Morison, Sir Alexander [acquired, PG 2623]
PGL 318   Landing at Aboukir [acquired, PG 2681]
PGL 319   Battle of Alexandria [acquired, PG 2680]
PGL 320   Scott, Francis George
PGL 321   Malcolm, Sir John
PGL 322   George IV at the Lord Provost's Banquet in Parliament House, Edinburgh [loan returned]
PGL 323   Henderson, Joseph Morris
PGL 324   Macgregor, Alasdair Alpin
PGL 325   Pryde, James Ferrier
PGL 326   George IV at a review of cavalry on Portobello Sands
PGL 327   Forbes of Callendar, William
PGL 328   Gathering at 7 London Street

PGL 329   Hyndford, 4th Earl of [loan returned]
PGL 330   Carmichael, Sir John Gibson
PGL 331   Baird, Sir David
PGL 332   Burns, Jean with Sarah Burns
PGL 333   Erskine of Torrie, Sir William, with his family
PGL 334   Glenshiel, Plan of the Battle of
PGL 335   Bucklitsch, John
PGL 336   Winton, 3rd Earl of, with Lord Seton and 1st Viscount Kingston
PGL 337   A Meet of the Fife Hounds
PGL 338   Kintore, Countess of
PGL 339   Kintore, 4th Earl of
PGL 340   Stewart, Prince Charles Edward, with Prince Henry Benedict Stewart

ARTISTS INDEX

BRODIE, William (*continued*)
  Constable, Thomas PG 1612
  Dunfermline, 1st Baron PG 330
  Maclaren, Charles (after) PG 281
  Miller, Hugh PG 255
  Nelson, William PG 1435
  Russell, Alexander PG 557
  Smith, Alexander PG 883
  Victoria, Queen PG 1068

BRODZKY, Horace (1885–1969)
  Murdoch, William Garden Blaikie PG 2430

BRONCKORST, Arnold (fl. 1565–83)
  Buchanan, George PG 2678
  James VI and I PG 992
  Morton, 4th Earl of (attributed to) PG 1857

BROWN, Helen Paxton (1876–1956)
  King, Jessie Marion PG 2406

BROWN, J.
  Siddons, Sarah PG 2542

BROWN, John (1749–87)
  Anderson, William PGL 67
  Barclay, George PGL 68
  Baxter, John PGL 69
  Brown, Alexander PGL 70
  Brown, Dr John PGL 71
  Buchan, 11th Earl of PGL 72
  Cardonnel, Adam de PGL 73
  Carlyle, Alexander PG 1975
  Caw, John PGL 84
  Cummyng, James PGL 86
  Daer, Lord PG 1685
  Dalrymple, Sir John PGL 74
  Deuchar, David PG 980, PGL 75
  Dick, Sir Alexander PGL 83
  Drummond, Alexander PGL 76
  Duncan, Andrew PGL 77
  Erskine, John PGL 78
  Glencairn, Countess of PG 359
  Gordon, Rev. Alexander PGL 79
  Gordon, Duchess of PG 1153
  Gordon, Duchess of, with Lady Wallace PG 927
  Henderson, Sir John PGL 80
  Hunter, John PG 218
  Jeans, William PGL 82
  Little, William Charles PGL 85
  Logan, Rev. John PG 154
  Monboddo, Lord PG 362
  Montgomery, Sir James William PGL 87
  Paton, George PG 200, PGL 66
  Robertson, Roger PGL 65
  Runciman, Alexander PGL 88
  Smellie, William PGL 64
  Unidentified PG 2413; PGL 54, 55, 56, 57, 58, 61, 62, 63

BROWN, Mather (1761–1831)
  Bridport, 1st Viscount PG 2256
  Buller, Sir Francis PG 357

  Pole, Sir Charles Morice PG 2242
  Rosslyn, 1st Earl of PG 861
  Smart, John PG 2254
  Soldier, Study of a PG 2264
  Tebbs, Sir Benjamin PG 2248
  Unidentified PG 2239, 2240, 2241, 2243, 2244, 2245, 2246, 2247, 2249, 2250, 2251, 2252, 2253, 2255, 2257, 2258, 2259, 2260, 2261, 2262, 2263

BROWNE, Mrs Marmaduke
  Atkinson, James PG 435

BRYDEN, Robert (1865–1939)
  Caw, Sir James Lewis PG 1158
  Smith, John PG 1201

BUCHAN, David Steuart Erskine, 11th Earl of (1742–1829)
  Belhaven, 2nd Lord (copy by) PG 1639
  Buchan, Countess of (copy by) PG 1645
  Buchan, 6th Earl of (copy by) PG 1635
  Buchan, Earl of (copy by) PG 1617
  Buchanan, George (copy by) PG 1622
  Cardross, 2nd Lord (copy by) PG 1636
  Crichton, James (copy by) PG 1623
  Elphinstone, William (copy by) PG 1619
  Erskine, Alexander (copy by) PG 1634
  Erskine, Sir Alexander (copy by) PG 1625
  Fletcher, Andrew (copy by) PG 1642
  Forbes, William (copy by) PG 1629
  Fraser, Sir Alexander (copy by) PG 1627
  Gordon, Robert (copy by) PG 1632, 1633
  Gregory, James (copy by) PG 1637, 1640
  Hope, Sir Thomas (copy by) PG 1526
  James II (copy by) PG 1618
  Johnston, Arthur (copy by) PG 1630
  Knox, John (copy by) PG 1620
  Lennox, 1st Duke of (copy by) PG 1624
  Leslie, John (copy by) PG 1626
  Maclaurin, Colin (copy by) PG 1643
  Maitland, William (copy by) PG 1621
  Mar, 2nd Earl of (copy by) PG 1628
  Mar, Countess of (copy by) PG 1631
  Newark, 1st Lord (copy by) PG 1638
  Ruddiman, Thomas (copy by) PG 108
  Short, James PG 1644
  Trail, Robert (copy by) PG 1641
  Wallace, Sir William (copy by) PG 1616

BUCK, Adam (1759–1833)
  Suvorov, Count (attributed to) PG 2338

BURCH, Edward (1730–1814)
  Hunter, William PG 2647

BURR, John (1834–93)
  Burr, John PG 1319

BURRELL, Benjamin (fl. 1790–1828)
  Leith, Sir James PG 122

BURTON, Sir Frederick William (1816–1900)
  Faucit, Helen PG 695

PG 3071

MofCat x McDerm PG 3072

PGPK.33Q Jessie Kesson

PGP 16.21

} Bay 6 Store

PG 2778

PG 2900

Bay 5 Store

A/44401